Raya Dunayevskaya
Philosopher of Marxist-Humanism

Raya Dunayevskaya

Philosopher of Marxist-Humanism

Eugene Gogol

Resource Publications
An imprint of Wipf and Stock Publishers

Raya Dunayevskaya: Philosopher of Marxist-Humanism

By Eugene Gogol

Copyright —2004 by Eugene Gogol

ISBN:
Hardcover: 1-59244-771-6
Softcover: 1-59244-770-8

Library of Congress Control Number: 2004110272

Resource Publications
An imprint of Wipf and Stock Publishers
199 W 8th Ave, Suite 3
Eugene, Oregon 97401

Table of Contents

Abbreviations   ix

Introduction -- Hegel, Marx, Lenin, Luxemburg, and Revolution in the Thought and Passion of Raya Dunayevskaya   1

Part I: 1941-1956, From the Origins of State Capitalist Theory to Letters on Hegel's Absolutes to the Founding of News and Letters Committees

Chapter 1 -- The Hitler-Stalin Pact, the Outbreak of the Second World War, and the Theory of State Capitalism: Manuscripts from Its Initial Projection, 1941-43   21

Chapter 2 -- Translation and Initial Probing of Lenin's Notebooks on Hegel's *Science of Logic*: Theoretical Ramifications, 1949-51; Relation to the 1949-50 Miners' General Strike   45

Chapter 3 -- Dunayevskaya's 1953 Breakthrough on Hegel's Absolutes in Relation to Momentous World Events: the Death of Stalin and the June 17, 1953 East German Revolt   65

Chapter 4 -- Founding of News and Letters Committees, 1955-1957, in the Context of East European Revolts, Workers' Struggles against Automation, and the Montgomery Bus Boycott 83

Part II: 1955-1964, Marxism and Freedom ... from 1776 until today

Chapter 5 -- Origins of *Marxism and Freedom* as World Events Unfold: Montgomery, Alabama 1955-56, Hungary 1956, Mao's China, 1957 109

Chapter 6 -- Elucidating the Philosophical Foundations of Marxism: The Structure and Content of *Marxism and Freedom* 125

Chapter 7 -- Projection and Concretization of *Marxism and Freedom* as Objective-Subjective Turning Points Develop: the African Revolutions, Automation Battles, and the Civil Rights Movement 159

Part III: 1960-1976, Philosophy and Revolution: From Hegel to Sartre and from Marx to Mao

Chapter 8 -- 1960-1973: The Process of Writing *Philosophy and Revolution* with Focus on Hegel's Absolutes 183

Chapter 9 -- Working out the Dialectic of Hegel's Absolutes for Our Age: The Structure and Content of *Philosophy and Revolution* 203

Chapter 10 -- Philosophic Concretization and Projection: Organizational Ramifications and Contradictions 227

Part IV: 1975-1982, Rosa Luxemburg, Women's Liberation, and Marx's Philosophy of Revolution

Chapter 11 -- Development of Luxemburg Book, 1975-1982: Strands from Women's Liberation, Luxemburg, and Marx; Relation to Iran's Revolution/Counter-Revolution, and to *News & Letters* as Theory/Practice 239

Chapter 12 -- The Categories Post-Marx Marxism and
Revolution-in-Permanence in Relation to the
Structure and Content of the Luxemburg Book   249

*Part V: 1980-87, Reaching for the Future: Dunayevskaya's
Re-examination of a Half-Century of Marxist-
Humanism, and the Projection of a New Work
On Dialectics of Organization and Philosophy*   269

   I. Projecting and Extending *Rosa Luxemburg, Women's
Liberation, and Marx's Philosophy of Revolution*
   II. Retrospective of Marxist-Humanism—Its Origins and
Development
   III. Towards Dialectics of Organization and Philosophy

Bibliography   309

Acknowledgements   317

Expanded Tables of Contents and Index   319

About the Author   329

Abbreviations

ACOT	*American Civilization on Trial*
M&F	*Marxism and Freedom*
MSTSC	*The Marxist-Humanist Theory of State-Capitalism*
N&L	*News & Letters*
P&R	*Philosophy and Revolution*
PON	*Power of Negativity*
RLWLKM	*Rosa Luxemburg, Women's Liberation, and Marx's Philosophy of Revolution*
RDC	*The Raya Dunayevskaya Collection*
SRDC	*Supplement to The Raya Dunayevskaya Collection*
WBA	*Workers Battle Automation*
WLDOR	*Women's Liberation and the Dialectics of Revolution*
WWFF	*Working Women for Freedom*

Introduction

Hegel, Marx, Lenin, Luxemburg, and Revolution in the Thought and Passion of Raya Dunayevskaya

Facing the Present Moment

The present moment at the dawn of the twenty-first century is quite different from the one Raya Dunayevskaya faced in mid 20th century. The state-capitalist Soviet empire which had emerged post-World War II to challenge the United States for single world mastery for almost four decades has collapsed. We are no longer in the bi-polar world that Dunayevskaya continually analyzed, but in a world of a single superpower hegemony. The possibility of revolutionary subjectivity as expressed in leftist social movements and revolutions, vibrant in the 1950s, 60s and 70s, has faded, while various religious fundamentalist movements are on the rise. As opposed to an era where Marxist ideas were openly and eagerly discussed and debated, much postmodern thought denies the idea of revolution, denounces any revolutionary role for dialectical thought, and questions the existence of revolutionary subjectivity.

And yet if we briefly examine three dimensions that characterize the present moment—(1) a rampant globalized capitalism under *Pax Americana*; (2) the threatened eclipse of dialectic thought; and (3) the apparent lack of a concept of revolutionary subjectivity—then the kind of new beginnings Dunayevskaya was compelled to search for six decades ago, seem necessary for this moment.

Globalized capitalism under a neo-liberal banner has been fused with *Pax Americana* in its latest manifestation, the war against terrorism. Marching through the opening created by the inhuman horror of the 9/11/01 terrorist attack, the Bush administration—first with the destruction of the Taliban in Afghanistan, and then the invasion and occupation of Iraq—completed the decade-long movement from "the war on Communism" to "the war on terrorism" as the organizing principle for establishing an unchallenged United States dominance abroad as it undermines civil liberties at home.

Der Spiegel, the German news magazine, summed up the moment: "Throughout the history of mankind, certainly no country has existed that has so thoroughly dominated the world with its politics, its tanks and its products as the United States does today" (Quoted in *The New York Times*, April 14, 2003, B13). While some have written as if a "hegemonic internationalism," or global dominance exists almost for its own sake, the US's narrow nationalism with a global reach should not be considered outside of the context of the current stage of capitalism, and of the militarized state's role in implementing it. The drive for an American *imperium* is a unification of the economic, the political, and the military.

A United States-led globalized capitalism is rampant and at the heart of the U.S. drive for single world mastery. Encroaching economically upon each continent, particularly in the technologically less developed lands, this virulent neo-liberal form of capital imposes privatized "free market" forces upon any and all activity. Commodification of every dimension of human life and labor, and of each expression of nature's diversity, has reached a previously unimagined intensity.

In the "First World," a capitalist-directed technology continually transforms industrialized, automated, computerized, production. The living worker more and more becomes capital's disposable Other, either thrown out of work, or entrapped in routinized, fragmented, alienated labor. The continually transformed *appearance* of capital wedded to technology, blinds some theoreticians to the *essence* of capital—the extraction of value and surplus value from the living laborer. A so-called "information age," as opposed to an industrial age, or to an automated age, has deepened the illusion that the worker's creation of value and surplus value is no longer the central core of capital accumulation. Not alone bourgeois thinkers, but would-be radical thinkers and social scientists, have moved away from a view of the material conditions of labor and production as primary determinants of our social existence.

At the same time, the neo-liberal rule of capital in the "Third World" has meant hundreds of millions of human beings, consigned to a marginalized existence, mired in extreme poverty, a degradation of the Other. As capital develops for capital's sake, enormous stretches of "the developing world"—indigenous villages in Chiapas and the *barricadas* of Lima, vast swaths of sub-Saharan Africa and North African shantytowns, Bangladesh countryside and New Deli slums—stagnate and fester. Globalized capitalism, as it gobbles up the world's resources, seems incapable of providing potable water, adequate nutrition, medical care, education, and meaningful work in much of the African, Asian, Latin American world. The International Monetary Fund and the World Bank, the economic enforcers of the neo-liberal mantra of "structural adjustment" via privatization, deregulation, unrestricted movement of capital and lower taxes, have assigned the nations and peoples of the Third World their "place" in globalized capitalism.

Nature too becomes capitalism's degraded object. The despoliation of the land, the water, and the air, intensifies under the rule of capital with a global reach. More and more, the earth's flora and fauna undergo commodification. No natural resource on earth seems immune from transformation into capital. Nature has become another of capitalism's Others.

A number of commentators, bourgeois as well as radical, see the current moment of globalization as indicating the demise of the nation-state. Forgetting that historically capitalism's globalizations have been under the international reach of one or another state power, they point to the rise of multi-national corporations in the post-World War II world as today's determinate. Far from the current moment of globalized capitalism manifesting a lesser role for the nation-state, it is more accurately characterized as an intensification of militarized state-power reaching for global dominance. Certainly this is true with respect to the United States today. Indeed, its intensified global reach is driven precisely by the objective fact of capital's increased globilization. State-power and the free market with its neo-liberal prescriptions and multi-national corporations, are not irreconcilable opposites, but moments of a whole. In this sense a theory of state-capitalism has meaning after the collapse of those state-capitalist regimes calling themselves Communist.

Faced with rampant globalized capitalism under *Pax Americana*, there is a need for a mode of thinking that breaks with the non-viability of current reality, and reaches to forge a pathway toward a new human society. Dialectics in the hands of revolutionary thinker-activists has historically been such a pathway. Yet today we live in times of the threatened eclipse of dialectical thought. Various intellectual currents—structuralism, post-structuralism, pragmatism, deconstructionism, post-Marxism and vulgar Marxism, post-modernisms —have, from different perspectives, hit out against the idea of dialectical thought. Within postmodernism, some have taken the view that reality is so complex and fragmented, that there is no overarching world view that can begin to comprehend the development of capital, not alone in the economic sphere, but also in the cultural and social spheres. For them, philosophy and theory cease to matter in today's world ("The Latest Theory Is That Theory Doesn't Matter," *The New York Times*, April 19, 2003, A17). But others ask, "Is theory simply just a nice, simple intellectual exercise, or something that could be transformative?"

The attempt to eclipse dialectical thought threatens to leave us philosophically rudderless in the currents of today's unfree reality. Our crisis is thus philosophic as well as economic, political and military—a crisis in the very innards of humanity's social existence. As we approach the 200th anniversary of the publication of Hegel's first comprehensive unfolding of his philosophy, *Phenomenology of Spirit*, two decades after the centenary of Marx's death, can dialectical thought re-emerge from its abandonment and dismissal by many social thinkers?

The question is not posed for reasons of academic interest, but because, living within a vacuum in revolutionary thought, not only is much of the Left mystified as to the essence of capitalism (though it was discerned with great profundity almost a century and a half ago!), but they have become trapped in and blinded by capitalism's very notion—the fetishism of commodities. The need for radical thinker-activists to wage two interrelated battles—against capitalism and against a threatened eclipse of dialectic thought—stands before us. Does the power of negativity, the heart of the Hegelian dialectic, have a voice here?

The threatened eclipse of dialectic thought is not unrelated to the lack of a concept of revolutionary human subjectivity. Where previously, vulgar Marxism had dismissed Marx's view of masses as reason, reducing subjectivity to the elitist party to lead, significant segments of today's postmodernism declares the fragmentation of the subject, and denies the possibility of a concept of revolutionary human subjectivity. What Marx had restored to dialectical thought—the human subject—many of today's intellectuals deny. Some recognize human subjectivity, but deny it any dialectical vantage point. Others dismiss both dialectical thought and a revolutionary subject.

The problematic of revolutionary organization also appears in disarray. While the vanguard party-to-lead is today in disrepute, the alternative that is often focused upon, spontaneity in and of itself, confines the discussion to the question of *form* of organization. As important as the rejection of the elitism of the vanguard party and a recognition of the mass self-activity from below are, we need to encompass as well a different sphere, not only form of organization but *philosophy* of organization. The burning question is to work out a dialectics of organization inseparable from a dialectics of philosophy. Revolutionary organization as flowing from a dialectics of organization and philosophy remains an unexplored pathway for the movement today.

•

In exploring the work of the Marxist-Humanist philosopher Raya Dunayevskaya in face of the present moment of globalized capitalism, the threatened eclipse of dialectical thought, the lack of a concept of revolutionary subjectivity, and the void in working out revolutionary organization in relation to dialectical philosophy, we are not trying to point to any direct relationship between today's tasks and those she undertook. Rather, we are probing the labor of working out dialectics anew undertaken by a revolutionary philosopher over almost half a century. Tracing her journey through the development of the Marxist-Humanist Idea can help us comprehend and practice dialectical thought today.

The present study makes no pretence of presenting the totality of her work. Rather, it seeks to be an opening for discovering Dunayevskaya's Marxist-Humanism. How her labors illuminate the present moment can only be answered in fullness by revolutionary thinker-activists who feel compelled to take their own thought-dive directly into her body of ideas in responding to today's stifling reality of unfreedom.

Readers of Raya Dunayevskaya's ideas will find neither a dispassionate academic nor an armchair Marxist. She was a passionate philosopher of the barricades who was engaged in a continual philosophic dialogue with Hegel, and Marx, and Lenin, while immersed in the class and social struggles of her time: Black civil rights struggles and rebellion, labor upsurges in the coal fields and auto shops, the emerging women's liberation movement, and the anti-war youth outpouring. Her prose, while of philosophic rigor and deep probing, was a language of revolutionary commitment—partisan, provocative, and far from neutral.

To enter into the life work of Dunayevskaya is to enter into a world of deep intellect and passionate revolutionary commitment. To have heard her lecture in public was not to have witnessed a finely-tuned, smooth discourse, but to have been present at an original creation, often rough-hewn, always overflowing with ideas, at times journeying into untrodden territory. It was often a spontaneous moment born of prodigious philosophic labor. To read Dunayevskaya is to be in the company of one who is thinking out the future, not as a Utopian project, but as emerging from human passions and forces of the time, the masses in motion. She was actively engaged in the movements of her time.

In both her writing and speaking, Dunayevskaya entered into a battle of ideas with various Marxist and Hegelian thinkers and tendencies in presenting her ideas. At the same time, she entered into a different kind of interchange with Hegel and Marx, with Lenin and Luxemburg. It was a critical look, but critical in the sense of an intent to discern and bring to the fore the full revolutionary dimension embedded in their thought as well as contradictions. In that sense she was having the most intimate, revolutionary conversation with them. For her, they were "alive" in the moment of her conversation. The subject was always revolution. Yes, the revolutions in thought and action of their day, but even more so, the revolutionary moments of her day. She was continually "integrating" them into the last half of the 20th century. Her immersion was so deep within their thought that the dialogue was here and now.

Antonio Gramsci's expression—"The philosophy of praxis is consciousness full of contradictions in which the philosopher himself, understood both individually and as an entire social group, not merely grasps the contradictions but posits himself as an element of the contradictions and elevates this element to a principle of knowledge and therefore of action," (quoted by Dunayevskaya in her third book, *Rosa Luxemburg, Women's Liberation and Marx's Philosophy of Revoution*)—embraces the spirit of her inquiry.

Though she did not have the opportunity to participate in an ongoing revolution in the manner that Marx, Lenin, Luxemburg and Trotsky did in their lifetimes, Luxemburg's expression—"The revolution is everything, all else is bilge"—speaks to the passionate, deep commitment of Dunayevskaya's life work.

These twin dimensions—ceaseless critique, (including of her own ideas), and passion for emancipatory social revolution—form vantage points for our exploration of Dunayevskaya as philosopher of Marxist-Humanism. We hope to present her passionate journey as self-development through contradiction, critique, self-critique of the Marxist-Humanist idea as it developed.

A Biographical Note, 1910 to 1941

I come from Russia 1917, and the ghettos of Chicago, where I first saw a Black person. The reason that I'm starting that way—it happens to be true—but the reason that I'm starting that way is that I was illiterate. You know, you're born in a border town—there's a revolution, there's a counter-revolution, there's anti-Semitism—you *know* nothing, but experience a lot. . . . That is, you don't know that you're a revolutionary, but you're opposed to everything.

Now, how does it happen that an illiterate person, who certainly didn't know Lenin and Trotsky, who as a child had never seen a Black, had begun to develop all the revolutionary ideas to be called Marxist-Humanism in the 1950s? It isn't personal whatsoever! If you live when an idea is born, and a great revolution in the world is born—it doesn't make any difference *where* you are; *that becomes the new stage of development of humanity* (News and Letters Convention, September 2, 1978, *Raya Dunayevskaya Collection [RDC]* microfilm #5818).

Dunayevskaya (Rae Spiegel) was born in 1910 in the Ukraine close to the Romanian border. She came with her family to the United States in 1922, to the city of Chicago, where her father had arrived several years earlier.

For a moment, let us turn away from all these philosophic-sociological-political-economic developments, to a story from my personal life. I am doing so to illustrate the difference between an idea in embryo and in full development: between process and result, as well as the whole question of a child's perception, when great revolutions occur and for how long these impressions last. The incident I'm diverting to happened when I was thirteen years old and had been but a single year in the United States. I was leading a strike against the school principal. Her name I still remember—Tobin. And she exacted corporal punishment for so little an infraction as coming five minutes late. Also, she forced all to memorize Shylock's speech, where he demands his pound of flesh. . . .

The event took place in 1924 in the Cregier public school in a Chicago ghetto. I credited my supposed bravery to the Russian Revolution of November 1917, which had left an indelible impression on me of great doings, like equality and comradeship. I was an illiterate child then, living in the Ukraine, who had refused, two years previous to 1917, to engage in khabar (bribery) in order to be among the one percent of Jews who gained the "privilege" of being able to sit in the back of the school room ("Dialectics of Revolution: American Roots and Marx's World Humanist Concepts" March 21, 1985, *RDC* #10218).

In the mid and late 1920s Dunayevskaya worked with the Communist youth organization in Chicago, the Young Workers League, writing material for its newspaper, the *Young Worker*. She distributed *Harvest Worker*, the Communist shop caucus paper at International Harvester in Chicago.

Black Chicago was the other area of Dunayevskaya's political activity as a teenager. She worked in the offices of the American Negro Labor Congress' newspaper, *Negro Champion*, during its Chicago years (1925-27). She wrote book reviews, and corresponded with a number of Black writers of the period.

> [A]s a senior in high school I led a protest against the segregationist policies of Medill High School. I was still a teenager when the American Negro Labor Congress was organized in 1925 and I was allowed to become a member of it. I was also the literary editor of the journal *Negro Champion*, which was published here in Chicago (Interview, *Chicago Literary Review,* March 15, 1985, RDC #10228).
>
> I remember Illinois in the 1920s, where every Sunday was Red Sunday for going down to the mine region for distributions of papers and for talk. . . . [I]n the 1920s, the Blacks may have been speaking Marcus Garvey language—to me it was the Russian Revolution (News and Letters Perspectives, 1984-85, *RDC* #8228).

After being expelled from the Young Workers League in 1928, for questioning a resolution to denounce Leon Trotsky, Dunayevskaya left Chicago, searching out "Trotskyists," first in New York. Over the next several years she worked and wrote for the Communist League of America and its newspaper, the *Militant,* and with its youth group, Spartacus Youth Clubs, and their newspaper, *Young Spartacus*. She served as business manager of the *Russian Bulletin of the Opposition* in 1933-34 and again in 1938. Her travels during the Great Depression of the 1930s took her all over the United States, seething with labor struggles, organizing of the unemployment, and Black protest.

> Before the CIO . . . the labor struggles reached their highest point in the San Francisco general strike of 1934. While San Francisco had always been a union town, the strike posed not just a union question or a strike in a single industry—the longshoremen—but a political, revolutionary, general strike in which I was very active. I was then the organizer of the Spartacus Youth Club in Los Angeles. In order to show that these types of revolutionary strikes, far from being "foreign," as the Hearst papers were screaming, were very America, I wrote an article for the *Young Spartacus* (June 1934) which went back to the railroad strikes of the 1870s, concentrating on the very first General Strike in St. Louis—1877—when "the strikers took possession of the city and ruled for an entire week."

The Depression certainly shook up America, and the strike struggles of the 1930s created both industrial unionism and introduced new paths in cognition itself. Far from pragmatism and American thought being one and the same, Marxian dialectics was very much on the American scene and was reflected in the multifaceted discussions engaged in by workers as well as intellectuals. I experienced this when I was conducting classes in Los Angeles on Marxism for the youth. I then returned Midwest, East and finally to Washington, D.C. (Hitchhiking was the main mode of transportation in those years.)

By 1936, when I was living in Washington, D.C., I became active in support of sharecroppers' struggles in the South. Interracial relationships became a key question during the Depression. In Washington D.C., for example, which was still a "Jim Crow" town except for streetcars, Ralph Bunche . . . was instrumental in establishing, with the Communists, a new National Negro Congress, and helped the socialists, who had organized the Southern Tenant Farmers Union, to establish the Washington Committee to Aid Agricultural Workers as a support group for the 1936 Arkansas sharecroppers' strike. I was a member of this committee, which included Carter G. Woodson, founder of the *Journal of Negro History*, and Prof. Dorsey, a political economist at Howard, who was to become the Washington chairman of the International Defense Committee for Leon Trotsky in 1937. The Black Dimension here opened the two-way road between the U.S. and Africa for me, especially since Nnamdi Azikwe was then in the U.S. writing his *Renascent Africa* ("Introduction/Overview to Volume XII *RDC*, February 28, 1986).

In 1937 Dunayevskaya traveled to Mexico to become Trostky's Russian language secretary. (For documentation of this period see *RDC* #2210-2407; #8783-8834.) She returned to the United States in 1938, later breaking with him on the analysis of the class nature of the Soviet Union, as the Hitler-Stalin Pact (August 1939) catalyzed her journey to rethink Marxism for her day.

> In 1936, I had wanted to join the Americans who were fighting the fascists in Spain. But I was turned down because I was a woman. That was when I went to Mexico to work with Trotsky as his Russian secretary.
> This was the period when the greatest frame-up trials in history were taking place in Russia, two years during which Stalin killed off the General Staff of the Russian Revolution. Inside Russia the workers faced the most Draconian anti-labor laws, including forced labor camps. And in foreign policy it was the period which ended in the signing of the Hitler-Stalin pact, an agreement which in effect gave the green light to Hitler to start World War II.
> To my utter shock and disbelief, I realized that with the outbreak of the war, Trotsky, who had been fighting the Stalinist bureaucracy for over a decade, would now turn to the workers and ask them to defend Russia, because it was a "workers' state though degenerate." Here was this man who had helped make two revolutions, the 1905 and the 1917 Revolutions, and I couldn't believe that I was saying to Trotsky, "You are wrong and I am right." Actually I lost my power of speech for two days.
> But precisely because it was so great a break and challenge to what I used to consider Marxist, *I had to prove it*. I was not only opposing the Hitler-Stalin pact, I was opposing Trotsky's conception that nationalized economy equaled workers' state.
> I was quiet for three long years, and then I went back to the three original Five Year Plans of the Russian economy, which had been published at the outbreak of World War II, but I also returned to Marx, because I felt Trotsky

did not understand Marx, especially the philosophic Marx (*Chicago Literary Review*, March 15, 1985, RDC #10228).

Facing the Crisis in Marxism as Capitalism Took New Form and Revolution Became Transformed into Opposite

In the mid-20th century a generation of Marxists faced the challenge of responding to the grave contradictions that arose in the decades following the Russian Revolution. With Stalin's consolidation of power came the single-party totalitarian state in the "Soviet" Union, established in the name of Marxism. In the West there emerged massive state-intervention as a "stabilizing" force for private Depression-ridden capitalism, the rise of Nazism and other forms of fascism. At the same time there was the emergence of new revolutionary forces, particularly with the Spanish Civil War. Finally the 1939 Hitler-Stalin Pact between a fascist state and a supposed workers' state opened the door to the Second World War and the resultant holocaust. The unfolding of these world-shaking events challenged revolutionary thinker-activists to reorganize their thought and action.

Foremost among these was Leon Trotsky. Yet Trotsky, despite his 15-year critique of and fight against Stalin, felt no compulsion to reexamine the economic nature of Russia, even after the shock of the Hitler-Stalin Pact. Nationalized property remained the defining dimension of socialism for Trotsky.

In contrast, for Dunayevskaya, the Hitler-Stalin Pact signified the need to begin a study of the nature of the Russian economy. In 1941, under the name Freddie James, she submitted an initial document "The Union of Soviet Socialist Republics Is a Capitalist Society," to the 1941 Workers Party national convention.

[Independently, C.L.R. James, under the name J.R. Johnson, submitted a document to the Workers Party calling Russia state-capitalist. James and Dunayevskaya would subsequently form the State-Capitalist Tendency, which renamed itself the Johnson–Forest Tendency in 1945. James (Johnson) and Dunayevskaya (under the party name Forest), joined by a third co-leader Grace Lee, remained leaders of the Tendency for more than a dozen years, first in the Workers Party, then, after a short interim period in 1947, as a minority in the Socialist Workers Party, and finally in 1951, as an independent group, Correspondence Committees. In 1955 the Tendency broke apart, with Dunayevskaya and colleagues founding News and Letters Committees.]

Starting with her 1941 designation of Russia as a state-capitalist society, Dunayevskaya was compelled to make a new beginning in revolutionary Marxist thought. Over the next decade and a half, she interwove three strands: (1) Economically, she discerned a new world stage of capitalism, state-capitalism. (2) Philosophically, she explored Hegel's Absolutes and brought to the fore Marx's Humanism, exploring both as crucial vantage points for creating revolutionary Marxism anew. (3) In relation to class and social movements and revolutions, she reconcretized and expanded a concept of revolutionary human subjectivity for the post World War II world. Out of these strands the philosophy of Marxist-Humanism was born in America. Part I of this book follows these developments from the period of the Spanish Civil War to the founding of News and Letters Committees.

The post-World War II world gave rise not alone to an age of state-capitalism dominated by the U.S.-U.S.S.R. super-power rivalry that threatened humanity's very survival, but to the birth of movements for revolutionary change. From Eastern Europe and within Russia, revolt and outright revolution became manifest in East Germany, Vorkuda, Poland, and Hungary. In the United States there arose workers' struggles against automation, and a Civil Rights movement sparked by Black masses within the segregated South followed by the dimensions of anti-war youth and a women's liberation movement. From colonial countries and other technologically underdeveloped lands came the birth of what became know as the Third World. The Afro-Asian-Latin American Revolutions opened up new vantage points. In addition, Mao's China claimed the mantle of Marxism and subsequently challenged Russia as leader of the Communist orbit.

Independent, revolutionary Marxists had to face these new realities. From the mid-1950s to the mid-1980s Dunayevskaya responded through the development of Marxist-Humanism as philosophic tendency, political practice and organizational expression. Her three books—*Marxist and Freedom*, *Philosophy and Revolution*, and *Rosa Luxemburg, Women's Liberation, and Marx's Philosophy of Revolution*—were written in the context of these objective/subjective world events. Parts II, III, and IV of the present study trace the development of the idea and practice of Marxist-Humanism through the lens of each of these works. For her, the self-determination of the Idea of freedom was crucial to the self-determination of peoples and nations.

Throughout this half century from the Depression years to the mid-1980s, Dunayevskaya was an American revolutionary—the revolutionary subjectivity of worker, Black, woman, and youth, were the here and now of her life. Beginning in the 1940s, she wrote continually on African-American struggles as crucial to social transformation in the United States. Her *American Civilization on Trial—Black Masses as Vanguard* (first edition, 1963) posed the integrality of Black and labor struggles inseparable from Marx's American roots. Her concrete activities with coal miners in West Virginia, with auto workers in Detroit wildcats and automation battles, with the founding of a Marxist-Humanist newspaper whose editor was a mass production worker, found philosophic expression in the "Automation and the New Humanism" chapter of her first book, *Marxism and Freedom*. Dunayevskaya wrote and thought about the "Woman Question" well before the emergence of the modern women's liberation movement, vigorously joining the movement as it became an idea whose time had come. She challenged that movement to work out its revolutionary philosophic dimension as it recovered its hidden history. "The Needed American Revolution" was not a Utopian dream, but a concrete perspective Dunayevskaya thought deeply about and fought to bring toward realization.

At the same time she was a persistent internationalist. Africa, the Middle East, Iran, Europe East and West, China, Japan, Latin America, were not only focuses of her analysis, but places to reach out to meet the human subjects of social transformation. Everywhere the determinant was revolution.

•

Two interrelated dimensions of Dunayevskaya's Marxist-Humanism can serve as signposts for our exploration of her thought and activity: (1) The concept of "battle of ideas" as a driving force for her development of Marxist-Humanism. (2) Her 1982-87 reexaminations of the origins and development of Marxist-Humanism undertaken under the impact of the category of "post-Marx Marxism as a pejorative," which were integral to her work on "Dialectics of Organization and Philosophy" in the last years of her life.

The Concept of Critique: Battle of Ideas and the Development of Marxist-Humanism

In 1986, Dunayevskaya looked back to the period of the Spanish Civil War: "[O]ut of the Spanish Civil War there emerged a new kind of revolutionary who posed questions not only against Stalinism but against Trotskyism, indeed against all established Marxists." That new kind of revolutionary included certainly Dunayevskaya herself, still in her twenties at the time.

For over half a century she battled not only the ideological obfuscation of capitalism, but with equal vigor, conceptions of Marxism which were truncated, half-way dialectical, indeed sometimes anti-dialectical in content. She rediscovered, translated, and rooted her thought in Marx's humanism, which she saw as the core of his revolutionary dialectic. She broke free of "mind-forged manacles" within the Marxist movement, to create and develop the concept of Marxist-Humanism in the United States.

The process was far from being a unilinear one. It involved theoretic differences and sharp breaks. First, with Leon Trotsky, "the man of October," beginning with her independent analysis of the class nature of the Soviet Union, and reaching to critically examine Trotsky as a theoretician; second, with organized Trotskyism, which she felt was not a viable Marxist alternative; and finally, with her co-leaders in the State-Capitalist Tendency over philosophic, political and organizational issues. She established Marxist-Humanism as a body of ideas and organization in the mid 1950s.

At the heart of this journey was her concept of critique, including a self-critique. The development of Marxist-Humanism was a contradictory process, involving a battle of ideas with other thinkers and tendencies, Marxist and non-Marxists alike. We can get a preliminary sense of how critique meant at one and the same time a battle with others and the growth of the Marxist-Humanist idea if we look briefly at four manifestations: (1) her exchanges with C.L.R. James, co-leader of the State-Capitalist Tendency for a dozen years; (2) her correspondence with the Hegelian-Marxist philosopher Herbert Marcuse in the 1950s and 60s; (3) her sharp critique of the thought of Mao Tse-tung; (4) her continual return to and probing of Lenin's Philosophic Notebooks on Hegel's *Science of Logic*. Each relationship will be discussed in more detail in the chapters that follow.

• In the late 1940s and early 1950s James and Dunayevskaya, (along with Grace Lee), were leaders of the State-Capitalist Tendency. They were striving to re-think and re-formulate Marxism for their day. What emerged, were sharply differing philosophic, political, and organizational attitudes to revolution on the part of Dunayevskaya and James. Where James first probed Hegel's absolutes but then stopped, Dunayevskaya continued digging into those absolutes, seeing there new beginnings for our age; where Lee and James dismissed humanism, seeing it only as a bourgeois category, Dunayevskaya plunged into the humanism of Marx; where the mass self-activity of the coal miners in 1950-51 was seen by Dunayevskaya as a basis for revolutionary organization and newspaper, James practiced a deep depoliticalization in the early 1950s, wanting no public presentation of the Tendency's ideas.

In one sense the differing attitudes and resulting tensions were a divergence from political-organizational work, particularly in the last period of the Tendency's existence when such tensions meant not responding as a tendency to ongoing objective/subjective events. At the same time however, it was Dunayevskaya's determination to work through the contradictions within the Tendency, which led to leaps in the development of Marxist-Humanism. Her 1953 breakthrough on Hegel's absolutes, her focus on the humanism of Marx, the new kind of organization and newspaper she would found with colleagues in 1955, were created in opposition to the direction James had sought to give the Tendency. The differences with James, even when not always expressed as an open battle of ideas, compelled Dunayevskaya to concretely work out what Marxist-Humanism represented philosophically, politically and organizationally.

• From the 1950s into the 1970s Dunayevskaya corresponded with the Hegelian-Marxist philosopher Herbert Marcuse. In the first period leading to the publication of *Marxism and Freedom* (1957), Marcuse's responses to her writing were important in Dunayevskaya's shaping of this first work. Their disagreements centered on the "translation" of the dialectic into the political realm, which was related to their differing views on the potential revolutionary role of the proletariat in post-World War II industrial society. These in turn, were inseparable from their contrasting view of the relevance of Hegel's Absolute Idea for a liberatory future, which could be seen primarily in their correspondence of the 1960s as Dunayevskaya was working on her second work *Philosophy and Revolution*.

Marcuse did not see the need for a philosophic return to Hegel's Absolutes in the post-war world. In Dunayevskaya's correspondence with Marcuse, one can trace her labor to develop a new philosophic vantage point within Hegel's absolutes, and to find the absolutes' expression in ongoing political events be they the African Revolutions or workers battling automation.

• Dunayevskaya's ongoing critique of the thought of Mao Tse-tung led to important developments in Marxist-Humanist philosophic thought. Indeed, the designation of her philosophy as Marxist-Humanism in 1957 came in the same period that she added a footnote to the galley proofs of her just completed *Marxism and Freedom,* critiquing Mao's just released text of his speech "On Contradiction" as sophistry.

By 1964 she had developed a full chapter, "The Challenge of Mao Tse-tung," for the 2nd edition of *Marxism and Freedom.* She singled out Hegel's abstract philosophic development of "Spirit in Self-Estrangement" in *Phenomenology of Mind*—"the absolute and universal inversion of reality and thought, their entire estrangement one from the other"—as representative of Mao's thought.

In the final section of her added chapter she posed the question of "Two Kinds of Subjectivity" as characterizing the age of state-capitalism and workers' revolts: "One is the subjectivism that we have been considering—Mao's—which has no regard for objective conditions. . ." The second type of subjectivity was represented by millions struggling for freedom. Dunayevskaya saw probing these two types of subjectivity as the focus of her new philosophic work in progress.

Over the next decade she developed these ideas in what became *Philosophy and Revolution* (1973). Her discussion of Mao therein was related to the section on "Spirit in Self-Estrangement" as well as to Hegel's discussion of intuitionism in the "Third Attitude to Objectivity" section of the *Encyclopedia Logic.* Dunayevskaya saw these sections as speaking to the contradictions developing in the freedom movements of the post-World War II world. With Maoism becoming a pole of attraction to many of these movements, her critique was a battle of ideas against what she saw as a grave diversion within the freedom struggles. At the same time her discussions of the Hegelian dialectic's relation to the latter part of the 20th century became part of the crucible from which the Marxist-Humanist idea was forged.

• On a quite different level was Dunayevskaya's "battle of ideas" with Lenin. From the 1940s to the end of her life, she had the richest, most revolutionary "conversation" and "critique" with Lenin. His *Abstract on Hegel's Science of Logic,* which she translated into English for the first time in the 1940s, was a crucial point of departure for her own journeys into the Hegelian dialectic. From the 1940s into the 1980s there was an outpouring of notes, letters, talks and book chapters on Lenin. These began with her commentary that accompanied her 1949 translations of Lenin. Her May 12, 1953 letter on Hegel's Absolute Idea (see Chapter 3) pointed to where Lenin halted within the Absolute Idea chapter, and raised the need to probe further into Hegel's writings.

In *Marxism and Freedom* (1957), her discussion of Lenin focused on the philosophic breakthrough his Hegel notebooks presented. She regarded them as his philosophic preparation for the Russian revolution. In *Philosophy and Revolution* (1973), she raised a question of Lenin's "philosophic ambivalence" with regard to his Philosophic Notebooks. (See Chapter 9.) In her *Rosa Luxemburg, Women's Liberation and Marx's Philosophy of Revolution*, Lenin was seen by Dunayevskaya as part of the category she created of "post-Marx Marxists." (See below) Finally in 1986-87 came new probing of Lenin's philosophic journey. This led to a sharp critique of Lenin's failure to fully enter into Hegel's Absolute Idea section of the *Science of Logic*.

Dunayevskaya continual returns to Lenin were central to the development of Marxist-Humanism, an evolving view of Lenin, including critique, which became points of departures for her own philosophic growth.

•

Dunayevskaya's concept of critique, of a battle of ideas, did not stop with a critique of other thinkers and tendencies. The half-century development of the Idea of Marxist-Humanism was itself a contradictory, self-critical, dialectical process. In her most expansive discussion of Hegel, Dunayevskaya wrote of the need to subject Hegel's Absolutes to Hegel's own method of Absolute Negativity (*Philosophy and Revolution*, 6). Out of this labor, a central philosophic category of Marxist-Humanism was created, "Absolute Negativity as New Beginning." (See Chapters Eight and Nine below for discussion.) At the same time, the New Beginnings that she discerned within Hegel's Absolutes could only have come to the fore through subjecting her own body of thought to absolute negativity. If Absolute Negativity as New Beginning was characteristic of the movement of human history, it was characteristic of revolutionary Marxism—or so Dunayevskaya thought and practiced in the continual self-examination and testing of her own work.

Dunayevskaya's 1980s Philosophic Labors as Our Vantage Point

When at the beginning of the 1980s Dunayevskaya created the category "post-Marx Marxism as pejorative," it marked a leap in the concept of critique as a battle of ideas. The category arose out of her re-examination of the Marx-Engels relationship as she was writing *Rosa Luxemburg, Women's Liberation, and Marx's Philosophy of Revolution*. In probing how different were Marx's and Engels' methodologies, Dunayevskaya pointed to the difference between a follower and a continuator. No one was a more loyal follower of Marx than Engels. But to be a continuator of Marx's ideas meant grasping the totality of Marx's Marxism, his philosophy of revolution as one's point of departure for creating the dialectic anew. The category became a way of measuring not only Engels, but all post-Marx Marxists, from Lenin to Luxemburg to Trotsky, against

Marx's philosophy of revolution. (See Chapter 12 and Part V for discussion of post-Marx Marxism as a pejorative.)

During the 1980s of President Ronald Reagan's "ongoing retrogressionism and his super-patriotic fanaticism," Dunayevskaya turned not only to analyze these objective events but to the whole body of Marxism-Humanist thought, developed over the course of more than four and a half decades, what she termed a Retrospective/Perspective

With the category of post-Marx Marxism, she subjected not only others but her own lifework to a self-critique that this category necessitated. The new category cast powerful illumination not only on Marxism post-Marx outside of Marxist-Humanism, but *inside* Marxist-Humanism. Part V begins by exploring Dunayevskaya's 1982-87 reexaminations of the Marxist-Humanist philosophic tendency she founded. These gave her a crucial way of viewing Marxist-Humanism in contrast to post-Marx Marxism, as well as a critical perspective on Marxist-Humanism's origins and development. Her return to the multi-layered, at times contradictory processes in developing the Idea of Marxist-Humanism, was unprecedented in the revolutionary Marxist movement.

She probed Marxist-Humanism's multi-linear origins: (1) in participation/analysis of mass movements ranging from the 1949-50 Miners' General Strike, to the 1952 Bolivian Revolution, to the 1953 East German Revolt; (2) in diving deeply into the Hegelian dialectic through working out Absolute Idea and Absolute Mind as containing a movement from practice to theory as well as from theory to practice. She would call this 1953 breakthrough, "The Philosophic Moment of Marxist-Humanism;" (3) in establishing a continuity with Marx's Marxism first as "economics" in developing the theory of state-capitalism, and then reaching to the fullness of bringing to the fore his humanism as characterizing a life-body of revolutionary dialectical thought and action.

At the same time, she continued to deepen her concept of post-Marx Marxism, particularly working out a new view of Lenin's journey into the Hegelian dialectic. She critically questioned whether Lenin had been philosophically immersed fully within Hegel's Absolute Idea, and asked what ramifications flowed from that.

Dunayevskaya challenged the revolutionary organization she founded—News and Letters Committees—to project the fullness of the Marxist-Humanist body of ideas in ongoing movements of women's liberation, anti-war youth, the Black dimension, and rank-and-file labor struggles. She critiqued the manner in which the Committees had projected the category post-Marx Marxism in the mid-1980s, and sought pathways to aide her colleagues in taking organizational responsibility for the Idea of Marxist-Humanism.

In 1986-87 she was engaged in writing a new book tentatively titled "Dialectics of Organization and Philosophy: the 'Party' and forms of organization born of spontaneity," a work halted by her death. She spoke of working out the dialectic of organization and philosophy as "the untrodden path," of the revolutionary movement.

Dunayevskaya's manner of creating, following out, and interweaving these 1980s threads gave birth to new revolutionary beginnings for Marxist-Humanism. Her journey opened the door for this present study. We have striven to have her 1980s view inform the content and structure of *Raya Dunayevskaya—Philosopher of Marxist-Humanism.*

•

In the end, the exploration of Dunayevskaya's thought and activity cannot be limited to undertaking a study in and of itself in isolation from our ongoing world and its crisis. Our moment is the one in need of deeply uprooting social transformation. Yet we cannot hope to be able to do so without rooting ourselves in the historical-philosophic antecedents of dialectic thought and in today's possibilities of revolutionary human subjectivity. Only thereby can the dialectic be recreated. Dunayevskaya's 50-year body of revolutionary ideas and activity can cast a powerful illumination on that needed task. This book is structured to present an opening to exploring that body of thought further.

Dunayevskaya's Archives as she organized them during her lifetime consist of more than 10,000 pages. After her death, close to 7,000 pages have been added as a Supplement to the collection. To do justice to such a collection, even if only in survey form, is a project beyond the scope of the present work. Instead, I have endeavored to present an opening for readers to begin an exploration of Dunayevskaya's thought, in the hope that it will encourage their own journeys into her major writings and archives.

Dunayevskaya was one of the foremost creative Hegelian-Marxist thinkers of the Twentieth Century. However her body of work is not well known in the world of radical thought at the beginning of the Twenty-first Century. The present work strives to give an indication of the vast depth and breath of Dunayevskaya's theoretical and activist-organizational labors. Its structure is both chronological and centered around her major writing projects. It is as well centered on certain crucial themes, nodal points, which emerged from those years. But concentration on nodal points alone, may at the same time lead to distortions, gaps in seeing the multi-linearity of her development, including the, at times, contradictory nature of the process. The development of Marxist-Humanism cannot be fully caught in moving from high point to high point. Thus, I have sought to present a range of developments and contradictions, some of which may turn out in the end to be crucial moments in self-development of the Idea of Marxist-Humanism.

•

Though I knew and worked with Raya Dunayevskaya over several decades, this book is neither a memoir nor a conventional intellectual biography from a critical distance. I do not have a desire to write the former, nor sufficient distance to write the latter. Rather, I seek to give an opening to her ideas to those who have not yet had the opportunity to become deeply acquainted with her revolutionary thought. I have sought not to rush to "interpret" her writings, though I know, of course, that by selecting certain writings and sections to take up and leaving others aside, as well as by setting a certain form to this book, I am indeed making an "interpretation." However, I trust that an interested, intelligent reader will not substitute my labors, for her or his own digging into the body of Marxist-Humanism that Dunayevskaya created. To the extent that my work can open the door for others' journeys, I hope it will be welcomed.

Dunayevskaya was an epochal thinker in the last half of the 20th century. Because she participated in important mass movements from below—workers against the new stage of automated production, the Black civil rights struggles and rebellion, the emergence of a women's liberation movement, and the actions of anti-war youth—but did not have the opportunity to test those ideas in epochal revolutionary moments—as did Marx, 1848, 1871; Lenin, 1905, 1917; Trotsky, 1905, 1917; Luxemburg, 1905, 1919;—her development of Marxist-Humanism, while known in many circles throughout the world, did not become a large pole of revolutionary attraction in her lifetime. Nor can we yet answer as to the viability of Marxist-Humanism in the future. The challenge is thus in presenting the dialectic of thought of her Marxist-Humanism as it was born and developed, out of world objective events and the dialectic of Hegel and of Marx, but as well, out of contradiction and self-critique. In the end this can be done in fullness only in its re-creation as ground and methodology for New Beginnings by living revolutionary practitioners of the Idea as needed for transforming reality. As Dunayevskaya noted:

> Only live human beings can recreate the revolutionary dialectic forever anew. And these live human beings must do so in theory as well as in practice. It is not a question only of meeting the challenge from practice, but of being able to meet the challenge from the self-development of the Idea, and of deepening theory to the point where it reaches Marx's concept of the philosophy of "revolution in permanence."

Dunayevskaya's body of work can be found in the books first published during her lifetime and in her vast Archives available on microfilm. Additional collections of some of her writings on state-capitalist theory and on the dialectic in Hegel and Marx are also available in book form. This present study restricts itself to an attempt to shine a light upon the existence of those studies, an opening for a new generation of thinker-activists to take their own voyages of discovery, to hear Dunayevskaya "thinking aloud," and perhaps discern ways that those ideas might speak to us today.

Part I

1941-1956, From the Origins of State-Capitalist Theory to Letters on Hegel's Absolutes to the Founding of News and Letters Committee

Chapter 1

The Hitler-Stalin Pact, the Outbreak of the Second World War, and the Theory of State-Capitalism: Manuscripts from Its Initial Projection, 1941-43

Prologue: The 1930s—The Spanish Civil War and Dunayevskaya as Secretary to Leon Trotsky

"Where to begin?" in relation to the body of ideas that comprises Marxist-Humanism, is not easily answered. Dunayevskaya grappled with this question when she initially placed her documents in the Wayne State University Archives of Labor History and Urban Affairs in July 1969. *The Raya Dunayevskaya Collection* was initially sub-titled "Marxist-Humanism: Its Origins and Development in the U.S., 1941 to Today." As an appendix to Part 1 of the Collection, she included documents from her earlier work with Leon Trotsky, including her translations of Trotsky's writings and correspondence from Dunayevskaya to Trotsky.

In 1986, Dunayevskaya deposited volume XII "Retrospective and Perspective—The Raya Dunayevskaya Collection, 1924-1984," creating what she called "a 1980s view of the Marxist-Humanist Archives," and changing the Collection's sub-title to "Marxist-Humanism: A Half-Century of Its World Development," in order to more fully reflect its range. She wrote an "Introduction/Overview" to the new volume, discussing the new additions in relation to the revolutionary movement in each of the decades.

From the 1920s came material which documented her activity as a teenager in the Chicago area, both her labor work and work in the Black struggle, including with the newspaper of the American Negro Labor Congress, the *Negro Champion*. From the 1930s, material was added in relation to her activity in American labor struggles, in work with the *Russian Bulletin of the Opposition*, and further documentation of her work with Leon Trotsky.

The Spanish Civil War was of particular significance, and Dunayevskaya called attention to the addition of three articles of Trotsky's on the Spanish Revolution that she translated. As well, she was translating part of Trotsky's *How the Revolution Armed Itself*. These activities "were part of making the 1917 Russian Revolution so relevant to the 1937 Spanish Revolution that Trotskyists should become both active participants and theoreticians" (Introduction to Vol. XII of *The Raya Dunayevskaya Collection*).

A few weeks after writing the 1986 Introduction/Overview to Vol. XII, Dunayevskaya added a post-script, further explaining the new title, and reflecting her thoughts as to Marxist-Humanism's initial development: "Put differently, the 1930s are the focal point now. The Depression signaled the end of private capitalism, while out of the Spanish Civil War there emerged a new kind of revolutionary who posed questions not only against Stalinism but against Trotskyism, indeed against all *established* Marxists."[1]

To Dunayevskaya in the 1980s, the Spanish Civil War had become key to the origins of her body of thought, including consciousness of the creative mass self-activity from below. The Civil War manifested the new revolutionary subjectivity of workers, while at the same time, it exposed the insufficiency of Trotskyism to meet that mass upsurge, or to fully confront the Stalinist stranglehold on the revolutionary impulses emerging from Spain. Spain became the dress rehearsal for the events that would unfold in World War II. It was a crucial catalyst for the emergence of "a new kind of revolutionary."

Early Writings on State-Capitalism in Relation to Marx's Writings

For the present study, we begin with the outbreak of the Second World War and Dunayevskaya's writings on state-capitalism. These were her first sustained writings at the time of her break with Trotsky's view of the nature of the Russian state.

The year 1939 saw the outbreak of the Second World War. Among its major catalysts was the Hitler-Stalin "non-aggression" Pact that had been rapidly negotiated and signed on August 23, only days after the negotiations Russia had been having with England and France ground to a halt. On September 1, Germany invaded Poland. On September 3, England and France entered the war.

The fact that an ostensibly communist country would open the door to war by signing a pact with a fascist state was a shock for the revolutionary movement. The major Left opposition to Stalin, Trotskyism, opposed the Pact. Yet for Trotsky, the Pact did not signal the need to alter his economic analysis of the Soviet Union. In the year that remained before his death by assassination at the hand of Stalin's agent, Trotsky continued with his view of Russia as a workers' state.

Within the Trotskyist movement, there were revolutionaries who felt that no authentic workers' state would sign a pact with Nazi Germany. Among them was Dunayevskaya, who began to study the nature of the Russian economy.

•

From the vantage point of today, when Russia is no longer the challenger to the United States either ideologically or in economic/military terms, it may seem of only archival interest to focus on Dunayevskaya's path breaking analysis of Russia as a state-capitalist society. However, three dimensions of her analysis speak to the contemporary relevance of her 1940s studies. First, though the concentration was on the economic nature of the "Soviet" Union, her analysis came to encompass state-capitalism as a world phenomenon that arose in the 1930s in such diverse spheres as Nazism in Germany, the New Deal in the United States, and the Co-Prosperity sphere in Japan. The linking of economics and politics, including the military, via the state, speaks to today's drive of the U.S. for hegemonic, single-world domination, in a world of neo-liberal rhetoric and a solo superpower.

Second, Dunayevskaya's theory of state-capitalism was never limited to a strictly economic analysis. The theory embraced state-capitalism's opposite—the human forces of rebellion. This was manifest by pinpointing the opposition within Russia to Stalin's state-capitalist terror and dictatorial rule. It extended to showing opposition within Russia's capitalist rival, the United States. In the midst of World War II, Dunayevskaya was also writing a number of studies on the Black question in America under the impact of uprisings in Detroit and Harlem, as well as a miner's strike which included large numbers of Black miners. Her methodology was one of searching out, listening to, and analyzing the forces of revolt in opposition to the evolving stage of capitalism.

Third, Dunayevskaya's theory of state-capitalism had within it, implicitly at first and then quite explicitly, Marx's philosophic categories as integral to his economics. Marx's humanism was in embryo in her theory of state-capitalism, later developing into the philosophy of Marxist-Humanism.

While Dunayevskaya's theory of state-capitalism was rooted in an analysis of the Soviet Union's economic reality in the mid-20th century, it developed to encompass a world dimension, a concept of revolutionary subjectivity, and a philosophic expression of Marx's humanism.

•

Two questions were at the heart of Dunayevskaya's studies of Stalinist Russia in the early 1940s: (1) What kind of a society was Russia if it was not a workers' state? (2) What was a workers' state if Russia no longer was one?

In examining Russian society, she used the economic categories Marx had discerned in *Capital*—(a) the fact that living labor took the form of a commodity, labor power; (b) the preponderance of the production of the means of production over the production of the means of consumption; (c) the organic composition of capital reflecting the domination of dead labor (machines) over living labor (workers)—to reach the conclusion that Russia was a state capitalist society.

In probing what was a workers' state, Dunayevskaya examined Marx's writings on the Paris Commune, his *Critique of the Gotha Program*, and discussed material from what later became known as the 1844 *Economic and Philosophic Manuscripts*. (In their initial publication in Russian, the manuscripts had been identified as "Preparatory work for *The Holy Family*.")

In the early 1940s she translated excerpts from his "Private Property and Labor," "Private Property and Communism," and "Critique of the Hegelian Dialectic" (*RDC* #8845). Her essay "Labor and Society," which was to be the introduction for her economic analysis of Russia, had begun to investigate the question of what was a workers' state from the vantage point of her reading of Marx's early humanist writings. Dunayevskaya's analysis of the reality of Russian society in the midst of Stalin's Five Year Plans was not limited to the here and now of Russia's economic statistics. In reaching back to Marx's economics, she found she was taking initial steps onto Marx's humanist, philosophic terrain.

"The Union of Soviet Socialist Republics is a Capitalist Society"

Responding to the Hitler-Stalin Pact and the Soviet Union's participation "in the Second Imperialist World War," Dunayevskaya began a series of studies on the nature of the Russian economy. "The Union of Soviet Socialist Republics is a Capitalist Society," (1941) was the title she gave to her first publication on the theory of state-capitalism. It was written before she discovered Marx's 1844 writings.[2]

This short essay had three sections. "Political and Social Rule," began by noting Trotsky's contention that statified property was sufficient to characterize Russia as a workers' state, despite the Stalinist bureaucracy. In contrast, Dunayevskaya described a twofold character of the Russian state in the first years after the Revolution: (1) workers' *political* power, "a state controlled by them through their own organs—the trade unions, the Soviets, the Bolshevik Party," and (2) *social* power, "practical participation in the management (Lenin)" of the state, so that "political and social rule of the proletariat are merged and *that* guaranteed power in the hands of the proletariat." This, she argued was not present in the Soviet state of 1941: "I deny that the social conquests of October . . .

are to be narrowly translated into mere statified property . . . which in no way resembles the Marxian concept of a workers' state, i.e., 'the proletariat organized as the ruling class' (Marx)" ("The Union of Soviet Socialist Republics is a Capitalist Society,"2,3).

In the second section, "State Capitalism or Bureaucratic State Socialism?" Dunayevskaya critiqued an alternative analysis of Russian society, the concept of "bureaucratic state socialism" put forth by Max Shachtman, the leader of the Workers Party. At the time, Dunayevskaya was a member of the Workers Party. She noted that the manner by which the mode of production in "this presumably new exploitative society," bureaucratic state socialism, differed from that of a capitalist society was never explored by Shachtman.

Not the ownership of the means of production, but "whether the means of production are *capital*, that is, whether they are monopolized and alienated from the direct producers," was decisive in exploring the class nature of a society (3). The term "bureaucratic state socialism," later called "bureaucratic collectivism," obscured the real economic relations.

Dunayevskaya returned to an analysis of Trotsky's view that state capitalism did not exist in Russia, "since the ownership of the means of production by the state occurred in history by the proletariat with the method of social revolution and not by the capitalist with the method of state trustification" (3). She pointed out that this path to state ownership did not prevent usurpers from transforming these statified means of production to capital: "It is high time to evaluate 'the economic law of motion of modern society' as it applies to the Soviet Union" (4).

In the final section, "No Defense of the Capitalist Society Existing in Russia," Dunayevskaya argued that because the class nature of Russia was misunderstood by the Trotskyist opposition, it was not prepared for "the Soviet Union's integral participation in the Second Imperialist World War. . . . The Red Army's march on Poland, the bloody conquest of part of Finland and the peaceful conquest of the Baltic states proved that the Stalinized Red Army had no more connection with the spirit, purpose and content of October than has the Stalinist state, whose armed might it is" (4). "The Russian masses bore the brunt" of the state's transformation that had begun long before the outbreak of World War II. The piecework system, speed-up, labor reserves, ten-fold income disparity between factory worker and factory director—all were characteristic of "the whole mode of production [that] produces and reproduces the capitalist production relations. State capitalism it is true, but capitalism nevertheless. . . . It is the real economic relations that leads to: no defense of the capitalist society existing in Russia" (5).[3]

"An Analysis of the Russian Economy"

After the initial political analysis made in her first essay, Dunayevskaya undertook "to evaluate 'the economic law of motion of modern society' as it applies to the Soviet Union." Her original study "The Nature of the Russian Economy," a 121-page typescript, was completed in November, 1942. To facilitate publication, Dunayevskaya divided the study into two parts: "An Analysis of the Russian Economy," ("concerned primarily with a factual and objective analysis of the evolution of the Russian economy from 1928 to 1941"), and "Politics and Economics," ("to analyze the nature of contemporary Russian economy in the light of basic Marxist principles"). Due to the restrictions placed upon a minority tendency within the Workers Party, Dunayevskaya was not able to present the full sweep of her work as it evolved. The only part of the study that was published at the time was Part I, "An Analysis of the Russian Economy."[4]

Because "An Analysis of the Russian Economy" was the first to document Russia's transformation to a state-capitalist society using statistics from the first three Five Year Plans, it is examined here in some detail. Its core was a study of "the *direction* in which [the] Russian economy has proceeded during that period [1928-1941]." This involved probing (1) the relation of the production of the means of production to the production of the means of consumption; (2) the organic composition of capital in Russia, and (3) the living standards of the Russian masses.

Instead of submitting to Trotsky's premise that "nationalized property equals socialism," or accepting the facile designation, without any comprehensive economic analysis, of Russia as a new social form, "bureaucratic collectivist," Dunayevskaya began her work by examining the relation between Marx's economic categories and the Russian economy. She first created a statistical abstract of the USSR. In constructing an index of industrial production Dunayevskaya had to discard the index produced by the state economists in Russia, which presented total production based on the value of the ruble, since it was found to be "utterly useless as an index of production or purchasing power in the internal economy" (*The Marxist-Humanist Theory of State Capitalism*, 37). Instead, she compared "physical output of selected sections of both heavy and light industry as well as agricultural production, against a background of statistics on population and national income" (37). Using such an index to measure the production of the means of production (electrification, petroleum, coal, iron, steel, tractors, length of railroads), and the production of the means of consumption (cotton materials, woolens, linen, paper, sugar, leather footwear, rubbers), Dunayevskaya found that the actual production for both types of goods based on volume was far short of the claimed accomplishment of the first Five Year Plan (1928-1932) based on ruble value.

Furthermore, the official figures were additionally skewed by including the level of past production as part of the present accomplishment, (that is, they counted work done before the initiation of the first Five Year Plan). When she created an index using both volume of production and computing the percentage of actual increase in production in relation to planned increase over the years covered by the plan (excluding past production), the actual accomplishment of the Five Year Plan dropped dramatically. For example, instead of construction of railroads being measured at 92.5% accomplished, the true value was 49%. Production of the means of production was shown to be considerably less spectacular than claimed by the government.

The difference between claimed results and actual achievement was even more dramatic when production of means of consumption was examined. When planned increases were measured against actual accomplishments, "the production of means of consumption not only failed to meet its goals, not only showed no increase in production, but starkly reveals a *decrease* from even the 1928 levels" (41). When measured by volume of production, a stagnation and even decrease in the production of means of consumption in such items as cotton and woolens occurred, (cotton decreasing from 2742 million meters in 1928 to 2417 million meters in 1932). Yet when measured by the standard of value output in terms of rubles, the gross output of articles of consumption falsely appeared to be nearly doubling, (8.7 billion rubles in 1928; 16.3 billion in l932).

Dunayevskaya showed that the accomplishments of the Russian economy were quite ordinary and, in terms of the production of means of consumption, even disastrous. When the overall composition of the Russian economy over the first two Five Year Plans and half of the third Five Year Plan was examined, the production of the means of production outdistanced the production of the means of consumption in a manner that was indistinguishable from that of a private capitalist society.

The value of the production of the means of production increased from 44.3% of the economy in 1928 at the initiation of the first Five Year Plan to 61% by 1940, whereas the production of the means of consumption decreased from 55.7% to 39.0%. Dunayevskaya commented; "Here we note a phenomenon characteristic of the whole contemporary world: the preponderance of the means of production over means of consumption" (39).

It was not that this preponderance was the open aim of the plan. But once the determination was made to "catch up with and outdistance the capitalist lands," and Russia entered the environment of the world market, the trend was established: "There was the necessity of producing machinery with the most modern technique. The low productivity of Russian labor conflicted with the high productivity of international labor. Consequently, the reality of the world market and world prices constantly forced the state to increase the amount of capital investments going into the production of means of production" (42).

The Russian planners saw the results of the plan and proclaimed an additional goal for the second Five Year plan: "to achieve a yet better improvement in the living standards of the masses." No matter that no time could be spared for such a concern. The drive for increasing the production of the means of production would brook no "diversion" in order to raise the living standards of the Russian people. As Dunayevskaya noted: "[T]he high organic composition of capital on a world scaled *imposed* this law of motion on the Russian economy" (43). Russia too would follow the law of capitalist industrial development discerned by Marx: the use of more and more dead labor (machines) relative to living labor (workers).

Dunayevskaya wrote: "The fact that is of utmost importance is that, despite the comparative backwardness of both Russia and Japan, both countries reflect the high organic composition of capital characteristic of *all* important industrially developed countries"(46). Russia followed what Marx had demonstrated to be characteristic of capitalist countries—the preponderance of the production of means of production over means of consumption. This characteristic was being driven by the continual change in the organic composition of capital on a world level. To compete, Russia could only move in the direction of a dominance of dead labor over living labor.

The goal of the third Five Year Plan, begun in 1939, was once again to catch up with the capitalist lands. The Russian leadership announced that this catching up needed to be measured not only as rate of growth or even the volume of output, but as per capita productivity. Russia was far behind the advanced capitalist countries in terms of the productivity of its labor. In capitalist terms, there are only two ways to change this: the introduction of more and more machinery (dead labor), or the speed-up of the working class. Russia intended to do both.

Dunayevskaya showed that the drive to "catch up with the capitalist lands" manifested itself in numerous ways. To expand their industries, the rulers needed accumulation, "socialist accumulation." The crucial principle was to obtain it from the Russian working class. As the chairman of the State Planning Commission stated:

> The plan for 1941 provides for a 12 percent increase in the productivity of labor and a 6.5 percent increase in wages per worker. This proportion between the increase in labor productivity and average wages furnishes a basis for lowering production cost and increasing socialist accumulation and constitutes the most important condition for the realization of a high rate of extended socialist reproduction" (quoted, 46).

However, this direct exploitation of its working class did not provide sufficient accumulation for Russia's rulers. Soon after the appearance of the first Five Year Plan came a decree for "a single tax on profits." Dunayevskaya explained: "'The single tax on profits' turned out to have two sections: (1) a tax on profits which comprised 9-12 percent of the state budget and (2) a turnover tax which comprised 60-80 percent of the state budget. It is the latter tax which is crucial—sufficient to finance all industrialization and militarization" (46).

The turnover tax could raise such enormous sums because unlike the usual sales tax, which is a fixed percentage of the base price of a commodity, the turnover tax is a fixed percentage of the total sales value, including the amount of tax. "This means that whereas a 90 percent sales tax raised the price of merchandise 90 percent, a 90 percent turnover tax increases the sales price *tenfold*" (47).

Dunayevskaya cited figures to show that the tax was unbalanced, light on means of production, heavy on articles of mass consumption. The tax was highest of all on bread and agricultural produce. Thus, not only was there direct accumulation from the working class at the point of production, but further accumulation from their consumption:

> [T]he whole cost of industrialization and militarization has been borne by the people through that ingenious scheme known as the turnover tax, which provided 79 percent of the total state revenue in 1937. . . . The "national wealth" grew from 19 billion rubles in 1931 to 178 billion in 1940; the per capita national income increase from 52 rubles in 1928 to 198 in 1937. But the real wages of the proletariat *decreased to half* of what they were in 1928! (48)

In the beginning of her study Dunayevskaya had pointed to three factors in looking at the direction of the Russian economy: (1) the preponderance of means of production over means of consumption; (2) the need for the organic composition of capital to continually move in the direction of more machinery and less living labor; and (3) the rapid deterioration of the living standards of the masses. The early sections of her essay examined the first two tendencies, while the latter sections probed the third factor of the Russian economy.

Dunayevskaya began examining the deterioration of the living standards by focusing on agriculture. In the section "The Economics of Russian Agriculture, 1928-41," she traced the vicissitudes of Stalin's agriculture policy from forced collectivization (and the resultant famine) to the subsequent free market resulting in the rise of a few rich collective farms and a multitude of impoverished ones, to the introduction of mechanization and increase in unemployment. She asked: "What is the economy of Russian agriculture and what is its law of motion?"

In 1931, Stalin had ordered a complete reversal of the New Economic Policy that allowed the peasantry a degree of private accumulation. Faced with immediate forced collectivization of agriculture, the reaction of the peasantry was to slaughter its livestock. This occurred in the context of the beginning of the Depression:

> The world crisis adversely affected the price Russian agricultural produce could command on the world market. If we take 1928 to be 100, prices on the world market dropped to 67.2 and on agricultural produce, which is what Russia wished to sell in order to buy machinery, they dropped to 45.5. Tractors, which were not manufactured rapidly enough in Russia to take place of the draft animals slaughtered, could not be brought in sufficient quantity because of lack of capital. The disorganization on the agricultural front was accompanied by a famine that stalked throughout the Soviet land. Millions died (52).

Faced with this extreme crisis, the government retreated to a free market, calling it a "collective farm market." This set the stage for a growing differentiation between various collectivized farms, and amongst the collectivized peasantry. While the slogan put forth in the Russian press was "Make all *kolkhozy* (collectivized farms) prosperous," the reality was far different. Dunayevskaya cited statistics which indicated that "the millionaire *kolkhozy* comprise *one-third of one percent* of all *kolkhozy* (610 *kolkhozy* out of 2,424 thousand *kolkhozy* in the USSR)," while pauper *kolkhozy* were twenty times as numerous.

Among the collectivized peasants, enormous differences in the amount of distribution of farm products as compensation for labor prevailed. In 1937 the amount of grain allotted per labor-day to an individual farm worker ranged from one and a half kilograms to over fifteen kilos. A labor-day was not a calendar working day, "but a piece rate unit accorded the various categories of skilled and unskilled labor. A field hand's working day is 'worth' one-half a labor-day and a tractor driver's day is worth five labor days. Moreover, a labor-day does not command the same price in all regions." Dunayevskaya recorded a fourfold difference per labor unit paid to different collectivized farm peasants for the same work. Social differentiation became government policy.

While unemployment was officially declared abolished after 1930, Dunayevskaya demonstrated through Russian statistics the enormous surplus of labor in the countryside, particularly under the impact of mechanization. Thus the needed number of man-days per hectare of land under grain crops fell by 50 percent from 1922-25 to 1937. But "no scientific proof that much of labor was surplus to agricultural requirements, not even the appeal of 'The Leader' himself, proved powerful enough to move the peasant off from his half acre plot of land and willingly give himself over to the factory regime" (58).

The regime's response to unemployment was state labor reserves. On October 2, 1940 a decree was promulgated requiring the *kolkhoz* and city soviets to give up to one million youths between the ages of 14 and 17 for compulsory vocation training, after which they had to work for the state for four years. Such was the lot of the peasantry and "surplus peasantry." For the vast majority, there was deterioration in their conditions of labor and life.

But what of the proletariat? What had the Five Year Plans meant for him or her? Dunayevskaya began the final major section, "Social Classes in Russia," by tracing the various anti-labor laws instituted by Stalin's Russia:

1929—a decree making workers responsible for damaged goods;

1930—a law making it obligatory "for a factory director to insert into the worker's paybook the reason for his dismissal" (60). In the same year, came the creation of a "special list" of those who left their jobs on their own volition, which denied them unemployment compensation. Because of food scarcity, rationing was introduced in 1930. The worker's ration card was put into hands of the factory directors. Unemployment insurance was abolished.

1932—A new decree allowed a worker to be fired for a single day's absence without permission. "Moreover, the factory director thereupon could deprive him not only of his food card *but also* of the right to occupy the premises owned by the factory, that is, the worker's living quarters" (60).

1933—the Council of Labor and Defense, which had tried to protect workers' rights, was absorbed into the Economic Council. No trade unions independent of the state existed.

1938—Labor passports were introduced to prevent absenteeism and forbidding workers from leaving their work.

1940—When labor passports did not have the desired effect, a new decree was issued. "It forbade the worker to leave his job. Truancy and other infractions of the law were punishable by six months 'corrective labor'—labor in the factory, that is, with a 25 percent reduction in pay" (59).

This series of labor law legislation attempted to force the submission of the Russian working class to the will of Stalin's state.

There was another major approach used by the regime in its attempt to fit the working class to the designs of the state: the ending of depersonalization and the creating of Stakhanovism.

In 1931 Stalin had called for the end of depersonalization. What did that mean? It was not until 1935 that, with great fanfare, the government provided the face and the method to carry out depersonalization: Stakhanovism. Dunayevskaya quoted the chairman of the State Planning Commission's explanation:

> A plain miner, the Donetz Basin hewer, Alexei Stakanov, in response to Stalin's speech of May 4, 1935, the keynote of which was the care of the human being and which marked a new stage in the development of the USSR, proposed a new system of labor organization for the extraction of coal. The very first day his method was applied he cut 102 tons of coal in one shift of six hours instead of the established rate of seven tons (61).

The press and photographers were there to record and propagandize this staged feat. Now depersonalization had a face and a method. Stakhanovism was instituted in other industries as the regime sought to impose the Stakhanovites' one-day miracles as the "norm" for the mass of workers. Dunayevskaya noted, "Piecework was made the prevailing system of work in Russia. In the state of Lenin-Trotsky, where the *Subbotnik* (the worker who volunteered his Saturday services without pay to *his* state) was the hero, the range of pay was one to three; in the Stalinist state, where the Stakhanovite is the hero, the range of pay is one to twenty" (62).

The end of depersonalization and creation of wide differentials in pay in industry and agriculture could only have meaning if there was something for this new aristocracy of labor to buy. The abolition of rationing and increased production of luxury goods served the purpose. Now a small group, Stakhanovites, and those peasants from the tiny fraction of rich collective farms, could spend their money on real goods.

But what of the vast majority of workers? The abolition of rationing for the mass of ordinary workers meant a huge increase in the price of goods and thus a decrease in their standard of living. Dunayevskaya constructed a series of tables that showed the cost of food in Czarist times, in 1928 before the imposition of the Five Year Plans, and in 1940 in the midst of the third Five Year Plan with rationing abolished. She then constructed an index of real wages by dividing the nominal weekly wage into the real cost of food. The standard of living of the worker in 1940, as measured by ability to purchase basic food products, was shown to have fallen to 50% of the 1928 level. Contrast this decrease with the fact that "'national wealth' leaped from six billions in 1928 to 178 billions in 1940, and you have the most perfect polarization of wealth in an 'industrially advanced' society" (66).

In conclusion, Dunayevskaya examined the Russian intelligentsia: "The Social Physiognomy of the Ruling Class." Behind the Russian leadership's determination to hide its "classless intelligentsia" under the category of "workers and employees" she found factory directors and managers, the supervisors, army intelligentsia and the like:

> The 'most advanced' of the intelligentsia, 'the genuine creators of a new life,' as Molotov called them—those, that is, who are the real masters over the productive process—constitute a mere 3.4 million or 2.05 percent of the total population. . . . The Central Administration of National Economy Statistics, needless to say, did not reveal the exact share of surplus value appropriated by this 'advanced' intelligentsia. But at least we know who this group is and what it does. The part it plays in the process of production stamps it as clearly for the ruling class; it is as if, indeed, it had worn a label marked 'Exploiters' (70).

"Politics and Economics"

"An Analysis of the Russian Economy," examined above, was Part I of a two part study on "The Nature of the Russian Economy." Part II, written as part of a single manuscript with Part I, (dated November 1942) was titled "Politics and Economics," but was never published in its original form. (*RDC* #102-163).

The first paragraph of this unpublished manuscript demonstrated Dunayevskaya's determination to extend her study beyond a factual analysis of the Russian economy:

> Part One of this article was concerned primarily with a factual and objective analysis of the evolution of [the] Russian economy from 1928 to 1941. Part Two has a broader and more fundamental purpose—to analyze the nature of contemporary Russian economy in the light of basic Marxist principles. The facts in Part One are necessary to elucidate and prove my conclusions[,] but

here I shall not confine myself to that period (1928-1941). It is necessary to turn the pages of history further back.

Dunayevskaya turned to the workers' state of the October revolution, "the first historic instance when the workers not only gained power but held it" ("Politics and Economics" *RDC*, #102). Her discussion of the debate on the role of trade unions in a living workers' state contrasted sharply with the closed, rule by decree, forced collectivization, state labor reserve state she had analyzed via the motion of the Russian economy, 1928-1941.

In following the trade union dispute of 1920-21, Dunayevskaya presented the positions of Lenin and Trotsky on the role of trade unions in what Lenin had characterized as a workers' state in "the transition from capitalism to Communism." Concerning Lenin, Dunayevskaya summed up his central motif after the conquest of power: "*the conscious participation of the masses* is quintessential in directing the state and in managing [the] economy *if* the workers state was to be transitional to socialism" (#106). According to Lenin, the trade unions played a crucial role in this transition: "[W]e must utilize these workers' organizations for the purpose of protecting the workers from their own state and in order that the workers may protect our state" (#106).

Turning to Trotsky, Dunayevskaya first presented Lenin's view that Trotsky did not grasp the ramifications that Russia was a transitional state, "not altogether a workers' state," and thus the need to have the trade unions as "transmission belts," as opposed to Trotsky's call for absorbing them into the state. She called attention to "Lenin's reproach of Trotsky for acting as an administrator in his trade union thesis [that] appeared in Lenin's Will as a characterization of Trotsky" (#108).

Dunayevskaya then took up her own analysis and critique of Trotsky with regard to the role of the workers' own organizations in a workers' state. She cited Lenin's view of workers in this nascent workers state—"their *conscious participation* in the process of production would establish the proper production relations and be the best guarantee against the bureaucratization of the apparatus"(#113)—and used this to counter Trotsky's view—"Trotsky considered that once the social foundation had been laid by the October Revolution that the proletariat need not fear for his interests, for his *state* would protect them. . . . [H]e retained his position that in a workers' state the trade unions have a limited role and the state would take care of the workers interests" (#112).

Dunayevskaya demonstrated that whether it was the period immediately after War Communism—when Trotsky wanted to statify the trade unions to help enforce production—or the period of the New Economic Policy (NEP), with its free market retreat—when Trotsky argued that a market economy excludes the possibility of practical participation of the trade unions in the management of the enterprises—the *constant* for Trotsky was making the workers' state into a fetish. This would blind him to the grave *internal* dangers to that workers' state. He did not see the concrete day to day self-activity of the masses as the crucial thread that could reveal the direction and grave contradictions facing the new workers' state.

Dunayevskaya reorganized this section of her manuscript into a section called "Role of Labor in a Workers State" (*RDC* #94-101). She also presented the position of the leader of the Workers Opposition, Shlyapnikov, who advocated turning the management of the national economy to a congress of producers. Dunayevskaya showed that Lenin opposed this approach as unrealistic, and argued that Shlyapnikov *and* Trotsky were making "an abstraction of the workers' state."

She saw the Trade Union Debate as a nodal point for examining the nascent Russian workers' state. Indeed, her discussion of the immediate post-1917 years would become a key category in the development of the Marxist-Humanism. In *Marxism and Freedom* (1957), the category "What Happens After?" achieving power, would be discussed as characteristic not only of Russia, but of the entire post-Russian Revolution age.

Trotsky's fetishism of the Russian workers' state neglected the reality of the Russian workers' relationship to that state, and was linked with his equating nationalized property to socialism. In so doing, he failed to detect Russia's transformation into a state-capitalist monstrosity as Stalin's Five Year Plans unfolded. It is to this fetishism of state property that Dunayevskaya turned in the "Politics and Economics" essay.

Dunayevskaya critiqued Trotsky's position at considerable length and asked: "Will the revolutionary workers' movement, after freeing itself of the fetishism of the *form* of a product of labor (commodity) create a new fetishism of a *form* of property (statified property)?" She argued that "it was this fetishism of statified property that blinded Trotsky from seeing the real content of the counter-revolution when it came."

•

Dunayevskaya's unpublished manuscript, "Politics and Economics" served as the basis for a rewritten "The Nature of the Russian Economy," which was completed and submitted for publication in 1943. However, it did not appear in the *New International* until December 1946 and January 1947, and then only after she was obliged to resubmit it in considerably abbreviated form.[5]

In addition to further analysis of the transformation of a Russian workers' state into state capitalism, "The Nature of the Russian Economy," discussed state capitalism as more than a Russian phenomenon: "Germany has achieved the statification of production through fascist methods; Japan through totalitarian methods began its Five Year Plans. Both these methods are the more recognizable capitalist methods of achieving the extreme limit of centralization" (*Russia as State-Capitalist Society*, 26).

Later, Dunayevskaya would use the expression "the age of state-capitalism," to characterize the era that began with the transformation of the Russian workers' state into a state capitalist society, and continued with massive state intervention in the economy to prop up private capitalism from the New Deal in the United States, to the Co-Prosperity Sphere in Japan and fascism in Germany. She saw state-capitalism as characterizing the post-World War II age.

Marx's early writings in relation to "Labor and Society"

The length of the original two-part manuscript on Stalinist Russia discussed above, if studied in isolation, can obscure the depth and breadth of Dunayevskaya's studies of the early and mid-1940s. The publishing limitations of being a minority tendency within the Workers Party did not allow the full scope of her work to be self-evident. A sense of the revolutionary ground of Dunayevskaya's investigation can be seen by examining her translations of the early Marx and their impact upon the essay "Labor and Society," which she had submitted as the Introduction for "The Nature of the Russian Economy." The Workers Party did not publish this Introduction.

"Labor and Society" together with "Role of Labor in a Workers State" were to serve as a springboard—a discussion of Marx's thought and a view of the concrete practice of the early Russian workers' state—for examining the nature of the economy in Stalin's Russia. What was entirely new was her use of recently discovered sources in Marx—what became known as Marx's *Economic-Philosophic Manuscripts* of 1844. In the early 1940s Dunayevskaya had translated several pages from three of these essays: "Private Property and Communism," "Alienated Labor" and "Critique of the Hegelian Dialectic" (*RDC* 8845-8858). Her source had been the Marx-Engels Archives published in Russian by Ryazanov.

"Labor and Society," the first part of Dunayevskaya's Introduction to a revised Part II of "The Nature of Russian Society," contained two sections, (1) the "Concept of Labor" and (2) the "Concept of Property." "Concept of Labor" focused on the centrality of labor in the history of humanity, how labor developed mankind and nature, and the necessary interrelation of the two. Dunayevskaya began by quoting from her translated excerpts of Marx's "Private Property and Communism": "[T]o socialist man *all of history* is nothing else than the production of man through human labor." She was tracing Marx's concept of historical materialism.

"Labor and Society" testified to the division between mental and manual labor as the characteristic of class society, and argued that in a socialist society, "the division between mental and manual labor would be abolished and the two aspects of labor thus united would make it possible for 'freely associated men' consciously to plan production, and what would assert itself would be the 'free individuality of the laborer himself.'" Dunayevskaya argued that this was not Utopia. Rather, this "new mode of activity will create the new type of human being, socialist man" (*MHTSC*, 19-20).

She quoted Marx on the relation of industry, nature and the possibility of human freedom: "Industry is the *actual* historical relation of nature, and consequently of the science of nature, to man." And then continued, "The industrial revolution, the progress of natural science and the general technological advances revolutionized the mode of production that finally there arose a basis for a true freedom, not only freedom from exploitation, but freedom from want" (19).

In "Concept of Property," Dunayevskaya's focus was to demonstrate that the form of property did not determine production relations: "You cannot dissociate property forms from production relations. . . . Property is the power of disposal over the labor of others" (22). She quoted from Marx's 1844 essay on "Alienated Labor:" "When one speaks of private property, one thinks of something outside man. When one speaks of labor, one has to do immediately with man himself. The new formulation of the question already involves its solution" (21). She added that in Marxism "all economic categories are social categories and thus in the science of economics it incorporates the subjective element, the receiver of wages, the source of value, in other words, the laborer" (21).

Dunayevskaya's recognition of the worker as "the subjective element" grew out of her unification of the categories from Marx's *Capital* with the *Economic-Philosophic Manuscripts* of 1844. She commented on her early 1940s work in 1984:

> [A]s early as 1941, when I was completing work on the Five Year Plans from original Russian sources, I found an article by Marx on 'Alienated Labor.' It is true I did not know that this was part of the famous 1844 *Economic and Philosophic Manuscripts*. But I quoted it . . . [in] 'Labor and Society,' both in order to show the transformation into opposite of that workers' state into a state-capitalist society *and* to point to new forms of workers' revolts ("Not by Practice Alone: The Movement From Theory," 1984. Reprinted in *MHTSH*, 4).

In tracing Dunayevskaya's initial discovery of the 1844 writings of Marx within her early working out of state-capitalist theory one can find the beginning moments of Marxist-Humanism, including a concept of worker as revolutionary subject. The work of state-capitalist theory was transformed by her initial study of excerpts from Marx's *Economic-Philosophic Manuscripts*. Dunayevskaya's categories in examining the nature of Russia were thus not only economic, but began to encompass philosophy.

•

An additional indication of the scope of Dunayevskaya's investigations can be seen by noting other writings of the period, some parts of her ongoing studies of the Russian economy not published; debates with tendencies within the Trotskyist movement, and analysis of Stalin's attempt to revise Marx's analysis of the law of value: (1) "Is Russia a Part of the Collectivist Epoch of Society?" (*RDC*, #8888); (2) "A Restatement of Some Fundamentals of Marxism Against Carter's Vulgarization" (*RDC* #167), which explored Marx's economic categories; (3) a manuscript excerpt, "The Law of Value and Capitalist Society"(*RDC*

#8895-8921*)*, which may have served as part of a section to appear before her concrete analysis of Russian state capitalism; and (4) "A New Revision of Marxian Economics" (*RDC* #209). Below we examine the latter two documents.

Writings on Marx's Economics, Particularly the Law of Value

Dunayevskaya's writings "to evaluate 'the economic law of motion of modern society' as it applies to the Soviet Union" were rooted in Marx's explication of the law of value in capitalist society. In her original plan, she intended to present Marx's concept of the law of value prior to her concrete analysis of Russian state capitalism. The typescript "The Law of Value and Capitalist Society" was a draft for such a discussion.[6]

Dunayevskaya straight away noted what determined that production was capitalist commodity production: "It is only from the moment that the direct producer must 'instead of a commodity sell his own capacity of labor as a commodity' that commodity production becomes capitalist commodity production. Hence it is more correct to call Marxist theory of capital not a labor theory of value, but a value theory of labor" (*RDC* # 8896).

Everything is linked to production because it is only within production that there can be the augmentation of value. To demonstrate this, Dunayevskaya drew on Marx's labors. In addition to translating excerpts from the Marx of 1844, she had translated excerpts from the unpublished "Chapter 6" of *Capital* ("The Results of the Direction Process of Production"). She quoted from the translation on the "*characteristic specific nature* of the capitalist process of production":

> The *magnitude of the value* must grow, i.e. the present value must not only preserve itself, it must create an *addition*. . . . In this simple, rudimentary value or money expression of capital (rather, that which must become capital) where it is divorced completely from the use-value to which it was bound, it is furthermore abstracted from every disturbing force and subsequently confusing incidental factors of the *real process of production* (the production of commodities, etc.) there is revealed abstractly and simply the *characteristic specific nature* of the capitalist process of production (*RDC* # 8897).

Within the production process, Dunayevskaya focused on Marx's concept of "socially necessary labor time" to demonstrate (1) the necessity of paying a worker only at value in a value producing society, "which means the *minimum* time required for the production and reproduction of labor power. In other words, he is given just that amount of wages which he requires to live and reproduce his kind, with all the necessary modifications brought about by trade unions, the historic standard of living in the country, etc" (*RDC* # 8898). For the capitalist to do otherwise and raise wages would mean his market would be captured by another capitalist who obeyed the law of a value producing society.

And, (2) that such a society was specifically a capitalist society, not a slave or feudal society. Dunayevskaya showed that Marx had created "socially necessary labor time" as a specific characteristic of a capitalist, that is, a value-producing society.

To underscore the fact that the law of value referred to a capitalist and only a capitalist society, Dunayevskaya created a section titled "What the Law of Value is Not," and posed an "imaginary socialist society," to demonstrate how labor time would be distributed in a society that did not produce according to value.

"What the Law of Value is Not," was followed by a section called "What the Law of Value Is," in which Dunayevskaya explained value production and the fact that the cost of the laborer was of first consideration in a capitalist society. That was because living labor was the only power that could augment the value of capital, that is, create surplus value, "to gain a value greater than the value which he [the capitalist] expands. That is the essence of capitalist production. That is what Marx called the *characteristic specific nature* of capitalist production" (*RDC* # 8903).

In sub-sections on "Abstract and Concrete Labor" and "Accumulated and Living Labor or the Real Subordination of Labor to Capital," Dunayevskaya discussed these crucial categories of capitalist production established by Marx and used examples from modern-day production to illustrate these categories' manifestations in the capitalism of the 1940s. She explicated Marx's discussion on "the real barrier of capitalist production is capital itself," wherein the capitalist was only the agent or the personification of capital. This brought her to the "General Contradiction of Capitalist Production."

The general contradiction revolved around the fact that to augment his value, the capitalist, on the one hand, was driven to reorganize his production system by increasing the amount of dead labor (machinery), and on the other, by so doing he decreased the relative amount of living labor used. Since the surplus value was extracted only from living labor, the capitalist was continually faced with a fall in the rate of profit. On one side the capitalist must constantly develop his productive forces, otherwise they are no longer capital. On the other side, he is unable to break though the barrier to fully do so because the surplus value needed to allow this to occur can only come through living workers (variable capital), whose labor is needed less and less as the productive process demands more and more machinery, automation, computerization (constant capital). "In a value-produced society," noted Dunayevskaya, "the productivity of labor turns against the laborers," who end up as a reserve army of unemployed (*RDC* # 8913).

Dunayevskaya ended this unpublished manuscript by critiquing those who argued that the disappearance of the market meant the disappearance of capitalism. She noted that in considering the concrete development of capitalism, "we could trace the disappearance of the market in any advanced capitalism" (*RDC* # 8818-19). Using examples from the U.S., Germany, and Japan, she showed that the development of large scale industry, the tendency toward integration of the entire process of production, often eliminated the need for the products of labor to pass through the market, "since exchange of means of production is a *market for capitalists*. . . . Should even *all* products of labor not pass through the market, should planning cover the whole of the economy and the entire social capital be concentrated in the hands of single society, it would be a capitalist society *so long as labor power remains a commodity bought at value*" (*RDC* # 8920).

The manuscript "The Law of Value and Capitalist Society" presented the key categories Marx had created in his presentation of the law of value as "the *characteristic specific nature* of the capitalist production process." Dunayevskaya was thus poised to present her specific analysis of the nature of the Russian economy.

"A New Revision of Marxian Economics"

In 1943, there appeared in the Russian theoretical journal *Pod Znamenem Marxism* (*Under the Banner of Marxism*) an article "Teaching Economics in the Soviet Union." Rather than simply a critique of the methods of teaching political economics in the Soviet Union, Dunayevskaya, who translated the article for the *American Economic Review* (Vol. 34: 3, September 1944), saw a far deeper significance. As she wrote in her accompanying commentary, "A New Revision of Marxian Economics:" "Its *raison d'etre* is contained in the argument that the law of value, in its Marxian interpretation, functions under 'socialism'" (*MHTSC*, 83).

Such an admission represented a significant turning point for state-capitalist theory. Dunayevskaya's original focus had been to prove that the law of value, which Marx had shown was characteristic of capitalist society, operated in the Russian economy. Now, "'*Some Questions of Teaching of Political Economy*,' [the literal translation of the title], contends that although the law of value operates in Russia, it functions in a changed form, that the Soviet state subordinates the law of value and consciously makes use of its mechanism in the interest of socialism."

As proof of the existence of the law of value operating in a socialist society, the authors cited Marx's expression from *Critique of the Gotha Program* that the laborer will receive for a given quantity of work the equivalent of such labor in means of consumption. But Dunayevskaya noted that Marx meant that only as a transition for a socialist society "as it emerges from capitalist society." Further, she pointed out that where Marx noted "labor will be paid by 'the natural measure of labor': *time*," the Russian economists argued that there will be "distribution according to labor." She then added: "It should be noted that they thereby completely identify 'distribution according to labor' with distribution according to value" (84).

Marx's emancipatory expression had been "From each according to his ability, to each according to his need." The Russians transformed it into quite something else: "From each according to his ability, to each according to his labor." The new formula did meet with the experience of Russia, but as Dunayevskaya had shown in her study of the Russian economy, it was an experience of sharp class differentiation of workers and peasants on the one hand, and the managers of industry, an aristocracy of labor and an intelligencia on the other. Needless to say, the pay range was not based on hours of labor, but varied enormously with the kind of labor performed. Thus the authors of the article could write: "The measure of labor and measure of consumption in a socialist society can be calculated only on the basis of the law of value" (84).

Dunayevskaya responded: "The whole significance of the article, therefore, turns upon where it is possible to conceive of the law of value functioning in a socialist society, that is, a non-exploitative society" (84). To combat such a false conception, she proceeded to demonstrate that the operation of the labor theory of value in a society was not an isolated, ahistorical phenomenon. Marx drew his theory of surplus value from the law of value. The seeming equality found in the market place—the buying and selling of labor power—yielded, in the process of production, the inequality of alienated, or exploited labor, captured as surplus value. This occurred because human labor power, the worker at the point of production, was the one commodity under capitalism that could produce more value than was necessary for the worker's reproduction, hence a surplus value was created. Dunayevskaya concluded: "*In its Marxian interpretation, therefore, the law of value entails the use of the concept of alienated or exploited labor and, as a consequence, the concept of surplus value*" (85).

Concluding her critique of the article, Dunayevskaya noted how the admission that the law of value applied in Russia was tied to a proposal for teaching *Capital*. *Capital* began straight away with the category of a commodity. Marx had shown how the dual value of a commodity, use value and exchange value, was a result of the two kinds of labor, concrete labor and abstract labor, which were found only in a capitalist society. Within the capitalist commodity lies the secret of capitalist development. Marx unwrapped this mystification, this fetishism of commodities. As for the Russians, they needed to obscure the dialectical beginning moment of Marx's greatest work. Hence, they called for skipping Chapter One on Commodities as the beginning point for teaching *Capital*. Dunayevskaya noted: "It is because of their need to divest the commodity of what Engels called 'its particular distinctness,' and turn it into a classless, 'general historic' phenomenon applicable to practically all societies" (87).

The publication of Dunayevskaya's translation of the original article from a Russian economic journal, together with her commentary, in the *American Economic Review*, stirred an open debate within the pages of the *AER* from a number of Left academic specialists on the Russian economy (*RDC* #213).

•

A turning point in Dunayevskaya's development had been reached. As she would note later: "After the Russian admission, in 1943, that the law of value operates in Russia, there was no further point to continue the detailed analysis of their State Plans" (*Marxism and Freedom*, "Introduction to the Second Edition," November 1, 1963).

Drawing Together Strands from the Theory of State-Capitalism Documents of the 1940s[7]

The uniqueness of Dunayevskaya's theory of state-capitalism lay in how her economic analysis of the Russian economy did not stand in isolation as "economics." From early on it was multi-linear in its origin and projection. Three dimensions characterized Dunayevskaya's development of state-capitalist theory of the early and mid 1940s: (1) Her analysis of the economic nature of Russia drew upon the economic categories that Marx had worked out in *Capital*. At the same time her discovery and excerpt translations of the Marx of 1844 meant there was a philosophic dimension to her analysis early on. Marx's "Private Property and Communism" helped to inform Dunayevskaya's state-capitalist theory, though it would be a full decade before state-capitalist theory became expressed as the fullness of Marxist-Humanism.

(2) Her theory of state-capitalism developed a world dimension. For Dunayevskaya, the US's New Deal capitalism, as well as of Germany's and Japan's state-forms, were seen as developing simultaneously in response to the economic crisis of the Great Depression. Though Russia's transformation—from a worker's state into a totalitarian state-capitalist society—was a unique manifestation, the emergence of state-capitalism on a world level became evident.

State-capitalist theory would help Dunayevskaya to forge a worldview of the political landscape of the post-World War II world. In topics ranging from the rise of Mao's China, to the ideological and economic factors within and without the Afro-Asian Latin American Third World of revolt, revolution and post-colonial societies, to the Sino-Soviet split, to critiquing of Left intellectuals in the age of state-capitalism such as Ernest Mandel and Herbert Marcuse, and to the super-power struggle of the United States and Russia, Dunayevskaya's commentary and analysis would take place within a framework of state-capitalist theory.

This is not to say that "state-capitalism" was an abstract generalization that she applied to every situation. Rather, the contradictory objective phenomena of diverse world realities could often be elucidated with the aid this overarching theory. Dunayevskaya did not view state-capitalist theory as a sufficient response to the objective and subjective realities which unfolded in the post-World War II world. As we will see, state-capitalist theory came to be situated within the philosophy of Marxist-Humanism developed from the 1950s to the 1980s. As she wrote: "Without Marx's Humanism, the Theory of State-Capitalism Is No Great Divide"("New Beginnings that Determine the End" July, 1978. Reprinted in *MHTSC*, 140). At the same time, in 1984 Dunayevskaya would write: "Heretofore we criticized the theory of state-capitalism by stressing that, without developing into the philosophy of Marxist-Humanism, it was incomplete. While this is true, it would have been impossible to get to the philosophy of Marxist-Humanism without the theory of state-capitalism" ("Not by Practice Alone: The Movement From Theory," July, 1984. Reprinted in *MHTSC*, 3).

(3) The other unique dimension of Dunayevskaya's theory of state-capitalism as it developed in the 1940s was her focus on the human forces that not only felt the blows of capitalism's new, world appearance, but stood in opposition and rebellion. Her view encompassed opposition from within Stalinist Russia, where of necessity it remained underground. It was also reflected in writings on the Black struggle and revolt in the United States, as well as militant labor struggles, all in the midst of World War II (*RDC* #259-323). And it extended to what would later be called the Third World, as seen in her contact with an African revolutionary from the Cameroon in the immediate post-war world (Letter of August 18, 1947, *RDC* #675).

•

The development from the theory of state-capitalism to the philosophy of Marxist-Humanism runs through Dunayevskaya's translation of Lenin's *Abstract* on Hegel's *Science of Logic*, and the State-Capitalist Tendency's participation on the 1949-50 Miners General Strike. It is there where her first deep probing of the Hegelian dialectic occurred, as well as her relation to the American proletariat at a time when it was on the threshold of a new stage of revolutionary subjectivity. We turn to this in Chapter 2.

---

[1] Post-script to 1986 Introduction/Overview to Vol. XII can be found in *The Myriad Global Crises of the 1980s and the Nuclear World since World War II*, 12.

[2] Written by Dunayevskaya under the pen name of Freddie James in February 1941. Issued by the Workers Party in an internal discussion bulletin, March 1941. Reprinted by News and Letters, October 1992.

[3] As noted in the Introduction, independently of Dunayevskaya, C.L.R. James, under the name of J.R. Johnson, wrote a "Resolution on the Russian Question," Sept 19, 1941, submitted to the same Workers Party National Convention as Dunayevskaya's initial document. Dunayevskaya and James began a collaboration that would last more than a decade inside and then outside the Trotskyist movement. Initially called the State-Capitalist Tendency, it would be renamed the Johnson-Forest Tendency in 1945. Outside Trotskyism, it was named Correspondence Committees (1951-1955). These developments will be taken up in Chapters Two and Three.

[4] *The New International*, organ of the Workers Party, December 1942, January 1943, February 1943 (*The Raya Dunayevskaya Collection* (*RDC* #69-86). Reprinted in *The Marxist-Humanist Theory of State Capitalism*, News and Letters, 1992.

[5] See her letters to the Political Committee of the Workers Party of May 8,1944, February 2, 1946, October 30, 1946 for discussion of the changes made and the difficulties in publishing the study (*RDC* # 8982-86). The published study is available in, *Russia as State-Capitalist Society*, News & Letters, 1973. Reprinted from the original study in *New International*, December 1946, January, 1947.

⁶ This typescript, which has some pages missing, has a handwritten date at the top of August, 1943. However, this could indicate not the date of its writing, but the date of its placement in a larger manuscript, as the pagination and footnotes are changed also in handwriting. The changes indicate that the typescript, which originally began as page 11 of a larger piece, now began as page 35 of a manuscript, which does not exist fully intact. The last sentence of this surviving 26-page typescript, (having some repetition and missing pages toward the end), read "Now for a concrete analysis of Russian state capitalism."

⁷ A truncated misreading of Dunayevskaya's theory can be found in Stephen Resnich's and Richard Wolff's *Class Theory and History*, (2002. New York: Routledge). So anxious are they to present "a new interpretation of the USSR's birth, evolution, and death," that they reduce her contribution to being part of those who defined Russian society primarily in terms of power and property forms, and not class structure (See *Class Theory and History*, 111-112).

Chapter 2

Translation and Initial Probing of Lenin's Notebooks on Hegel's *Science of Logic*: Theoretical Ramifications, 1949-51; Relation to the 1949-50 Miners' General Strike

Dunayevskaya's 1949 translation and initial probing of Lenin's 1914-15 Notebooks on Hegel's *Science of Logic*[1] became a catalyst for her life-long immersion into the Hegelian dialectic, and vantage point for exploring Lenin's revolutionary practice as leader of the Russian Revolution and first workers' state. Her interpretation of Lenin's philosophic development and its relation to his revolutionary political practice post-1914 stands as one of her singular contributions to Marxist thought.

In *Marxism and Freedom* she wrote of the objective events that surrounded Lenin's 1914 return to Hegel:

> The holocaust of World War I erupting after a century of near peace and general optimism, shook the world to its foundations. It brought about the fall of the world Socialist organization known as the Second International. The German Social-Democracy had voted war credits to the Kaiser. So incredible did this appear, so completely unexpected, that the *Vorwarts*, which announced this fact, was thought by Lenin to be a forgery of the German Imperial Office. When it was proved to be true, the theoretical ground on which he had stood, and which he had thought so impregnable, gave way under him.
> Prior to August 1914, all Marxists agreed that material conditions create the basis for the creation of a new society; that the more advanced the material conditions, the better prepared the proletariat would be for taking power. Now, these same mass labor parties—in the most advanced countries, where technology was most fully developed and the proletariat most highly organized—took an action which hurled masses of workers across national boundaries to slaughter each other "in the defense of the Fatherland." Germany was only the

first. The Marxists of the other warring European countries soon followed suit. The German Social Democracy was not an organization of bourgeois liberals or of deviating reformists. It was, in the main, an organization of *avowed* revolutionary Marxists. Before the outbreak of war, they had taken an unambiguous stand against any imperialist war that might break out. The war no sooner broke out than they were part of that mobilization for destruction. *Why?* They betrayed, yes, but betrayal wasn't merely "selling out." What were the *objective* causes for such total *ideological* collapse? The fact was overwhelming, totally unforeseen, incontrovertible. Confronted with the appearance of counter-revolution *within* the revolutionary movement, Lenin was driven to search for a philosophy that would reconstitute his own reason.

He began reading Hegel's *Science of Logic* (*M&F*, 167-68).

From State-Capitalist Theory to Philosophic Correspondence Via Lenin's Hegel Notebooks[2]

Dunayevskaya translated Lenin's notebooks on the Hegelian dialectic while she was a co-leader of the Johnson-Forest Tendency. Her initial article on state-capitalism, "The Union of Soviet Socialist Republics is a Capitalist Society," had been written independently as a Trotskyist within the Workers Party. That same year C.L.R. James also wrote on the state-capitalist nature of Russia. Under their organizational names, Freddie Forest (Raya Dunayevskaya) and J. R. Johnson (C.L.R. James), they established the State-Capitalist Tendency within the Workers Party. In 1945 the Tendency renamed itself the Johnson-Forest Tendency. A third leading member was Ria Stone (Grace Lee Boggs).

While first formed on the basis of a state-capitalist analysis of Russia, the Tendency over the period of more than a decade—within the Workers Party (1941-1947), the Socialist Workers Party (1947-51), and as a separate organization, Correspondence Committees (1951-1955)—explored questions concerning the nature of revolutionary Marxism. Studies on Marx's *Capital*, on the Negro Question in America, on the nature of Trotskyism, translation of and commentary upon Lenin's Hegel Notebooks of 1914-15, readings and discussion of Hegel's *Logic*, as well as the first English translations of essays from Marx's 1844 writings, were among the theoretical work undertaken by the Tendency.

With the transformation of Russia into a state-capitalist society, the Tendency was seeking its bearings within the Marxist movement. This contrasted with the majority of the Trotskyist movement, which was trapped economically within Trotsky's formulation that nationalized property equals socialism, and which thus moved away from production relations and towards property forms as the lens for viewing economic relations. The Soviet Union under Stalin was still seen as a workers' state. The Trotskyist movement was trapped politically in a position that called for critical defense of the Soviet Union. Within the main currents of the movement, there was no compulsion to search out a philosophic new beginning for revolutionary Marxism.

The Johnson-Forest Tendency, which by the mid-1940s had clarified economically the nature of the Soviet Union and refused to politically support this state form of capitalism, began a search for new philosophic beginnings. In 1947 Dunayevskaya wrote an 80-page outline, "State-Capitalism and Marxism," as part of the Tendency's work to restate Marxism for their day (*RDC* #472). In 1948, James wrote "Notes on the Dialectic," focusing on Hegel's *Science of Logic*, and included discussion of Marx's and Lenin's relation to Hegel. Lenin's 1914-15 writings on Hegel were taken up based on excerpt translations that Dunayevskaya made earlier in the 1940s.

In response to "Notes on the Dialectic," Dunayevskaya decided to translate the entire *Abstract* on Hegel's *Science of Logic* as well as Lenin's notes on Hegel's *History of Philosophy*. Her translation became catalyst for a three-way correspondence between Forest, Johnson and Stone in the late 1940s and early 1950s. The leaders of the Tendency were seeking new philosophic starting points within Hegel, Marx, and Lenin, seeing the necessity for a restatement of Marxism in what they viewed as the era of state-capitalism. The correspondence encompassed a digging into the philosophic categories of *Science of Logic*, particularly in relation to Lenin's Notebooks and his post-1914 writings, and into Marx's *Capital*.

The three-way correspondence was a high point of the Tendency's philosophic development. The interchange on Lenin's Notebooks, on the Hegelian dialectic, and on the structure of Marx's *Capital* in relation to the dialectic, were the Tendency's reaching to become a philosophic nucleus. (See *RDC* #1595-1744, and #9209-9327, for surviving letters, 1948-1951.)

At the same time, Dunayevskaya would later see that embedded within the correspondence was the beginning of the Tendency's end, as differing attitudes toward Lenin's Notebooks, Hegel's Absolutes, and humanism as a philosophic category came to the fore.[3] These differing philosophic attitudes would subsequently become sharp political differences, which, by the end of 1954, resulted in the demise of the Tendency. The three way correspondence was thus at one and the same time the high point and the "perishing" of the Tendency.

Below we follow Dunayevskaya's contribution to the three-way correspondence, first in the letters that accompanied her translation of Lenin's 1914-15 Hegel Notebooks; second, in her exploration of Lenin's breakthrough in subsequent letters; and third, in her correspondence on Marx's "dialectic plan for *Capital*."

Letters Accompanying the Lenin Translations

As Dunayevskaya completed translations of each of the three major sections of Lenin's comments on the Doctrines of Being, Essence, and Notion from

Hegel's *Science of Logic*, she sent them to James and Lee accompanied by a letter giving her first commentary. In her letter of February 18, 1949, sent with her translation of Lenin's commentary on the Introduction, the Prefaces and the Doctrine of Being, Dunayevskaya began by pointing to Lenin's comment at the climax to the Doctrine of Being, the category Measure: "gradualness explains nothing without leaps," and to the further notations of "Leaps!" Lenin made. She then noted his comment about the "transition of being to essence is analyzed doubly obscurely," and added her own comment, "How much that man knew and how much more he was searching for" (*Power of Negativity*, 346).

In hindsight, it can be seen that in Dunayevskaya's view of Lenin, "Leaps!" was not only Lenin's *comment on Hegel*, but was the profound reality of Lenin's 1914-15 *voyage into Hegel*. In *Marxism and Freedom*, she would characterize Lenin's Notebooks as "The Break in Lenin's Thought," "Lenin and the Dialectic: A Mind in Action," and "The Great Divide in Marxism." Throughout her life, she returned to discuss Lenin's Notebooks on Hegel's dialectic. Significant commentaries on Lenin can be found in each of her major works, *Marxism and Freedom, Philosophy and Revolution* and *Rose Luxemburg, Women's Liberation, and Marx's Philosophy and Revolution*, as well as in her last writings on "Dialectics of Organization and Philosophy."

In this February 18 letter, Dunayevskaya returned to Lenin's earlier notes on the Doctrine of Being, praising what she termed "this firm grasp of the dialectic at its simplest," and cited Lenin's remark on appearance and essence after he read Hegel's section on "The Objectivity of Appearance, the Necessity of Contradiction." "Is not this the thought, that appearance is also objective, since it is *one of the sides* of the objective world? Not only *Wesen* [Essence], but also *Schein* [Appearance] are objective. Even the distinction between subjective and objective has its limits." She then commented: "No wonder that man could write of *appearance* so profoundly! *Imperialism: A Popular Outline*. Need I harp on my favorite peeve: compare this analysis of appearance to Rosa's [Luxemburg] analysis of essence in her *Accumulation* [*of Capital*]" (346).

Dunayevskaya took up Lenin and method: "Another thing that struck me anew was emphasis on Method, Method, Method, 'the dialectic which it has [comprises] in itself.'" She cited Lenin's reference to *Capital* as he quoted Hegel on not posing a mere abstract Universal, but one which "comprises in itself a full wealth of Particulars." She commented that Lenin was reading the *Logic* while having in mind both economic conditions—"*Capital* plus the *Imperialism* he was going to work out"—and "Ideology"—in terms of the Bernsteins, Kautskys, "and yes, Rosa Luxemburg since in that very period he also made notes on her book. What rich years were 1914-16 for Lenin in his 'study room!'"

After brief further comments on Lenin's evident realization of how "materialistic" Hegel could sound, Dunayevskaya ended this letter on the Doctrine of Being notes by quoting Lenin on the movement and all-sided universal flexibility of concepts in Hegel, when objective "it is dialectic, it is the correct reflection of the eternal development of the world" (348).

In Dunayevskaya's letter accompanying her translation of Lenin's Notes on the Doctrine of Essence (February 25, 1949), one sees she was not alone a translator, but an active participant in a "dialogue," particularly with Lenin, but also with Hegel and Marx. She began by noting the combination of "deep richness" and "utter simplicity" in Lenin's Notes. She cited Lenin's comments on Hegel working out dialectics as "purely logical" in relation to induction and deduction in *Capital*, and then added: "Not for one instant does he [Lenin] permit you to think that to compare the dialectic 'merely' to the deductive and inductive method of *Capital* is 'narrow,' for the comment occurred as an addition to: 'The continuation of the work of Hegel and Marx must consist in the *dialectic* working out of the history of human thought, science and technique.'"

In response to Lenin's singling out universal movement and change first in *Science of Logic* (1813), then in the *Communist Manifesto* (1847), and finally in *Origin of Species* (1859), Dunayevskaya would write: "Whoever is still so foolhardy as to look for a 'primary cause' may do so if he has enough time to waste; Lenin will have none of that—he will have only totality and movement and break-up and movement" (349).

Turning to the whole of the Doctrine of the Essence she proposed a "summary" in three words—"If the three sections of the Doctrine of Essence had to be summarized in three words, I'd say *Manifoldness* for Show (Reflection), *Law* for Appearance, and *Totality* for Actuality."—and noted the importance of Manifoldness considering "Lenin wrote his Notes when the world was being rent asunder" (349).

This short letter—as it swept into the Law of Contradiction, jammed together Lenin's comments on Causality with Dunayevskaya's view of his *Imperialism*, returned to the *Phenomenology*, related the Law as Essential Relation to Marx's "absolute general law" of capitalist accumulation—does not lend itself to summary. What one is witness to, is Dunayevskaya's own leaps in cognition, her willingness to "grappl[e] with the law of motion of capitalist society in philosophic rather than in value terms," as she translated and commented upon Lenin's leaps.

She ended the letter with Lenin: "He is full of 'all-sidedness and all-embracing character of world connection.' Always it is: Connection, relation, mediation, necessity, motion, unity of opposites, break-up of identity, transition and motion, motion and transition, and that is totality. I believe I am ready to follow him into Notion" (351).

Dunayevskaya's translation of Lenin's Notes of the Doctrine of the Notion were completed in early March. In her letter to James of March 12, she singled out the difference between Lenin's Notes and James' "Notes on the Dialectic": "Lenin was looking for a new Universal. He found Hegel's Idea . . . . [T]he thing you [James] chose most to stop at . . . was the Law of Contradiction in Essence."

Dunayevskaya then summarized Lenin's reading of the Doctrine of the Notion:

> Just as the LEAP characterized Lenin's comprehension of the Doctrine of Being, LAW as Essential Relation his grasp of the Doctrine of Essence, so PRACTICE characterizes his very profound analysis of the Doctrine of the Notion, and why he chooses to single out the section on the Idea.
> Lenin begins with the fact that "The dialectic road to cognition of truth is from living observation to abstract thinking and from this to practice" and never lets go of this for a single second (352).

She proceeded to present a series of Lenin's comments on "practice, practice, practice" and concluded: "His *whole* emphasis on the *end*, and *Subjective* notion is that the aims of man are generated by the objective world but that he changes, subjectively desires change and acts; there he goes so far as to call the objective world non-actual and the desires of man *actual*, and the reason he hangs on so to the Idea is that 'it not only has the dignity of a universal, but also the simple actual'" (353).

To emphasize Lenin's creativity in reading Hegel's chapter on "The Idea" in the Doctrine of the Notion, Dunayevskaya proceeded to present her own reading of what she termed Lenin's seventeen definitions, "more correctly, manifoldednesses: (What a word I just made up!)" of the Idea. Although drawn from Lenin, the definitions were also Dunayevskaya's expression of the "Idea." In translating and commenting upon Lenin's *Abstract* on Hegel's *Science of Logic*, Dunayevskaya was herself reading Hegel in a most concrete and creative way. Through her labor on Lenin's Notebooks, Dunayevskaya's *own* internalization of Hegel found a profound point of departure.

She ended her commentary by calling attention to Lenin's remark that none of the Marxists had understood Marx's *Capital*. This was in reference to their not "having studied and understood the *whole* of Hegel's *Logic*" (Lenin, *Collected Works* Vol. 38, 180). She then expressed her own desire to concentrate on two areas flowing out of the translation and commentary she had just completed: "1) the American economy . . . 2) to Marx's *Capital*."[4]

•

At the time of her translations of Lenin's Notebooks, Dunayevskaya was not conscious of philosophic differences within the Tendency. However her comments to James in the letters accompanying the translations called attention to differences between Lenin's and James' reading of Hegel. Thus in her first letter, on the translation of the Doctrine of Being (Feb. 18, 1948) she wrote of the fact that James' Notes had "practically skipped over the first book," in comparison to Lenin's commentary. And after completing the translations of Lenin's Essence and Notion notes, she wrote (March 12, 1949):

[T]he outstanding difference between the two 'versions' [James' Notes and Lenin's *Philosophic Notebooks*] is striking. You will note that Lenin's notes on the Notion are as lengthy as those on the Introduction, and Doctrines of Being and Essence combined . . . although you spend that much time on Notion, and included its practice, the thing you chose most to stop at and say: *hic Rodus, hic salta* to was the Law of Contradiction in Essence . . . (but Lenin) chooses to single out the section on the Idea (*PON* 351).

That James did catch his differences with Lenin *and* with Dunayevskaya's reading of Lenin on Hegel, can be sensed from his letter to her of June 10, 1949, which finally acknowledged the translation of Lenin's *Philosophic Notebooks* of the previous February and March, and Dunayevskaya's commentaries: "You are covering a lot of ground and it is pretty good. But after conversations with [Grace Lee] & reading (carefully, this time) your correspondence, I feel that we are still off *the* point."

Though Dunayevskaya did not comment on differences of interpretation with James in this immediate period, her view of the insufficiency of James' "Notes on the Dialectic" can be gleaned from her determination to continue her own digging into Lenin's *Notebooks*, her exploration of the impact of the dialectic on Marx's *Capital*, and her determination to probe further into the Hegelian dialectic, including the Absolutes.

While James' 1948 Notes had been an important initial catalyst for their work, by 1949-50 it was Hegel, Lenin and Marx she was probing. A minor remark in the opening sentence of the February 25 letter discussed above was revealing. In explaining being able to translate faster than she had anticipated, Dunayevskaya noted: "I had thought it would take time 'to find' the quotations but now find that as I myself internalize Hegel I nearly always flip open the right page" (348).

Exploring Lenin's Breakthrough

In her 1949-1951 correspondence with James and Lee, Dunayevskaya's internalization of Hegel found expression in her commentaries on Lenin pre- and post-1914. Between January and the end of August 1949, Dunayevskaya wrote a series of letters exploring Lenin's philosophic breakthrough. Although she had extensively studied many of Lenin's works earlier,[5] her new correspondence had the distinct vantage-point of his Philosophic Notebooks. In Dunayevskaya's letters after the translation of the Notebooks, we witness her 'thinking aloud' to clarify the meaning of Lenin's philosophic breakthrough. Her aim was "to follow through the major 'discoveries' of Lenin's dialectics," particularly with regard to his post-1914 activities (#1608).

In a letter of January 27, 1949 accompanying the *Philosophy of History* excerpts, two points were particularly striking: (1) Dunayevskaya singled out Lenin's comment that despite writing nearly 1,000 pages on philosophy, Plekhanov had nil about the *Science of Logic*, the dialectic proper as philosophic science. She added, "In other words, Lenin has decided that not only can you not understand *Capital* without the *Logic* but you cannot understand philosophy without the *Logic*" (*RDC* #9213). (2) she noted Lenin's work on the dialectic proper meant seeing contradiction not only in appearance, but in essence. She added that this could be seen easily enough when applied to capitalism—use value and value, concrete and abstract labor—"but when it comes to applying this same principle to revolution, we [revolutionaries] shy away from this contradiction in essence, and wish to fight only capitalism" (*RDC* #9213). This realization would aid in clarifying the Johnson-Forest Tendency's analysis of Trotskyism.

Concepts that Lenin singled out in his reading of Hegel's *Logic*—the immanent emergence of difference, the necessary connection or all sides of a given phenomena, transformation into opposite—Dunayevskaya saw concretized in Lenin's working out of the apparent oppositeness of competition and monopoly, of imperialism emerging out of monopoly, and of the emergence of difference in relation to two fundamental tendencies within the working class. He saw a contradiction in the essence of monopoly capitalism that divided the proletariat into an aristocracy of labor and the mass in general.

To interpret Lenin's new reading of *Capital* as he explored Hegel, Dunayevskaya summed up eight different references to *Capital* that appeared in Lenin's Notebooks on *Science of Logic*. She wrote of the need to approach Lenin "from a new angle:"

> to connect what was new in his *Imperialism* with his conclusion that none of the Marxists had understood *Capital* and particularly its first chapter for it is impossible to understand that without comprehension of the whole of Hegel's *Logic*. It seems to me that what Lenin means by that is that no one had seen imperialism "growing out of" capitalism, specifically, the concentration of production "out of which" w[ould] come monopoly any more than they had been aware of the unity of opposites in the commodity (May 17, 1949).

In a number of her letters, Lenin's post-1914 writings were taken up and commented on in relation to his philosophic breakthrough: (1) his massive Notebooks on Imperialism, the content of which she enumerated in detail; (2) the actual booklet *Imperialism*; (3) the articles on Junius, and on the fall of the Second International; (4) "Letters from Afar," (5) the "April Thesis," (6) *State and Revolution*.

An extensive letter of July 6, 1949 listed a series of categories discussed in Lenin's writings—imperialism, the economic stage of capitalism, socialization of labor, opportunism in the movement, self-determination of peoples and nations, dialectics—and then divided each category into mini-summaries of Lenin's pre-1914 and post-1914 views.

In grappling with Lenin's Hegel Notebooks, Dunayevskaya sowed a vast array of seeds. Over the next months and years she would cultivate a significant number of them to arrive at what she would later term "The Great Divide in Marxism" (*Marxism and Freedom*, 1958). These returns to the rich garden of Lenin's thought became crucial soil for her own philosophic growth.

"The dialectic of Marx's plan for *Capital*"

The translation and exploration of Lenin's *Abstract* on Hegel's *Science of Logic* not only deeply enriched Dunayevskaya's view of Lenin, but was also an important catalyst for a new exploration of Marx's *Capital* from the vantage point of Hegel's *Logic*. As noted above, Dunayevskaya had singled out the many times Lenin commented on the relationship of the *Logic* and *Capital*. At the beginning of 1949 she had written one of her colleagues, Grace Lee, proposing a correspondence involving a new kind of reading of *Capital*:

> I wish to propose that we begin a correspondence regarding that oft (and not by accident) postponed article on *Capital*, and in the spirit of the new me, I propose no such abstract title as the Materialism and Dialectics of *Capital*, but the dialectically concrete The Significance of *Capital* for our Day. And this proposal includes within it the conception, not that you write on dialectics and I on materialism, but that we each write both (January 5, 1949).

In her emerging philosophic probing, Dunayevskaya was determined not to separate dialectics and materialism in her reading of *Capital*. In a letter of October 5, 1949, she expressed it as wanting "to write my notes of the first ch[apter] of *Capital* from the new dialectical view of it."

Throughout the 1940s she had been writing on Marx's *Capital*, first working with it intensely while preparing her analysis of Russia as a state-capitalist society. In the mid-1940s she had prepared an *Outline of Marx's Capital, Volume One*, a series of 14 lectures coving all eight parts of *Capital* for the Educational Department of the Workers Party (*RDC* #324). An *Outline of Marx's Capital, Volume Two* followed as part of a class she taught (*RDC* #385). She had also translated a number of previously unavailable writings of Marx, including "Chapter 6," the original unpublished ending of *Capital*. And yet now, in the course of her work with Lenin's *Philosophic Notebooks*, Dunayevskaya felt the necessity to return to Marx, with new, philosophic eyes.

From 1949-50 there are a dozen extant letters of Dunayevskaya in which the major thrust is a reading of *Capital* with Hegel's *Logic* in hand. Two themes predominated: (1) A singling out of a number of Hegelian categories that Dunayevskaya saw in sections of Marx's *Capital*; (2) A tracing of changes Marx made in the structure of *Capital* through various drafts—"the dialectic of Marx's plan for *Capital*"—undertaken in part through Marx's rereading of Hegel. Both themes were developed as Dunayevskaya established the historic circumstances surrounding the writing of *Capital*.

In the letter of January 5, 1949 that proposed a correspondence on *Capital*, Dunayevskaya took up the categories of "abstraction," "fixed particular" vs. "universal," as well as the Hegelian categories of Being, Essence, and Notion within a philosophic reading of *Capital*. She briefly contrasted the "violent abstraction" (Marx's expression) of Ricardo in his transforming rate of surplus value into rate of profit with what she termed the "true abstraction" of Marx, who traced the concrete transformation of surplus value to profit. She did this not to prove the difference between the two, but to show the need for the category of surplus value. She then turned to Rosa Luxemburg to point out her substitution of imperialism—what Dunayevskaya termed her "fixed particular"—for Marx's universal of capitalism. Later in the letter, she posed a possible reading of the various parts of Volume I of *Capital* in relation to the categories Being, Essence, and Notion, as well as reading of Volume III of *Capital* in terms of the Notion.

A few weeks later, in her letter of February 1, 1949, she continued integrating Hegel's categories within Marx's *Capital*. She related Marx's discussion of "crisis" to "Actuality;" the "Law of Accumulation" to Hegel's concept of "Notion;" "shapeless Essence" as perhaps value; and "unstable Appearance" as possibly boom and bust. She also took up Hegel's "infinite in the finite," where, "to me it seems to say: if infinite production is the real, then the finiteness of capitalist production is that it cannot be real, it cannot plan, because it is *conditioned* (Ground?) on (1) class relations, (2) self-expansion of existing values. In other words, planning, social planning, can only exist when not grounded within class relations."

One category that she probed through several letters was Hegel's section in "Determinant Being" on Barrier and Ought from the *Science of Logic* in relation to the general contradiction of capitalism:

> An analysis of the general contradiction of capitalism, in dialectic terms, still remains unwritten, but in the process of laboring on it I came across the section in Determinate Being on Barrier and Ought which I believe poses the problem. . . . Let me first state it in political terms. One of the *limits* of capitalist production is the consumption of the proletariat paid at value. That is the alpha and omega of the underconsumptionists. But the real *barrier* says Marx is capital itself. Now heretofore we have used the terms practically inter-changeably; underconsumptionists saying it is consumption and the decline in rate of profit theorists saying, no it is capital; but neither side made any distinction between limit and barrier. Now, with the help of Hegel let us introduce that distinction (February 10, 1949).

Dunayevskaya then quoted from Hegel on Determinate Being, and added:

Skip a couple of lines on same page and we come to "The proper limit of Something, thus posited of it as something negative and also essential, is no longer Limit as such but Barrier." We have here then not just limit of laborer paid at value or "the poverty and restricted consumption of the masses," but the barrier, capital itself, which consists of the preservation of the existing capital, self-expansion, unconditioned production—that is, all contradictory and mutually exclusive.

She continued the discussion in the following letter (February 17, 1949). After receiving a cautionary note from Grace Lee, Dunayevskaya wrote, "Naturally we must be very wary before we rush to fill the logical categories of Hegel with specific class content." She added: "Marx not merely 'applied' the dialectic to the economic laws of capitalism," which did not stop him from working with the dialectical categories. She ended her discussion on barrier and limit in relation to *Capital* as follows:

> The tendencies in capitalist production whose evolution results in the general contradiction are in constant struggle between the tendency to expand and the tendency to preserve the existing values. Our problem is when does the limit of underconsumption turn into the barrier of self-expansion. I will not myself ride further, but I know I hit upon something in the ought and barrier and I would like to see you develop [that] in logical context.

Our point is not to present in detail Dunayevskaya's development of each of these readings of Marx with the eyes of the Hegelian dialectic. Many of the readings were only developed in a preliminary way by Dunayevskaya. Others would become central to her first full public discussion of all three volumes of *Capital* in *Marxism and Freedom*. What comes to the fore in these letters is a recognition of how the dialectic was becoming deeply embedded in Dunayevskaya's reading of Marx. A critical return to earlier studies, to the original Marx, but with *her* eyes immersed in Hegel and in Lenin's reading of Hegel, led to new leaps and understandings of these "old" Marx texts.

This "new dialectical view of it" was not exhausted in a one-to-one correspondence between Marx's discussion and Hegel's categories. Rather it meant a different kind of reading of Marx. Thus in a letter of October 5, 1949 she proceeded to present ideas on (1) the contrast between private and social not as private and social property, but between private or individual labor and social labor; (2) to show that "exchange value now turns out to be the *only form* of value able to express the true nature of its content, abstract labor;" (3) writing about this capitalist social form of production, she noted that "what this social form of production, with its value form, hides is that it is a form worthy of the content, the mastery of process of production over man."

Another way to see Dunayevskaya's new philosophical reading of *Capital* is to note her expansive, patient tracing of the changes Marx introduced into the various drafts of *Capital*, what Dunayevskaya called, "the dialectic of Marx's plan for *Capital*."

In a letter of January 24, 1950 Dunayevskaya began extensive notes on "the structural development of *Capital*." She traced changes from *Critique of Political Economy* (1859) forward, citing Marx's letter of January 14, 1858 to Engels, "I have thrown over the whole doctrine of profit as it has existed up to now. In the *method* of treatment that by mere accident I have again glanced through Hegel's *Logic* has been of great service to me."

Dunayevskaya then described Marx's plan to present an analysis of the bourgeois economy in six books and then noted:

> BUT THIS STRUCTURE WILL BE CHANGED, not merely in order to put all theories [of other theorists] "at the end" in a separate book, but for the more important and actual reason that nothing will interfere either with the dialectical development of Marx's own theory nor with the actual development of capitalist production for whatever history will be included within the body of the work itself, will be not the history of *theory* but the history of *production relations* arising out of technological development and resulting in the struggle of the workers for the shortening of the working day.

Here in embryo was the new vision, the vantage point that Dunayevskaya would fully develop in the chapters on *Capital* which form Part IV of *Marxism and Freedom*: "The Humanism and Dialectic of *Capital*." This would include the impact of the Civil War and its Black struggle for freedom to the working class struggles of the period, particularly the fight for the shortening of the working day, on Marx's *Capital*. Dunayevskaya's 1940s writings on the Black dimension in America would become inseparable from her writings on *Capital*. "The dialectic of Marx's plan for *Capital*," became her dialectical method.

Quoting from a later letter of Marx's (June 27, 1870), she showed that this new method allowing freer movement of the material itself was what Marx called "*the dialectic method*." She proceeded to follow the development of the *Capital* manuscript from August, 1861 to June, 1863. Much of her discussion here would be presented in a more developed form in *Marxism and Freedom*.

Towards the end of her letter she wrote:

> The revolution in the plan of *Capital* was not as a result of the absolute *conclusion*—the antagonism between labor and capital which was the very basis of every word he ever wrote from 1843 on—but that the conclusion arose not out of history alone but of the very dialectical development of the production of value and which, both in its surplus value and wage forms, finds embodiment in the *social product*.

One week later, Dunayevskaya followed with a letter noting "The dialectics of Marx's plans for *Capital* must be worked out in great detail" (January 30, 1950). She brought forth Marx's discussion of the Civil War in the U.S., quoting his expression in *Capital* on the Civil War sounding the tocsin for the European working class. The historical circumstances surrounding the writing of *Capital*, among them, the U.S. Civil War,[6] the Polish insurrection (1863), and the birth of the First Workingman's International, were discussed.

On June 7, 1950, in a 12 page single-spaced letter Dunayevskaya commented in great detail on: (1) structural changes in the evolution of *Capital*; (2) development of a number of specific concepts within *Capital*, including debates with Adam Smith, rate of surplus value and rate of profit, differences between value and cost price, theory of rent, and machinery; and (3) the historical circumstances surrounding the writing of *Capital*. No summary can substitute for an individual probing of this letter.

A later letter, (October 20, 1950), explored the differences between *Critique of Political Economy* and *Capital*, stating "the complete victory of Marx of *Capital* over Marx of the *Critique* is contained in the analysis of the fetishism of commodities." But Dunayevskaya objected to any dismissal of *Critique* through the "brutal method you [C.L.R. James] wish me to employ."[7]

The massive amount of material Dunayevskaya wrote, both on Marx's *Capital* and Lenin's *Philosophic Notebooks*, was a major source for what would become *Marxism and Freedom*. But other philosophic developments, particularly Dunayevskaya's reading of Hegel's Absolutes and a further probing of the Marx of 1844, would come to the fore before the form and content of *Marxism and Freedom* would emerge.

•

Of great significance for her writing would be what she termed "my deeper comprehension of the world objective connections" (Letter of October 12, 1949). The Miners' General Strike of 1949-50, the March 1953 death of Stalin, the June 17, 1953 East Germany Revolt, and the 1955-1956 Montgomery Bus Boycott, were among those world objective connections that Dunayevskaya strove to comprehend in the period leading to *Marxism and Freedom*. These philosophic and objective developments would give form to her theoretic labors. In this chapter we take up the Miners' General Strike as discussed by Dunayevskaya and Andy Philips in *The Coal Miners' General Strike of 1949-50 and the Birth of Marxist-Humanism in the U.S.*[8]

The Coal Miners' General Strike and the New Form of the Book-To-Be

From the vantage point of the 1980s, Dunayevskaya wrote of the impact of the Miners' General Strike on her work: "The dialectic of the 1949-50 Miners' General Strike, as it was transformed from a Lewis-authorized strike that already had lasted some six months into a challenge to John L. Lewis himself, laid the ground for new ways of thinking." How did this come about?

Andy Phillips, who at the time of the strike had recently begun working in the mines and was a member of the Johnson-Forest Tendency within the Socialist Workers Party, wrote a personal account of the strike and its ramifications—"A Missing Page from America Labor History" for *The Coal Miners' General Strike* pamphlet. The description of the strike the follows is based on his account. Direct quotes are from his article.

The Lewis authorized strike had begun in the middle of 1949 under the shadow of the Taft-Hartley Act, that severely limited union organizing power and the right to strike. Facing fines if the Act was violated, Lewis outmaneuvered the coal operators and government by using a short three-day work week rather than a full-blown strike to limit coal supplies. However, this violated a long held principle of "No Contract, No Work" by the United Mineworkers Union. Several weeks into this short work-week strategy, the United Miner Workers' Health and Welfare Fund was been rapidly exhausted, as the coal operators were refusing to make their royalty payments. After Lewis announced payments from the Fund were suspended, workers from two of the largest mines in West Virginia decided to strike until the Fund's problems were solved. Union miners in northern West Virginia and southwestern Pennsylvania with the support of their local union leaders joined the walkout.

"No Contract, No Work," was thus made concrete by the workers. Phillips described the activity of miners: roving pickets from throughout the region who went from mine to mine, including non-union mines, to halt all production and transportation of coal. The strike spread throughout Appalachia. But after more than 50 days out, Lewis ordered the workers to resume the three-day workweek. It was now mid-November, more than four months since the expiration of the contract. Maneuvering between coal companies, the government and the union continued. Meanwhile the miners and their families were going deeper in debt on the three-day-work week.

A turning point was reached in January, 1950:

> Consolidation Coal Co. brought court action against the UMWA in Ohio, demanding an injunction against the three-day work week and payment for lost production. Lewis promptly called out the miners in six Consol mines in the Morgantown-Fairmont area on Monday, January 9 . . . only to have most of the other area miners spontaneously walk out as well" (*Coal Miners' General Strike*, 19).

It was now that the wildcat strike took a path independent of Lewis. Though Lewis "suggested" the workers return to work, a number of locals in the area decided not to return, even as district union officials were urging them to do so. Again roving pickets were sent out and honored, even when union officials tried to force miners to cross the picket lines.

A meeting of local union officers was called for the following Thursday, January 19. Some 1,800 rank-and-file miners converged on the local union hall in Monongah: "There had been a number of mass meetings before this one, of course, but never had I been at such a huge mass meeting with so many angry rank-and-file miners. . . . The turning point . . . reached irrevocable completion at the Thursday Monongah meeting. The rank-and-file were now in control of the strike" (21).

Both before the actions of 1949-50 and throughout the months of the mine workers' militant activity, members of the Johnson-Forest Tendency, mine workers and supporters, were deeply involved in the coal country of northern West Virginia. Philips wrote of them: "The miners responded to the work of the young group, but among the most responsive were the Blacks—both miners and women. They persistently brought together their friends and neighbors to participate in meetings where we discussed what we all could do together to fight against racial discrimination in the community as well as the oppression in the mines" (7).

Phillips described the self-activity of the miners as they took charge of the wildcat strike, which not only opposed the coal operators, but challenged Lewis himself. Of particular importance was the formation of a miners' relief committee that established worker to worker contact with workers in other industries and states. It also involved the participation of Johnson-Forest Tendency members:

> But what truly became a transition point for the strike was the rank-and-file Miners Relief Committee. With all established avenues of aid dried up or cut off, the top priority became relief, massive relief to help feed the miners and keep the operators from starving us into defeat. Raya [Dunayevskaya], from her vantage point of being there, was able to gauge both the mood and needs of the miners and their families. Moreover, she also knew that workers in other industries were in complete sympathy with the miners and were very anxious to help. Her position was clear and simple—and revolutionary: have the miners go to other workers, but especially to those areas where other State-Capitalist Tendency (Johnson-Forest) members could help (25).

The Miners Relief Committee was able to make contact with other workers. From Detroit in particular, aid came from Ford autoworkers, with food, clothing and money. And importantly, autoworkers accompanied the aid and met with mine workers. The relief work gave the mineworkers a little breathing room. Soon, the coal operators gave in and on March 3 a new contract was signed.

Though the immediate issues of the strike were wages and payments into the Welfare Fund, a major stage in production was looming below the surface: automation. The continuous miner was just being introduced into mining operations. This first utilization of automation in heavy industry would have devastating affects on mine workers in the period ahead. Tens of thousands would be laid-off, while those left, would have to work at the pace and under the conditions created by introduction of the continuous miner.

The wildcat nature of the strike was an expression of the gulf separating Lewis from the rank-and-file miners. In writing of the strike's historic significance Phillips noted:

> The historic significance of the 1949-50 strike, however, was not only that the miners had revealed in the course of the strike that they were far ahead of their leaders—even such an able and militant leader as Lewis certainly had been. They had also demonstrated that to achieve their ends they had to create their own organization—the mass meeting. They had made their own decisions, carried them out in opposition to the power of the government, coal operators, a hostile press and their own union leadership, and at the same time had directly involved broad segments of the working class in the nation. To some, many of the things the miners did seemed spontaneous, as though the actions came from nowhere. Just the opposite is true. The spontaneity of the miners flowed from their own repeated collective thought and action that preceded their "spontaneous" activity (32).

Then Phillips added, "But the 1949-50 events also demonstrated that actual concrete activity in thought as well as in practice proves that philosophy is not merely subjective, but objective. The over-riding importance of philosophy was that *out of* the strike was born the passion for working out what the strike meant."

•

Dunayevskaya had first visited West Virginia in 1947 with the aim of establishing a miner and student local of the Socialist Workers Party.[9] In 1948 she moved to Pittsburgh to work with steelworkers there and miners in West Virginia. When the strike first broke out she had completed the translation of Lenin's Notebooks on *Science of Logic* and was engaged in the three-way correspondence discussed above. The correspondence:

> centered on the relationship of the dialectic to Lenin as well as to our age. While we seemed to be as one on the need to work out the relationship between objective and subjective for the state-capitalist age that Lenin had worked out for the monopoly stage of capitalism, that relationship between objective and subjective was spoken of only "in general." Now, however, with an ongoing strike in progress, what had been a discussion of ideas assumed, to me, concreteness and urgency. Indeed, it gained a whole new dimension through what the miners were doing and thinking ("The Emergence of a New Movement from Practice that Is Itself a Form of Theory" in *Miners' General Strike* 33-34).

In the midst of the strike Dunayevskaya proposed a new kind of meeting with James and Lee concerning the book they were jointly working on. For her, the strike and the Lenin translations meant the need to take up Marx's *Capital* in a new way, and thus she posed two new vantage points for her presentation: the American proletariat and Lenin's Philosophic Notebooks. To make this even more concrete she wished to invite a worker in the Tendency, Johnny Zupan, to be present for the discussion.

The proposal was a major turning point in Dunayevskaya's conception of the *kind of book* the Tendency would be writing. Its development would not be limited to a discussion among Marxist intellectual revolutionaries. Its audience would not be restricted to a debate among intellectuals. (1) The ideas and responses of a worker-member of the Tendency would become part of the process. (2) Lenin's *Philosophic Notebooks*, his philosophical preparation for revolution, would be a crucial point of departure for the Tendency's theoretical work.

The decision was as well a turning point in the *manner by which the book would be written*. The invitation to have a worker within the organization participate in the discussion foreshadowed the way *Marxism and Freedom* would be written, involving the deepest layers of society, and having the development of revolutionary Marxist philosophy *within* a Marxist organization.

Writing in the 1980s, Dunayevskaya characterized the period of the 1949-50 Miners' General Strike as "The Emergence of a New Movement from Practice that Is Itself a Form of Theory." While she did not use such an expression explicitly at the time of the strike, such a concept was implicit in her presentation to James and Lee with a worker, Zupan, present. Let's follow this briefly from the notes taken at the meeting.

She opened the discussion by singling out the new points of departure, beginning with the American proletariat. "[A]t present the struggle of miners and new content they have infused into 'No contract, no work' is what gave me impulse to go into the essential dialectical development of Marx himself." ("Discussion led by Raya Dunayevskaya on the new form of book-in-the-making from two vantage points: American proletariat and Lenin's Philosophic Notebooks." Feb. 15, 1950. *RDC* # 1585) The workers' action and thought, their praxis, had pushed the theoretician to a new way of thinking.

The second point of departure was on Lenin, "who was led to re-evaluate [his] whole method of thinking . . . by 1914 with the collapse of the Second International." After briefly taking up this development she added: "But even the 1915 Lenin with *Logic* does not see what this higher form to which the socialization of labor transits is. It is the proletarian action in 1917, which shows that form: the soviets. Concrete content assumes abstract form, all the while there is a new unformed substance—the proletarian revolution which begins to show the intellectuals the new form" (#1585).

Two intertwined moments were expressed: (1) the self-activity of the workers in 1949-50 helped give Dunayevskaya a way of seeing Lenin's philosophic preparation for revolution being brought to fruition by the proletarian revolution with its worker-created form of the soviet. (2) the same self-activity helped her to reach for a new form for thinking about her own age.

The new stage of proletarian consciousness that Dunayevskaya saw emanating from the Miners' General Strike—the implication of which meant her aligning herself as a theoretician with these new impulses from the workers—when combined with her probing of Lenin's Hegel Notebooks and the mass revolutionary proletarian activity of 1917, created a new way of approaching Marx's *Capital*.

The rest of Dunayevskaya's presentation moved to Marx: "He himself goes through a *development* and *transition*" (#1586). The sub-divisions of her talk demonstrated the attention to the relation of proletarian movement to theoretician's labor as central to Marx's development and transition: "I. 1843-7—Impending proletarian revolution; this is completed by the 1848 revolution. II. 1850-59—Critique of Political Economy—Period of Quietude; III. 1861-73—The period of the specifically proletarian revolution."

She summarized the 1841-47 period of Marx: "When he counterposes economics to politics, materialism to idealism, history to non-history—but all in the form of counterposings of one to the other and not of systematizing or reaching notion—[these] are climaxed by the 1848 revolutions, anticipated by Marx in his *Communist Manifesto*" (#1588).

Her treatment of the 1844 *Economic and Philosophic Manuscripts* of Marx here was limited. She briefly took up "Alienated Labor," which she characterized as a philosophic discussion in contrast to Marx giving "it the concrete form of the actual alienation of labor at the point of production, we will have [in] *Capital*" (#1587). Neither of Marx's essays, "Critique of the Hegelian Dialectic" nor "Private Property and Communism," (which would play a prominent role in her discussion of Marx's Humanism in *Marxism and Freedom*), were taken up.

The fact that Marx's early writings, which Dunayevskaya had found and excerpted in the early 1940s, did not play any substantive part in the Tendency's philosophic discussions from the mid-1940s to the mid 1950s break-up of the Tendency is important to note. It is true that Grace Lee's rough translations of essays from the *Economic-Philosophic Manuscripts* had been published by the Tendency in mimeographed form in 1947. But the humanism of Marx did not become a revolutionary philosophic category until after the split, and Dunayevskaya's 1955-57 work on the draft of *Marxism and Freedom*. Rather, humanism was rejected by Lee and James as merely Christian or existentialist.

In the Tendency's document, which summed up their experience in Trotskyism, *State-Capitalism and World Revolution* (1950), the philosophic section, written by Grace Lee, focused on Contradiction. Dunayevskaya later wrote, that the section "went no further philosophically then we had already worked out in economic and political terms for the decade of 1941-50" ("Not by Practice Alone: The Movement from Theory," 1984, *PON*, 281).

The collectivity of the Tendency, far from opening a new pathway to the early Marx in those years, imposed a barrier to his humanism, which Dunayevskaya would not overcome until after her 1953 plunge into Hegel's Absolutes, and the subsequent 1955 founding of News and Letters Committees.

In Part II of her presentation on Marx, the period of quietude, she moved from the defeat of the 1848 revolutions to Marx's economic studies, and noted that the 1857 crisis did not result in any class battles. *Critique of Political Economy* was written, "but the class struggle is missing" (#1591). At the same time she singled out Marx's 1858 re-reading of Hegel's *Logic*, and discussed its influence. However, her point of concentration was on the mass movement from below, so that even though she was still in Part II, she moved to the "proletarian revolution" concept of Part III. This was seen in her discussion of the effect the Civil War in the U.S. had on Marx—from movement of slaves before the war, and his comment on the effect a single Negro regiment would have on the war's outcome, to the international impact of the Civil War, particularly the actions of the English proletariat and the First International.

In Part III, she continued discussion of the Civil War, then proceeded to briefly trace Marx's reworking of *Capital*. Within her commentary she mentioned the Jamaica Negro Revolt of 1865 and the Polish revolution of 1863. And finally to the Paris Commune, "that complete, irreconcilable *opposite* form to that of Fetishism of Commodities" (#1591).

What was clear from her presentation on the book-in-the-making was that Dunayevskaya now viewed Marx's "dialectical plan of *Capital*" as inseparable from his immersion into Hegel, and from "objective world connections," particularly those stamped with proletarian revolt in the 1860s and 70s.

•

While there was no open opposition to Dunayevskaya's presentation on the part of her co-leaders in the State-Capitalist Tendency, what would soon emerge were differing attitudes both to the mass movement from below, and to other objective world connections. In 1951, when the Tendency made its final break with Trotskyism and began a new organization, tensions emerged more openly. A new newspaper was planned. But when Dunayevskaya proposed that its first issue be devoted to an ongoing 1951 miners' seniority strike, James opposed. He insisted that "our membership and their friends are the only audience I have in mind for the paper . . . If a mighty bubble broke out, 500,000 miners vs. John L. Lewis, and shook the minefields, I would not budge from our program."

In the 1980s Dunayevskaya wrote of this moment: "It is there, *precisely there*, where those two 'subjectivities'—Johnson and Forest—in their attitude to the *masses in motion*, acted totally differently" ("Not By Practice Alone: The Movement From Theory" 1985, *PON*, 275). Only a mimeographed paper was issued from 1951 to 1953. Dunayevskaya would term this period one of "deep depoliticalization."

•

The period of 1949-51—from a deep probing of Lenin's *Abstract* of Hegel's *Science of Logic*, to the new proletarian impulses manifest from below in the Miners' General Strike, to the discoveries about Marx's theoretical development towards and within *Capital*—was a crucial turning point in Dunayevskaya's development. Her immersion in Lenin's 1914-15 exploration of Hegel, and into Marx's dialectical plan of *Capital* as she had Hegel's *Logic* in hand, were quintessential preparation for Dunayevskaya's own reading of Hegel. In hindsight, it is possible to see the tensions that emerged and grew within the Tendency in this period. However, the philosophic leap that would fully launch Dunayevskaya on a unique revolutionary, political, organizational path had not yet taken place. We turn to that philosophic moment, her May 1953 Letters on Hegel's Absolutes, written six weeks after Stalin's death and on the eve of the June 17, 1953 East German Revolt.

---

[1] Dunayevskaya had undertaken sight translations of portions of Lenin's Notebooks earlier in the 1940s. This first complete English translation was published as appendix to the first edition of *Marxism and Freedom* (1958).

[2] For a study of Lenin's Hegel Notebooks, including the response to them among Western Marxists, see *Lenin, Hegel and Western Marxism* by Kevin Anderson, University of Illinois Press, Chicago, 1995. Anderson is a student of Dunayevskaya's thought.

[3] See Part V for Dunayevskaya's 1980s view of the Johnson-Forest Tendency.

[4] These two areas would come to realization in Dunayevskaya's *Marxism and Freedom* (1958) and *American Civilization on Trial* (1963). See Part II of the present study.

[5] In 1947 she had prepared an abbreviated commentary on the 12 volumes of Lenin's *Selected Works* (*RDC* #710, 721).

[6] Dunayevskaya made a number of different references in her letters to the attention Marx paid to the movement of slaves in America, to John Brown, and to the Civil War in this period.

[7] James wished to severely truncate the material taking up Marx's development towards *Capital* in the joint book envisioned by the Tendency. However, Dunayevskaya continued to present Marx's "dialectical plans" in the process leading to *Capital* as well as within *Capital* itself.

[8] See Dunayevskaya's contribution: "The Emergence of a New Movement from Practice that Is Itself a Form of Theory" in *The Coal Miners' General Strike of 1949-50 and the Birth of Marxist-Humanism in the U.S.*, News & Letters, 1984. For an additional Dunayevskaya discussion of the period 1949-1954 as "New stage of production, New stage of cognition, New kind of organization," see her Prologue to *25 Years of Marxist-Humanism in the U.S.—A history of worldwide revolutionary developments*, News and Letters, 1980.

[9] The Johnson-Forest Tendency had moved from the Workers Party to the Socialist Workers Party in 1947.

Chapter 3

Dunayevskaya's 1953 Breakthrough on Hegel's Absolutes in Relation to Momentous World Events: the Death of Stalin and the June 17, 1953 East German Revolt

The death of Stalin (March 5, 1953) was a momentous event objectively and subjectively. From within the Russian Empire, the ruling bureaucracy's fear of revolt post-Stalin would govern many of its actions. Within weeks of his death, revolt broke out in East Germany, and shortly thereafter in the Vorkuta slave labor camp in Siberia. The Russian ruling clique underwent a purge.

Outside the Empire, the shock waves were felt worldwide. In America, production workers talked of it on the shop floor, and theoreticians were challenged to give meaning to the event. From the vantage point of the 1980s, Dunayevskaya wrote of her response:

> The death of Stalin lifted an incubus from my brain, and it was inconceivable to me that it wouldn't do that for the Russian and East European workers. I looked forward to great explosions. Charles Denby [the auto worker colleague of Dunayevskaya who would later become editor of *News & Letters*, the Marxist-Humanist newspaper founded by Dunayevskaya and her colleagues] called as soon as his shift ended to tell me of the excitement in his factory as the radio blared the news of Stalin's death. Each worker was saying that he had just the

person to take Stalin's place—his foreman. I asked Denby to come over for a discussion.

When he came over we spent several hours talking both about Stalin's death and the affinity the American workers felt with the Russian workers, especially on the trade union question. The discussion made clear to me that, far from the American workers considering this a "Russian Question," they were relating it to their own working conditions in the shop and their relationship to their own bosses and union bureaucrats. . . .

Denby felt the workers he knew would not only understand the problems the Russian workers faced, but that they would find lessons for their own struggles against both the union bureaucrats and the company. He raised the question I had been discussing with him some time before, on the 1920-21 Trade Union debate between Lenin and Trotsky. He said that if I could put that story in the framework of what the workers were experiencing right then, he would be happy to distribute it to his fellow workers and tell me their comments. Outside of the two days it took me to write the political analysis of Stalin's death, I spent the next few weeks writing the essay on that debate, which I called "Then and Now" ("The Emergence of a New Movement from Practice that Is Itself a Form of Theory," p.38-9, *The Coal Miners' General Strike of 1949-50 and the Birth of Marxist-Humanism in the U.S.,* News and Letters, 1984).

Dunayevskaya's analysis, "Stalin: Why He Behaved as He Did," appeared in the mimeographed "practice" newspaper, *Correspondence*, that the Johnson-Forest Tendency was putting out. The article began: "Stalin's death does not end the period of ruthless totalitarianism, but it does close one chapter of a book on the labor bureaucracy in *and* out of Russia which can be entitled: Why Do They Behave As They Do?" (*Raya Dunayevskaya Collection* #2194).

In answering this question, Dunayevskaya posed two additional questions: "(1) why does any individual behave like that; what *objective* movement in the economy, what *class* impulses necessitate such brutality? (2) what specific characteristic in a man enables him to become the receptacle for and the executor of class impulses from an alien class, the very one he either challenged or actually helped overthrow?"

Her answer began with Stalin's bureaucratic attitude toward the masses, his "passion for bossing." Those traits "*coincided* with the objective movement of capitalist production looking for a *new form* by which it could continue to keep the workers enslaved." The "Total Plan and the Totalitarian Personality" coincided: "[T]his man of steel, we must repeat, won power not because of sheer ruthlessness but because that will and that ruthlessness emanated from an *objective* movement of the economy."

In opposition to such ruthlessness was "the constant revolt of the Russian workers," which she traced from the first Five Year plan onward. Dunayevskaya ended her analysis by turning to the American workers and their attitude toward their own labor bureaucrats. She saw a parallel with the Russian workers.

In this essay, Dunayevskaya related the meaning of Stalin's death to a discussion of leaders and ranks in workers' organizations. ("Then and Now, 1920 and 1953," *Correspondence* April 16, 1953, *RDC* #2184). The origin of this article on the 1920-21 Trade Union Debate in Russia came partly from the responses of American workers to Stalin's death—"I have just the candidate for Stalin's job: my foreman." It also came from what these workers were experiencing with their own trade union bureaucracy as they faced the day to day exploitative conditions on the shop floor. A study of the early Russian workers' state that Dunayevskaya had undertaken in the 1940s could now be shared with American workers in the context of questions they were raising in factory, mine, and mill. The article also focused on the relation of leaders and ranks within old radical organizations and on newly emerging radical forms of organization.

Dunayevskaya traced the facts of the Trade Union dispute in the new Russian workers' state, 1919-20. The article was perhaps Dunayevskaya's fullest analysis of the Trade Union debate. Its essence was later presented in *Marxism and Freedom* (1958) in the context of "What Happens After" a revolution has taken power, and the construction of a new society is on the agenda.

During this period, the Johnson-Forest Tendency did not have a unified position on the meaning of the death of Stalin. Dunayevskaya wrote of the Tendency's 1953 dispute in a 1980 essay:

> Lee (who was then on the West Coast and acting as editor that month) had a very different view of what kind of analysis of Stalin's death was needed, because—far from seeing any concern with that event on the part of American workers—she made her point of departure the fact that some women in one factory, instead of listening to the radio blaring forth the news of Stalin's death, were exchanging hamburger recipes. She so "editorialized" my analysis and so passionately stressed the alleged indifference of the American proletariat to that event, that the article become unrecognizable....
> In Detroit I was preparing ["Then and Now"] devoted to the 1920-21 debate ... The following issue ... described the dispute over the political analysis, told that it wasn't possible to substitute a description of the indifference of a few women in a single factory ... for the political analysis of the ramifications of a world event such as Stalin's death. That issue then reproduced the article on Stalin's death as originally written (*25 Years of Marxist-Humanism in the U.S.* p. 3. News & Letters, 1980).

In another writing from the 1980s, Dunayevskaya commented,

> [T]he death of Stalin ... brought about a political crisis also in the Johnson-Forest Tendency ... Suddenly what was disclosed was the apoliticalization which deepened when, after our final break with Trotskyism in 1951, we failed to face the public either with our theory of state-capitalism or the magnificent experience in the Miners' General Strike followed by the seniority strike in

1951" ("Not By Practice Alone: The Movement From Theory," 1984. Reprinted in *Power of Negativity*, 284-85).

The political divisions within the Johnson-Forest Tendency did not halt her philosophic explorations within the Hegelian dialectic. However, as we will see, those divisions *and* the emerging philosophic differences as Dunayevskaya created and explored a new philosophic terrain, meant that the Tendency, at one and the same time, spurred and hindered her path. It surely was not a uni-linear pathway free of contradictions and diversions. This was particularly true for the question of organization, which the Tendency was grappling with not alone theoretically but as the concrete practice of Correspondence Committees and its paper *Correspondence*. However, we need to begin with Dunayevskaya's probing of Hegel's Absolutes.

In May 1953, six weeks after Stalin's death, Dunayevskaya's explorations of the Absolute Idea chapter of *Science of Logic* and the Absolute Mind chapter of *Philosophy of Mind* resulted in two breakthrough letters on Hegel's Absolutes—what she would later call the Philosophic Moment of Marxist-Humanism.

The Letters on Hegel's Absolutes

On May 12, 1953, Dunayevskaya wrote to her colleague Grace Lee discussing the "Absolute Idea" chapter of Hegel's *Science of Logic*. This letter, and that of May 20, were different from the 1949-51 philosophic correspondence she had carried on with James and Lee. While Hegel's dialectic was taken up in those earlier letters, the subject matter focused primarily on Lenin's Hegel notebooks or the dialectic plan of Marx's *Capital*. In the May 1953 letters, it was Hegel's Absolutes in and of themselves that were probed in relation to the revolutionary problems of the post-World War II era. Lenin and Marx were discussed, but Dunayevskaya's reading of the Absolutes was the subject.

The May 12 and 20, 1953 letters on Hegel's Absolutes were at one and the same time a culmination of a philosophic journey of several years, and a new philosophic point of departure. The Johnson-Forest Tendency had been working on a book re-stating Marxism for their age. Dunayevskaya had written an 80-page outline, "State-Capitalism and Marxism"(1947) (*RDC* # 1735). James had composed a manuscript, "Notes on Dialectics," (1948) which took up the Hegelian dialectic. After her 1949 translation of Lenin's Notebooks on Hegel and the 1949-51 three-way correspondence (discussed in Chapter Two), Dunayevskaya wrote a second draft, "The Lenin Book" (1952). James, in his correspondence with Dunayevskaya and Lee, was busy assigning sections, including lengths, to the others, for the developing book, with Dunayevskaya being "the economist," and Lee "the philosopher." The goal was cracking the Absolute Idea with regard to "dialectic of the party."[1] In her writings, Dunayevskaya sought to breakdown divisions between "economist" and "philosopher." In any case, she felt compelled to take her own journey into Hegel's Absolutes.

Dunayevskaya was undertaking a philosophic journey into the absolutes which by the end of her May 20th letter would in fact burst through the confines of "dialectic of the party," to enter "the new society," beginning with the abolition of the division between mental and manual labor. At the same time her 1953 discussion of the party and dialectics set the ground for her 1986-87 work on "Dialectics of Organization and Philosophy." But let us begin with the May 12th letter.

May 12, 1953—From the Dialectic of the Party to the Threshold of the New Society

The initial framework for Dunayevskaya's exploration of Absolute Idea was the dialectic of the party. This seemed to coincide with what the Tendency had been exploring first within Trotskyism and then in its independent existence post-1951. As she wrote in the May 12 letter to Lee, "I brazenly shout that in the dialectic of the Absolute Idea is the dialectic of the party and that I have just worked it out" (*PON*, 15). At the same time, right from the beginning of her letters there was something beyond James' view of the party in Dunayevskaya's concept:

> (1) I am not touching upon the mass party; the workers will do what they will do and until they do we can have only the faintest intimation of the great leap.
> (2) This is not 1948, but 1953; I am not concerned with spontaneity versus organization, nor with Stalinism which the workers will overcome.
> I am concerned only with the dialectic . . . of the *type* of grouping like ours, be it large or small, and *its* relationship to the mass (16).

When Dunayevskaya wrote "this is not 1948 but 1953," she was moving beyond James' "Notes on the Dialectic," written in 1948, with its focus on spontaneity and organization. While not throwing out the question of spontaneity and organization, her exploration of Hegel's Absolutes probed additional dimensions of revolutionary organization and dialectical philosophy.

When she wrote, "I am concerned only with the dialectic . . . of the *type* of grouping like ours, be it large or small and *its* relationship to the mass," she was asking what was the role of a revolutionary group that had Marx's philosophy as its basis. How would dialectical philosophy impact upon its relation to the masses?[2]

Dunayevskaya then presented several quotes from the Absolute Idea chapter's opening paragraph on the Idea: as "the identity of the Theoretical and the Practical Idea," as containing "the highest opposition within itself," as "the only object and content of philosophy . . . containing every determinateness." These were juxtaposed to the party as, "the identity or unity of the activity of the leadership and the activity of the ranks;" and as "the only object and content of *our* philosophy" (16).

Continuing on the theme of the party, she focused on two discussions of the Other that Hegel developed in the Absolute Idea chapter. In the first discussion, Hegel related the "Notion . . . as person, is impenetrable and atomic subjectivity; while at the same time it is not exclusive individuality, but is, for itself, universality and cognition, and in its Other has its own objectivity for object" (*Science of Logic* 466). Dunayevskaya saw this Other as the proletariat outside.

She contrasted this description of the Other to Hegel's second discussion:

> The second or negative and mediated determination is at the same time the mediating determination. At first it may be taken as simple determination, but in truth it is a reference or relation; for it is a negative—the negative, however, of *the positive*, and includes the latter. It is not therefore the Other of a term to which it is indifferent, for thus it would be neither an Other nor a reference or relation; it is the Other in itself, the Other of an Other. It thus includes its own Other, and so is contradiction, or the posited dialectic of itself (*Science of Logic*, 476-477).

Dunayevskaya commented, "Other turns out to be, not the proletariat outside, but the party itself" (16-17).

In her May 12 letter Dunayevskaya now turned to the Absolute Knowledge chapter of *Phenomenology of Mind*, taking up the movement from universality to individuality through specification via "the mediated result," and related this to the question of the party. Was the party the mediation? Was the party itself mediated through its composition and by its relation to the proletariat and to the universal of socialism? She quoted Hegel on Spirit's externalization, and drew a parallel to Socialism externalizing itself in events such as the Paris Commune, the Soviets, and the CIO. She called attention to Hegel discussion of history at the end of Absolute Knowledge, quoting his expression of "Spirit externalized and emptied into Time," and relating this to the historic development of the party at different moments.

However, she noted that Hegel did not leave Spirit only as history, quoting the final paragraph of *Phenomenology* on History and Science, which together, "or History (intellectually) comprehended, form at once the recollection and the Golgotha of Absolute Spirit."

Returning to the *Science of Logic*, she noted parallels between early parts of the Absolute Idea chapter and the party, as well as organizational forms such as the CIO and the Soviets. Within the framework of the party, she related Hegel's philosophic discussion of internal intuition and sensuous intuition to the "internal intuition" of the leader, "which comes from the way he *thinks*" and the "immediate of sensuous intuition" coming from how the ranks live. However, far from such "internal intuition" being put on any pedestal, Dunayevskaya noted that "the self-development of socialism, objectively and subjectively, gave off impulses which come one way to the leader, another way to the *class* as a whole, but what is important is that it is *determined to appear* 'to hear itself speak'" (19). It was the movement, the self-development, which was crucial. Furthermore, "[T]he beautiful part about the 'internal intuition' is that this 'beginning must be inherently defective and must be endowed with the impulse of self development'" (19).

We are here far away from the "internal intuition" being the vanguard party-to-lead with its hierarchical division of leaders and ranks. Neither the word of the leader nor the immediate impulses of the class was the final determinant. Rather, movement within the Absolute, "determined to appear," and "self-development" were key: "Hegel's conclusion that nothing in life or in thought has a beginning so simple as is imagined but that 'every beginning must be made from the Absolute, while every progress is merely the exhibition of the Absolute. . . . The progress is therefore not a kind of overflow. . . . It is the Absolute only in its completion'. . . . The new society will not be until it is" (19).

Dunayevskaya proceeded to bring Lenin into her letter. It was a very different discussion of Lenin and Hegel than she had previously engaged in. Before, Lenin was, in a sense, her mentor for reading Hegel. Until May 1953, his 1914-15 Notebooks on the dialectic had been perhaps her most crucial source of illumination. With the letters on the Absolute Idea, the vantage point would be different. Now she was reading *Lenin* with the eyes of Hegel's dialectic.

Furthermore, though the initial subject of her letter was dialectic of the party, her interest in Lenin here was not in relation to his concept of the vanguard party, which Dunayevskaya and the State-Capitalist Tendency had already critiqued and separated themselves from politically. Rather, she was now discerning, probing, questioning aspects of Lenin's *philosophic* journey into Hegel, particularly his incomplete commentary on Hegel's Absolute Idea, at the end of his Notebooks.

After calling attention to Lenin's 16-point definition of dialectics, and summarizing its essence, she wrote, "[W]e can fit Lenin in ... here *historically*" (20). She pointed out that in commenting on the Absolute Idea chapter, Lenin developed objective world connections but not the creativity of cognition that he had singled out in the previous Idea of Cognition section. It was the creativity of cognition that Dunayevskaya sought to follow out. By doing so, she not only "fit Lenin in," but moved "to where we part from Lenin."

A key for moving "to where we part from Lenin" was her singling out mediation and second negativity, particularly within the last pages the Absolute Idea chapter. She reached the mediating determination that is a negative, "but the negative of the *positive* and includes that latter." This negativity was for Hegel, "the turning-point of the movement of the Notion." She quoted from this paragraph ending with, "The second negative, the negative of the negative which we have reached, is this transcendence of the contradiction, but is no more the activity of an external reflection than the contradiction is: it is the innermost and most objective moment of Life and Spirit, by virtue of which a subject is person and free" (20).

Dunayevskaya exclaimed all in caps, "SHOUT PERSONAL AND FREE, PERSONAL AND FREE, PERSONAL AND FREE AS LENIN SHOUTED LEAP, LEAP, LEAP," in his Notebooks.

Diving into Hegel on absolute method, where "the Notion preserves itself in its otherness. . . . and by its dialectical progress not only loses nothing and leaves nothing behind, but carries with it all that it has acquired, enriching and concentrating itself upon itself," Dunayevskaya read this as: "none of the other philosophies (parties to us) just degenerated or died, but their achievements have been incorporated in the new philosophy or party" (21).

Everything for Dunayevskaya was now about second negation in Hegel: "Each new stage of exteriorization (that is, of further determination) is also an interiorization, and greater extension is also high intensity" (21). It was the "absolute dialectic" that "liberates itself." However the steps to do so were not only "progressive further determinations," but a "regressive confirmation of the beginning."

Hegel had hit out against alternatives to this method of mediation and second negativity: "that impatience whose only wish is to go beyond the determinate . . . and to be immediately in the absolute, has nothing before it as object of its cognition but the empty negative, the abstract infinite—or else a would-be absolute" (21-22). Dunayevskaya seized on this expression and wrote: "[W]e are back at liberation and until the end of The Absolute Idea that will be the theme, liberation, freedom and *an absolutely uncompromising, Bolshevik attack on impatience*" (21).

The real stunner was that the "Bolshevik attack on impatience" included a critique of Lenin. Immediately after quoting Hegel on impatience she wrote, "I am shaking all over for we have come to where we part from Lenin." Dunayevskaya discussed how Lenin, in his Philosophic Notes on the Absolute Idea chapter, had failed to develop his expression, "Man's cognition not only reflects the objective world but creates it."

She pinpointed where in Hegel's final paragraph Lenin stopped: "For the Idea posits itself as the absolute unity of the pure Notion and its Reality, and thus gathers itself into the immediacy of Being; and in doing so, as totality in this form, it is Nature." Lenin had interpreted this as Hegel stretching a hand to materialism. He felt no need to follow Hegel further in the Absolute Idea chapter. Dunayevskaya argued the need to go further into this final paragraph where the Idea is an absolute *liberation*, and "freely releases itself in absolute self-security and self-repose."

She "dialogued" with Lenin on the difference between his age of transformation into opposite, competition into monopoly, where transition was sufficient, and the new age of Stalinism and the totalitarian one-party state, where one needs to follow Hegel who had passed *beyond* transition: "*[T]hat* is the new that must be overcome by a totally new revolt in which everyone *experiences* 'absolute liberation'"(22), "the object and subject as one fully developed" (22). The reality of the state-capitalist age compelled one to grapple philosophically with the relation of objectivity and subjectivity.

Dunayevskaya's philosophic parting from Lenin rested on following out second negation in Hegel. She refused to stop with a mere materialist translation of Hegel's idealism. She was determined to follow out the dialectic of second negativity to where it moved beyond "transformation into opposite," beyond any Party, moved to where the idea freely releases itself, to the threshold of the new society.

This did not mean organization was not a dimension of the dialectic. It meant that James' formulation of the dialectic of the party did not capture the relation of philosophy and organization. This would not become fully clear to Dunayevskaya until the mid 1980s when she began working on a book aimed at transforming the question to "Dialectics of Organization and Philosophy: 'the party' and forms of organization born out of spontaneity."

In preparation for taking the plunge into Hegel's final few sentences of the Absolute Idea chapter of the *Logic*, Dunayevskaya quoted the last two sentences of the penultimate paragraph of the Absolute Idea chapter that indicated where Hegel wished to begin again: "In so far [because] the pure Idea of Cognition is enclosed in subjectivity, and therefore is an impulse to transcend the latter; and, as last result, pure truth becomes *the beginning of another sphere and science*. This transition need here only be intimated." Dunayevskaya responded: "And then he [Hegel] goes into how the Idea posits itself and is liberation. That, he says, he cannot fully develop here; he can only intimate it" (23).

The question of "intimate" led her to return to Marx: "Now you will recall that that is precisely what Marx does in the [section on the] accumulation of capital when he reaches the laws of concentration and centralization of capital and socialization of labor" (23). She cited the expressions from *Capital* that testified to this point and explained: "[Grace], are you as excited as I? *Just as Marx's development of the form of the commodity and money came from Hegel's syllogistic UPI* [Universal Particular Individual], *so the Accumulation of Capital (the General Absolute Law) is based on The Absolute Idea*" (23).

The intimations from Marx on centralization of capital "in the hands of one single capitalist corporation," and the revolt growing out of "the very mechanism of capitalist production," were the ideas that, three-quarters of a century later, Dunayevskaya developed in her theory of state-capitalism.

She paraphrased Lenin's aphorism on Marx not leaving a Logic, but the logic of *Capital*, and wrote, "This is it—*the logic of Capital is the dialectic of bourgeois society*: the state capitalism at one pole and the revolt at the other" (23).

Concluding her May 12 letter, Dunayevskaya returned to the last paragraph of the *Logic*, quoting the movement of the Notion "to perfect its self-liberation in the Philosophy of Spirit." She now wished to explore *Philosophy of Spirit (Mind)*: "I have an instinct that we couldn't get very far there when we tried it before because we equated Mind to party, but now that I believe the dialectic of the Absolute Idea is the dialectic of the party, I feel that Mind is the new society gestating in the old" (23-24).

Dunayevskaya had begun her May 12 letter by looking for the "dialectic of the party" within Absolute Idea. By the end of the letter she had the new society in view. Neither the party, with its leader and its ranks, nor the mass movement and its various organizational forms, were the Absolute. The new society is, only on its completion. Philosophy in the Absolute Idea encompassed organization, but the dialectic stretched beyond, stretched toward the new society.

This did not mean that organization disappeared. Reaching toward the new society, at least in Dunayevskaya's philosophic labors, was taking place while she was a leader in the State-Capitalist Tendency and moving toward what she would call Marxist-Humanism, and which she founded as a philosophic-organizational tendency.

In discussing "the Party" in the context of the Absolute Idea chapter of *Science of Logic*, Dunayevskaya was raising a question that had been absent in the radical movement post-Marx: *the relationship of philosophy and organization*. It was not her particular formulations—of proletariat and party, leadership and ranks, of party as the only object and content of our philosophy—that was the central issue. (Dunayevskaya emphasized that she was expressing her views of the dialectic and the party "*at this moment.*") It was that *revolutionary organization needed be grounded in philosophy*. This was an untrodden path to be explored.

May 20, 1953 "We have entered the new society."

Exploring the final sentences of the Absolute Idea chapter in the *Logic* was not an end for Dunayevskaya but a new beginning as she decided to follow Hegel into *Philosophy of Spirit (Mind)*. She began her letter of May 20 by listing what she had reread in preparation for studying *Philosophy of Mind*:

> The Preface, Introduction, and Absolute Knowledge in the *Phenomenology of Mind*, the Introduction, Three Attitudes of Objectivity and the Absolute Idea in the Smaller Logic and the Absolute Idea in the *Science of Logic*. After that I read from cover to cover Lenin's phenomenal Vol. IX [*Selected Works*], which is the Absolute Idea in action, reread Marx's [section on] accumulation of capital and the fetishism of commodities in Vol. I of *Capital*, the final part in Vol. III [of *Capital*], and *The Civil War in France* (25).

After presenting an "outline of the development of the vanguard party and its relationship to the mass movements," she briefly discussed the Introduction by quoting from paragraph 385 on the three stages in the development of Mind: Subjective, Object, and Absolute, and from paragraph 386 on Mind as the infinite Idea, and "finitude here means the disproportion between the concept and the reality—but with the qualification that it is a shadow cast by the mind's own light—a show or illusion which the mind implicitly imposes as a barrier to itself, in order, by its removal, actually to realize and become conscious of freedom as *its* very being, i.e., to be fully *manifested*" (26).

She turned to the section on "Free Mind" where "we will meet with free will in a new social order" (26), and noted that this was "not the free will of the Ego, the unhappy consciousness, but the free will of the *social* individual, 'an individuality . . . purified of all that interferes . . . with freedom itself'" (27). She showed that "Hegel cannot avoid *history*, the concrete development," quoting his expression from paragraph 482 on individuals and nations obtaining the concept of full-blown liberty. But then Dunayevskaya added: "I'll be d—d if *for us* I need to stop to give the materialistic explanation here. I'm not fighting Hegel's idealism but trying to absorb his dialectics" (27).

Dunayevskaya's absorption of dialectics moved to Absolute Mind and her commentary on its concluding four paragraphs, 574-577. Paragraph 574 began, "This notion of philosophy is the self-thinking Idea, the truth aware of itself—the logical system, but with the signification that it is universality approved and certified in concrete content as in its actuality." Dunayevskaya wrote that this reminded her of Hegel's Introduction to the *Encyclopedia Logic* where, "the Idea is not so feeble as merely to have a right or an obligation to exist without actually existing." She "translated" this for her age as "Socialism 'is not so feeble as merely to have a right or obligation to exist without actually existing.' Quite the contrary, the new society is *evident* everywhere, *appears* within the old" (28).

In paragraph 575, the self-thinking Idea would make its first appearance in the form of a syllogism, Logic-Nature-Mind: "The Logical principle turns to Nature and Nature to Mind." Dunayevskaya, after quoting from the opening sentences of the paragraph, expressed her reading of this first syllogism: "The movement is from the logical principle or theory to nature or practice *and* from practice not alone to theory but to the new society which is its essence" (28).

This reading of paragraph 575—stating that within Hegel's Absolutes there is a movement from theory to practice, *and* a movement from practice that reaches out to theory and to the new society—would come to have enormous implications for the development of Marxist-Humanism.

Following Lenin, Dunayevskaya "translated" Nature as practice. But whereas Lenin had done so at the beginning of the last paragraph of the Absolute Idea chapter of the *Science of Logic*, and had not followed Hegel to the end of the chapter or into *Philosophy of Mind*, Dunayevskaya was doing so within the final paragraphs of Absolute Mind. Thus, Nature was not outside the Idea, an "answer" in the revolutionary practice of the masses alone. Rather, Nature was the mediation, "Nature is essentially defined as a transition-point and negative factor, and as implicitly the Idea" (paragraph 575). As such, Dunayevskaya noted, "that practice itself is 'implicitly the Idea'" (28). And such practice not only expressed theory, but reached toward the new society. This conception made philosophically explicit that the practice of masses was not only muscle of revolution, but Mind as well.

At the same time, Dunayevskaya noted, "[L]et us not forget that this is only the first syllogism," and proceeded to quote the second syllogism in which the form is Nature Mind Logic: "[T]hat syllogism is the standpoint of the Mind itself, which—as the mediating agent in the process—presupposes Nature and couples it with the Logical principle. It is the syllogism where Mind reflects on itself in the Idea: philosophy appears as a subjective cognition, of which liberty is the aim, and which is itself the way to produce it" (paragraph 576). With Mind now "the mediating agent in the process," Dunayevskaya's "translation" became:

> I cannot help but think of Marx concluding that the Commune is "the form at last discovered to work out the economic emancipation of the proletariat," and of Lenin in Vol. 9 saying that the workers and peasants "must understand that the whole thing now is *practice*, that the historical moment has arrived when theory is being transformed into practice". . . . And so I repeat Mind itself, the new society, is "the mediating agent in the process" (29).

Dunayevskaya now moved to "where Hegel arrives at Absolute Mind, the third syllogism:"

> The third syllogism is the Idea of philosophy, which has self-knowing reason, the absolutely-universal, for its middle term: a middle, which divides itself into Mind and Nature, making the former its presupposition, as process of the Idea's subjective activity, and the latter its universal extreme, as process of the objectively and implicitly existing Idea.

She summed up the dialectical movement she had discerned:

> No wonder I was so struck . . . with the Syllogism which disclosed that either the Universal or the Particular or the Individual could be the middle term. Note carefully that the "middle which divides itself" is nothing less than the absolute universal itself and that, in dividing itself into Mind and Nature, it makes *Mind* the presupposition "as process of the Idea's subjective activity" and *Nature* "as process of the objectively and implicitly existing Idea" (29).

Dunayevskaya's recognition that *either* the universal, particular, or individual could be the middle term, the mediation, a "middle which divides itself" and thus "the absolute universal itself," released the Absolute as an absolute movement of becoming. There was nothing static about the categories Universal, Particular and Individual—all was movement, self-movement through double negation, second negativity, both forward and rearward. Each of the terms, Universal, Particular and Individual—the new society as cognition and reality, the particular (specific) forms of practice and thought to get there, the social individual striving for liberation—could be the middle, the mediating agent, and thereby implicitly the whole.

She quoted the last sentences of paragraph 577—

> The self-judging of the Idea in its two appearances (paragraphs 575, 576) characterizes both as its (the self-knowing reason's) manifestations: and in it there is a unification of the two aspects:—it is the nature of the fact, the notion, which causes the movement and development, yet this same movement is equally the action of cognition. The eternal Idea, in full fruition of its essence, eternally sets itself to work, engenders and enjoys itself as absolute Mind.

—and ended her letter: "We have entered the new society."

•

The response of Dunayevskaya to Stalin's death was a leap in cognition, her breakthrough on Hegel's Absolutes. The masses in Eastern Europe and Russia had their own response. On June 17, 1953, East German workers rebelled against new work norms and totalitarian overlordship.

One month earlier, May 18, the East German Communist government had announced an increase in work hours. In the following two weeks open strikes broke out. By mid-June, workers in East Berlin were assembling on the streets to hold open discussions. On June 16, construction workers organized a protest march against speed-up. "Down with the Government," was shouted in the streets. The government revoked its speed-up order, but the demonstrations did not stop.

On the morning of the 17th, thousands took to the streets, attacking major government buildings. Symbols of Communist power—flags, posters and pictures of Communist party leaders—were torn down. For several hours the strikers were the only power in East Berlin.

The Russian military, the real power behind the East German government, sent 10,000 troops to East Berlin and martial law was decreed. By June 20, the Russians had put 25,000 troops in East Berlin. Over 20,000 were arrested. But strikes continued in other cities: on June 22, Leipzig was still on general strike.

What Dunayevskaya had discerned in Hegel's Absolute Mind in her May 20, 1953 letter—"The movement is from logical principle or theory to nature or practice *and* from practice not alone to theory but to the new society which is its essence"—was taking on flesh and blood existence in the streets.

The same issue of *Correspondence* (October 3, 1953) that reported on the East German Revolt also carried Dunayevskaya's analysis of the purge of Lavrenti Beria, the Russian ruler who had been most directly in charge of the satellite countries. "There is no getting away from it," she wrote, "the Russian masses are not only ill-fed, ill-clad and ill-housed. *They are rebellious.* . . . We are at the beginning of the end of Russian totalitarianism." Though not known in the West at the time, ten thousand miners in the slave camps at Vorkuta had burst into an open strike in July 1953. Three years later came the Hungarian Revolution.[3]

Dunayevskaya's article on the Beria Purge was met by hostility from her co-leaders Johnson and Lee similar to that provoked by her analysis of Stalin's death. A critique by their followers appeared in subsequent issues of *Correspondence*. These divisions within the Tendency occurred as McCarthyism was sweeping the country.

The Letters on Hegel's Absolutes and the Break-Up of the State-Capitalist Tendency, 1953-54

The letters on Hegel's Absolutes would signal the demise of the State-Capitalist Tendency. However, this was by no means clear in 1953. There was no straight-line to the establishment of a Marxist-Humanist tendency in 1955, nor to *Marxism and Freedom* in 1957. Although Grace Lee quickly responded to the May 12 letter, C.L.R. James' response was silence, and Lee, under his tutelage, subsequently made no further commentary.

Furthermore, the letters were quite unknown within the Tendency, whose organizational form was now Correspondence Committees. They were not to be shared and discussed with other members. Within her own organization, Dunayevskaya could not pursue her path-breaking breakthrough on the relationship of Hegel's Absolutes to the problem of revolutionary organization. Rather, the philosophic dialogue halted, and organizational warfare primarily conducted by Grace Lee, but with James' concurrence, appeared in the pages of *Correspondence*. Critiques of Dunayevskaya's political analysis of the events in Russia continued for several issues.

Dunayevskaya would later refer to 1954 as the "lost year." This was not only a description of what she saw as the diversionary disputes of the leadership, which continued the depoliticalization within the Tendency as seen in its incomplete response to objective/subjective world events. The term perhaps also included an element of self-critique on the part of Dunayevskaya. In that lost year, no discussion of the 1953 letters occurred at the Correspondence Committees national gathering. Instead, James' view of revolutionary organization consisting of "three layers" took center stage.[4] At the time, Dunayevskaya, in a presentation to the national meeting entitled "Our Organization," did not dispute the formulation, staying within its framework.

Objective events, particularly within America, soon intervened sharply in the Tendency's life. With war clouds over Formosa (Taiwan) building abroad, and McCarthyism raging at home, the Johnson-Forest Tendency was listed by the Attorney General as a subversive grouping. James chose that moment, at the end of 1954 and the beginning of 1955, to breakup the organization. Less than a month after the break-up, a new organization, News and Letters Committees, was founded by Dunayevskaya and her colleagues. They began publishing a newspaper, *News & Letters* on June 17, 1955, the 2nd anniversary of the East German Revolt.[5]

•

The 1953 letters were not only the philosophic divide within the State-Capitalist Tendency, they established Dunayevskaya's philosophic trajectory. The letters became the critical source for her philosophic-political-organizational labor as a Marxist revolutionary over the next three and a half decades, 1953-1987. The 1953 letters were the birth of what she would later call "the Philosophic Moment of Marxist-Humanism."

The first public presentation of the 1953 Letters emerged with the founding of News and Letters Committees, after the break up of the Johnson-Forest Tendency. Along with establishing the newspaper *News & Letters*, the first publication of the Committees was a mimeographed pamphlet (1955) consisting of the first English translation of Lenin's *Abstract* on Hegel's *Science of Logic* and the 1953 Letters on Hegel's Absolutes. The second edition of this pamphlet, *Philosophic Notes*, was issued in 1956, as Dunayevskaya was in the process of writing *Marxism and Freedom*. Each edition had introductions by Dunayevskaya (*RDC* #2433-4, #12061-12063).

In these introductions Dunayevskaya situated her letters in two new moments in the objective-subjective situation that had emerged in the first half of the 1950s: (1) the death of Stalin followed by the "new era of struggle for freedom . . . opened by East German revolt . . . by a revolt in the slave labor camps of Vorkuta inside Russia itself;" (2) "a new era in production with the first serious introduction of automation in the form of the continuous miner. . . . [t]he second industrial revolution," in America, inseparable from the fact that workers began to question the very mode of labor.

In the 1955 Introduction, Dunayevskaya characterized this period as "a new humanism," and commented: "The maturity of the age could be seen in the fact that the average man on the street and the philosopher were asking one and the same question: *Can* man be free in this age of totalitarian bureaucracy?" It was during this moment that Dunayevskaya first probed Hegel's Absolutes: "I turned to philosophy and saw in the Absolute Idea the breakdown of the division between theory and practice in the movement for total freedom. What was *new* was that there was a dialectic not alone in the movement from theory to practice, but *from practice to theory*."

Here lay the philosophic root of the division within the Johnson-Forest Tendency: "Without this universal philosophic form, state capitalism as a tendency would remain economist and incomplete." The leaders of the State Capitalist Tendency had for several years seen their task as "the working out materialistically of Hegel's last chapter on *The Absolute Idea*," but "were unable to relate the daily struggles of the workers to this total conception."

The 1956 Introduction built on the 1955 Introduction. Dunayevskaya quoted from Hegel's warning: "It is certainly possible to indulge in a vast amount of senseless declamation about the idea absolute. But its true content is only the whole system, of which we have been hitherto examining the development." For Dunayevskaya "the true content," the concretization, "was a study of working class struggles and working class thought." Her reading of Hegel's Absolute Idea in 1953 cast the greatest illumination, identifying these struggles "with a concept of the new society and the struggle for total freedom."

•

For more than three decades, the May 1953 letters on Hegel's Absolutes were returned to again and again by Dunayevskaya in developing new points of departure in response to unfolding world events and concrete organizational needs.

As the same time, Dunayevskaya's focus on the relation of revolutionary organization to philosophy that she had found in Hegel's Absolute Idea—what in 1987 she would see as part of "the many universals inherent in [the 1953 Letters]"—would not be theoretically explored by her for more than three decades. The long span of time before returning to the letters specifically on the question of dialectics of organization is complex. Dunayevskaya's breakthrough on Hegel's Absolutes had opened up a vast array of vistas on the re-creation of Marxism for the latter half of the 20th century. At the same time, the need to free the new organization and her own thought from the last vestiges of "Johnsonism," perhaps meant such a sharp movement away from "dialectic of the party," as to partially obscure the new dialectical relationship of organization and philosophy inherent in her letters. One sees this ambivalence towards the formulations on organization in the 1953 letters in one reprinting in 1974 (*RDC* #5041). This re-publication of excerpts did not include the first pages of the May 12 letter on the relation of dialectics and organization. Was this 1970s ambivalence on the early part of the May 12 letter due to its many references to organization as the dialectic of the party?

As we have seen, though Dunayevskaya wrote of "the party," what she arrived at was far different from James' dialectic of the party. While not spelled out explicitly, what was implicit, and would become concretized by Dunayevskaya over more than three decades, was that neither the party nor the spontaneous self-organization of the masses was the totality. Dialectical philosophy, in its highest expression, the absolutes, was the key determinant for organization, for a radical group's relation to the self-activity of masses in motion.

The philosophic journey Dunayevskaya took in 1953 burst through the confines of "dialectic of the party" to reach toward the new society. This did not mean that "dialectic of the party" was annihilated. Hegel's expression *aufhe-*

ben—a term with intertwining meanings: (1) to raise, to hold, lift up; (2) to annul abolish, destroy, cancel, suspend; (3) to keep, save, preserve;—can perhaps help us to grasp the transcendence which "dialectic of the party" underwent in Dunayevskaya's hands, first in the 1953 letters, and then culminating in 1986-87 as "Dialectics of Organization and Philosophy: 'the party' and forms of organization born out of spontaneity." This is no mere substitution of the word "organization" for the word "party." Rather, it was a re-creation of the dialectic in philosophy in its organizational manifestation/expression.[6] It would form part of what Dunayevskaya called "the long trek and process" in the development of Marxist-Humanism.

It would take three decades of work within the revolutionary organization News and Letters Committees—as well as her further probing of Marx on organization from the Communist League to his *Critique of the Gotha Program*, and her examination of the Marx-Engels relationship resulting, in the 1980s, in the category post-Marx Marxism as a pejorative—before she explicitly took steps to transcend the historic barrier on organization/philosophy that Marx did not live to leap over, and that Lenin did not attempt to work out. Only in 1986-87 would Dunayevskaya fully return to the question as a "Dialectics of Organization and Philosophy," and find that its origins were philosophically embedded in the 1953 Letters on Hegel's Absolutes.

•

With the 1953 Letters on Hegel's Absolutes and the break-up of the Johnson-Forest Tendency, a new organization, newspaper, and projected restatement of Marxism for the age, were at hand. It is to these developments we now turn.

---

[1] In 1986-87 when Dunayevskaya returned to the question of organization, she sharply critiqued the formulation "dialectic of the party" as trapped within the State-Capitalist Tendency framework, but saw in her May 12 letter points of departure for the notion of a "Dialectics of Organization and Philosophy."

[2] As we will see, the founding and experience of News and Letters Committees from the mid 1950s through the mid 1980s would become the practice of her new point of departure. Theoretically, the seeds she was planting on organization in her 1953 Letters would not be fully returned to until the mid-1980s were her work on "Dialectics of Organization and Philosophy."

[3] For Dunayevskaya's writing on the East Germany and Vorkuta uprisings, and on the 1956 Hungarian Revolution, see especially "The Beginning of the End of Russian Totalitarianism," Chapter 15 of her *Marxism and Freedom*.

[4] The editors of *Power of Negativity* described the "three layers" in a footnote: "C.L.R. James developed a concept of 'three layers' after the Johnson-Forest Tendency left the Socialist Workers Party, patterned on his interpretation of Vol. XI of Lenin's *Selected Works*. The term 'first layer' referred to the 'intellectual leadership;' 'second layer' referred to the 'experienced politicos;'

'third layer' referred to the rank-and-file workers, women, Blacks and youth" (*PON* 30n4).

[5] See *25 Years of Marxist-Humanism in the U.S.* News and Letters, 1980, and *The Coal Miners' General Strike of 1949-50 and the Birth of Marxist-Humanism in the U.S.*, News and Letters 1984, for two of Dunayevskaya's discussions of the Tendency's differences and eventual breakup. See also Part V of the present study.

[6] As noted early this will be further explored in Part V of the present study. It is, as well, a subject I hope to return at greater length in a future study.

Chapter 4

Founding of News and Letters Committees, 1955-1957, in the Context of East European Revolts, Workers' Struggles Against Automation, and the Montgomery Bus Boycott

In three intense years, 1955-1957, the theoretical and practical foundation for Marxism-Humanism, as book, newspaper and organization was established:

• At the end of 1954 and the beginning of 1955 Correspondence Committees was broken up by followers of James. Even though the group supporting Dunayevskaya constituted a majority of the membership, they did not have legal title to the newspaper *Correspondence*. A conference was held by Dunayevskaya and her colleagues to establish News and Letters Committees and begin a new newspaper, *News & Letters* (named after the Boston *Newsletter* from the time of the American Revolution). The first issue was published in June 1955, commemorating the second anniversary of the East German uprising (June 17, 1953).

• In the fall of 1955, the new organization published its first pamphlet. Its contents were Dunayevskaya's translation of Lenin's *Abstract* of Hegel's *Science of Logic* and her Letters of May 12 and 20, 1953 on Hegel's Absolutes. By the spring of 1956, News and Letters Committees began issuing a series of discussion bulletins in preparation for its first national convention. Among the bulletins issued were "Johnsonism: A Political Appraisal," "The Need for a Workers' Paper," "What Form of Organization," and a discussion bulletin that contained a preliminary draft of a constitution as well as articles on Dunayevskaya's forthcoming book. Dunayevskaya wrote a bulletin on finances, as well as a "Rough Draft of International Memo." (See *RDC*, Vol. IV for documents.)

- At the founding Convention of News and Letters (July 1956), Dunayevskaya delivered the opening presentation, "Theoretical and Practical Perspectives: Where to Begin" (*RDC* #2568-86). The gathering took place seven months after the start of the Montgomery Bus Boycott and five months before the Hungarian Revolution erupted—events that would contribute to the development of the new organization. A constitution was written; a National Editorial Board was elected as the leadership and as the committee responsible for continuing the publication of *News & Letters*; Dunayevskaya was assigned the task of writing a restatement of Marxism in book form.
- At the first News and Letters Plenum (1957), Dunayevskaya gave the perspectives talk, "The American Roots of Marxism in the World Today and Our Development" (*RDC* #2597), with the galley proofs of *Marxism and Freedom* in hand. This restatement of Marxism for the mid-20th century would be the primary statement of Marxist-Humanism throughout the 1960s and into the 1970s.

Thus a decade and a half after the 1941 origins of state-capitalist theory and the establishment of the State-Capitalist Tendency, News and Letters Committees was founded and became the organizational home for Marxist-Humanist philosophy. These crucial first years as organization, newspaper, and philosophy are discussed below, principally through the focal point of Dunayevskaya's Perspectives Reports to the founding Convention and to the first Plenum of News and Letters. *Marxism and Freedom* will be taken up in Part II of this study.

Where to Begin? Theoretical and Practical Perspectives

The opening of Dunayevskaya report, "Theoretical and Practical Perspectives: Where to Begin" (*RDC* #2568-86), laid out the major themes for discussion, particularly concerning newspaper, organizational form and the book-to-be. These were the major threads for the foundation and praxis of News and Letters Committees in its initial years:

> My topic, THEORETICAL AND PRACTICAL PERSPECTIVES, sounds very imposing. The sub-title, WHERE TO BEGIN, sounds simple. Yet both mean one and the same thing. It is a matter of laying a solid foundation for the decisions we are to make at this, our founding convention, on the following topics:
> (1) the continuance of *News & Letters* as a workers' paper, as the recorder of the impulses from the deepest layers of the population which is at the same time a new form of unity of theory and practice;
> (2) the FORM OF ORGANIZATION we wish to establish for ourselves, and its relationship to the working class as a whole;
> (3) our relations with workers abroad—the hunger of the European workers and the colonial masses have for contact with the American working class *as it is*, not as it is portrayed by the Voice of America, is matched by the American workers' desire for knowledge of the world working people. Nothing for example, got such a rise out of Negro auto workers as the information we carried,

and which no one else carried, on the struggles of the Kenya people for their freedom;

(4) finally, the book on Marxism as both theory and a weapon in the class struggle.

Except for the book, these topics were discussed at separate Convention sessions. A major focus at this opening session was on the material to be developed for the book. However, "the basic foundation we are laying here at this session, as the reason for our being" was inseparable from a paper, form of organization, and international relations.

Among the participants at this founding Convention were miners from West Virginia, auto workers from Detroit, and a steelworker from Pittsburgh who had just participated in wildcat and regular strikes. The recording of those actions and the thoughts of the workers taking part in them "was the type of activity which is the essence of theory and organization." In speaking of the wildcat strikes, Dunayevskaya laid out two different attitudes towards automation: (1) that of the management, who felt the men were "expendable," while "the machine can almost run by itself;" (2) the attitude of the workers that "the machine was a man-killer," throwing men out of work and sweating mercilessly those who still had a job.

As noted in Chapter Two, the concrete struggles emerging from the Miners' General Strike of 1949-50 helped give form to the book-in-progress. Dunayevskaya noted "the present experiences [of the workers' attitudes toward automation] will enrich the book on Marxism further."

The non-worker participants at the Convention were spoken of as intellectuals: "Since I [RD] am one myself, I feel free to tell you that the task of grasping for full significance of this book will not be as easy for you as for the workers. It took me ten years of direct work on Marxist theory before the miners' strike of 1950 illuminated for me the form the book must take." She attributed that kind of difficulty to what was "so inherent in our society—that monstrous division of mental and manual labor."

To illustrate her point Dunayevskaya quoted from Karl Kautsky's statement (which, she noted, Lenin had quoted approvingly in 1902) that "Socialist consciousness is something introduced into the proletarian class struggle from without, and not something that arose within it spontaneously." Not only did the newly formed News and Letters Committees reject the separation of Marxism and the proletariat, but, such a concept would have sounded fantastic to Marx. Dunayevskaya took the matter further: "And yet in knowing that, how many of us grasp that so ACTIVE are the relations of theory and practice that there are moments when they can actually change sides with each other and indeed they do?"

This last expression of the unity of theory and practice showed the movement, not as an external imposition, but *within* theory and *within* practice. In fact, so *active* was the movement, that each side could become a form of the other within a revolutionary process. The divisions that characterize class society—between thinking and doing, mental and manual labor, subjectivity and objectivity—begin to break down in such a process.

Dunayevskaya began to present historical manifestations of this, ranging from Marx's recognition of the workers' struggle for a shorter working day as a new philosophy and the philosophic axis of *Capital*, to Trotsky's failure to recreate this active relationship between theory and practice after the death of Lenin, when he insisted on defending Russia as a workers' state at the time World War II broke out. Her concentration though, was on more than a decade of experience of those who did recognize the specific new stage of capitalism, the State-Capitalist Tendency, and yet who could not fully work out the active relation between theory and practice.

The Tendency had "connected the new stage of capitalism with the *specific* form of workers' revolt and hailed the 1943 miners' strike and Negro demonstrations that took place in the midst of war as well as the general strike movement, the soldiers movements to return home, and the colonial revolts that followed World War II." Yet, as an independent tendency breaking from Trotskyism, they did not move further. Why not?

Dunayevskaya pointed to the two years of "hibernation," when the Tendency (then called Correspondence Committees) did not try to work out the political reality they faced. However for her, the most crucial factor was facing the challenge of working out the active relation of theory to practice that rests on "the theoretician's relationship to the working class itself as IT evolves new forms of revolt to this new stage of capitalist domination." In the 1940s and 1950s, this involved not only the new world stage of state-capitalism as it evolved out of the 1929 economic crash, but also from the subsequent stage of production, automation, *and the workers' response to it*:

> Something new had arisen in 1950. I CALL IT THE MOVEMENT FROM PRACTICE TO THEORY. IT WAS BORN OUT OF, OR RATHER REACHED A NEW INTENSITY WITH AUTOMATION WHEN THE WORKERS ON THEIR OWN BEGAN TO QUESTION NOT ALONE THE FRUITS OF LABOR BUT THE MODE OF LABOR, THAT IS, THE KIND OF LABOR ITSELF.

Instead of grasping the specificity of this new stage of production, Dunayevskaya pointed to the fact that two of the leaders of the State-Capitalist Tendency (James and Lee) confined themselves to generalizations "about this being the age of absolutes." In contrast, understanding the meaning of the new stage of revolt, its specificity as "the movement from practice to theory" meant an active new working out of the relation of theory and practice. Catching this stage of revolt in the Letters on Hegel's Absolutes anticipated not only the break-up of the Johnson-Forest Tendency, but the new beginning that would become News and Letters Committees.

Dunayevskaya argued that it was not enough to reach the generalization that this was the age of absolutes. One must also answer the question "What is *your* task?" Here she made a sharp division between what she saw had happened in the radical movement in the past and the new unity of theory and practice that must be actually worked out. Those who claimed "only the proletariat can" make the revolution were evading the question of the necessary task of revolutionaries as much as any "philosopher's retreat to the ivory tower."

The old vanguardist conception that workers needed to reach the theoretical level of the "leaders" was smashed to smithereens in 1917. With the transformation of the Russian Revolution into its opposite "this concept of the alleged backwardness of the working-class to achieve its own emancipation became the face of the counter-revolution." The Johnson-Forest Tendency rejected that concept. But something more was needed: "IF we had had a truly total view of this movement *from* practice *to* theory, our theory in turn would have developed to the point where it could have met this movement from practice to theory on *its* level."

This was the challenge Dunayevskaya laid out at the founding Convention. It was the challenge for the newspaper, for the organization, and for the book. The need to see the book not as a popularization of the old, but as a conception of Marxism emerging out of this new unity of theory and practice—and thus a concept which would set the ground for the role of a radical Marxist group in its relationship to the working class—compelled a further detailing of her ideas.

In three sections of her presentation—"How Marxism Began," "How Marxism Developed," and "The Great Divide in Marxism"—Dunayevskaya took up many of the themes that would become central to *Marxism and Freedom*[1]:

- In "How Marxism Began," Marx's relationship to Hegel, to classical political economy, and to Utopian socialism were examined.
- In "How Marxism Developed" the focus was on two moments of Marx's work on *Capital*: (1) the active relationship of theory and practice as seen in how the Civil War entered his theoretical labors, and how the spontaneous outburst of the Paris Commune "stripped the fetishisms off all forms of rule: economic, political, intellectual" for Marx. (2) his tracing the law of motion of capitalism, which centered on the capital-labor relationship.
- "The Great Divide in Marxism" briefly discussed Lenin's post World War I philosophic foundations of Marxism, asking what constituted "*his* preparation for actual revolution *as well as* his preparedness to break with his co-leaders" when a new bureaucracy emerged.

Despite the important heritage of the Russian workers' action in 1917-1923, "workers of today must find a NEW BEGINNING." Dunayevskaya took up that new beginning in the section "Practical Perspectives," starting with the concept of "two worlds:" "I do not mean Russia and America. These two capitalist giants out for world domination, each day look like one another . . . No, the two worlds

I mean are right within our own country. Each country has two such worlds in it." The two worlds were those of "exploitation and degradation and crises and wars," and "the second world . . . striving for a new freedom, a total freedom, worthy of human beings." As part of the second world, including wildcat strikes and colonial revolts, she singled out the ongoing Montgomery Bus Boycott with its

> self-activity of the Negroes in Montgomery, who easily enough found they could organize without any big brass to draw up blueprints for them. Not alone to take care of their transportation needs, but to rise to the full dignity as human beings who will not be shoved around. The other day, I heard that when the NAACP [National Association for the Advancement of Colored People] was outlawed from the state of Alabama, the ingenuity of the Negroes to remain organized, quickly enough evolved a new form of organization. I understand they now call themselves The Alabama Christian Movement for Human Rights.

The concept of "two worlds" also became manifest in Dunayevskaya's writing for *News & Letters*. She called her column "Two Worlds." We will explore her journalism below.

The new beginning needed to answer the question, "What is Marxism today, 1956[?]" This meant probing the concrete stage of capitalist production—automation—and catching the proletarian impulse. Dunayevskaya quoted a worker and News and Letters member, Angela Terrano, on her attitude toward automation:

> Work will have to be completely new. Man likes to work, to build something, but today work is so separate from everything else in your life. Each day is divided: you work, then you have some time in which to rest, forget about work, escape from it. What will be with automation? There is less work for man (as I think of work today). But there will be more time. I am scared of more time the way things are now because more time for the worker might be seven days a week with no pay check at the end of the week.

Dunayevskaya linked the needed new beginning with the new News and Letters Committees in the final section of her presentation, "Indivisibility of the Book and the Paper:" "The indivisibility of the book and the paper as the life of the organization, its foundation and its expression is the answer to the question, where to begin."

The next several pages of her presentation focused on the indivisibility of the book and paper in the life of the organization. The year 1955 witnessed simultaneously the publication of the new paper *News & Letters* and a speaking tour on the book by Dunayevskaya. She explained the need to write the book as a *collective* venture, and that it was the workers, even those who had never read a word of Marxism, who in that first year contributed more to the writing of the book than the organization's intellectuals. She referred to the kinds of writing and questions being posed by workers, which showed that they did not separate themselves from Marxism, whereas others were creating such a division by saying the paper can't be "just" a forum for workers, as if that wasn't a contribution to Marxism for 1956. The intellectuals did have a contribution to make once they understood the new in the age of absolutes: the movement from practice to theory that releases a new role for the movement from theory that no one else was doing. It was out of looking at the creative, thinking dimension of workers and intellectuals that a concept "specifying that the two poles of the book would be Automation and the Absolute Idea" came to be.

Dunayevskaya pointed out "the new type of intelligence in the world, Proletarian Reason," which was reflected in *News & Letters* worker columnists. She continued:

> Everyone is ready to lead. No one to listen. YET THIS AGE OF AUTOMATION DEMANDS TO BE RECORDED AS PROLETARIAN IMPULSE. This is what *News & Letters* is doing. There is nothing but intellectual sloth on the side of the vanguard parties.
> WHAT THEY ALL FORGET IS THAT A NEW SOCIETY IS THE HUMAN ENDEAVOR OR IT IS NOTHING AT ALL.

Though proletarian reason propelled Dunayevskaya's thrust, it did not mean an abdication of the revolutionary's responsibility. Rather, "We also have something to say . . . We have Marx to build on. We have the great divide in Marxism to absorb. We have the experience of more than three decades of working-class struggles since Lenin's death." She ended her presentation as follows:

> All the knowledge of the past does is to lay the foundation for the present and infuse us with the confidence that this continuous thread from history is a sort of WIRELESS COMMUNICATION THAT WILL FIRST BE DECODED IN OUR AGE WHICH WILL SEE TO IT THAT THE IDEA OF WORKERS' FREEDOM IS NOT SO FEEBLE THAT IT WILL NOT ACTUALLY COME TO BE IN OUR DAY.

News and Letters Committees: Its Constitution and Organizational Form

The founding Convention of News and Letters passed a constitution. Its three page Preamble began: "People everywhere, today, are looking for a new way of life under which man can be free to guide his own destiny: to set and establish his own way of living, his own conditions of work, and his own forms of association with his fellow-man."

The Constitution characterized the age lived in as the age of state capitalism, both "in its totalitarian form and its capitalist-democratic form." It singled out working people as "the only force in the world capable of changing present-day society and of evolving the forms and shape of future society." With the advent of automation, American working people at the point of production were posing the question, "What *kind* of labor?" Abroad, the June 17, 1953 revolt of East German workers, followed by the revolts in the Vorkuta prison camps, and the 1956 Polish workers' uprising, "answered affirmatively the question: *Can man be free in this age of totalitarianism.*" The document linked opposition to war to the vision of a new society. It singled out the struggle of the Negro people, who "occupy a place of special significance in American life."

The Constitution established News and Letters Committees and the newspaper *News & Letters*, "whose editor shall be a worker and the articles for which shall be written on a decentralized basis." The paper and the committees sought "to promote the firmest unity among workers, Negroes and other minorities, women, youth and those intellectuals who have broken with the ruling bureaucracy of both capital and labor." Youth were singled out as organizationally independent and having space available to them in the paper to write and edit for themselves.

The Constitution stated the need for News and Letters Committees to present an interpretation of Marxism on native grounds in book form: "We hold that the *method* of Marxism is the guide for our growth and development." In less than two years, the book would be completed and published as *Marxism and Freedom... from 1776 until today.*

On organizational form, the Constitution noted: "We make no pretense of being a political party. We constitute ourselves as News & Letters Committees whose members come together to promote their ideas in an organized manner."

The By-Laws provided for an elected leadership, the National Editorial Board (NEB). Dunayevskaya was elected chairperson of the NEB.

All of Dunayevskaya's political life had occurred within radical organization: the Workers (Communist) Party as a youth in the 1920s; the Trotskyist movement in the 1930s, including Russian language secretary to Leon Trotsky in exile in Mexico 1937-38; as co-founder of the State-Capitalist Tendency within Trotskyism in the 1940s; and as the independent existence of Correspondence Committees, 1951-1955.

After being in various Marxist "vanguard parties" throughout the 1930s and 1940s, she developed, along with those in the State-Capitalist Tendency, a decentralized form of organization, first manifested as Correspondence Committees. With the split within Correspondence Committees and the formation of News and Letters Committees (1955), the committee form of organization became united with a philosophic foundation of Marxist-Humanism and journalistic expression in *News & Letters*. Dunayevskaya continued to head News and Letters Committees until her death in 1987.

In 1955 a News and Letters Conference decided to begin issuing *News & Letters*, and assigned Dunayevskaya responsibility to complete her book on Marxism. Thus paper and book were being worked out in an organizational forum before the Constitution was adopted in 1956. The Constitution formalized the new philosophic form of organization and paper, holding that "the method of Marxism," as it was in the process of being interpreted in the book, would be the foundation for organization. A year after the founding Convention, in a meeting of the National Editorial Board of News and Letters, Dunayevskaya expressed the aim and challenge as "the organization of thought . . . which determined . . . organizational life ("The American Roots of Marxism in the World Today and our Development," *RDC,* #2609).

"Organization of thought, which determines organizational life," expressed the original and creative manner in which Dunayevskaya was an organization person. From the founding of News and Letters Committees to the end of her life, Dunayevskaya strove to practice this concept, not just individually, but in the very being of the Committees by sharing the process of thought and the necessity for its concretization in organizational life with her News and Letters colleagues.

Almost all of her political-philosophic labors became expressed through News and Letters Committees. The most comprehensive philosophic expressions presented publicly—her three books, *Marxism and Freedom*, *Philosophy and Revolution*, and *Rosa Luxemburg, Women's Liberation, and Marx's Philosophy of Revolution*—were collaborative in the process of development through circulation of draft chapters, oral presentations, discussions and correspondence with Committee members. After publication of each work, ramifications were most often made explicit within News and Letters Committees. These included pamphlets by herself and other members, new ways of writing for the paper, classes and discussions on each of the books, seeking ways to reach outside the organization with the book's ideas.

As chairperson of the National Editorial Board of News and Letters, Dunayevskaya was not only the founder of the philosophic tendency of Marxist-Humanism, but practiced the philosophic process in the Committees on a continuous basis. Every year she gave the Perspectives talk to the national gathering of News and Letters Committees. This came after presenting a Draft Perspectives with the collaboration of the Resident Editorial Board of News and Letters (REB, those members of the NEB who resided at the Center) in the months before the bi-annual Convention. At the Convention, she participated vigorously in the ongoing discussions, and deivered a final Executive Session presentation on different aspects of dialectics of leadership. In alternate years she addressed the gathering of the NEB, writing a Draft Perspectives in the months prior to the meeting, and giving a Perspectives report at that meeting.

On a bi-weekly basis, she chaired meetings of the REB (which assumed responsibility for the functioning of News and Letters between conventions and gatherings of the NEB). The full minutes of the REB were shared with the local committees of News and Letters. They often reported philosophic-political-organizational presentations by Dunayevskaya and discussion by her colleagues. Other times, members of the REB would make reports and Dunayevskaya was among those who contributed to the discussion.

News & Letters, a Marxist-Humanist Newspaper

News & Letters began publishing in 1955 during the period of McCarthyism. From the vantage point of the 1980s, Dunayevskaya wrote a "Retrospective/Perspective: Thirty Years of *News & Letters*."[2] She began by examining the first year of the paper's existence in order to reveal: "first, what we heard, and second, the meaning we gave to what we heard by declaring it to be 'a movement *from practice* that is itself a form of theory.'"

"The uniqueness of the simultaneity of act and of thought in the 1950s—in such events as the 1949-50 Miners' General Strike and the 1953 East German Revolt—gave a spur to the publication of *News & Letters*." News and Letters had a local committee in the heart of the West Virginia coal country, and in its first years the paper had a section entitled "Coal and Its People." "That section had been born," noted Dunayevskaya, "from the *kind of questions* posed by the 1949-50 Miners' General Strike . . . they asked what *kind* of labor man should do." A "World Comment" section in the first issue of the paper discussed the East German Revolt. "*News & Letters* demonstrated our international dimension in its very appearance in June, 1955, to commemorate the second anniversary of the June 17th East German Revolt."

Dunayevskaya described the unique features of the paper during its first years:

• The editors were two workers, Johnny Zupan and Charles Denby. Denby soon became sole editor. "This was the first time a U.S. Black production worker became the editor of a Marxist paper."

• The Black Dimension was present in the pages of the paper, from the Black South—Charles Denby went to Alabama and met with participants in the Montgomery Bus Boycott; a front-page article on the murder of Emmett Till in Mississippi reported on the Black mass reaction to it—to Africa, with the first issue publishing "a picture of Njeri, a Kenyan woman who was a central figure in the Mau Mau struggle for freedom against British imperialism."

• "Women's Liberation as Reason as well as revolutionary force" found expression through the presence of a number of columnists in the paper. Ethel Dunbar, a Black Woman, authored a column she called "We Are Somebody." Jerry Kegg appeared on the Labor Page, and Angela Terrano, a woman worker, wrote "Working for Independence," first on the Youth page and then on the Labor page.

- There was a Youth column first written by Robert Ellery, "who edited the page and called his column "Thinking It Out."
- A section called "Readers' Views" "was created to give priority not merely to letters to the editor, but also to unwritten letters, i.e., to views of non-members, often only spoken. . . . [I]t was a question of our members needing to be alert to what the masses said to each other, what they thought, how they felt, whether at work or just on public transportation. Involved here is the whole concept of oral history."
- "An 'MD' column was written by a doctor [Louis Gogol]. It did not limit itself to medical problems, though central to the column would be specific questions about industrial illnesses and about the social nature of illness." Among the topics taken up was a view of "The Biological Basis of Marxist-Humanism," developed in a series of articles.
- Dunayevskaya's column was called "Two Worlds" with an over-line, "Notes from a Diary."

The Revolutionary Journalism of Raya Dunayevskaya

Dunayevskaya's revolutionary journalism stretched back to the 1920s, when she wrote, at age 13, new words to the "Pledge of Allegiance" published in the *Young Comrade*, newspaper of the sub-15 age group of the Workers (Communist) Party. She worked in the office of the *Negro Champion* (newspaper of the American Negro Labor Congress) in Chicago in the mid-1920s and wrote book reviews for the paper. She wrote a review of E.B. Reuther's *The American Race Problem* that appeared in the *Young Worker*, the newspaper of the Young Workers League, the youth section of the Workers Party.

In the 1930s she wrote for the Trotskyist newspapers, *The Militant*, *The New Militant*, and the *Young Spartacus* on issues ranging from the *Russian Opposition Bulletin*, the wave of strikes occurring in the U.S. in 1934, to the organizing campaign of home relief workers in New York City in 1934.

In the 1940s, her articles appeared in the Workers Party journal *New International*, including articles on the theory of state-capitalism, which were subjected to continual battles with censorship. Other articles included one on Luxemburg's *Theory of Accumulation* in relation to Marx and Lenin, and "Negro Intellectuals in Dilemma," a critique of Gunnar Myrdal's *An American Dilemma: The Negro Problem and Modern Democracy*." She also wrote for the paper *Labor Action* on the Russian economy and on the Black dimension. From 1948-50, she wrote for Socialist Workers Party's *Militant*. Her articles discussed the Black question and the 1949-50 Miners General Strike.

Chapter 3 discussed some of Dunayevskaya's writing from both the mimeographed and printed *Correspondence* in the early 1950s.

Despite the considerable amount of writing for the radical press in the pre-*News & Letters* era, it is only from 1955 onwards that the revolutionary journalism of Dunayevskaya became fully realized. Her *News & Letters* journalism was post the 1953 breakthrough on Hegel's Absolutes containing a movement from practice as well as from theory. This new vantage point of philosophic expression in revolutionary journalism was also free from the obstacles that Dunayevskaya faced when writing for *Correspondence*.

A concept of revolutionary journalism as a unity of theory and practice had been implicit in Dunayevskaya's breakthrough on the Absolute Idea. The challenge was to practice it on an ongoing basis in an 8-page bi-weekly or monthly newspaper. Far from being an immediate accomplishment, it was a concept that needed to be concretized and re-concretized.

Dunayevskaya's revolutionary journalism was not only a matter of her own writing—the "Two Worlds" column that appeared in each issue—but the whole of *News & Letters*. She was chairperson of the National Editorial Board of *News & Letters* and participated in discussions, classes, and correspondence in working out revolutionary journalism as a concrete process of giving meaning to ongoing objective-subjective world events. At the same time, her writings in the paper were its central axis. We cannot here follow the trajectory of those writings for thirty plus years. For our purposes we will briefly concentrate on the writings from her "Two Worlds" column in the founding period of *News & Letters*.

In the first two years of the paper's existence, the "Two Worlds" column covered a wide array of topics: One of the most frequent was the two poles of world capitalism. Russian state-capitalism was taken up with articles on the revolt in the slave labor camp in Vorkuta, the worker struggles within Russia, the Hungarian Revolution of 1956, and the maneuvers of the Russian bureaucracy. The U.S. was taken up in articles on the workers' struggles against automation and the labor bureaucracy, "anti-Communism" used against freedom and peace struggles in America, the old radical's and labor bureaucrat's attraction to "the Plan," and on the Negro struggles in the South. Many times the columns were not solely on one superpower or the other, but on the relation between the two. Sometimes her discussion revolved around the fact that, while not identical twins, Russia and America were the twin poles of capitalism. Other times, the link was the struggles of workers in both countries against capital at the point of production.

Other topics of her first columns included Africa (the Mau Mau revolt in Kenya against British imperialism), and China (a lead article giving an analysis of Mao's revealing speech on contradiction, which Dunayevskaya discussed in relation to the historical development of the concept of contradiction in the Hegelian dialectic). Various social forces and social types were discussed: the emergence of youth as a revolutionary dimension in the 1950s alongside workers; scientists in the atomic age; the ex-radical's alienation and rootlessness; the Abolitionist dimension before the Civil War.

Dunayevskaya's journalism in 1955-57 was inseparable from the writing of *Marxism and Freedom*. In part, this was because she discussed certain contemporary themes in her column that were incorporated into the book—the 1953 Vorkuta prison revolt, the 1956 Hungarian Revolution, American workers' attitudes toward automation, and the Montgomery Bus boycott. Sometimes, historic themes were taken up, such as Lenin's activities in post-1917 Russia. The book and paper were also inseparable because Dunayevskaya's method of writing her philosophic works, beginning with *Marxism and Freedom*, did not involve a retreat to the library or study hall. Her sustained philosophic probing was accompanied by intense engagement in ongoing world events.

"Letter Writing and New Passions"

Dunayevskaya's first column, "Letter Writing and New Passions" (June 24, 1955), expressed the need for "a workers paper, one written, edited and circulated by workers themselves." She began the column as follows: "As we were preparing to go to press with this, our first issue, I was asked why I had placed so much emphasis on letters to and from news committees as well as to and from workers outside these news committees."

> It is a matter of new passions as they are expressed in the daily lives of ordinary people. It is these that need to be heard. When fundamental changes are shaking society to its depths, the need for communication forces its way up, finds all sorts of unique ways of realization. One of these is letter writing.

Historically, the letter writing in the American Colonies expressed the struggle for independence from Great Britain. Later, the opposition slavery could be expressed in William Lloyd Garrison's Abolitionist newspaper the *Liberator*: "[T]he *Liberator* was the *expression* of these new passions and forces for freedom which brought on the Civil War."

She continued: "The American working people, with their great capacity for free association in industry and in politics, have in the press created an almost unique form of communication, an inter-communication . . . [T]he worker considers letters the oft-spoken conversation that has finally been written down *to be heard*." "It seldom is nowadays." The daily press instead reflected the views

> of the very people—the political leaders, the big industrialists, the labor bureaucrats—who have brought the world into the state of total, never-ending crisis in which it now finds itself, while the rank and file people are not heard at all. . . . [T]he first necessity is that rank and file have the paper in their hands to *say what they want to, how they want to*. It is in the expression of the working people, on whose back the total weight of state capitalism rests, that we will find the new passions and forces for a new society.

In this first column Dunayevskaya did not write all she would have to say about the revolutionary journalism of a workers' newspaper. Her concept of revolutionary journalism grew and deepened over the next three decades. However, she was determined from the inception of *News & Letters* not only to break with the bourgeois concept of a newspaper, *but also with the old radical concept.* It was not a newspaper *for* working people but one "written, edited and circulated by workers themselves." The concept of "a movement from practice that was itself a form of theory," needed to be concretized in the form of a workers' newspaper. Once that concept became the practice of the paper, the other moment of the breakthrough on the Absolute Idea—the movement from theory that was grounded in philosophy and reached to unite with the movement from practice—could find fuller expression. Dunayevskaya's revolutionary journalism within the pages of *News & Letters* was the crucial form of that expression.

Charles Denby: Autoworker, Editor of *News and Letters*, "Worker's Journal" Columnist, Author of *Indignant Heart: A Black Worker's Journal*, Colleague of Raya Dunayevskaya

For more than a quarter century, Charles Denby, a founding member of News and Letters Committees, was a member of its National Editorial Board, the worker-editor of *News & Letters*, and the front page "Worker's Journal" columnist. For thirty-five years he was a political, organizational colleague of Raya Dunayevskaya. Both his *Indignant Heart* (1952, written under the pen name of Mathew Ward) and his *Indignant Heart: A Black Workers Journal* (1978, includes 1952 *Indignant Heart* as Part I. Part II was written after almost a quarter century as editor of *News & Letters*) have been recognized as classics in the field of Black and Labor Studies. The concept of a Black production worker speaking for himself, not only telling his life story, but his thoughts on world reality and his projection of a different world, were path breaking. At the time of his death (1983), Dunayevskaya wrote and delivered an In Memoriam. It was subsequently published as an afterward in a new edition of Denby's book. We draw from it here to show Denby's revolutionary life as seen through the eyes of his colleague Raya Dunayevskaya:

> I first met Denby in 1948 when he had already become a leader of wildcats, a "politico," but the talk I heard him give of tenant farming in the South and factory work in the North was far from being a "political speech." Listening to him, you felt you were witnessing an individual's life that was somehow universal, and that touched you personally (Published as an Afterward to the Wayne State University Press edition of *Indignant Heart—A Black Worker's Journal*, 1989).

Denby was working in a Chrysler plant in Detroit when miners from the 1949-50 Miners General Strike came to town to appeal for help: "I remember that the bureaucrats were not too hot about the idea. They didn't dare come right out and oppose it, but you could tell they weren't enthusiastic, like the rank-and-file were. But our enthusiasm was so strong that by the time the meeting ended the bureaucrats had to triple the amount they had intended to give."

Shortly after the strike Denby began dictating his life's story, *Indignant Heart*. "It became a turning point in his life," wrote Dunayevskaya, "because in telling his life story he gained confidence that he could express himself in a way that carried meaning for other workers as well."

In 1953 she moved to Detroit: "[I]t was then I first broached the question of having a worker as editor of a new type of paper we were planning, instead of forever bestowing that prerogative on an intellectual who would speak 'for' the workers. Denby was at first non-committal."

At the same time Dunayevskaya had been having political-philosophic discussions with Denby, including on the nature of the early Russian workers' state and its meaning for U.S. workers. This was the same year Stalin had died (1953), and she described Denby's reaction, calling her immediately after he got out of the job and reporting what workers were saying: "Every worker was saying, 'I have just the man to fill Stalin's shoes—my foreman.'" For Dunayevskaya it became a starting point for her article on the trade union debate in the early Russian state and its relationship to workers in America. (See Chapter 2.) Denby saw to it that the article came into the hands of workers in his shop.

The June 17, 1953 East German workers' revolt quickly followed: "[T]he fact that it broke out against speed-up meant so much to Denby, that our discussions on philosophy became discussions about concrete actions of workers."

Two years later, when a new kind of workers' paper was going to be launched, Denby accepted editorship of *News & Letters*. Nineteen fifty-five was also the year the Montgomery Bus Boycott began. Denby, who had been born in Alabama, went south and reported on this new stage of freedom in the pages of *News & Letters:*

> I have recently come back from a trip to Alabama, where I was born and raised. Montgomery is my hometown. From what I've seen and feel, there is a social revolution going on in the South that has it in a turmoil of a kind that hasn't been seen since the days of Reconstruction.

Over the next quarter of a century, Denby would write on a vast array of social and political issues in his Worker's Journal column, ranging from the shop floor to Black caucuses in the unions, from the anti-Vietnam War Movement to the 1967 Detroit Uprising, and the freedom struggles in South Africa.

As editor of *News & Letters,* Denby helped to elicit a broad range of voices for the paper, from other sectors of the labor movement to other dimensions—Black, youth, women, international—of the freedom movement. This was shown in the pamphlet *Workers Battle Automation* (1960), that Denby wrote in concert with workers from other industries.

His fellow autoworker and Marxist-Humanist labor columnist, Felix Martin, wrote of Denby's *Indignant Heart: A Black Worker's Journal*:

> In the mountains where I grew up, those who couldn't get a job in the mines, and who needed something to eat sharecropped. They were the really poor, and used the corn raised to buy a few other things and for moonshine. The cropping in our area meant you supplied your labor while the man furnished the land, the tools and the seed. Where I was raised it was only white. There weren't any Blacks.
> How much rougher it is when your skin is Black. Charles Denby, my friend and editor of *News & Letters*, had one chapter dealing with sharecropping. In the deep South, there was not white and white, but Black and white, the plantation owner gave only the land. The tools and seeds and everything else was for the cropper to supply, and you always wound up in a hole to the plantation owner. Certainly the struggle of Appalachian white and Southern Black is similar, but the struggle is deeper and rougher if you are Black.
> All through the first part of *Indignant Heart* I felt this kinship with Denby's life, that part of my life resembled his, and at the same time had the depth of experience and struggle which was profoundly Black.

Denby and Dunayevskaya represented something very special and rare in the American radical movement—that combination of worker and intellectual, of Black and white, which, when fused within Marxist-Humanist philosophy, meant important leaps in philosophical-organizational action. Their relationship speaks to the question of how freedom ideas developed in Marxist-Humanism.

• They carried on a continual philosophic as well as political and organizational dialogue. One example was a letter Dunayevskaya wrote to Denby on the French philosopher Merleau-Ponty's "Marxism and Philosophy," which she wished to discuss with Denby in relation to automation and the thoughts of workers on the job (Letter to Charles Denby, March 10, 1960. Reprinted in *Power of Negativity*). Other manifestations of this dialogue came in their work on the Resident Editorial Board of News and Letters Committees.

• Denby helped to call, and then chair, a Black/Red Conference in Detroit in 1969. At this conference, Dunayevskaya presented ideas on revolutionary philosophy and the Black dimension in the process of working on her book *Philosophy and Revolution*. Denby began his welcome:

> This is the first time that such a conference of Black youth, Black workers, Black women and Black intellectuals will have a chance to discuss with each other as well as with Marxist-Humanists, who lend the red coloration not only for the sake of color, but for the sake of philosophy, a philosophy of liberation.

- Denby co-authored an Introduction with Dunayevskaya to a News & Letters pamphlet, *Frantz Fanon, Soweto, and American Black Thought* (1976).
- Denby wrote a Part II to *Indignant Heart* that had first been published in 1952. This new book, *Indignant Heart: A Black Worker's Journal*, came after more than two decades as a Marxist-Humanist editor during the time when Dunayevskaya was chairperson of the National Editorial Board. As Denby wrote in the Forward:

> It isn't only that 25 years separate Part I and Part II. More importantly, the great events of the 1960s that gave birth to a new generation of revolutionaries could but give a new direction to my thoughts and actions as a Black production worker who became the editor of a very new type of newspaper—*News & Letters*.

The Organization of Thought, which Determines Organizational Life: News and Letters Perspectives as *Marxism and Freedom* Is Completed

In a letter of August 5, 1957, a few weeks before the 1957 News and Letters Plenum, Dunayevskaya wrote: "*MARXISM & FREEDOM* BEING THAT ORGANIZATION OF THOUGHT WHICH WILL DETERMINE OUR FUTURE ORGANIZATIONAL LIFE."[3] This category—the organization of thought which determines organizational life—was the focus of her Perspectives talk, "The American Roots of Marxism in the World Today and Our Development" (*RDC* #2597).[4] In her presentation, delivered September 1957, she developed the category's historical and political roots as part of the need to work it out anew in relation to News and Letters Committees.

For the presentation, Dunayevskaya had before her the galley proofs for *Marxism and Freedom*. In exploring what the book would mean for the two-year old News and Letters Committees, she began with the objective situation, starting with the fact that Russia had just tested an intercontinental ballistic missile able to hit a target 5,000 miles away. Responding to the test, the U.S. Secretary of State John Foster Dulles had attempted to explain the size of a "target area" in an attempt to allay fears. Dunayevskaya hit out against his "stupidities," noting that this "brink of war strategist" had only recently "unhinged the Suez crisis . . . which nearly catapulted us into World War III."

In contrast to a world where "anything, *anything at all* can trigger off the war," as Russia and America maneuvered, she posed two fundamentally opposed worlds, not the two nuclear-armed states, but the two worlds of "the workers and the capitalists in *each* country." She continued:

The point is are you with the people struggling for a totally new way of life or with capitalism fighting to perpetuate itself, although it has long outlived its usefulness. So universal were the feelings against war among working people that even the rulers play the game of peace and disarmament conferences. . . . What does distinguish us from them is not what we are against, but what we are *for*. To the barbarism of the war we pose *the new society*.

The two worlds within each country and the vision of the new society was the vantage point from which Dunayevskaya wished to discuss the newly completed book and the organizational tasks that fell upon News and Letters Committees. The aim was to be with the workers in their opposition to war, as "they and only they are the future society." At the same time the plenum report argued that "TO ACHIEVE A TRULY HUMAN LIFE . . . WE DO NOT SHIFT TO THE SHOULDERS OF THE WORKERS WHAT IS OUR TASK, THE THEORETIC CLEARING OF THE GROUND FOR THE RECONSTRUCTION OF SOCIETY ON NEW HUMAN BEGINNINGS."

Marxism and Freedom cleared new theoretical ground, and Dunayevskaya spelled out the new point of departure of Marxist-Humanism: "To stand for a new society to us, means to see that not alone as practice *when* it will come, but as *theory* that helps discern the movement before it comes and thus become part of the *new* evolving realty." She was beginning to concretize for organization what she had posed in her May 12, 1953 Letter of the Absolute Idea: "I am concerned only with the dialectic . . . of the *type* of grouping like ours, be it large or small, and *its* relationship to the mass."

News and Letters Committees, with its newspaper, and now on the eve of publication of *Marxism and Freedom*, was reaching to a new relationship to the mass movement—to become a part of the new evolving reality. For News and Letters "practice INCLUDES THEORY, which is tested in practice."

How did these concepts come to be born in America? They began to rise with the working out of the theory of state-capitalism that consisted of two poles: the evolution from private to state monopoly, and as a consequence, the unity of political and economic power. This meant not less, but more oppression for the worker. While state capitalism had its fullest expression in Russia, its tendency existed in America, and partly manifested itself through a labor bureaucracy to discipline the workers. Thus the necessity to daily fight the labor bureaucracy.

Those without a theory of state-capitalism, including many of the intellectuals in Western Europe, could not help the European workers find a way out from either pole of world capital. Such intellectuals acted as a brake when workers wanted to move away from the mass Communist parties and their labor bureaucracy.

ONLY IN AMERICA, where the proletariat was unshackled by mass parties, only in America the labor bureaucracy has no more standing with the workers now than during the war when they were actually bound down with the no-strike pledge. Only in America therefore, the workers' attitude toward Automation quite freed from the labor bureaucracy's conception of "progress," and only in America was a state-capitalist grouping able to catch the impulse from the workers and move *theory* forward from its political-economic context of state-capitalism to the fully philosophic concept of FREEDOM. In a word, only here could the movement from theory to practice meet the movement from practice to theory and start anew.

What we were witness to was not American exceptionalism, but American specificity. Because the United States was the most industrially advanced post World War II, this new stage of production, automation, was born on its shores. The American workers had in the 1949-50 Miners' General Strike taken a stand against labor bureaucracy and the coal mine operators by infusing new meaning into the slogan "no contract, no work" and conducting a wildcat strike. (See Chapter 3.) They thereby opened the door to questioning the kind of labor they were being forced to undertake as the continuous miner began to be introduced into the coal mines in the early 1950s.

For Dunayevskaya, this struggle, not only around the length of the working day and higher wages, but of workers questioning the very mode of labor they had to engage in, meant a breakthrough in the concept of theory. No longer was theory the private preserve of intellectuals. She saw in the workers' thoughts and actions a movement from practice that was itself a form of theory. In turn, this demanded a new responsibility for theoreticians to meet that movement from practice. The writing of *Marxism and Freedom* undertook that responsibility. How would News and Letters Committees further concretize and develop it? This was the heart of the Perspectives presentation.

Dunayevskaya called the American working class, "the true heirs to Marxist philosophy." "The American Roots of Marxism" were not only history, but were "In the World Today." "The heritage of Hegelian dialectics and the Marxist world view of history has fallen to American workers."

In the second section of the perspectives talk, The Birth Time of History, Dunayevskaya discussed historical roots of Marxism in America, beginning with a quote from the Preface to Hegel's *Phenomenology*: "Our epoch is a birth-time, and a period of transition . . . But this new world is perfectly realized just as little as the new born child—A building is not finished when its foundation is laid." She related this to American historical development: the Committees of Correspondence at the time of the American Revolution, and the fight for the eight hour day that commenced once the Civil War ended, had international repercussions, which Marx took up in *Capital*. Later, she would discuss the heritage of Abolitionism.

These historical roots of Marxism now had new beginnings: American workers in the 1950s asking, What Kind of Labor? and *Marxism and Freedom* laying "the *theoretic foundation*, the NEW GROUND FOR MARXIST HUMANISM in this native soil, and yet extending the world over."

Dunayevskaya was putting forth the proposition that the American working class, together with a small Marxist grouping that was catching the workers' new departure in thought and action, and working out its meaning philosophically, were the inheritors, the continuators, the new manifestation of Marx's Marxism in America.

In a section called "It Is Indeed a Birth Time of History," Dunayevskaya summarized the theoretic foundation of *Marxism and Freedom* as "both the history *and* quintessence of man's struggle for freedom:"

- It breaks down the division between the *struggle* for freedom and the *idea* of freedom.
- [I]n showing that philosophy is fashioned out of the activity of *common* man, it puts a prius, a FIRST on what the common man thinks and does, and points next to the genius [Hegel] who *organized* this thought into a system of philosophy, so that the organization of thought *sums up* the previous stages of man's activity.
- When part I of *Marxism and Freedom* entitled From Practice to Theory, 1776-1848 ends, we see a new BIRTH OF THEORY WHICH DOES *CONSCIOUSLY* what Hegel did unconsciously. . . .
- Because, on the other hand, Marx *consciously* extracted his dialectic from the mass movement, his philosophy was not only a summation of the past, but an anticipation of the future. The *Communist Manifesto* was published on the eve of the 1848 revolution and determined the organizational life of the Communist League.

The League perished with the defeat of the 1848 Revolutions. "We get here, in the period of defeat, a still different view of the relation of the worker and intellectual, for the attitude to the state creates a division within the unique combination of worker-intellectual type of political organization. We see a new type arise in this new organization, which was created. The type of the worker-dictator, Lassalle." Lassalle could not simple be dismissed, for at a turning point in history he represented "*millions* of workers—workers Marx did not have." Only a different kind of thinking creates a new pathway for intellectuals. "[I]f anyone thinks thinking WHEN IT MEANS parting with your class origins is easy, history has passed them by altogether."

"Thinking in general is hard work," she noted, quoting Hegel on philosophy being "the labor, patience and suffering of the negative." Then Dunayevskaya made a startling statement on Marx's great labor of the negative:

- Marx's *Capital* that entirely NEW ORGANIZATION OF THOUGHT upon which no new organization has been built.
That may sound like a fantastic contradiction, a complete untruth, the throwing out of the history of the Second International and hence the

years 1889-1914. Nevertheless, among the new things in *M&F* . . . is that history under the title *Organizational Interlude*.
• What we did in the book in pinning down ORGANIZATION, when organization of thought is just peripheral—something you do Sunday, while daily, hourly it is not thought but organization which preoccupies you, EVEN AS IT DOES CAPITALISM ITSELF AS IT REACHES THE MONOPOLY-IMPERIALIST STAGE.

Not only was there no new organization built upon Marx's *Capital* among the first generation of Marxists post-Marx, but the organization that was built, the Second International, reflected instead the new organizational manifestation of capitalist development—imperialism.

Dunayevskaya ended her summation of *Marxism and Freedom* by taking up Herbert Marcuse's Preface to her work as "proof of what happens to the Marxist theory when the Marxist METHOD of beginning from where the workers are, building on their impulses, is passed over as something that belonged to his time, not ours. You can't divide theory from method." Without method you cannot build theory anew for your own day.

She appealed to the members of News and Letters Committees to think out what it means to be founders of a new movement called Marxist Humanism. As a manifestation of such a founding, she returned to the movement of Abolitionism.

New England intellectuals had surrounded themselves with militant ex-slaves: "WITHOUT THE RUNAWAY SLAVE FOLLOWING THE NORTH STAR TO FREEDOM the abolitionist intellectuals were ineffectual. With them they gave a new dimension to the American character and created America anew." The Abolitionists were not just "against" slavery, but did something about it. "It wasn't just any radicalism, it was the specific radicalism which tied up with the daily activity of men who wanted their freedom." The Abolitionists were a different kind of intellectual:

> [E]ven though you [the Abolitionists] were petty bourgeois you were part of what today we would call Marxist Humanism AND THEY CERTAINLY WERE HUMANISTS. Not a single relationship—whether between Negro and white or man and woman—merely retained its conventional stamp. The new, human relations that were to mark the new non-slave *society* already marked the behavior and relations of the Abolitionists. In their movement, those relations were changed. That is what we mean that the ideal is not very far from the real.

In the final section of her Perspectives report, Philosophic Innocence & New Humanist Proletarian Maturity, Dunayevskaya proceeded to trace how News and Letters was born, from the 1941 origin of the theory of state capitalism, through "the actual birth of News and Letters Committees or Marxist Humanism as the new theory, *1955-57.*" The first period, 1941 to 1949-50 she characterized as "the development of that political tendency as a development from theory to practice." At the time, the theory was not tested in practice, and was built on statistics from the Russian economy and past theory, that is, "Marx's concept of capitalism's development and the revolt of the workers." It all took place "*within* the radical movement itself."

The period 1949-50 began a new epoch, the Miners' General Strike:

> [S]omething TOTALLY NEW APPEARS: the movement *from practice to theory.* . . . Not that there wasn't always that movement in life, in history, but no theoretician was *fully* conscious of it. (a) Even the founder of Modern humanism, Marx who broke with the bourgeois concept of theory, and reconstructed his major theoretical work on that movement *from practice*, nevertheless made a separation between theory and practice. *It could not have been otherwise until the proletariat itself matured philosophically.* (b) The proof of that is that the 32 years after Marx's death, when the proletariat was readying for the greatest revolution in history—overthrow of Tsarism—and Lenin came to philosophy, he saw the essence of the dialectic in the unity of opposites, the transformation of one into the other, and not the AI [Absolute Idea], or new society.

The next period, 1950-55, included both automation, and "the break from totalitarianism signaled by the June 17, 1953 revolt in East Germany." But these movements from below could not be fully responded to without the break with Johnson (C.L.R. James). This only came with the birth of News and Letters Committee and Marxist Humanism that "*compelled* us to shed our philosophic innocence in the face of the workers demand for a total approach, but we have just begun. He who thinks otherwise will never build an organization, which cannot be built *seriously* without first of all being based on organization of thought that is both new and continued from Marx's day."

The rest of the Perspectives presentation was an outpouring on the Organization of Thought and its relation to actual organization. Dunayevskaya took up bourgeois organization of thought, which tried to endow "MAN MADE INSTITUTIONS with ETERNAL, UNCHANGEABLE LAWS OF THEIR OWN, taking them out of their *historic, human* determinateness, and thus make a FETISH of it." Marx developed this most concretely as the fetishism of commodities. Dunayevskaya wrote, all in caps: "That is why Marx opposed not only the capitalists as a class and their ideology as rationalization for their exploitation of the working class but insisted that all human consciousness up until then was a *false* consciousness." The worker, who could gain a "TRUE consciousness," could end,

> the *pre*-history of humanity . . . Gaining a mind of his own MEANT AN ENTIRELY NEW, UNPRECEDENTED ORGANIZATION OF THOUGHT, and this organization of thought was elaborated by Marx in the *Communist Manifesto*, which determined the organizational life of the Communist League.

WITHOUT SUCH AN ORGANIZATION OF THOUGHT organizations are nothing but factional groupings to be manipulated by unscrupulous politicians.

The final paragraphs of Dunayevskaya's presentation encompassed how News and Letters Committees could actualize Marxist Humanism, practice it in its organizational life. Here she stressed the need to practice philosophy, concretized for today:

> [I]t cannot be too often repeated that Marxism is not what Marx wrote in 1843 or 1883, but what it is *today*. What 1843-1883 created was the *theory* and the *method*. *We* must unite theory, method and practice, so the workers can actualize it and make it real, or there will be no new society. . . The whole organization . . . has just gained its philosophic wings, but it is not yet *practiced*.

Viewing News and Letters, 1955-57, Under the Shadow of the Johnson-Forest Tendency

In drawing together the threads of the first years of News and Letters Committees and its newspaper, *News & Letters*, we need to keep in mind the dual heritage of the years of the State-Capitalist Tendency. Without the State-Capitalist Tendency, as theoretic expression and organization, there could not have been the development to Marxist-Humanism. At the same time, there had to be a sharp struggle, particularly in the last years of the Tendency, as it manifested a deep depoliticalization, and a void in discussing the philosophic breakthrough of 1953, before the new philosophic beginnings could be developed organizationally, politically, and journalistically.

There was no straight line from state-capitalist theory to Marxist-Humanist philosophy, from translation of Lenin's *Philosophic Notebooks* to Dunayevskaya's Letters on Hegel's Absolutes, from the discovery of Marx's 1844 economic-philosophic writings to singling out the category Marx's Humanism, from a rejection of the vanguard party to the committee form of organization with a philosophic content, from *Correspondence* with its depoliticalization to *News & Letters* newspaper projecting and seeking to practice a unity of theory and practice.

Furthermore, the dualities and contradictions existed not only within the State-Capitalist Tendency. The vestiges, as a mode of thought and practice, could be found *inside* News and Letters Committees in 1955-1957. "Johnsonism," was not over and done with as soon as News and Letters Committees was founded. Dunayevskaya faced the question of "rearming" the organization in its first years:

(1) News and Letters Committees sought to be a unique combination of workers and intelectuals, based on the dual movement within Hegel's Absolutes that the 1953 Letters had forged—a movement from practice to theory that was

itself a form of theory, and a movement from theory to meet that movement from practice. This had to be worked out concretely in organizational practice as opposed to Johnson's "three layers" theory of organization, with its static roles for each layer.[5]

(2) *News & Letters* was to be a weapon in the class struggle, and to do so by having working people and all forces of revolution writing and speaking for themselves, and by having intellectuals writing political and theoretical analysis under the discipline of writing in a workers' newspaper. This concept of revolutionary journalism differed sharply from *Correspondence*, which James and Grace Lee saw as only recording voices from below, and without working out any concept that a worker be editor of the paper. The attacks on Dunayevskaya's political analysis of Stalin's death and later the Beria purge were part of a refusal of the other leaders of the State-Capitalist Tendency to take theoretical responsibility for working out the idea of freedom for the age. *News & Letters* as a theoretical journal and as a paper that could express masses as reason would only be developed when a theoretical statement on the meaning of Marxism for the post-World War II period was worked out.

(3) The working out a restatement of Marxism in book form, not as a private enclave, but as an individual and organizational responsibility, "the organization of thought which determines organizational life," was undertaken immediately, inseparable from organizational tasks and the newspaper's ongoing class struggle political analysis work. The crucial theoretical and practical foundations, laid in 1955-57, arose from the organization of thought Dunayevskaya had been laboring on for 16 years. *Marxism and Freedom* was its first full expression. We turn to its origins, structure and content, and ramifications in Part II.

---

[1] Because the material in all three sections became manifest in *Marxism and Freedom*, it is only briefly discussed here. See Part II on *Marxism and Freedom* for further discussion.

[2] See *The Myriad Global Crises of the 1980s and the Nuclear World since World War II*, News & Letters, 1986.

[3] Note to Olga [Domanski] appended to Letter to Saul [Blackman], August 5, 1957, *SRDC* #12186.

[4] Here in embryo was the category that would become the focus of Dunayevskaya's work in 1986-87: "Dialectics of Organization and Philosophy." See *SRDC* Volume XIII, as well as Part V of present study.

[5] See chapter 3, endnote 4, for description of "three layers."

Part II

1955-1964, Marxism and Freedom
... from 1776 until today

Chapter 5

Origins of *Marxism and Freedom* as World Events Unfold: Montgomery, Alabama 1955-56, Hungary 1956, Mao's China, 1957

The origins of *Marxism and Freedom* can be traced as far back as Dunayevskaya's 1941-43 studies on Russian state-capitalism. The studies were the beginning of a 16-year journey in which three turning points played determinant roles in shaping the form and content of the book:[1] (1) Dunayevskaya's 1949 translation of Lenin's *Abstract* on Hegel's *Science of Logic* followed by the 1949-50 Miners' General Strike, out of which she decided to present the book from two vantage points: the American proletariat and Lenin's Philosophic Notebooks; (2) her 1953 Letters on Hegel's Absolutes, which discerned a movement from practice that was itself a form of theory as well as a movement from theory within the absolutes. (3) the break-up of the Johnson-Forest State-Capitalist Tendency at the end of 1954 and the beginning of 1955, followed by the formation of News and Letters Committees, which in its first conference assigned Dunayevskaya the task of completing the book on Marxism.

In this chapter the focus will be on three developments that speak to Dunayevskaya's process of writing in the period of 1955-1957:[2] (1) her discussions with News and Letters colleagues as recorded in the form of book outlines, draft chapters, letters, and in-person presentations; (2) her dialogue on the book in-the-making with the "outside" in presentations and discussion to audiences that included Detroit autoworkers, Pittsburgh steelworkers, and West Virginia miners, as well as students on a number of campuses; and (3) Dunayevskaya's relationship with intellectuals, manifested in this period by a correspondence and in-person dialogue with Herbert Marcuse, a relationship that continued for more than two decades.

In this same period world events impacted the content and form of *Marxism and Freedom*: (1) The Montgomery Bus Boycott was recorded in the pages of *News & Letters*. Charles Denby made an in-person trip to Alabama. Dunayevskaya took up Montgomery in her presentation at the founding Convention of News and Letters Committees. Within *Marxism and Freedom*, the closing chapter, "Automation and the New Humanism," had a section on the bus boycott, which in conclusion echoed Marx's statement about the Paris Commune, "the greatest thing of all in this Montgomery Alabama, spontaneous organization was its own working existence." In the Preface to *Marxism and Freedom*, Dunayevskaya wrote that, "the Negro struggles of 1956-57 no less illuminated the road to a new society," than did the Hungarian Revolution of 1956.

(2) The Hungarian Revolution, which took place in the midst of Dunayevskaya's final writing of *Marxism and Freedom*, was singled out in the chapter, "The Beginning of the End of Russian Totalitarianism," along with the East German Revolt of June 17, 1953, and the Vorkuda prison uprising of July 1953. She saw the Hungarian Revolution as raising a banner of humanism, the dimension that was at the core of her presentation of Marxism anew in book form.

(3) A speech of Mao Tse-Tung, "On Contradiction," was released and caused significant world controversy as *Marxism and Freedom* was already going to press. Dunayevskaya added a footnote briefly critiquing Mao's concept of contradiction. She called attention to this footnote in a postscript to the completed preface. The second edition of *Marxism and Freedom* (1964) would include a chapter on "The Challenge of Mao Tse-tung."

A Collective Effort in the Writing of *Marxism and Freedom*: News and Letters Colleagues and Committees; Working People as Co-authors

Three months after the Founding Conference of News and Letters, Dunayevskaya wrote a letter to News and Letters Committees "on the relationship of the writing of *Marxism and Freedom* to the work of the organization:"

> Because we live in an age where the movement *from practice* to theory is richer than any other age, we have the opportunity to write the book as a collective effort not alone as regards the relationship of the individual author and the newspaper committee, but as regards the so-called outside and the inside. At no time in history will they in turn have had the opportunity to be the actual collaborators in *every process* of the writing of the book. Thus the present tour is scheduled when the author will have no more than a bare outline of what she wants in the book on which she has spent some 15 years. This will be vitally influenced by the discussion of the groups of that unique combination of worker and intellectual that so characterize the news committees *and* their friends. And there will be another chance for the whole organization in convention to act on it after the writing of a draft (Dear Friends letter to all local committees of July 28, 1955. *SRDC* # 12055).

This letter, written a month and a half before Dunayevskaya would begin a national tour, laid out the historic framework that compelled a restatement of Marxism:

> At each break in world history, from the Civil War in the United States through World War II, Marxists have had to re-examine their principles, enrich them, and move forward with history—or fall under the weight of the old society, as did the Second International.
> That was true of Marx himself who first in the period between the Civil War in the United States and the Paris Commune in 1871 completed his life's work, *Capital*. This was true of Lenin who had to go back to the philosophic foundations of Marxism in Hegel himself, just when the whole world was collapsing about him with the outbreak of the First World War.
> It was not true of Trotsky who thought it sufficient merely to hold the banner of 1917 aloft. . . .
> Political theses—and the political thesis based on the theory of state capitalism is among these—are good, but not good enough. Lenin's statement that there can be no revolution without a revolutionary theory means something far different in our age than in his. We have lived through three decades in which the workers have done everything from the CIO and the Spanish revolution to the resistance movement and the East German revolt without the Marxist theoreticians contributing anything new. It is high time to begin.

Dunayevskaya began a book on Marxism whose structure and content would be based on movement from practice to theory that appeared historically. As well, that movement from practice, as it was then taking place, would be a decisive catalyst for her theoretic labor on the book. First came her tour that involved speaking to and listening to coal miners, steelworkers, and auto workers, as well as student youth as participant discussants. Only then did she begin to draft chapters. Those initial draft chapters were then shared with News and Letters local committees and friends. Taped discussions and transcripts of discussions were shared with the author. She presented further developments on the book to the first (1956) National Convention of News and Letters. The final drafts of chapters were then written.

Dunayevskaya's interchange with West Virginia coal miners was central to the chapter, "Automation and the New Humanism." As she planned an initial fall 1955 tour of several cities with News and Letters locals to have presentations and discussions on the book, she wrote to Olga Domanski, a News and Letters colleague then living in West Virginia:

> It dawned upon me that rather than start in Detroit in fall with the lectures on the book, I would like to start in West Virginia . . . The truth is that objectively as far back as 1947 when we established ourselves in West Virginia we said it was *the* key place to the most revolutionary and basic proletariat. . . .

> Well, here it is 1955 . . . [w]e are leaping ahead in 1) first and foremost reinterpreting Marxism for our generation, for our age, for our country, and for the world, 2) from a level—Absolute Idea—it never had except in the most general terms and that solely in the hands of Marx himself and Lenin himself, and 3) doing something that not even these founders could, for they did not live in our age, and that is taking up the book *with the public* before the author ever lays hands to it, which of course means that when she does it will be a collective work in the highest sense and ready to be rechecked by what masses we have contact with before publisher. Now for such a high journey of discovery someone who has a grasp of what is involved and does not take it as "an extra meeting" is the one who should lay the groundwork. That someone or someones is you and Andy [Philips] (Letter of August 24, 1955 *SRDC* #12050).

Two points were involved: (1) while Dunayevskaya was going on tour without a draft of the book in hand, she was going with a theoretic-philosophic framework from which to present ideas *and* to elicit responses from her working class audience. (2) the relationship between the News and Letters Committees as newspaper committees and friends who had been helping to write articles for *News & Letters* was going to be key in establishing an audience for Dunayevskaya's "taking up the book with the public," in this case West Virginia miners.

In a letter of August 24, 1955, Dunayevskaya further developed the concentration on West Virginia:

> I felt that no place could take the place of West Virginia for the type of audience that is a necessity for the book. In working through automation at one pole and the absolute at the other—the two poles of the book on Marxism—I first realized that although we did not have the *word*, automation in 1950, actually the continuous miner and the strike then had all the elements of the wildcats and the feelings on automation here [Detroit], and that therefore they feel and grasp clearest the problem of which I am talking about when I say our age has matured so that the movement now is *from theory to practice*. [Likely Dunayevskaya meant to write *from practice to theory*] . . . Do tell Andy [Philips] I am looking forward to seeing and talking with him in particular and really cracking both Hegel's Absolute Idea, Marx's freedom and the Working Day, and the West Virginia coal miners being right in on it all from the ground floor and making their contribution (*SRDC* # 12057).

After beginning in West Virginia, Dunayevskaya toured various News and Letters locals, speaking to both working class audiences and on university campuses.[3] Following the tour, Dunayevskaya drafted a number of chapters in March, April, and May 1956, and sent these to News and Letters locals who discussed the book-in-the-making among themselves and with friends. Of particular importance was the meeting the West Virginia News and Letters Committee had in the spring of 1956. It was from this meeting that the miners' voices emerged that appear in the Introduction to *Marxism and Freedom* and in the "Automation and the New Humanism" chapter.[4]

These discussions with non-member workers were fundamental in the shaping of the book. As well, the dialogues Dunayevskaya had with workers and others inside the Committees were decisive. These included worker-colleague News and Letters members, Charles Denby and Angela Terrano, who contributed to the discussions on automation.

In addition to presentations made by Dunayevskaya to News and Letters locals while on tour, a stream of letters flowed from her to the Committees and to individual colleagues on various aspects of the book. They were often on the relationship between a small radical grouping and its theoretical-organizational responsibility for restating and practicing Marxism anew, and allowed Dunayevskaya to "think out loud" in relation to the book.

By April 1956, a number of draft chapters and a brief "Outline of Contents" began to be circulated. By mid May, Dunayevskaya completed "The French Revolution and German Philosophy," a draft chapter, which, in rewritten form, would become the opening chapter of the book. In July, Dunayevskaya presented the thesis "Theoretical and Practical Perspectives: Where to Begin," to the founding News and Letters Convention. (See Chapter 4 for a discussion of this thesis.)

At the end of October, Dunayevskaya addressed a letter to the leadership of News and Letters, the National Editorial Board (NEB), writing on what she felt was "a void" in the leadership when it came to "the question of establishment of committees as the *form* of combining *News & Letters* and the book": "We alone have restored theory to its genuine Marxist foundation both philosophically and as it gains its source from the actual developing class struggle," and reminded the leadership that, "the most prodigious work theoretically was just when [Marx] was organizationally active and, not accidentally, in turn, the First International had, as its Statutes, the essence of the movement of *Capital*" (*SRDC* #11823).

The letter continued on the necessity for the NEB to assume on a voluntary basis, the financial responsibility for the publication of *Marxism and Freedom*. Dunayevskaya felt this was a *political* question tied to the meaning of a small group's relation to Marxist tradition:

> There are moments in history when a small group holds in its hands certain threads of continuity with Marxist tradition that demand of the group the greatest exertions and creativity. They cannot appear until the inner conviction of what it is we are doing has permeated us to our very bone and marrow.

She ended the letter by presenting "the outline of the book as it had changed in the process of reworking."

By the end of November 1956, the book was completed. Dunayevskaya's correspondence with News and Letters Committees now revolved around how to both absorb and project *Marxism and Freedom*. On May 5, 1957, Marx's birthday, and shortly after she had signed a contract for publication, Dunayevskaya gave a talk on "The New Stage" that this signified. Her concentration was on how to make "*Marxism and Freedom* real, that is to say, concrete for ourselves [News and Letters Committees]." Several letters to the Committees in the following months took up questions of promotion, financial responsibility, study and projection of the book. Dunayevskaya tackled directly "the relation of theory to membership growth."

Of central concern was how "the organization of thought" that was *Marxism and Freedom*, would "determine the organizational life" of News and Letters Committees. (See Chapter 4 for discussion of Dunayevskaya's fullest development of this theme at the July 1957 News and Letters Plenum.) The fact that the book was structured on the movement from practice to theory, did not mean theory would simple resolve itself based on practice. Rather, "the time has come when the movement from practice to theory must finally meet theory itself" (Dear Friends letter, December 5, 1957, *SRDC* #12192). With *Marxism and Freedom* off the press in less than a month, such theory, Dunayevskaya argued, became an organizational responsibility.

•

In addition to the presentations and letters to the organization as a whole or to its leadership, Dunayevskaya carried on extensive individual correspondence with members of News and Letters Committees on aspects of *Marxism and Freedom* as it was being written. Among the letters:

• An exchange with Olga Domanski. Domanski wrote a seven page letter commenting on the initial draft of Dunayevskaya's chapter on Hegel's Absolute Idea in which she took up both the structure and content of the chapter and the covering letter Dunayevskaya had sent with the chapter. Dunayevskaya drafted a reply expressing appreciation for "the serious piece of criticism you did on the chapter." She then proceeded to discuss with Domanski the working out of a section of the book "the so-called [organizational] interlude—that is the Second International."[5]

• To Bessie Gogol, October, 20, 1956 (*SRDC* #12316). This letter was written in the midst of translating Marx's "Critique of the Hegelian Dialectic" (printed as an appendix to *Marxism and Freedom*) on the relationship between where Marx stopped his commentary on Hegel's *Philosophy of Mind* and where Dunayevskaya had begun hers in her Letter of May 20, 1953 on Hegel. Without knowing where Marx had stopped, she had begun on the very next paragraph in Hegel (paragraph 385). She wrote to Gogol "I feel . . . as if I had been in communication with Karl [Marx]. I swear there is such a thing as communication between the ages, not only in general as each generation inherits the civilization up to it, but in particular as a *class and its thought*, develops its problems."[6]

• To Domanski, June 23, 1957. The letter was commentary on Mao Tse-tung's speech "On the Correct Handling of Contradictions Among the People" in relation to Hegel's discussion of "Spirit in Self-Estrangement." The ideas in this letter formed the basis for a footnote on Mao that Dunayevskaya added to *Marxism and Freedom* on galley proofs. (See footnote 17, *Marxism and Freedom*.)

Dialogue with Herbert Marcuse

In the late 1940s and early and mid 1950s Dunayevskaya sought out a dialogue with a number of intellectuals in America and abroad on the ideas she was working on. Among them were Robert Cohen, Chaulieu (Cornelius Castoriadis), Joseph Buttinger, Meyer Schapiro, Alexander Ehrlich, E.H. Carr, and Joan Robinson. Of particular significance was her correspondence with Herbert Marcuse. She had read his *Reason and Revolution* in the 1940s and felt it made an important contribution to Hegelian-Marxism. In 1954 they began a correspondence which continued to 1978.[7]

Much of the Marcuse-Dunayevskaya correspondence was characterized by a respect for, but often, deep disagreement with, their respective philosophic labors. In the period 1954-57, leading to the publication of *Marxism and Freedom*, Marcuse's responses to Dunayevskaya's writing, including critique and questions, were important in Dunayevskaya's shaping of this first work. In addition, he assisted her in trying to obtain a publisher. Their disagreements centered on the "translation" of the dialectic to the political realm which was related to their differing views on the potential revolutionary role of the proletariat in post-World War II industrial society. This, in turn, was inseparable from their contrasting views of the relevance of Hegel's Absolute Idea for a liberatory future. In addition, they differed on the relation of Lenin and Stalinism, that is, on the nature of the Russian state, which Dunayevskaya held was no longer socialist, but state-capitalist.

In one of the first letters, Dunayevskaya wrote of her desire to meet and talk on the question of dialectics:

> I had been working for quite some time on the Absolute Idea, Absolute Knowledge, Absolute Mind which, to me, is "to *be* free" rather than merely "to *have* freedom" and answers the question of the man on the street who wants to know whether in this totalitarian age: *can* man be free? We have indeed reached the age of absolutes that are not in heaven but concretely in life when the question that bothers philosophers is the same that the ordinary worker asks in his everyday workaday world (February 12, 1955 *SRDC* #12036).

Dunayevskaya's concretization of dialectical thought in the "everyday workaday world" formed one dimension of the "battle of ideas," which began early in their correspondence. In a letter of April 3, 1955, she posed the framework and the philosophic origin for the book she wished to write:

> The twin poles to me of any fundamental work [on Marxism] must have, automation at one end, and the absolute idea or freedom at the other end. I'm very anxious to hear your response to those two letters [of May 12 and 20, 1953] where I first posed the question of the absolute idea in term[s] of a movement from practice to theory as well as from theory to practice (*SRDC* # 12038).

Marcuse responded:

> I have now read the notes on Hegel which you lent me. This is fascinating, and I admire your way of concretizing the most abstract philosophical notions. However, I still cannot get along with the direct translation of idealistic philosophy into politics: I think you somehow minimize the "negation" which the application of the Hegelian dialectic to political phenomena presupposes (April 14, 1955; # 12039).

Dunayevskaya, who had earlier extended an invitation to Marcuse to come to Detroit and meet with the production workers who wrote for a Marxist workers' newspaper, replied:

> [P]erhaps you will take that trip to Detroit, and thus see that it is not a question of "my" direct translation of idealistic philosophy into politics, but the dialectical development of proletarian politics itself as its struggles to rid itself of its specifically class character in its movement to a classless society. That is why I "translated" Absolute Mind as the new society (May 5, 1955; # 12047).

Dunayevskaya then noted that Lenin had "sort of put a period" in the Absolute Idea chapter when he interpreted Hegel's transition of the Idea to Nature as "stretching a hand to materialism." But that was 1915 she added, and we were in a different age:

> What is needed in this age of absolutes is not the separation of politics from philosophy but their integration . . . 1955 compels that where Hegel made it the job of philosophy to elicit necessity under the semblance of contingency, today's intellectuals must elicit the new society present in the old by seeing the human freedom totally unfolded in freely associated labor alone deciding its own fate. . . . The reason this is the age of absolutes is that the objectivity, all objectivity, is now in the proletariat himself. That is how I read Hegel on the Absolute Idea freely releasing itself.

Their debate continued. On June 22, 1955, Marcuse wrote, "I read your draft re Marxism and State Capitalism and found it most needed and useful. The whole thing is excellent." He then added:

Your answer to my brief remarks re Hegel does not satisfy me. Certainly you do not suspect me of ignoring the substantive connection between philosophy and praxis. BUT it is—*sit venia verbo*—a dialectical connection, not an immediate one. What is the meaning of the explicit or implied "is" in your statement: "the dialectic of the Absolute Idea is the dialectic of" the proletariat or whatever it may be? Is this a mere analogy? An equation or identification? You cannot just "apply" Hegel's text to an essentially different sphere without demonstrating why and how (# 12051).

Dunayevskaya immediately responded:

Naturally I do not mean when I go further in the *Logic* and say the Absolute Idea "is" the proletarian self-emancipation or liberation from the party that there is a direct relationship between the laws and movement of the logic and the field of human freedom. It is always a dialectical relationship and will need to be developed in all its manifoldedness. But that "is" is an absolute necessity to cut through not only detail and the gibberish of so much that passes for Marxism these days but to open up those closed intellectual ears of ours to the fresh impulses from the workers. That is why I dropped any work on the book for two years and came here [Detroit] to work on the paper. As soon as *News & Letters* gains a certain momentum of its own, I will return to the work. But note how I mean to return to it so that you will see what I mean by method of work and impulse from the only *theoretically new thoughts* from the proletariat itself. This is not simple movement from theory to practice—I'm sure you above all know that in both Hegel and Marx—but one *from practice to theory* not as mere verification of the latter but its creator (June 28, 1955; # 12052).

She then explained her plan for working on the book, which included lectures and discussions with small groups of workers and intellectuals followed by further input from them.

Throughout the rest of 1955, Dunayevskaya wrote Marcuse of the attempts to obtain an English language publisher for Marx's *1844 Manuscripts* and Lenin's *Philosophic Notebooks*, and of her fall lecture tour. Marcuse, upon reading some of Dunayevskaya's notes, wrote, "I must encourage you to go ahead with the elaboration. Your ideas are a real oasis in the desert of Marxist thought" (December 2, 1955; # 12064).

In 1956 after Marcuse's *Eros and Civilization* was published, Dunayevskaya commented:

Your *Eros and Civilization* has broken down my adamant refusal lasting two decades "to have a position on sex." Because your work is of such an original character it of necessity invalidated the self-defensive gesture of an old politico who feels it necessary not to get embroiled in every question "intellectuals" feel called upon to thrust into a political argument to deflect from the main point (September 6, 1956; # 12129).

In the fall of 1956 Marcuse returned from Europe and commented upon parts of the *Marxism and Freedom* manuscript that Dunayevskaya had sent him. He stated that her chapter on the Second International was "too sketchy and does not [do] justice to the historical problem." He argued again his view of the modern proletariat: "In the development of late industrial society in the advanced countries, this class *qua class* has changed its position, structure, consciousness, etc." Finally, he disagreed, "with your assumption of a complete break between Leninism and Stalinism."

Marcuse and Dunayevskaya met at the end of November 1956, and discussed parts of the book. Marcuse outlined ideas for the Preface he would write. (For Dunayevskaya's account of this meeting see letter to John Dwyer of Nov. 27, 1956; *SRDC* # 12148.) In June 1957, Dunayevskaya wrote a two and a half page summary of *Marxism and Freedom* in response to Marcuse's request for a recapitulation of the "gist" of the book to assist him in writing the Preface to the book. (See appendix to this chapter.)

Marcuse's Preface singled out Dunayevskaya's recapturing Marxian theory in its foundation as humanistic philosophy, and his disagreement with some parts of her analysis of post-Marxian developments.

In calling for a reexamination of Marxist theory, Marcuse argued that the theory had "accurately anticipated the basic tendencies of late industrial society," but drawn "incorrect conclusions from its analysis." Twentieth century capitalism "did not explode in the final crisis;" the "construction of socialism in the communist orbit exhibits hardly any of the substance of the Marxian idea." However, if modification of the Marxian theory were necessary "the modifications must be demonstrably related to the theoretical basis, that is, to the dialectical-materialist concept of industrial society." Much discussion of Marxian theory, argued Marcuse, did not "elucidate the function and the full content of dialectical materialism." In contrast,

> Dunayevskaya's book discards these and similar distortions and tries to recapture the integral unity of Marxian theory at its very foundation: in the humanistic philosophy . . . .
> Dunayevskaya's book goes beyond the previous interpretations. It shows not only that Marxian economics and politics are throughout philosophy, but that the latter is from the beginning economics and politics.

Marcuse proceeded to discuss Marxian theory in which "humanism" was a "historical possibility":

> Marxian theory does not describe and analyze the capitalist economy "in itself and for itself" but describes and analyzes it in terms of another than itself—in terms of the historical possibilities which have become realistic goals for action. As *critical* theory, Marxism is two-dimensional throughout: measuring the prevailing society against its own, objective-historical potentialities and capabilities. This two-dimensional character manifests itself in the union of phi-

losophy and political economy. . . . [E]very one of the economic categories is a philosophical category.

Marcuse pointed out how Dunayevskaya's discussion of *Capital* brought out this union and thus showed Marx's humanistic philosophy as firmly here as in his critique of Hegel or theses on Feuerbach.

Marcuse then discussed his view that for Marx, "the realization of freedom is a problem of *time*: reduction of the working day to the minimum which turns quantity into quality. A socialist society is a society in which free time, not labor time is the social measure of wealth and the dimension of the individual existence." This free time would be the basis for "the development of those human faculties which make for the free (in Marx's words—'all-round') individual, especially the development of 'consciousness.'" For Marx, Marcuse noted, it was "*revolutionary* consciousness, expressing the 'determinate negation' of the established society, and as such proletarian consciousness."

What happened in the 20th century to that proletarian consciousness, to the development of Marxism itself post the Russian Revolution, and to capitalism's form with the Depression and the rise of Stalin became major fault lines between Marcuse and Dunayevskaya:

> While the author of this Preface agrees in all essentials with the theoretical interpretation of the Marxian *oeuvre* in these first parts [of *Marxism and Freedom*], he disagrees with some decisive parts of the analysis of post-Marxian developments, especially with that of the relationship between Leninism and Stalinism, of the recent upheavals in Eastern Europe, and, perhaps most important, with the analysis of the contemporary position, structure and consciousness of the laboring classes.

Despite deep disagreements on many fundamental issues, (including the significance of Hegel's Absolutes for the post-World War II world that will be taken up in a subsequent chapter), Dunayevskaya had a great appreciation for Marcuse's willingness to engage in philosophic dialogue with her. (See her In Memoriam, "Herbert Marcuse, Marxist Philosopher," *News & Letters*, Aug.-Sept. 1979 *RDC* # 5985.)

Appendix:
A 1957 Dunayevskaya Commentary
on *Marxism and Freedom*

Responding to a request from Herbert Marcuse for a summary of the gist of Marxism and Freedom *as he was preparing his Preface, Dunayevskaya wrote the following letter (SRDC #12176):*

June 11, 1957

Dear Herbert Marcuse:

It was good to hear from you. I'm sure that you are well acquainted with the fact that it is much easier to write 100, if not 500, pages than it is to summarize the gist of a book on which one has worked [on] for some 15 years, in a page or two. But I will try.

I. *The* central point, the pivot around which everything else in *Marxism and Freedom* revolves, is, of course, the philosophic foundation of Marxism. As I put it in my introductory note, "The aim of this book is to re-establish the original form of Marxism which Marx called [a] "'thoroughgoing Naturalism or Humanism.'"

This runs like a red threat throughout the book. Thus Part I begins with the French Revolution and Hegel and ends with Marx's Early Economic-Philosophic Essays: A New Humanism. It constitutes his answer to classical political economy as well as to the utopian socialists and vulgar Communists of his day and establishes a new world outlook, Marxian philosophy, which is distinguished from the Hegelian dialectic and closely knit with it. What is established as the thesis of the young Marx then reappears in Part III, Marxism: the Unity of Theory and Practice, where, in The Dialectical Humanism of Volume I, I show that not only are Marx's economic categories social categories but they are thoroughly permeated with the humanism that came out of the working class struggles for the shortening of the working day. As Marx put it, the mere question, when does my day begin and when does it end, was on a higher philosophic level than "the pompous catalogue of the Declaration of the Rights of Man." What is true of Volume I of *Capital* is true of the Logic and Scope of Volumes II and III, including Theories of Surplus Value, where I show that all of history to Marx was the struggle for freedom, which, as its basis, is the shortening of the working day, and only from there do we go from the realm of necessity to that of freedom.

Lenin learned the critical importance of the philosophic foundations the hard way—when the Second International actually collapsed and, to reconstitute his own reason, [he] had to return to Hegel's *Science of Logic*. The chapter, A Mind in Action, then traces what the philosophic foundations meant to Lenin and the Russian Revolution[,] and ends with the thought that just as Marxism without its philosophic foundation is meaningless, so is Leninism. Neither is an "economist." Finally when we come to our own age, which I call Automation and the New Humanism, I show the *methodology* of Marxism and the compulsion of our own age for a total outlook.

II. Subordinated to this main theme of the book, and running parallel with it, is the division between the radical intellectual like Proudhon and the Marxist intellectual. I contend that Marxism is not only the theoretical expression of the working class striving to establish a new society on socialist beginnings, but it is that which gave intellectuals a new dimension. That new dimension arose precisely because he did not divide theory from history, including the current class struggles. The relationship of theory to history is seen as a live element that changes the very structure of Marx's greatest theoretical work. In 1863 and 1865 when he fundamentally revised that structure and 1872-75 when he wrote the French edition of *Capital*—the period from the Civil War in the United States through the Paris Commune—is proof of this relationship of theory to history and at the same time shows that what the young Marx established in the Early Essays when he held that never again must society be counterposed to the individual and which in 1848 he emblazoned on his *Communist Manifesto* as the thesis that the development of the individual is the condition for the development of all[,] reappears in his "most economic" work which is preferred by the academic economists—Volume III of *Capital*.

Again, when I move from Marx's time to that of Lenin's time I show that the contribution of the Second International—Organization—was taken over by Lenin in his concept of the so-called Vanguard Theory in 1902-03, but as the actual Russian Revolution occurred, he threw it overboard—or at least radically revised his theory no less than 6 times so that in 1917 he says the workers on the outside are more revolutionary than the vanguard party and by 1923 says that unless the party work is checked by the *non-party* masses the bureaucracy will yet bring the workers state down and they will retrogress to capitalism. In any case, our problem is certainly not will there be a revolution: but *what will happen after*: are we always to be confronted with a Napoleon or a Stalin? In a word, without relating the spontaneous self-organization of the proletariat and its quest for universality in the manner in which Marx did it for his time, we can expect nothing but totalitarianist results.

III. In my introductory note I state that the 3 main strands of thought in the book are: 1) Classical Political Economy, Hegelian Philosophy, and the French Revolutionary doctrines in relationship to the actual social and economic conditions of its time, the Industrial Revolution, the French Revolution and to the first capitalist crisis. 2) Marxism in relationship to the class struggles of his day, the period of his maturity, 1843-1883, as well as Marxism in the period from 1889-1923; and 3) The *methodology* of Marxism to our era which I call the period of state capitalism and workers revolt, the analysis of the Five Year Plans of Russia and the revolts of East Germany, and Vorkuta following Stalin's death; finally the analysis of Automation but this is a comparative free and easy essay. I think this too in a way can be summed up in the introductory note where I explain the method in which this book is written—that research began in 1939 when I broke with Trotsky over the "Russian Question" but that it did not assume the form of *Marxism and Freedom* until 1950-53 when the miner's strike on automation and the revolts in Eastern Europe from their separate vantage points led me to present all my ideas to groups of workers who checked and discussed the material. "No theoretician, today more than ever before, can write out of his own head. Theory requires constant shaping and reshaping of idea on the basis of what the workers themselves are doing and thinking." I return to Hegel (page 73 ftn in the *Science of Logic*) where he shows that those who took Kant's *results* without the process did so as a "pillow for intellectual sloth" and that if the intellectual sloth which has accumulated in the Marxist movement concerned only Marxists then we wouldn't be confronting the H-bomb threat without ideological backwardness showing. The need is for a new unity of theory and practice which must begin with the new impulses coming from the working class, that this, far from being intellectual abdication, would mark the actual fructification of theory. Once the theoretician gets that, his work does not end, but first *begins*.

In a word, I have no prescriptions or rhetorical conclusions. I show a method at work and appeal to the intellectuals to use that dialectic method as a basis to view the contemporary scene, to get out from under domination of either the Russian totalitarian of the American "democratic" bomb threats in their thinking. The workers by themselves can do a lot but they too have not achieved a new social order, but if the movement from practice to theory met the movement from theory to practice, then a *serious* start could be made.

There are naturally other points in the work—from the American roots of Marxism to the Communists perversions both of Marx's Early Works and *Capital*—since it tries to deal with our machine age since the Industrial Revolution to Automation, but I do not believe anything germane to the book is lost once one grasps the central point, the philosophic foundations.

I know the effect that your *Reason and Revolution* had in 1941. They could neither treat Hegel as an "old dog" nor Marx's Early Writings as mere humanitarian adjuncts to "the great scientific economic theories." But then it was a philosopher speaking and not "a solid economist" like me. When the two were combined, glory, hallelujah—there was havoc. But the academicians need not think themselves any smarter—they all fell into the "Popular Front;" it is not possible to fight Russian totalitarianism or any other kind without some solid theoretic foundation and social vision.

I naturally cannot say whether I succeeded in doing which I aimed at but *if* intention were indeed achievement then I could say that what was *new* in *Marxism and Freedom* was 1) the re-establishment of the philosophic foundations of Marxism in Hegel in so concrete a way that the origins of our machine age as well as the latest period of automation came alive; 2) the summation of all three volumes of Marx's *Capital* in a manner that the reader knows Marxism both as theory and as methodology; and 3) the new dimension Marxism endows the intellectual with became so real to him that he could indeed discern the movement from practice to theory and as eagerly long for the unity of the two as does the worker.

I hope this is some way answers what you wanted me to do in recapitulating the gist of the work. I also enclose the introductory note to the bibliography so that you can see all my problems there.

Looking forward to your Preface *very* eagerly.

[1] During the existence of the State-Capitalist Tendency, Dunayevskaya wrote two draft outlines, "State capitalism and Marxism" in 1947 (*RDC* # 472) and "The Lenin Book" in 1952 (*RDC* #1735).

[2] Dunayevskaya wrote most of the draft chapters in 1956, followed by publication at the end of 1957. To explore the full available range of draft chapters, outlines, correspondence, notes, and presentations in the process of writing *Marxism and Freedom* see *RDC* # 2410-2619; *SRDC* #11785-12196.

[3] Dunayevskaya spoke on topics ranging from Marx as a Philosopher, to Hegel's Philosophy, to An Analysis of the 20th Congress on DeStalinization, at campuses including UCLA, UC-Berkeley, and CCNY. For listing see *SRDC* #12060.

[4] For the actual material incorporated, see Olga Domanski's letter to Dunayevskaya, April 21, 1956, *SRDC* #12091.

[5] See the following documents "The French Revolution and Classical German Philosophy" *SRDC* #11834; "Dear Friends", May 18, 1956, #12105; Domanski letter to Dunayevskaya, July 29, 1956, #12109; Unfinished letter to Domanski, August, 4, 1956, #12126.

[6] See *SRDC* # 12136. See also letter on translation Oct. 18, 1956 *SRDC* #12134; "Critique of the Hegelian Dialectic," draft translation, #12015.

[7] See RDC # 9889-9975 for Dunayevskaya-Marcuse correspondence in Archives. For a discussion of the correspondence, see Kevin Anderson, "The Marcuse-Dunayevskaya Dialogue," *Studies in Soviet Thought*, Vol. 39:2 (1990). pp. 89-109. See my Chapter 8 for discussion of the correspondence in relation to writing of *Philosophy and Revolution*.

Chapter 6

Elucidating the Philosophical Foundations of Marxism: The Structure and Content of *Marxism and Freedom*

> *The twin poles . . . of any fundamental work [on Marxism] must have automation at one end, and the absolute idea or freedom at the other end.*
>
> *The aim of this book is to re-establish the original form of Marxism, which Marx called "a thoroughgoing Naturalism, or Humanism"*

Part I, From Practice to Theory: 1776 to 1848

The title Dunayevskaya gave to Part I of *Marxism and Freedom*, "From Practice to Theory" characterized the structure of the whole work. The book showed "that philosophy is fashioned out of the activity of *common* man" ("The American Roots of Marxism in the World Today and Our Development," Perspectives Talk to News and Letters, Sept, 1957. RDC #2603). She pointed to the masses' practice as a movement toward theory, indeed, as the source of philosophic thought: "There is nothing in thought—not even in the thought of a genius—that has not previously been in the activity of the common man" (*Marxism and Freedom*, 23). To recover the *philosophic foundations* of Marxism, buried under historic debris of 20th century revolutions aborted and transformed into their opposite, one needed the vantage point of the masses' movement from practice.

This first became manifest in Chapter One, "The Age of Revolutions: Industrial, Social-Political, Intellectual," where Dunayevskaya discussed the activity of the Parisian masses, and its impact on dialectical philosophy's development, "Freedom and the Hegelian Dialectic." "The revolutions in thought can be fully understood only in the light of the revolutions in action, particularly the development of the great French Revolution" (28). Hegel's organization of thought became a system of philosophy that summed up the previous stage of man's activity. This was so even as he "was unconscious of this *human* factor" ("The American Roots of Marxism in the World Today and Our Development," *RDC* #2603).

In *Marxism and Freedom* Dunayevskaya traced the mass self-activity that arose during the French Revolution:

> The truth is that precisely the spontaneity of 1789 and of 1793, especially 1793, bears both the stamp and the seal of the demands of the mass movement and the *method* by which the masses meant to construct a new society in place of the old. . . . There is a double rhythm in destroying the old and creating the new which bears the unmistakable stamp of the self-activity which is the truly working class way of knowing. This, in fact, was the greatest of all the achievements of the great French Revolution—the workers' discovery of their own way of knowing (28-29, 31).

After a discussion of the masses' praxis in the revolution, she followed Hegel's reorganization of the premises of philosophy under its impact: "[The French Revolution] had revealed that the overcoming of opposites is not a single act but a constantly developing process, a development through contradiction. He called it dialectics. It is through the struggle of opposites that the movement of humanity is propelled forward" (34). Though Hegel worked out the contradictions in thought alone, this should not be read to mean that he remained in a closed ontological system. Rather, "Hegel drew history into philosophy, thereby revolutionizing the concept of philosophy." Thus human freedom, even if present only in abstract form, was nevertheless present.

"Freedom is the animating spirit, the 'Subject' of Hegel's greatest works. All of history, to Hegel, is a series of historical stages in the development of freedom" (35). To obtain that freedom, human beings had to fight, "thereby is revealed 'the negative character' of modern society" (35). "The *Science of Logic* may be said to be the philosophy of history established by the French Revolution, namely that man in temporal history, that is, on this earth, can achieve freedom" (41).

Dunayevskaya's concentration was on Hegel's Absolutes—Absolute Knowledge, the Absolute Idea, Absolute Mind: "Brought out of their abstractions, Hegel's 'Absolutes' have applicability and meaning for every epoch, ours most of all" (36). This became the center of the last section of the chapter, "Hegel's Absolutes and Our Age of Absolutes," where Dunayevskaya presented a two-way road. She quoted Hegel to show how his concept of freedom as a dimension of humanity's being was contemporaneous to our age: "If to be aware of the idea—to be aware, i.e., that men are aware of freedom as their essence, aim, and object—is a matter of *speculation*, still this very idea itself is the actuality of men—not something which they *have*, as men, but which they are" (36).

At the same time, she wished to show what was necessary *from our age* to grasp the fullness of Hegel's dialectic: "Paradoxical as it may sound, the greatest impediment in the way of the intellectuals discerning the new society in Hegel's 'Absolute Mind' is their isolation from the working people in whose lives the elements of the new society are present." This intertwining of our age and Hegel's, became fully developed when Chapter One's discussion of Hegel's Absolutes was fused with the final Chapter Sixteen's "Automation and the New Humanism." It was then that "the two poles of the book," the Absolutes and Automation, were spelled out in their fullest form.

That Hegel's dialectical historical method spoke to the mid 20th century world could also be seen in Dunayevskaya's discussion of the Russian Communists' attempt to replace Hegel's development through contradiction with a "new dialectical law" of "Criticism and Self-Criticism" (39-40). Far from being a remote academic discussion, the foisting of such a "law" as "a powerful instrument in the hands of the Communist Party," (Andrei Zhdanov, Central Committee of the Communist Party, 1947), was a way of trying to subsume the objectivity of the Hegelian dialectic under the Communist Party's narrow subjective purpose of maintaining exploitative class rule in their so-called "classless, socialist society."

Dunayevskaya would return to the Hegelian dialectic with respect to Marx's creation of a new Humanism in Chapter Three. In Chapter Two she turned to "Classical Political Economy, the Revolts of the Workers and the Utopian Socialists." The chapter had embedded within the concept of "From Practice to Theory" in relation to two groups of intellectuals, the classical political economists and the Utopian socialists. Each would be tested against the activity of a newly emerging class—the proletariat.

She began with classical political economy: "The labor theory of value created as great a revolution in man's thinking as the industrial revolution had in man's conditions of living" (44-5). Labor, the greatest force of production, was a source of all value. In revealing that the laborer was paid at value, classical political economy had "revealed the *innermost* law of bourgeois production. . . . The laborer was getting only what was *necessary* to produce him, and all the *surplus* he produced was appropriated by the capitalist. From the *equality* of exchange *in general* arose the *inequality* of exchange of the *particular* 'commodity'—labor" (45-46).

Dunayevskaya pointed to classical political economy's first major assumption, "a *given* class society, capitalism, which it took for the eternal natural order" (45). Its second assumption was to conflate labor and labor*er*, that is, to accept as natural the reduction of the living worker to a commodity, a thing. Once labor was substituted for laborer, classical economy was blind to the revolt of the workers. In briefly tracing "the Continuous Revolt of the Workers" which helped to signal "the End of Classical Political Economy," she called attention to the first form of trade unions, combinations, as well as the uprisings and revolts that challenged industrial production. Trade unions sprung up and with them strikes: "The labor*er* who had been left out of Ricardo's analysis loomed very large in the actual development of capitalist society. From the very birth of industrial capitalism the laborer has been in constant revolt. . . . [T]he workers were striking not against the machine but against the *uncontrolled power of capital*" (46, 47). The revolt of the workers and the general capitalist crisis, which had its first appearance in the 1820s, exposed the grave contradiction of classical political economy's "single economic law"—a theory of labor value that devalued the laborer.

Dunayevskaya showed how Marx separated himself from Smith and Ricardo. On the one hand, he appropriated their epic-making discovery of labor as the source of value in a capitalist industrial society. On the other, he critiqued them for their refusal to deal directly with the labor*er*; for seeing private property as a separate entity rather than arising from the fact that the workers' activity in the factory was an alien activity; for treating the capitalist method of production as a natural eternal order, rather than a social order which was historic and transitory.

While classical political economy's blindness to a movement from practice was to be expected—they were intellectuals who did not want to uproot capitalism, but to put it in on a solid, economic footing—the same cannot be said for the Utopian socialists. These intellectuals, who witnessed the inequalities of distribution that arose from the capitalist method of production, sympathized with the proletariat. "Being *outside* of production, however, the intellectual could not see that the working class had *power* to overthrow the contradictory conditions of production. For the intellectual, the proletariat existed only as a suffering class" (49). Instead of exposing the root error of classical political economy, "a crop of utopian socialists arose who wanted to 'use' the classical theory of labor as the source of value 'for' the working class. . . . The utopian socialists stayed away from the living movement of the working class" (49).

Foremost among these socialists was Pierre Proudhon. Dunayevskaya noted that he opposed strikes and worker combinations as well as political movements; that in place of any workers' independent activity he had a few abstract moral ideas on "justice" and "equality." She quoted Marx's critique of Proudhon: "In place of the great historic movement arising from the conflict between the productive forces already acquired by man and their social relations, which no longer correspond to these productive forces. . . . Monsieur Proudhon supplies the evacuating motion of his own head" (50). "The division between the radical intellectual like Proudhon and the Marxist intellectual" was one of *Marxism and Freedom's* important themes (Letter to Herbert Marcuse, *SRDC* #12176).

Proudhon's proposed schemes, from "people's banks" to "reunited labor and property," were all *"within the present system of production*, which was to remain intact" (51). Dunayevskaya pointed to Marx's profound response in *Poverty of Philosophy*: "Marx argued that to try 'to organize exchange,' in a society based on factory production, *must* mean its organization according to the division of labor in the factory where the authority of the capitalist is undisputed. To try to bring that 'principle of authority' into society as a whole could only mean subjecting society to one *single master*" (51-52). She called this Marx's "profound prediction of the totalitarianism to which abstract planning would inevitably lead" (52).

Dunayevskaya turned to Marx's early economic-philosophic writings, calling them "A New Humanism." She saw these manuscripts as so central to Marx's development, and so relevant for the contemporary radical movement, that she translated two essays from the *Economic-Philosophic Manuscripts* of 1844 into English. "Critique of the Hegelian Dialectic" and "Private Property and Communism" were published as appendices to the first edition of *Marxism and Freedom*.

It was not until almost completing *Marxism and Freedom* that Dunayevskaya had decided to publish these two essays by Marx as an appendix. The lateness of the decision perhaps spoke to the influence of the movement from practice to theory upon Dunayevskaya. With the East European revolts and revolutions of the mid-1950s, Marx's *Economic-Philosophic Manuscripts* were taken out of the archives and onto the world stage. Marx's humanism was found to speak to the revolutionary moment of the mid-twentieth century. It was as the writing of *Marxism and Freedom* was ending that Dunayevskaya created the category Marxist-Humanism to characterize her philosophic labors and the organization she founded.

In 1844, Marx wrote profoundly on the Hegelian dialectic while calling his own view a "thoroughgoing Naturalism or Humanism." For Dunayevskaya, this period was no mere "phase" that the young Marx "outgrew." Rather, his 1844 writings were "the foundation of historical materialism."[1] She saw these essays as closely tied to Marx's *Capital* and titled a later chapter, "The Humanism and Dialectic of *Capital*, Vol. I."

Dunayevskaya's discussion of the *Manuscripts* concentrated first on the integrality of Marx's response to the new proletarian impulses arising in the 1840s with his immersion in the Hegelian dialectic:

> The year 1844 saw new proletarian impulses literally reach up from the earth of the turbulent 1840's. . . . It was the same year of 1844 when Marx wrote his *Economic-Philosophic Manuscripts*. Here Marx posed dialectically the fundamental problem—what *kind* of labor. . . . [He] made this self-same question pivotal, *the* new theoretical response to the workers' revolt against the tyranny of factory labor. . . . He now saw the core of the Hegelian *method*—the self-movement which is internally necessary because it is the way of the organism's own development—in the self-activity of the proletariat (54-55).

In Marx's "Critique of the Hegelian Dialectic," Dunayevskaya noted how:

Marx criticizes Hegel's idealism. . . . But Marx praises, takes over, develops, the dialectic method. . . . absorbed and recreated the principle of "the negation of the negation"—or the revolutionary overcoming of real contradiction, that is to say, opposing class forces—not only in his early writings, but in *Capital* itself" (57).

A second theme Dunayevskaya discussed from these Essays was Marx's critique of the Utopian communists of his day for their one-dimensional view of tying all alienation to the fact of private property. She showed that when Marx appropriated "transcendence as objective movement" and "negation of the negation" from Hegel's *Phenomenology*, and looked at the reality of his day, he was able to draw the line between "vulgar communism," limited to the mere negation of private property, and his own philosophy of "positive Humanism beginning from itself." "In a word, another transcendence, *after* the abolition of private property is needed to achieve a truly new, *human* society" (58).

When Dunayevskaya took up Marx's essay "Private Property and Communism," she continued the discussion of Marx's conception of a new human society verses the Utopian communists' "total preoccupation with the question of private property." Quoting from Marx—"In the alienation of the object of labor is only crystallized, the estrangement, in the very activity of labor"—she returned again and again to his view of the needed emancipation of labor rather than a mere change of property forms. She felt the need to do this not only to set the record straight as to Marx's view, but also to clear the debris that had been piled upon Marx's concept in the 100 years since he had written his essays. Marx's emancipatory vision reached to the mid-20th century. It was "the totalitarian Communists of our day" that she battled.

This battle continued in the final section of the chapter, "Communism's Perversion of Marx's Economic-Philosophic Manuscripts." Dunayevskaya critiqued the attempt at "a total perversion of Marxian philosophy" on the part of a Soviet ideologue, V. A. Karpushin, who had written an article in Russia's leading philosophic journal denigrating the concept of transcendence through negation:

> Where Marx saw the negation of the negation, the Hegelian transcendence, as an *objective* movement, Karpushin made it "mystic" and "subordinate" to the struggle of opposites. Where Marx writes how "throughgoing Naturalism or Humanism distinguishes itself from both Idealism and Materialism and is at the same time the truth uniting both," Karpushin tried to turn Marx into a vulgar materialist, a practical man concerned with "practical problems"(63).

Here, as when critiquing Zhdanov's earlier attempt to put forth a new dialectical law of "criticism and self-criticism" in place of the Hegelian development through overcoming contradictions, Dunayevskaya was not simply pointing to an obscure academic debate. The reason for the attack on Marx's early writings was most concrete: "It is that actual world of Russia with its forced labor camps that compels this Russian attack against Marxism. It is not the idealism of Hegel that worries them. It is the revolutionary method of the dialectic and the Humanism of Marx that threatens their existence in theory even as the working class does in life" (63).

Only an individual reading of her chapter can do justice to the breadth and depth of her discussion of the young Marx. She strove to present the formation of the radical revolutionary intellectual Karl Marx as he emerged in the early and mid-1840s. She discerned what set him apart from the other radical intellectuals of this period—his mastery and re-creation of the Hegelian dialectic in fusion with the revolutionary activity of the proletariat discovering itself as a class. The Hegelianism and Humanism of Marx were inseparable. The *Economic-Philosophic Manuscripts* of 1844 were the process and result. Later, Dunayevskaya would call the period 1843-44, "The Philosophic Moment" of Marx.

•

In *Marxism and Freedom's* Part I "From Practice to Theory: 1776 to 1848," Dunayevskaya had opened with "The Age of Revolutions: Industrial, Social-Political, Intellectual." She traced the strands in thought that led to Marxism—French revolutionary doctrines, classical political economy, and German idealistic philosophy of Hegel. She concentrated on the triple break in thought Marx was compelled to make: (1) with the classical political economists' conclusions as they ignored the labor*er* in their labor theory of value; (2) with the Utopian socialists and communists of his day who were abhorred by and often fought against the abominable conditions the proletariat faced, but who failed to recognize the workers as self-actualizing subject of social transformation; and (3) a critique of Hegel for his "dehumanization of philosophy," but at the same time the deepest appropriation/re-creation of the dialectic as Marx encountered a new revolutionary element, the living working class struggles of the 1840s. The first great test in practice was at hand, the 1848 Revolutions. Dunayevskaya turned to that historic moment.

Part II, Worker and Intellectual at a Turning Point in History: 1848 to 1861

So crucial a turning point were the 1848 Revolutions and their aftermath that Dunayevskaya created an entire part, "Worker and Intellectual at a Turning Point in History: 1848 to 1861," for a single chapter, "Workers, Intellectual and the State." The chapter revolved around the role of the worker and the role of the radical intellectual in a period of revolutionary upheaval and consolidation of bourgeois state power. It was a turning point wherein the irreconcilable nature of the bourgeoisie and its state with the proletariat was demonstrated.

In the first section, The 1848 Revolutions and the Radical Intellectual, Dunayevskaya drew upon a number of Marx's works of the period—*The Communist Manifesto, The Class Struggles in France,* 1848-1850, "Address of the Communist League," and *The Eighteenth Brumaire of Louis Bonaparte*—to sharply contrast the self-activity of the French working masses, who exposed the irreconcilable class antagonism between themselves and the rising bourgeois state with the plans and schemes of the radical intellectuals, who were "blind to the creative energies of the masses." At the same time, she showed the separation between those radical intellectuals and Marx, who kept "his eyes glued instead to the activity of the masses," and "was able to generalize their creative activities into a *theory* of liberation" (74).

The chapter continued the structure of Part I, From Practice to Theory, in describing the activity of the Parisian workers and students in 1848, first in February in forcing the newly formed Provisional Government to declare a Republic and demanding the formation of a Labor Ministry, and then in June, challenging the state, raising the slogan "Down with the bourgeoisie!" Though brutally defeated, a new historic moment had arisen:

> The true essence of the 1848 revolutions was now revealed: it was the emancipation of labor. . . . [T]he bloodletting could not erase the accomplishments of those few months: 1) abolition of slavery in the colonies; 2) abolition of the death penalty; 3) abolition of imprisonment for debt; 4) universal suffrage; 5) the ten-hour day (72).

Through the eyes of Marx, Dunayevskaya followed the events of 1848-1851:

• In the *Communist Manifesto*, Marx had anticipated the working class nature of the revolt, "Workingmen of the world, unite! You have nothing to lose but your chains. You have a world to gain." Dunayevskaya noted that none of the other radical intellectuals had anticipated this mass uprising from below. They had focused on a conspiratorial *coup* or schemes. Instead, the revolution released new activities and talents: "In a few weeks, 171 newspapers appeared. . . . [R]evolutionary workers' clubs sprung up all over Paris—145 of them in the first month" (71).

• Quoting Marx's *Class Struggles in France,* Dunayevskaya drew from his description "of this first great battle between the two classes" (72).

• From Marx's "Address to the Communist League" she pointed to Marx's conclusion of a revolution in permanence, when in June 1849 the workers, "fought the bourgeoisie, the capitalistic order and fought it by *their own great combined resources*" (72-3): "They placed themselves in violent contradiction with the very conditions of existence of bourgeois society by declaring the revolution permanent" (Marx, quoted 73).

- From the *18th Brumaire of Louis Bonaparte*, she caught Marx's sharp dismissal of the petty-bourgeois thought of the radical intellectual of the period as she pointed to Marx's very different sensitivity to proletarian creativity.

Dunayevskaya summed up the meaning of 1848 in the activities of the workers and in the thought of Marx as he responded:

> The true essence of the 1848 revolutions was now revealed: it was the emancipation of labor. . . . Marx's discovery—that the objective movement itself produces the subjective force for its overthrow—transformed utopian socialism into scientific socialism. It drew a sharp class line between the intellectuals (utopians) who would continue with their schemes and the proletariat itself which had now separated itself from these sects and was creating movements of its own . . . The division between the creative energies of the masses on the one hand, and the plans of the radical intellectuals, on the other, widened and deepened in the 1848 revolutions because the proletariat had gained consciousness of itself as a class (72-3).

In the second part of the chapter, Dunayevskaya discussed "Ferdinand Lassalle, State Socialist." Here was a revolutionary intellectual who did consider himself a follower of Marx's thought and yet, "Marx had to separate himself sharply from this perverse progeny of his" (74). Dunayevskaya wrote of Lassalle's determination to find a "short-cut to socialism" through a compromise with Bismarck, the chancellor of the Prussian absolutist state:

> It is not that Lassalle misunderstood the class nature of the State. But he could not rid himself of the concept of the "backwardness" of labor, despite the glorious pages it wrote in nineteen century history. . . . Lassalle conceived it to be his duty to "bridge the gulf between the thinkers and the masses" (74).

Lassalle was able to build what Marx never had, a large independent political party of the German proletariat, the German Workers Association. Dunayevskaya pointed out that Lassalle was no armchair socialist, but an activist. Nor was he a "traitor:" "He could not have been bought. He fought for his principles, went to prison for them and would have been ready to die for them" (76). Nevertheless, because "he did not believe in the masses ability to overcome their conditions of labor" (75), and felt that Marx was "too abstract," he had nowhere to go except collaboration with the Prussian government. Dunayevskaya quoted Marx's view of Lassalle:

> "His attitude," wrote Marx, "is that of a future workers' dictator. He resolves the question between labor and capital as easily as play. The workers are to agitate for universal suffrage and then send people like himself armed with the shining sword of science into Parliament. They will establish workers' factories, for which the state will put up capital, and by and by these institutions will embrace the whole country" (77).

For Dunayevskaya, the period 1848-61 shed illumination "on the relationship of the worker and intellectual," disclosing "the administrative *type* long before the administrators are armed with power." Lassalle was "the anticipation of the State Socialist administrator of our day" (77). Marx, as Dunayevskaya showed us, viewed his role as revolutionary intellectual/activist in a quite different manner. It would come to its fullest expression in *Capital*.

Part III, Marxism: The Unity of Theory and Practice

The four chapters that focused on the historical moment in which *Capital* was written and subsequently deepened, and then discussed the structure and content of all three volumes, form one of the most cogent expositions of Marx's greatest theoretical work written in the twentieth century. Dunayevskaya presented Marxism as the unity of theory and practice from the opening sentences: "The decade of the 1860's was decisive for the structure of Marx's greatest theoretical work, *Capital*. . . . *Capital* . . . is proof of the creative impact of masses in motion on theory" (81).

The first two chapters of Part III, "The Impact of the Civil War in the United States on the Structure of *Capital*," and "The Paris Commune Illuminates and Deepens the Content of *Capital*," spelled out concretely the impact of masses in motion on Marx's theoretical labor. Dunayevskaya placed these two chapters on the historical framework of *Capital* before the two chapters that discussed the content. The unity of theory and practice began with recognition of the movement from practice to theory.

Dunayevskaya's opening section on the impact of the Civil War took up "The Abolitionists, the Civil War, and the First International." She singled out Marx's 1860s concentration on the abolitionist John Brown, and on a slave rising, and then, in the midst of the Civil War, his propagandizing abroad the ideas of the Abolitionists, and calling for the use of Black troops in the war.

Dunayevskaya traced the relation of the origins of the First Workingman's International, which Marx helped to found and was a central figure within, to the Civil War: "It was under the impact of the Civil War and the response of the European workers as well as the Polish insurrection, that the International Working Men's Association, known as the First International, was born."

It was not only as propagandist and organization man that Marx had a relationship to the anti-slavery movement and Civil War in America, but as theorist as well. She discussed Marx's bringing the Civil War directly into the pages of *Capital*:

> His analysis of the struggle for the shortening of the working day comes to a climax . . . when he writes of the relationship of the end of slavery to the struggle for the eight hour day: "In the United States of North America, every independent movement of the workers was paralyzed so long as slavery disfigured a

part of the Republic. Labor cannot emancipate itself in the white skin where in the black it is branded. But out of the death of slavery a new life at once arose. The first fruit of the Civil War was the eight hours' agitation, that ran with the seven-leagued boots of the locomotive from the Atlantic to the Pacific, from New England to California" (84).

In the second section of the chapter, "The Relation of History to Theory," Dunayevskaya turned to detail the impact of the working class activities of the 1860s on the structure of *Capital*. She contrasted Marx's 1859 *Critique of Political Economy*—what she termed "The Limits of an Intellectual Work"—to "The Working Day [section of *Capital*] and the Break with the Concept of Theory." In *Critique*, Dunayevskaya showed that Marx had worked out the duality of use-value and exchange-value inherent in the commodity as originating in the two-fold nature of labor in capitalist society: concrete and abstract labor. At the same time, she noted: "The truth is that the work, both in its special and in its general aspects, lacks a structure, a shape that can come only out of the developing class itself."

The 1850s, following the defeat of the 1848 Revolutions, were a quiescent period in terms of workers' activity:

> What happens to a theoretician, to any theoretician, even to a Marx, when the proletarian revolutions are crushed, is that he must watch the laws of economic development of the old social order without being able to see the *specific* form of revolt with which the workers mean to meet the new stage of production (87).

Dunayevskaya thus called *Critique* an "intellectual," a "remote" work. She characterized it as an "application" of dialectics rather than "the *creation* of the dialectic that would arise out of the workers' struggles themselves."

Turning to the structural changes within *Capital*, Dunayevskaya concentrated on "The Working Day" chapter, which Marx had not formulated until 1866. The chapter traced capitalism's werewolf appetite for surplus labor, obtained by ever lengthening the proletariat's working day, and then followed the workers' historic struggle for the shortening of their working day. Marx's creation of this chapter represented a break with the concept of theory as a debate among intellectuals:

> "The establishment of a normal working day," [Marx] wrote, "is the result of centuries of struggle between capitalist and laborer." Marx's method of analysis was revolutionized thereby. Where, in his *Critique*, history and theory are separated, with a historical explanation attached to each theoretical chapter; in *Capital*, history and theory are inseparable. Where, in *Critique*, history is the history of theory; in *Capital*, history is the history of the class struggle (89).

The working class activity of the 1860s, particularly the renewed struggle for a shorter working day, had released in Marx a new concept of theory. Theory now became the revolutionary interchange between the self-activity of a working class in motion and the radical intellectual having all his senses attuned to that self-activity. As Dunayevskaya wrote:

> Marx's shift from the history of *theory* to the history of *production relations* gives flesh and blood to the generalization that Marxism is the theoretical expression of the instinctive strivings of the proletariat for liberation. . . . Marx, the theoretician, created new categories out of the impulses from the workers (89, 91).

Leaving the crucial addition of the chapter on the Working Day as illuminating Marx's new concept of theory, Dunayevskaya took up how Marx "turned everything around" from the first draft of the *Capital* manuscript to what was finally published as Volume I, in Marx's lifetime, and Volumes II and III, via Engels following out Marx's plan. The key was Marx's shifting the discussions on the history of theory out of Volume I. "*He is breaking with the whole concept of theory as something intellectual, a dispute between theoreticians*" (91). *Capital* now becomes "a *new philosophy, the philosophy* of labor" (90).

Dunayevskaya's chapter was a discussion of the relation of theory and practice, of the *meaning* of theory for Marx and thus for Marxism today. She sharply posed her conclusion: "He who glorifies theory and genius but fails to recognize the *limits* of a theoretical work, fails likewise to recognize the *indispensability of the theoretician*" (89).

In beginning Chapter Six, "The Paris Commune Illuminates and Deepens the Content of *Capital*," Dunayevskaya posed a crucial contradiction of capitalist production that the Paris Commune brought to the fore: "The Despotic Plan of Capital vs. the Cooperation of Freely Associated Labor." The plan of capitalist production showed itself in the labor process to be despotic, to be "the undisputed authority of the capitalist" (92). Aligned against it was the cooperative plan of freely associated labor—working women and men deciding amongst themselves what they would produce and how they would go about the production process. What was theoretically posed by Marx in *Capital* before the Paris Commune—the creativity of freely associated cooperative labor—became reality in the Commune. It was a reality that exposed the mind-forged manacles that adhered to the despotic plan of capitalist production as the Commune proceeded through "its own working existence" to present a different manner of organizing work.

Dunayevskaya wrote of how, "the despotic plan inherent in capitalist production reveals itself in a form all its own—*the hierarchic structure of control over social labor*" (92). An army of foreman, managers and superintendents "to force labor out of the many laborers." This capitalist-directed cooperation was in opposition to cooperating laborers: "The opposition is between the *nature* of the cooperative form of labor and the capitalist *form* of value production." Because cooperative labor under capitalism was confined to the production of value, it could not develop freely.

Even machinery, technology, was not developed to express its full potentiality. Its development was not classless, but narrowed to "the single purpose of extracting ever greater amounts of surplus, unpaid labor from the workers" (93). Thus, the workers' initial resistance to the machine accurately reflected the fact that "the first appearance of machinery as a handmaiden of capital was its *true* appearance" (94). Through further struggles the worker turned from fighting the instrument of labor to opposing "the capitalistic employment of it—the conditions of production which transformed him into a cog in the machine" (94). The struggle of the workers against the capitalist conditions of labor was not an opposition to science and technology but to capitalism's degrading of science. "The workers thus at one and the same time fight for their emancipation and against the capitalistic limitations of science and technology" (94).

Dunayevskaya now took up the Paris Commune. The Commune helped to illuminate capitalism's contradictions, particular the fetishism of commodities. In response to the experience of the Commune, Marx significantly enriched the French edition of *Capital*. In describing the Commune, Dunayevskaya contrasted the secret insurrectionary plans of the Blanquists and the Utopian schemes of the Proudhonists to the open, mass revolutionary activity of the Parisian men and women as they created something entirely new:

> The first act of the Revolution was to arm itself. The armed people struck out against the everywhere present state organs—the army, the police, officialdom—which were such a faithful copy of the hierarchic division of labor in the factory. The first workers' state in history, called the Commune of Paris, was born. . . . The armed people smashed parliamentarianism. The people's assembly was not to be a parliamentary talking-shop but a *working body*. . . . *[T]he power remained always in the hands of the mass as a whole* (96).

The Commune in its brief two months existence had reorganized all of society: public services were to be performed at workman's wages; education was to be open and free to all, involving the fullest participation of the whole people; political rule began with destroying the state form of capital's rule and replacing it with a commune-type of self-government—what Marx had called "the political form at last discovered to work out the economic emancipation of the proletariat."

Perhaps the most crucial reorganization was the Commune's form of cooperative production:

> The Commune's workshops were models of proletarian democracy. The workers themselves appointed the directors, shop and bench foremen. They were subject to dismissal by the workers if relations or conditions proved unsatis-

factory. Not only were wages, hours, and working conditions set, above all, *a factory committee met every evening to discuss the next day's work* (96).

The Commune's revolutionary working existence had "shed new insight into the perversity of relations under capitalism. . . . By exposing the bourgeois State as the public force of social enslavement that it was, the proletariat demonstrated how the *absolutely new form of cooperation*, released from its value-integument, expressed itself" (98). It was precisely here, from the Communards' self-activity in the workplace, that Marx gained new insight into the origins and nature of the fetishism of commodities, which characterized capitalist production. Because Dunayevskaya traced Marx's new discovery in a meticulous manner we quote from it extensively:

> Marx asks: "Whence then arise the enigmatical character of the product of labor, so soon as it assumes the *form* of commodities?" And he answers simply: "clearly from this form itself."
> Pervious to this edition [the French edition of *Capital*], this was not so clear to anyone, not even to Marx. The simplicity of expression achieved in 1872 is worth tracing, especially since the significance has been lost.
> There is nothing simple about a commodity. It is a great fetish that makes the despotic *conditions* of capitalist production *appear* as if they were self-evident truths of social production. Nothing could be further from the truth. Just as these conditions were *historically* determined and rest on the servitude of the laborer, so the commodity, from the start of capitalism, is a reflection of the dual character of labor. It is, from the start, a unity of opposites—use-value and value—which, in embryo, contains *all* the contradictions of capitalism.
> This simple relationship was beyond the perception of the greatest bourgeois economist, Ricardo, despite the earlier discovery of labor as the source of value. Although classical political economy had reduced value to its content, it had never once asked WHY did this *content*, labor, assumed this *form* value?
> Long before *Capital*, Marx had analyzed the duality pervading bourgeois society: "In our days everything seems pregnant with its contrary; machinery, gifted with the wonderful power of shortening and fructifying human labor, we behold starving and overworking it. The new-fangled sources of wealth, by some strange weird spell, are turned into sources of want. The victories of arms seem bought by the loss of character. At the same pace that mankind masters nature, man seems to become enslaved to other men or to his own infamy. Even the pure light of science seems unable to shine but on a dark background of ignorance. All our inventions and progress seem to result in endowing material forms with intellectual life, and in stultifying human life into a material force. This antagonism between modern industry and science on the one hand, modern misery and dissolution on the other hand; this antagonism between the production powers and the social relations of our epoch is a fact, palpable, overwhelming, and not to be controverted."
> In general, *but only in general*, the logic of content and form of labor was actual to Marx's thinking from the very beginning when he worked out the concept of alienated labor. Nevertheless, insofar as economic *categories* were con-

cerned, he accepted them, more or less, as worked out by classical political economy. That is true as late as the publication of *Critique of Political Economy* in 1859, when he still used exchange-value in the sense of value and not in the sense of value-*form*. He still was "taking for granted" that "everyone knows" that production relations are really involved in the exchange of things.

By 1867, in the first edition of *Capital*, he singles out the commodity-*form* as the fetish. Even here, the main emphasis is on the *fantastic* form of appearance of production relations as exchange of things. It is only *after* the eruption of the Paris Commune that his French edition shifts the emphasis from the fantastic form of appearance to the *necessity* of that form of appearance because that is, *in truth*, what relations of people *are* at the point of production: "material relations between persons and social relations between things."

Having located the trouble at its source, Marx sees that a product of labor *can have no other form than that of a commodity*. Thus, to the question: whence the fetishism of commodities?—the answer is simple and direct: "Clearly from the form itself" (99-100).

•

Dunayevskaya turned to discuss each of the three volumes of *Capital* as a whole, taking up Volume One, in Chapter Seven, "The Humanism and Dialectic of *Capital*, Volume I, 1867 to 1883." The title illustrated her view of *Capital* encompassing more than an analysis of bourgeois economic relations. For Dunayevskaya, the strands of humanism and the dialectic were not adjuncts to his economic analysis, but the core of Marx's critique of bourgeois society. The humanism was not an abstraction but emerged as historical: "There are two movements in *Capital*: the historical and the logical. . . . [They] . . . are not two separate movements: the dialectic contains them both. It is not that Marx has interrelated them. It is the very nature of one to contain the other" (117, 120). As she wrote in a letter to Herbert Marcuse, "[I]n The Dialectical Humanism of Volume I, I show that not only are Marx's economic categories social categories but they are thoroughly permeated with the humanism that came out of the working class struggles for the shortening of the working day." (June 11, 1957. See appendix to Chapter Five for text of letter.)

The dates of Dunayevskaya's chapter title—1867, the initial publication of *Capital*, and 1883, Marx's death—illustrated Marx's continuous rethinking. "Volume I, on which Marx never stopped working until the day of his death in 1883, is the one complete volume we have from his own hand" (134). As we have seen, she made a specific category out of the changes introduced by Marx to the French edition (1872-75).

Marxism and Freedom's chapter on Volume One of *Capital* was a crystallization of Marx's 800-page *oeuvre* in a scant twenty odd pages. One cannot "summarize" or excerpt the tightly woven presentation without doing damage to its dialectical structure. Here I only sketch out and list some of the topics covered for a reader to explore further.

A significant part in the chapter was Dunayevskaya's explication of Marx's three original categories:

In analyzing the economic system of capitalism, Marx wrote some five thousand pages, or about two million words. Throughout this gigantic work, he was able to use the categories already established by classical economy. He refined value—and with it surplus value—but he took over the categories themselves from classical economics. In three instances, *and in three instances only*, he had to *create entirely new categories*. These are: labor power, constant capital and variable capital (112).

Labor power was taken up in the opening section, "The Split in the Category of Labor: Abstract and Concrete Labor, Labor and Labor Power." Dunayevskaya straightforwardly followed Marx's movement from the duality of use-value and value of the commodity to his analysis of abstract and concrete labor:

> What is *new* in *Capital*. . . . is that Marx now goes directly to the labor process itself. The analysis of the capitalist labor process is the cornerstone of the Marxian theory. Here we see what *kind* of labor produces value—abstract labor—and *how* concrete individual labor with specific skills becomes *reduced*, by the discipline of the factory clock, to nothing but a producer of a mass of congealed abstract labor (104-05).

While there is no such organism as an abstract laborer, "the instrumentality of the machine, which expresses itself in the ticking of a factory clock" (105), turns all concrete, specific labor (of a machinist, tailor, or steelworker), into a mass of products turned out in a given amount to time, abstract labor. Abstract labor is quantified as the *socially-necessary* labor time to produce a given commodity. "Constant technological revolutions change *how much* labor time is socially necessary" (105).

Dunayevskaya contrasted capitalism's inhuman system of production to Marx's attention to the worker's quest for his/her wholeness:

> There is nothing intellectual or deductive about the worker's individual skills being alienated from him to become social labor whose only specific feature is that it is "human." It is a very real and very degrading labor process, which accomplishes this transformation. It is called the factory. Marx's concept of the degraded worker seeking universality, seeking to be a whole man, transformed the science of political economy into the science of human liberation (105-06).

Dunayevskaya followed Marx into the factory where labor power became manifest: "What he did that was new," was to show "what *type* of labor creates values and *hence* surplus values, and the *process* by which this is done. . . . how *inequality* arose out of the *equality* of the market. That is because, in the millions of commodities exchanged daily, *one and only one*, labor power, is incorporated in a living person" (106, 107). She added:

But in the factory "it" is no longer a commodity—"it" is the *activity* itself, labor. True, the living laborer is made to work beyond the value of his labor power. His sweat congeals into unpaid labor. That precisely is the "miracle" of surplus value: that labor power is incorporated in the living laborer, who can be, and is, made to produce a greater value than he himself is (108).

Dunayevskaya followed what the splitting of the old category labor into labor as activity and ability to labor, or labor power, the commodity, meant for Marx in his creation of a chapter on "Cooperation." Marx described a new social power: "Not only have we here an increase in the productive power of the individual by means of cooperation, but the creation of a new owner, namely, the collective power of masses. . . . When the laborer cooperates systematically with others, he strips off the fetters of his individuality and develops the capacities of his species" (quoted, 109, 110). However under capitalism, this natural form of cooperation was stifled and subverted to the capitalist Plan, wherein "the powerful will of" the capitalist subjected the workers' activity "to his aim."

Throughout the chapter, Dunayevskaya's view of the humanist dimension of *Capital* came to the fore:

> What characterizes *Capital* from beginning to end is the concern with living human beings. . . . Because Marx thought first and foremost of how the workers feel, he could anticipate the key question of our epoch: is productivity to be increased by the expansion of machinery or by the expansion of human capacities? (109)

Dunayevskaya discussed the Marxian economic categories, constant and variable capital in the second section of the chapter. She defined the terms—

> (1) *Constant capital* comprises the means of production and raw materials, the dead labor. They undergo no change in magnitude in the process of production . . . . (2) *Variable capital* is labor in the actual process of production. It does undergo a variation in the magnitude since it reproduces not only its own value, but an unpaid surplus. . . . Marx is most specific and adamant about naming *both* factors of production *capital* (112-13).

—and gave these terms corporal presence in describing how a worker works:

> The radio assembler whose line has to produce 75 to 90 radios an hour will not stop to inquire into its mechanics. He will know only that it means making eight connections per radio, and the wires mean to him only blue, red and green colors so that his eye can pick them out without stopping to consider. He will twist about 4800 wires per day, and his hands will handle the pair of pliers with such speed that the chassis do not pile up alongside his bench.
> This, Marx calls the real subordination of labor to capital. That is how accumulated labor [dead labor] dominates living labor. It is this domination which

turns accumulated labor into capital, a force divorced from the direct producer and exploiting him (113).

Capital demonstrated how accumulated labor and living labor—constant capital and variable capital—did battle as capitalism developed, historically and logically, extracting surplus value from living labor. Surplus value was first created by the extension of the working day, *absolute surplus value*. The worker resisted, fought for the shortening of the working day. Capitalism fought back with its most potent weapon, technological development, which made possible the extraction of greater surplus value within the same working day, *relative surplus value*. Dunayevskaya followed out these categories from Marx and laid out the parameters of the battlefield:

> [W]e can see how Marx's new categories—constant and variable capital—illuminate the ever greater contradictions of capitalist production. The constant capital—the machinery—undergoes no change in value, no matter how light or how hard it is worked. The laborer, with his concrete type of labor, can transfer the value of the machine to the new product only to the extent of its original value, that is to say, the socially necessary labor time it took to produce it. As dead matter, machinery is incapable of creating value and gains nothing from the labor process. The capitalist is therefore fully dependent on his other type of capital, variable capital—the labor power of the living laborer, who therefore, must be forced to produce ever more. When this can no longer be done through the lengthening of the working day, it must be done by speed-up. This is where the factory clock plays its part. It is now not merely a sort of counting machine for quantity of output. It has become a *measure of the intensity* of labor itself. The surplus labor or value thus extracted is related *directly* to the wear and tear of the laborer himself (115).

This battle to extract an ever greater amount of surplus value, and the workers' continual resistance were present at each stage in the development of capitalist production. The drive to gain a value greater than the value which the capitalist expends, "this is the essence of capitalist production. This is what Marx called 'the *characteristic specific nature*' of capitalist production'" (118).

Dunayevskaya ended this section by again returning to the historical and logical as one

> Having traced the dialectical development of the two opposites, living labor and dead labor, labor and machinery, from *"Cooperation"* through the *"Division of Labor and Manufacture"* to *"Machinery and Modern Industry,"* Marx concludes that there is no other than the *historical* solution to the "revolutionary ferments, the final result of which is the abolition of the old division of labor, diametrically opposed to the capitalistic form of production and to the economic status of the laborer corresponding to that form" (119).

In turning to "The Accumulation of Capital" she refused to separate Marx's analysis of capitalism's logic of development from posing its absolute opposite—"the New Forces and New Passions." Marx's discussion of each development of capital and capitalism was inseparable from his focus on the condition and revolt of the worker:

- An increase in the "organic composition of capital"—the preponderance of constant over variable capital—meant the further subjugation of worker to machine.
- The centralization of the means of production (capital) meant the socialization of labor. But socialization under capitalism meant the growth of "misery, oppression, slavery, degradation, exploitation, but with this too grows the revolt of the working class" (Marx, quoted, 122).
- "The end result of this relation of capital to the lot of the working class is the great, the insoluble contradiction which is wrecking the entire system—the unemployed army. Marx calls this *'the absolute general law of capitalist accumulation'*" (123).

The humanism of the text of *Capital* was what Dunayevskaya illustrated. Her ultimate paragraph of the chapter read:

> Thus the development of capitalism itself creates the basis of a new Humanism—the "new forces and new passions" which will reconstruct society on new, truly human beginnings, "a society in which the full and free development of every individual is the ruling principle." It is because Marx based himself on this Humanism, more popularly called "the inevitability of socialism," that he could discern the law of motion of capitalist society, the inevitability of its collapse. The Humanism of *Capital* runs like a red thread throughout the work. This gives it both its profundity and its force and direction (125).

•

In Chapter Eight Dunayevskaya takes up "The Logic and Scope of *Capital*, Volumes II and III." Again here, as for Volume I, we can only hint at the vast canvass Dunayevskaya painted. In writing of Volume II Dunayevskaya concentrated on two factors: (1) Marx's demonstration that the process of circulation was rooted in the process of production and reproduction. (2) the fact that the critics of Volume Two, including Marxists, were blinded by the market and emergence of imperialism in the late 19th century and early 20th century capitalism, and thus missed that the reality of capitalist economics was in concert with Marx's theoretical suppositions.

In taking up Marx's argument that circulation was rooted in production, Dunayevskaya described Marx's premise of the division of the entire social product into only two main departments: "Department I produces means of production, and Department II produces means of consumption. . . . The relationship between the two branches is not merely a technical one. It is rooted in the class relationship between the worker and the capitalist" (126). Surplus value did not float free. It was embodied within means of production and means of consumption. To obtain greater surplus value greater social product had to be produced. This could only occur through an increase in means of production, expanded reproduction.

> Marx established that the social product cannot be "either" means of production "or" means of consumption. There is a *preponderance* of means of production *over* means of consumption. Marx's point here is that the *bodily* form of value predetermines the *destination* of commodities: iron is not consumed by people but by steel; sugar is not consumed by machines but by people. . . . The use-values produced are not those used by workers, nor even by capitalists, *but by capital*. . . . Under *capitalism* the means of production form the greater part of the two departments of social production and, *therefore*, also of the "market." That is what Marx called "the real being of capital," and that is why the market was not the problem (127-28).

The consumption market could not be larger than the luxuries of the capitalists and the needs of the workers, paid at value. Therefore the only market that could expand was the capital goods market. "Means of production literally shot up to the sky" (128).

Dunayevskaya described Marx's construction of a closed capitalist society, "an isolated society dominated by the law of value" (128), consisting of only workers and capitalists. All other elements were subordinate, including foreign trade, though this closed capitalist society was in the environment of the world market, and hence had to continually compare its prices to those of the whole world. The purpose for such a construction was to demonstrate the direction of capital's development without getting caught in the phenomena of capital's appearance. In this closed capitalist society,

> each of the two departments of social production comprises three elements: (1) constant capital; (2) variable capital; and (3) surplus value. Just as the division of social production into two main departments was not merely technical, so this was not a merely technical division. It was rooted in the relationship of worker to capitalist, and was inseparable from the inherent laws of capitalist production (130).

Adam Smith had argued that the constant portion of capital would "in the final analysis" dissolve into wages. Dunayevskaya took up Marx's demonstration that the truth was the opposite—the continual growth of constant capital. "Marx's categories are so immutable for capitalism and apply to no other society. They assume that what is produced is consumed because it is *capitalist* production, and capitalist production is the production of capital and hence is *consumed by capital*" (131). Far from constant capital being dissolved into wages, Marx showed it would continually increase and dominate the living worker.

Other economists had argued that the crisis in capitalism came from overproduction, that the workers could never buy back all that was produced, hence there was underconsumption. "What Marx did in disproving the underconsumption theory was to demonstrate that there is no direct connection between production and consumption. . . . Volume II is both a critique of bourgeois and petty-bourgeois thought, and an analysis of the actual movement of capitalist society" (131, 132).

In the section titled "Appearance and Reality," Dunayevskaya discussed the reception of Volume II's publication, particularly among Marxists. Her concentration was on Rosa Luxemburg, whose *Accumulation of Capital* attempted to revise Marx's theory of accumulation. Dunayevskaya showed how Luxemburg was blinded by the appearance of imperialism into mistaking what was the reality of capitalism's mode of accumulation: "She was betrayed by the powerful historical development of imperialism that was taking place, to substitute the relationship of capitalism to non-capitalism for the relationship of capital to labor" (133).

Dunayevskaya ended her discussion of Vol. II by looking at Marx's projection of "a non-existence, fantastic society" in his day (the 1870's) in relation to the reality of her day. She noted his major premises—"The worker will be paid at value." "The means of production will far outdistance the means of consumption."—and looked at their viability in terms of the state-capitalist world that had emerged with the Depression. Far from being fantasy, she argued that Marx's idealized capitalist society spoke to the reality, the crisis, of capitalist production in Russia and in the U.S. "The only possibility of avoiding capitalist crises is the abrogation of the law of value. . . . What to Marx was theory is a most concrete problem now. Russia is proof of the fact that the logic and scope of Marxian theory are as integrally connected as are appearance and reality in life" (136-37).

In Dunayevskaya's discussion of Volume III of *Capital*, "The Breakdown of Capitalism: Crises, Human Freedom, and Volume III of *Capital*," she continually linked all three volumes of *Capital*:

> Marx develops his analysis of capitalism on different levels of abstraction and each level has its own dialectic. In Volume I, the categories which enabled us to comprehend the realities of production were: constant and variable capital (labor power). In Volume II, where we are on the surface of society, the categories which disclose the inner mechanism are: *means of production and means of consumption*. In Volume III, it is the decline in the rate of profit, "the general contradiction of capitalistic production that reveals its law of motion and points to its collapse" (139-40).

It was the crash of 1929 that alerted the academic economists to Marx's analysis of the breakdown of capitalism. They were attracted to his analysis of "real life"—rent, profit, competition, cyclical crisis. But what was the result?

> At the end of all these intricate transformations of surplus value into ground rent, interest and profit, as well as the conversion of values into prices, rate of surplus value into rate of profit, etc.—at the end of it all, Marx takes us back to that on which it is based: production of value and surplus value. . . .
> Nothing fundamental had changed; nothing whatever. Labor power, which is the supreme commodity of capitalist production because *it* alone creates capital, is still a commodity, sold at value, and—still *in* the process of production and *not* in the process of exchange or the market—creates a greater value than it itself is (141).

It was from within value production itself that the inherent contradiction in capitalism's development arose. Dunayevskaya quoted from Volume III of *Capital*:

> In order to produce the same rate of profit, when the constant capital set in motion by one laborer increases ten-fold, the surplus labor time would have to increase ten-fold, and soon the total labor time, and finally the fully twenty-four hours a day would not suffice, even if wholly appropriated by capital (Quoted, 141).

This was the logic of capital's development. It was what made the worker a producer of overproduction. On the one hand the constant revolutions in production and constant expansion of constant capital demanded a larger market, on the other it could not be larger. The decline in the rate of profit—"due to the fact of the relative ever-smaller use of living labor, which is the only source of surplus value, to ever-greater use of machines"—made it impossible to continually increase the market. Dunayevskaya quoted Marx: "The real barrier of capitalist production is capital itself."

In the last part of the chapter, Dunayevskaya again returned to the relationship of the three volumes of *Capital* and to what Marx had hoped to do with the uncompleted Volume III, as well as the unfinished rewriting of Volume II. But Dunayevskaya was not making an argument for what remained unwritten:

> *Essentially* Marx said what he wanted to say. This is true not only of Volumes II and III, which Engels edited with scrupulous care and presented exactly as Marx had written, but even Book IV, with the structure of which Karl Kautsky did tamper when he published it as *Theories of Surplus Value*. The reason is that Volume I, published by Marx is not only, as he put it, a whole in itself. *It is the whole* (146).

Dunayevskaya briefly discussed how Marx's reorganization of "Accumulation of Capital" showed where Volumes II and III "belong logically, *how* they are dialectically connected with Volume I and *what* is the law of motion of capitalism in general and the dialectic of his analysis in particular" (146).

Organizational Interlude

As *Marxism and Freedom* came off the press Dunayevskaya wrote:

> Marx's *Capital* that entirely NEW ORGANIZATION OF THOUGHT upon which no new organization has been built. That may sound like a fantastic contradiction, a complete untruth, the throwing out of the history of the Second International and hence the years 1889-1914. Nevertheless, among the new things in *M&F* . . . is that history under the title Organizational Interlude ("The American Roots of Marxism in the World Today and Our Development" *RDC* #2597).

Because she saw the International as never establishing continuity with Marx, Dunayevskaya decided not to place "The Second International, 1889 to 1914," as a Part. Rather, she considered that there had been an Organizational Interlude in the history of Marxist thought: "Despite [the Second International's] adherence to Marxist 'language,' *there was no organization of Marxist thought*" (*Marxism and Freedom*, 156). In arriving at such a conclusion, Dunayevskaya traced the origins and development of the Second, and in particular, its lack of response to the first great revolutionary moment of the 20th Century, the 1905 Russian Revolution: "When the great 1905 Revolution broke out and involved hundreds of thousands it was not on the agenda [of the 1907 Congress of the Second International] as a separate point. . . . In a word, the Second International was from the beginning to the end a West European organization" (151). It had been born only a half dozen years after Marx's death (1883), in 1889, on the 100th anniversary of the fall of the Bastille as the French Revolution began:

> For a quarter of a century the Second International was to experience unprecedented growth, be respected as a powerful organization and stand for established Marxism. Suddenly, and against the basis of its very existence as an opponent of capitalism, it collapsed in the face of Western Civilization's plunge into the chaos of the First World War (151).

While the fall of the Second was unexpected, even to as great a revolutionary as Lenin, Dunayevskaya argued that there was a "slow poisoning of Marxism, *long before* the collapse" (151). The origins were first of all in Second International Marxist theoreticians' methodology: "The *methodology* to be learned by rote, and disregarding the *process*, the relationship of theory to history, past and present, in the development of Marxism" (152). Central here were the writings of Karl Kautsky, including *Economic Doctrines of Karl Marx*, which set the ground for popularizations and applications of Marxism lacking any of the underlying philosophic concepts.

Second, was the International's concept and practice of organization, especially by its largest party, the German Social Democracy:

> The key word, in theory as well as in practice, was: Organization, organization, organization. It lived entirely in the realm of the difference between immediate demands and the ultimate goals of socialism. The ultimate goals of socialism could wait. Meanwhile, there was the "practical" struggle and in that they could show phenomenal gains (153).

In a section on "Achievements of the Second International," Dunayevskaya showed how trade union and political organization of the proletariat were indeed achieved, sending Social-Democratic deputies to parliament, and building trade unions with millions of members. However, the Social Democracy's idea of organization was narrowly constructed: "No word was used with greater contempt than 'unorganized'. . . . They had contempt not alone for small-scale enterprises but for the great mass of peasantry, and not only for the artisans but for the great mass of unorganized workers" (155).

The Second's concept of organization dovetailed with the new stage of capitalist production—monopoly with its extension into imperialism—and with the stratification of the proletariat. A section of the proletariat, the organized skilled trades—what Lenin would later call the aristocracy of labor—who objectively began to have a stake in capitalism's monopoly-imperialistic development, was the narrow segment of the working class that the Second International organized.

Because the monopoly stage would supposedly bring "order" to the markets, an "organized capitalism," "all" that was necessary was for the working class organized into trade unions and the political party of Social Democracy to take over the existing economic and social forms:

> There is no longer any sense of breaking the chains of the ubiquitous capitalist machine, nor is there the faintest glimmer of the idea that "the dictatorship of the proletariat" or "the workers organized as the ruling class" means the total reorganization of the relations of men at the point of production *by the men themselves* (163).

Dunayevskaya concluded: "The German Social Democracy had become part of the very organism of 'progressive capitalism' and was bound to fall with it" (163).

The revolutionary alternative to the Second International, which established continuity with "the whole concept of theory as Marx *lived* it[,] flow[ing] from the proletariat as its source," was the 1905 Russian Revolution and its "New Form of Workers' Organization: the Soviet." In the final section of the chapter, Dunayevskaya described the self-activity of the workers as it spread from the textile center, Ivanovo-Voznesensky in May, to Odessa, Warsaw, Moscow, and then St. Petersburg in October, "where a Soviet of Workers' Deputies was formed to direct and coordinate the strikes" (157).

Dunayevskaya listed the achievements of the fifty-day St. Petersburg Soviet that included a general political strike, freedom of the press, proclamation of the eight-hour day, support for *Kronstadt* sailors, creation of trade unions, call for a Constituent Assembly and autonomy for national minorities. The Soviets

> were spontaneous outbursts of the broad masses of people. . . . The Soviets of Workers' Deputies were *not* just a "name" for a Labor or Trades Council. . . . The revolutionary "overtones" expressed the natural revolutionary content that dared not only to challenge the Tsarist Autocracy, but to act as if they were indeed an alternative government (159).

When the Second International did not steep itself in the new impulses from the Russian working class revolt, it of necessity left itself open to impulses from the opposing force—capitalist production. That was so in 1907. It was so in 1914 (160).

Part IV, World War I and the Great Divide in Marxism

Two major objective-subjective events dominated this period: (1) the outbreak of the First World War, and with it the collapse of the Second International; (2) the Russian Revolution and the subsequent practice of this first ongoing workers' state in history. In the three chapters of Part IV, Dunayevskaya followed these events by examining Lenin's thought and practice before, during, and after the Russia Revolution. His theoretical and practical activity formed the basis for the Great Divide in Marxism. The chapters were an intertwining of Lenin and the Russian masses. We first witness Lenin's theoretical preparation for revolution, then his concretization of that preparation in the reality of the nascent Russian workers' state.

In Chapter 10, "The Collapse of the Second International and the Break in Lenin's Thought," the betrayal of established Marxism by taking sides in the imperialist war was taken up. This was followed by examining Lenin's response in returning to reading Hegel's *Science of Logic*: "It formed the philosophic foundation for the great divide in Marxism" (168). As we saw in Chapter Two, Dunayevskaya translated Lenin's *Abstract on Hegel's Science of Logic*, in 1949. Her translation was presented as an appendix to the original edition of *Marxism and Freedom*, its first publication in English. Dunayevskaya presented a brief commentary on the content of the *Notebooks*. The thrust of her analysis here explored the impact of Lenin's reading of Hegel on his political-philosophic views. She began by quoting Lenin's comment on "the importance of dialectics, the *movement of thought*":

> Movement and self movement (this NB) independent, spontaneous, internally necessary movement), 'change,' 'movement and life,' 'the principle of every

self-movement,' 'impulse' to 'movement' and to 'activity'—Who would believe that this is the core of 'Hegelianism,' of abstract and abstruse (difficult, absurd?) Hegelianism? We must disclose this core, grasp it, save, shell it out, purify it—which is precisely what Marx and Engels have done (169).

Dunayevskaya argued that through his exploration of *Science of Logic* Lenin broke decisively with his own philosophic past. No longer was dialectics just a "reference point in internal polemics." Instead, it became the ground Lenin stood on for all his revolutionary political activity:

• Lenin became dissatisfied with Rudolf Hilferding's *Finance Capital*, and began his own independent analysis. After writing voluminous notebooks he published *Imperialism*. "These preparatory notes show how, in the concrete economic study, he held tight to the dialectic. The published work itself was a demonstration in economics of the dialectic as the unity of opposites" (170).

• Where "prior to 1914 Marxists had treated cartels, trusts, syndicates as mere 'forms' of large-scale production, as part of a continuous development of capitalism. . . . now . . . Lenin treats monopoly not so much as a part of a continuous development, but as a development through contradiction, through *transformation into opposite*" (170).

• Lenin criticized his former teacher Plekhanov, the leading figure in the founding of Russian Marxism, writing that though he had written voluminously on philosophy, he had written "nil" on Hegel's *Science of Logic*.

• Lenin had earlier written profoundly on *Capital*, but would now write: "It is impossible completely to grasp Marx's *Capital*, and especially its first chapter, if you have not studied through and understood the *whole* of Hegel's *Logic*. Consequently, none of the Marxists for the past half a century have understood Marx!!" (Quoted, 171). Dunayevskaya commented: "Before 1914, Lenin had one view of *Capital* and philosophy. War and the collapse of the Second International made him turn to the dialectic and changed his views" (171).

Dunayevskaya concluded, "There is no major work of Lenin's from the *Philosophic Notebooks* until his death, that is not permeated with the dialectic. It is the very warp and woof of all his works from *Imperialism* to the *Split in the International*; from the *National Question* to *State and Revolution*; from the famous *Trade Union Debate* to his *Will*" (172).

Dunayevskaya ended the chapter by exploring Lenin and the dialectic in relation to the Irish Revolution, that is, on the question of self-determination of nations. His Bolshevik colleague, Nikolai Bukharin, had argued that in the age of imperialism one could only fight against capitalism in general, and thus, "the slogan of 'self-determination' is first of all *utopian* and *harmful*. . . . as a slogan which *disseminates illusions*." Lenin called such an analysis "Imperialist Economics." "Lenin stressed the *co-existence* of imperialism and the democratic tendencies among the masses" (173). The Irish rising in 1916 sharpened this debate. Dunayevskaya briefly described the rebellion and then turned to Lenin's reaction:

Lenin hailed the rebellion and accepted it as the real test of his thesis. In summing up the discussion on self-determination he concluded: "The dialectics of history is such that small nations, powerless as an *independent* factor in the struggle against imperialism, play a part as one of the ferments, one of the bacilli, which help the *real* power against imperialism to come on the scene, namely, the socialist proletariat" (174-75).

Dunayevskaya turned to examine "Forms of Organization: The Relationship of the Spontaneous Self-Organization of the Proletariat to the 'Vanguard Party.'"[2] In a chapter of a dozen and a half pages she took a journey through Lenin's concept of organization from his theory of the vanguard party in *What Is to Be Done?* (1902), through changes wrought from the workers' actions in the 1905 revolution, and the period of reaction post-1905 defeat, and finally to "the Relationship of the Masses to the Party," on the eve of October 1917.

What Dunayevskaya tightly followed was: (1) Lenin's relating his concept of organization to the specific economic and political realities of Russia at each moment, leading to his conclusion that "while the *economic content* of the revolution will be capitalistic, *the method will be proletarian.* . . . It was these two contradictory aspects of the content and method of the revolution that Lenin emphasized over and over again" (181); (2) Lenin's relationship to the Russian workers and peasants at each historic moment, the "red thread is this closeness to the Russian masses" (185); (3) the resolution of "the contradiction in Lenin between the practicing revolution dialectician and the thinking Kautskyan" (186), to arrive at "a new organization of thought in the true Hegelian-Marxian manner" (191), on the eve of October.

She began discussion of *What Is to Be Done?* by pointing to the intellectual origins—in the writings of Kautksy and earlier in Lassalle—of Lenin's statement that, by themselves, the workers could only reach trade union consciousness, that socialism must be introduced to them from the outside. Lassalle had argued for the need "to bridge the gulf between thinkers and the masses," which Kautsky later formulated as "the vehicles of science were not the proletariat, but the bourgeois intellectual." Prior to the 1905 Revolution, Lenin accepted this framework for organization. However,

> there was an element in Lenin's theory on organization which was *not* borrowed from the German Social Democracy, which was *specifically Leninist*—the concept of what constitutes membership in a Russian Marxist group. Indeed, the definition did not merely rest on a "phrase"—that only he is a member who puts himself "under the discipline of the local organization." The disciplining by the local was so crucial to Lenin's concept that it held primacy over verbal adherence to Marxist theory, propagandizing Marxist views, and holding a membership card (180).

The split that resulted in Mensheviks and Bolsheviks came from this concept. For Lenin, what constituted party membership was rooted in the particular economic-political conditions of Russia: "while the *economic content* of the revolution will be capitalistic, *the method will be proletarian*." Unless the Russian intellectual was disciplined by the proletariat in a local, the intellectual could be "veering in all directions at once, but pretty steadily *away* from the proletarian responsibility" (181).

Two years later, the 1905 Revolution became the initial expression of proletarian method. Dunayevskaya quoted Lenin's developed view of proletarian consciousness. In place of his pre-1905 view of workers reaching only trade union consciousness, he wrote: "The working-class is instinctively, spontaneously, Social Democratic. . . . The special condition of the proletariat in capitalistic society leads to a striving of workers for socialism; a union of them with the Socialist Party bursts forth with spontaneous force in the very early stages of the movement" (182).

If Lenin returned to underground, highly disciplined groups after the defeat of 1905, it was not from a retrogression in his view of proletarian consciousness, but as a result of the conditions that "reactionary Tsarism *forced any democratic* grouping to live" under (182). Meanwhile the proletariat had its own form of revolutionary activity, the Soviets, which would reappear in 1917.

> Just as the 1905 Revolution *and* counter-revolution prepared the Russian masses for the successful Revolution of 1917, so it shaped Lenin's mind. What runs through it like a red thread is this closeness to the Russian masses. He never at any time had any conception of the party as an elite in the sense in which our age uses the term (195).

With 1914 and the collapse of the Second International, Lenin had to face "transformation into opposite" not alone of the party, but of a segment of the working class. Dunayevskaya showed that Lenin was compelled to go "deeper and lower" into the working class and at the same moment to have the type of party which would not shirk taking power.

With the February 1917 Revolution, and the collapse of the monarchy, a new moment arrived. The Russian workers remembered what the intellectuals, including the Marxist intellectuals, did not—the Soviets. Soviets of Workers, Soviets of Soldiers, Soviets of Peasants came to the fore.

> Lenin's mind leapt forward with the surge of the spontaneous movement of the workers. . . . "a party of a *new* type, which must *in no way* resemble those of the *Second International*. . . . drawing in large masses *and* embodying in this organization, military, state, and national economic problems."
> What was to become the famous April Thesis was taking shape. Heretofore, the break had been against Kautsky, then against Bukharin. Now, the big break was to be with *his own past*. The contradictions had been *in himself*. . . . [T]o Lenin a vanguard party now was such *only because* in April, 1917, it represented the revolutionary masses(189, 190).

Dunayevskaya was showing a practicing dialectician on Russian soil, who discovered the need to overthrow not only the corporeal organization, but the organization of thought represented by the Second International. In its place Lenin forged "a new organization of thought in the true Hegelian-Marxian manner." He was no longer a "thinking Kautskyan," but could fully unite with the Russian masses' upsurge from below. November 1917 was at hand.

The category Dunayevskaya created for post November 1917—What Happens After?—was one of the most crucial to emerge from *Marxism and Freedom*. Though linked specifically to the Russian Revolution and discussed in that context, the category objectively-subjectively characterized not alone Russia 1917, but was a problematic for all revolutions of the 20th century. She saw the question raised with regard to Russia as reaching forward to our age of transformed into opposite and aborted revolutions. "What Happens After?" became a central question facing revolutionaries and revolutionary movements globally.

For the new Soviet State, Dunayevskaya posed the two biggest tasks it faced theoretically: "(1) *how* would labor assert its mastery over the economy and the state? And (2) since the dictatorship is supposed to be a transitional state—transition to socialism—*how* would it achieve its own 'withering away'?" (194).

She looked at these questions by: (1) discussing the trade union debate of 1920-21; (2) examining Lenin's concept of "Party Work to Be Checked by Non-Party Masses;" and (3) presenting Lenin's critique of his fellow Bolshevik leadership at the end of his life.

In Chapter One we took up an earlier Dunayevskaya discussion of the 1920-21 trade union debate. She saw Lenin's position in that debate as a crucial contribution toward grappling with "What Happens After?" How to fight the "bureaucratic distortions" that were plaguing the new workers' state, the "passion for bossing" among Communists in power was what Lenin was posing, not only in the trade union debate but in his every activity.

Dunayevskaya summed up this post-1917 period in Lenin's concept that "Party Work to Be Checked by Non Party Masses." In this extreme period of Civil War, Kronstadt mutiny, economic retreat with the New Economic Policy that permitted certain capitalist enterprises, and the failure of the German Revolution of 1919—with all that—she saw Lenin making "no fetishism out of the workers' state, neither did he of the Bolshevik Party which he founded" (205). This party man, who marshaled the party to seize power, was unafraid to speak of "Commmunlies," Communist lies, against that same party. The only way to fundamentally combat the growing bureaucracy was to go to the Russian masses:

> To put life into the Soviets, to attract the non-party people, to have the work of the party people checked by non-party people. . . . We are badly executing the slogan arouse the non-party people, check the work of the party by the non-party masses (quoted, 357, footnote 195).

Finally, Dunayevskaya took up Lenin's Will: "There is no greater indictment of the Party leadership that led the only successful revolution in history then Lenin's *Will*" (205). First came Lenin's assessment of Stalin: "He is 'rude and disloyal.' He *must be removed*." Then Trotsky: "the most able man in the present Central Committee," but he is "*far too much attracted by the purely administrative side of affairs*" (205-206).

Dunayevskaya focused on Lenin's comments on Burharin: "[H]is theoretical views can only with the very greatest doubt be regarded as fully Marxian, for there is something scholastic in him (he never learned, and I think never fully understood the dialectic)" (quoted, 206). Lenin said this about the man he considered "the most valuable and biggest theoretician of the party." "[Lenin's] criticism is all concentrated in the word, 'dialectic'" (207).

As Lenin critiqued the party leadership he raised the question that this reflected a more fundamental contradiction:

> Lenin states boldly that, if the *dual* nature of the Russian state—that of being a state of workers and peasants—is at the root of the dispute between the principal combatants—Trotsky and Stalin—then no force on earth could stop the class division from bringing down the workers' state. Its fall is inevitable. . . . [I]f the party dispute reflected actual class lines, nothing on earth can close up those divisive lines. The proletarian state would collapse. *So it did* (205, 209).

Part V, The Problem of our Age: State Capitalism Vs. Freedom

Part V was divided into two sections, The Russian Scene and The American Scene. The introduction to the Russian Scene concentrated on the question of the state Plan, and in particular on the fact that Trotsky, who had introduced the idea of "the single national plan" in 1920, had a decidedly administrative conception in which, "It is necessary to guarantee the unity of leadership in all economic commissariats" (quoted, 212). Dunayevskaya contrasted this to Lenin's view of a single national plan, "'but not administratively, not in uniting the commissariats;' rather in 'drawing in the broadest possible masses'" (213). What was at stake, "the two opposing conceptions of plan—which Marx in *Capital* had first analyzed as the despotic plan of capital and the plan of cooperative labor—were being fought out in life rather than in theory in the most unusual circumstances of a workers' state with bureaucratic distortions allowing private trade" (213).

After Lenin died and Trotsky was expelled, "the Plan, with a capital 'P,' was introduced. Stalin became the Planner extraordinary" (213). Dunayevskaya argued that, "To the extent that Trotsky clung to 'the Plan,' to that extent—despite his constant criticisms of 'the tempo'—he was in actually a prisoner of Stalin's Plan. In process the very concept of socialism was reduced to the concept of Plan." (213). Chapter 13, "Russian State Capitalism vs. Workers' Revolt," followed this concept of "socialism" in analyzing Stalin's State Plans from 1928 through the early 1940s. Dunayevskaya's analysis of Russian state capitalism was discussed here earlier in Chapter One.

The second chapter of the Russian Scene took up Stalin who "is only the Russian name for a phenomenon that is *world-wide*" (240). In this chapter she wished to explore two questions:

> (1) Why does any individual behave like that? *What objective movement in the economy, what class impulses, necessitate such brutality?* (2) What specific characteristics in a man enable him to become the receptacle and the executor of class impulses from an alien class—the very one he either challenged or actually helped overthrow?

Russia had just experienced an exhausting civil war, was economically in crisis, and isolated as the German Revolution failed. "[I]n Russia's exhaustion Stalin flourished. Stalin's outstanding trait was a bureaucratic attitude to the masses" (241). Dunayevskaya showed this was particularly true with regard to both workers and to Russia's many nationalities. Lenin opposed Stalin's attitude but lay dying. "The road to power seemed obvious: it was to get control of the Party which was the State which was the Economy" (242). Stalin maneuvered with one faction and then with another to become undisputed leader.

> Once the Russian people, "to a man," did not run the economy and the state; once the German Revolution too was defeated; once world capitalism regained its breath and the vortex of the world market had full sway, the logic of the Russian development was startling, unforeseen, but inevitable. The Revolution then found the really serious counter-revolution *inside itself*. Stalin was the perfect representative of that counter-revolution, not only because he personality suited the task so well, but above all, because he did come *from* the Revolutionary Party and did have command of the Marxist "language" (243).

As Stalin consolidated power he "became conscious of representing a new force—*State* power, the *State* Plan, the *State* economy, the *State* Party" (243). He was now the Russian personification of the newly-emergent world phenomenon of state capitalism.

In the last part of the chapter, Dunayevskaya traced the demise of Stalin's absolute power post-World War II: "[H]e no longer was responsive to the *objective needs* required for a struggle for world power" (244) *vis-à-vis* the United States.

The final chapter of the Russian Scene, "The Beginning of the End of Russian Totalitarianism," took up three pages of freedom against Russian state-capitalism: the East German Uprising, June 17, 1953; the Vorkuta slave labor camps strike of July, 1953; and the Hungarian Revolution of 1956. (In Chapter Three we briefly discussed Dunayevskaya on the East Germany Revolt.) Vorkuta was within Russia's borders. Dunayevskaya wrote that the uprising helped to destroy the myth of Russian invincibility. More than 10,000 miners went on strike, forming strike committees, creating slogans, issuing pamphlets. She quoted one of the inmates, "Russia is more than ever full of revolutionaries" (252).

As *Marxism and Freedom* was being completed the Hungarian Revolution broke out in October 1956. Dunayevskaya wrote an immediate description of the events, that was incorporated into Chapter 15, taking special note of the Hungarian workers' councils that sprung up even after defeat was reported. In subsequent writing, she would call attention to the crucial banner of Marx's Humanism that the revolutionaries had raised in their opposition to Russian totalitarian occupation.

•

"The American Scene," Dunayevskaya's introduction before the final chapter of the original edition, "Automation and the New Humanism," began by noting: "America is not exempt from the development of state capitalism" (258). At the same time she added, "Although America is headed in the same direction as Russia, Russia and America are by no means identical twins" (259). The specificity of America, particularly the response of its workers to the new stage of automated production, and the Black response to continued racism, formed the basis for this last chapter. If the Russian scene had its freedom pages in East Germany, Vorkuta, and Hungary, the American scene opened new pages in strikes and wildcats against automation, and in the Montgomery Bus Boycott.

In "The American Scene" Dunayevskaya pointed to the division between the rank and file and the labor leaders, who were transformed into a labor bureaucracy with regard to attitudes to production. In "Automation and the New Humanism," she turned over the beginning sections to what the workers were saying and thinking, their different attitude to automation vs. the capitalist, the labor bureaucrat, and the intellectual technocrat. To Dunayevskaya, "Workers Think Their Own Thoughts," and she sought out the views of miners, autoworkers, women workers, young workers.

In one sense we have come full circle since the opening chapter on the French Revolution and the Hegel's Absolutes. There, we were witness to the movement from practice of the great French Revolution and the reorganization of philosophic thought from Hegel who wrote under its impact. In this final chapter Dunayevskaya presents workers' practice in beginning a battle against automation, and emerging from it a philosophic category: "[F]rom the workers' experience with Automation comes a *new Humanism. . . . the movement from practice to theory, and with it, a new unity of manual and mental labor in the worker, are in evidence everywhere*" (275, 276). We are at the two poles of automation and the absolute.

For Dunayevskaya, labor continued to be the core of any reorganization of society: "The fundamental problem of true freedom, however, remains: What type of labor can end the division between 'thinkers' and 'doers'? This is the innermost core of Marxism" (275). She argued that "[T]he workers, the American workers, made concrete *and thereby extended* Marx's most abstract theories of alienated labor and the quest for universality" (276).

For America specifically, Dunayevskaya saw this joined by the Black question, historically in Abolitionism, and at that very moment she was writing her work on the Montgomery, Alabama bus boycott. In the concluding section to the chapter and to the original edition of *Marxism and Freedom*, "Towards a New Unity of Theory and Practice in the Abolitionist and Marxist Tradition," Dunayevskaya discussed the Montgomery Bus Boycott then erupting—fighting against segregated buses, lack of Negro bus drivers, and for human dignity. She pointed to the participants being "in *continuous* session: daily there are small meetings; three times weekly, mass meetings; at all times the new relationships;" to "the decision is always *their own*;" to the fact that "the organization of their own transportation, without either boss or political supervision, is a model organization." Dunayevskaya concluded: "Clearly the greatest thing of all in this Montgomery, Alabama spontaneous organization was its own working existence" (281).

In the final pages of her work she again reviewed some of the revolutionary events and contradictions of the first half of the 20th century, including within the Marxist movement, and concluded: "The creation of a new society remains *the* human endeavor. The totality of the crisis demands, and will create, a total solution. It can be nothing short of a New Humanism" (287).

---

[1] See Herbert Marcuse, "The Foundation of Historical Materialism" in *Studies of Critical Philosophy* New Left Books 1972.

[2] Thirty years after drafting this chapter, Dunayevskaya was engaged again in the deepest probing of organization. In this uncompleted study of 1986-87, she was in the process of examining spontaneous organizational forms and the "party to lead" in relation to what she called "Dialectics of Organization and Philosophy." This study included a changed perception of Lenin. See Vol. XIII of the *Supplement to the Raya Dunayevskaya Collection*, and Part V of the present work.

Chapter 7

Projection and Concretization of *Marxism and Freedom* as Objective-Subjective Turning Points Develop: the African Revolutions, Automation Battles, and the Civil Rights Movement

When *Marxism and Freedom* was published, Dunayevskaya faced the challenge of its projection and concretization in the face of ongoing world events. In the United States she undertook speaking tours on university campuses with the new book. This, in an era when McCarthyism's poisonous atmosphere of anti-Communism still remained in the country, and few intellectuals separated Marx's emancipatory projection and Communism's totalitarian practice.

She projected the ideas of Marxist-Humanism internationally, traveling to Europe in 1959 to seek out co-thinkers and organizational colleagues for Marxist-Humanism. She went to West Africa in 1962 to explore the continent's new revolutionary moments in relation to *Marxism and Freedom* and to a projected new book on philosophy and revolution.[1] She journeyed to Japan and Hong Kong in 1965, establishing and extending relationships with a number of revolutionary groups and numerous individuals. Foreign language editions of *Marxism and Freedom* were arranged in several countries including Italy and Japan.

Responding to ongoing world events, Dunayevskaya developed ways to concretize the theoretical ground of *Marxism and Freedom* in new political writings, as well as in a series of Marxist-Humanist pamphlets that spoke to the emergence of revolutionary forces and to the ideological battles taking place.

One dimension of this could be seen in relation to the 1959 Cuban Revolution. The Revolution threw down the gauntlet to U.S. imperialism, and marked a crucial divide in Latin America. U.S. imperialism responded with the Bay of Pig invasion of 1961. Dunayevskaya at once issued a Political Letter condemning the invasion. She wrote in support of the Cuban Revolution against U.S. imperialism, while critically questioning Castro's quick alignment with state-capitalist Russia.

Such political letters became a new category for responding to ongoing events: "Since we were too few in number, and too poor in finances to print more than a monthly paper, these mimeographed letters were offered to all readers, and initiated a new stage of development for us, testing us by measuring our philosophy against the actual objective developments as they were occurring weekly" (*25 Years of Marxist-Humanism in the U.S.*, 9).

Over the next year and a half, Dunayevskaya wrote some 40 Political Letters on topics which ranged from De Gaulle and the French Crisis, to the Sino-Soviet unity and rift, to the Syrian Revolt to "Crisis-Soon-To-Be in South Vietnam and the Sending of U.S. Troops." (For a complete listing of topics and the text of the letters see, *RDC #2907*.)

In October 1962, when the Cuba missile crisis brought the world to the edge of nuclear conflagration, she began a new series of political letters, condemning this threat to humanity's survival.

This chapter will examine Dunayevskaya's projection and concretization of Marxist-Humanism in the period after the publication of *Marxism and Freedom* in a series of pamphlets published on the Afro-Asian Revolutions, on the struggles of workers in relation to automation, and on the history of Black struggles as the touchstone of American Civilization. It will also focus on a new chapter added to *Marxism and Freedom* on Mao's China. Finally, the chapter will trace Dunayevskaya's work with News and Letters Committees to create a philosophic-organizational pole of attraction for the ongoing freedom movements in the 1960s.

Ideological-Philosophic Pulls as Africa Transformed Itself: *Nationalism, Communism, Marxist-Humanism and the Afro-Asian Revolutions*

In the late 1950s and early 1960s over twenty newly independent nations remade the map of Africa, opening a new page in worldwide freedom struggles. Dunayevskaya wrote on the meaning of these events in *Nationalism, Communism, Marxist-Humanism and the Afro-Asian Revolutions* (1959), which first appeared as a supplement in *News & Letters* and then as a pamphlet. An expanded edition was published in 1961.

Nationalism, Communism, Marxist-Humanism and the Afro-Asian Revolutions was an analysis of the Afro-Asian liberation struggles in relation to competing ideologies that sought to influence, and at times, dominate those struggles. Dunayevskaya asked whether the African Revolutions could "escape being torn between the two warring poles of state capitalism" when faced with "*a new form of struggle between the two nuclear titans, the Soviet Union and the United States.*" She probed various ideologies—nationalism in its pan-Africanist form, Communism Russian-style, as well as Trotskyism, and the thought of Mao.

She began with the concept of Pan-Africanism, tracing one of its origins to W.E.B. DuBois' 1919 concept of a "'thinking intelligentsia' *working through imperialist institutions*" (*Afro-Asian Revolutions*, 8), and posed its modern manifestation:

> Among the leaders who sprang up to lead the movement—and not a few of them were ex-Marxists—the question of a new nation's destiny was reduced to a question of administration and power. . . . [T]he espousal of such Pan-Africanism is for the purpose of channeling African movements and making them function *within the order of world state capitalism* (8, 9).

Turning to Russian Communism, Dunayevskaya argued that in reality it was, "The New Stage of World Capitalism: State Capitalism" (11). Advanced capitalism, whether of the U.S. or Russian variety, lacked the capital to industrialize the Afro-Asian world. Russia could not even provide for its own people, while in the West, "lush as the *mass* of profits are . . . the truth is that there isn't enough capital produced to keep the crazy capitalist system going with self-same profit motive on an ever-expanding scale" (13). The question of industrialization of Africa and Asia could not be solved either by "democratic capitalism" or by "totalitarian Communism, i.e. state capitalism."

Neither could industrialization be solved by "China with its Russian-styled Plans. . . . It soon turned out that whatever 'great leap forward' was made, was made on the bent back of the masses, not for them" (14-15). Whether in backward lands or advanced lands, it was not the masses whose thought and creativity was elicited. Rather, their sweated labor was what was wanted, controlled by "the intellectual bureaucrat . . . a firm ally of the labor bureaucrat" (16). The Chinese alternative led to Mao's "Army-Party cadre" and the "Communes" with their "barrack labor, barrack discipline, and barrack family life." "The Chinese path to industrialization" was no viable path for Africa.

As against these paths, Dunayevskaya turned to explore Lenin's Marxism, "developed in total opposition to any short cut to workers' power" (18):

> "Every citizen to a man must act as a judge and participate in the government of the country and what is most important to us is to enlist all the toilers to a

man in the government of the state. This is a tremendously difficult task, but socialism cannot be introduced by a minority, a party." (Lenin)
This was not said merely for outside consumption. It was said to a Party Congress. Nor was it said by a man on the way to power. It was said by a man in power in order to stress that the party should not, in the revision of its program, forget how and why it came to power (18-19).

Dunayevskaya argued that this concept of socialism, "impelled Lenin, two years afterward, when the colonial revolutions burst upon the historic scene, to make these a new point of departure in his theory" (19). To Lenin, "Colonial Revolts under Imperialism" did *not* inevitably have to go through capitalism: "[W]ith the aid of the proletariat of the most advanced countries, the backward countries may pass to the Soviet, and after passing through a definite stage of development, to Communism, without passing through the capitalist stage of development" (quoted, 19).

This leap in Lenin's cognition came from two world shaking events: "Firstly the 1917 Revolution had established a workers' state that could come to the aid of a land even more backward technologically than Russia, whilst secondly the colonial revolutions themselves illuminated the revolutionary role of the peasantry in the imperialist epoch" (19).

Dunayevskaya summed up the lessons from the Russian Revolution: "That revolution only underlined the truth of history's dialectic: just as small nations fighting for independence could unleash the socialist revolution, so the working class of industrialized countries achieving the revolution could help the underdeveloped countries avoid capitalist industrialization" (20).

Dunayevskaya pointed to Trotsky's failure to absorb these lessons from the first decades of the 20th century. Where Trotsky's theory of permanent revolution had been prescient in anticipating the 1905 and 1917 Russian Revolutions, that is, revolutions in technologically underdeveloped lands, it had a deep internal contradiction in not seeing the role of the peasant revolutionary subject. In fact, she noted, Trotsky's view later came to signify not the working class leading the peasantry so much as the Party leading the proletariat. She discussed how the hollowness of Trotsky's theory of permanent revolution was demonstrated in its failure to see the revolutionary role of the peasantry in China post the 1925-27 Revolution.

Dunayevskaya posed the alternative of Marxist-Humanism for the post-World War II era of revolutions in technologically underdeveloped lands. She wrote of "present-day Communist attacks on humanism" being rooted in their attempt to substitute state capitalism's exploitative practice for Marxism as a theory of liberation, and traced the opposition that developed in thought as well as practice *within* state capitalist countries as in Hungary's revolution against Communism's death grip.

In part, Dunayevskaya built Marxist Humanism's view of revolutions in underdeveloped lands on "Lenin's new departure in theory. The revolutionary initiative is not always with the working class. The road to Berlin may lead through Peking, said Lenin in the days of Sun Yet Sen. The overwhelming majority of the population of the world is in the East and one must take the new elemental force of the colonial revolutions as a new point of departure in theory" (28).

Almost four decades after Lenin, she wrote: "A people mature enough to fight for its freedom is mature enough to take destiny into its own hands in the matter of reconstructing its own society." This was not a Utopia, but depended on aid from workers' movements in technologically advanced lands. Dunayevskaya stated what she saw as part of a crucial alternative:

> [T]he African masses must turn directly to the workers in the technologically advanced countries whether they are Russia, West Europe, or America. . . .
> Without the aid of the majority of the workers of a technologically advanced country neither the African nor the Asian revolution can escape capitalist exploitation and the bureaucratic State Planner. . . .
> Powerful as the two big masses of world capital are, the new nations cease to be half-way houses doomed forever to stay at the cross-road of history *once their reliance passes from the governments to the common people of the technologically advanced countries.* This is neither mere wishful thinking nor a question of drifting on totally uncharted seas (7, 10).

She argued against false alternatives, whether Russian Communism or Chinese Communes. "Marxism is a theory of liberation or it is nothing" (23). A Pan-Africanism that claimed it was an "in-between road," would not be viable either: "The leaders of the African Revolutions are *not* relying solely on the creative energy of the masses, proletarian, peasant or primitive, not because they are independent of 'doctrinaire Marxism' *but because they are dependent upon the capitalist road to industrialization*" (28).

The opposition to Communist totalitarianism had taken "a humanist form both in theory and practice. The same is true of the Afro-Asian revolutions against Western imperialism. The same is true in the workers' movements in the technologically advanced countries" (28-9).

In *Nationalism, Communism, Marxist-Humanism and the Afro-Asian Revolutions*, the humanism of Marxism was posed as *the* alternative for the Afro-Asian Revolutions: "a unifying principle. It is the point of unity . . . between the masses in the underdeveloped countries and the common people in the advanced countries" (25).

The American Proletariat Speaking for Itself:
Workers Battle Automation

In American factories of the late 1950s, there was a rapid, intense introduction of automation, and a continuing series of strikes and wildcats by workers facing its consequences on the production and unemployment lines. *News & Letters* printed numerous articles written by workers on their struggles facing automation including their attitudes toward its development. Published in Detroit and widely distributed in its auto plants, the paper was on the cutting edge in giving voice to workers' thoughts. Charles Denby, its editor lived in Detroit and worked in the Chrysler Jefferson plant, frequently writing on automation in his "Worker's Journal" column. A number of autoworkers wrote stories for the labor page. News and Letters Committees had a local in West Virginia and carried a section in the paper on "Coal and Its People." A Black Pittsburgh steelworker member submitted stories on his mill.

With the publication of *Marxism and Freedom,* workers' voices were seen in a deeper, more profound way.[2] They were discussed as a source for theory, a unity of thinking and doing. Participation in strikes and protests was inseparable from writing about them by workers in the paper. At the same time, the pamphlet *Workers Battle Automation* (*WBA* 1960, *RDC* #2843) sought to concretize and project the ideas present in *Marxism and Freedom*, particularly its core structure of a movement from practice to theory that was itself a form of theory. Workers were seen as Reason of social transformation.

The principle author of *WBA* was Charles Denby. The voices of many workers, women and men, adult and youth, Black and white, from various industries including auto, steel and coal, were present. After a brief Introduction, "Let the Workers' Voices Be Heard," *Workers Battle Automation* had sections with voices from auto shops, steel mills and the mines. The workers spoke about speed up, the fragmentation of work, sickness from laboring on the belt line, the loneliness of the job, and the fight with the labor bureaucracy. There were discussions on the Negro Worker and on unemployed armies, as well as contributions from an office worker on early computers, a doctor responding to Denby's question on how much contamination from exhaust and gas in the plant can a worker stand, and from an engineer.

In addition to reporting on the conditions of labor from the workers' viewpoint, the pamphlet elicited a dialogue and debate on the future of automation. One worker, Angela Terrano, asked: "Why do people assume that Automation is the way people will want to work in a new society? Why do they assume that all that matters is that the workers will be in control? Will 'being in control' of the machine lighten the work, or make it less boring?" Charles Denby felt that the key was workers' control of production, workers' deciding all questions. Others joined the debate, including a 16 year old woman who wrote: "My vision is one of a new free society in which among other things, I will not have to wait until I am 21 to be admitted into the human race."

Workers Battle Automation became the first in a series of News & Letters pamphlets in which various forces of social transformation—African-Americans, youth, women—would speak for themselves.

American Civilization on Trial: Dunayevskaya and the Black Freedom Movement

The Civil Rights era that had opened with the Montgomery Bus Boycott of 1955-56, exploded with an outpouring of protests, new forms of freedom activity and organization on the part of African-Americans and their supporters throughout the 1960s. Sometimes the name of a city—Selma, Jackson, and Birmingham among others—signified not only locale, but the Movement for Black freedom.

From sit-ins at Woolworth lunch counters, to Freedom Rides and Freedom Unions, to the 1963 March on Washington and the 1964 Mississippi Summer Project, to the 1965 rebellions in Watts and Detroit, News and Letters Committees participated in events and wrote in-person reports in their newspaper. A number of pamphlets on specific manifestations of the Freedom Now! movement were written by Committee members and Movement participants. *Freedom Riders Speak for Themselves* (1961), *The Free Speech Movement and the Negro Revolution* (1965), *Black Mass Revolt* (1967), and *The Maryland Freedom Union, Workers Doing and Thinking* (1969), were all written under the impact of *Marxism and Freedom*.

The most comprehensive statement on the Black Dimension from News and Letters Committees in this period was *American Civilization on Trial: The Negro as Touchstone of History, 100 Years After the Emancipation Proclamation* (1963). Written by Dunayevskaya, the statement was issued by the National Editorial Board of News & Letters.

Dunayevskaya had developed a thesis of the Black struggles as central to social transformation in America in the mid-1940s. In the midst of the Second World War, there were Black uprisings in Detroit and Harlem. These revolts, together with Black worker participation in a major wartime miners' strike, posed anew for Marxists the role of the Black struggle within the revolutionary movement. In the Workers Party of the American Trotskyist movement, the majority position on the Black question held that the Negro struggle was only radical in relationship to the trade union question, not as independent struggles of the Negro masses. The minority Johnson-Forest Tendency, led by C.L.R. James and Raya Dunayevskaya, held a quite different view. It was centered on recognition of the crucial nature of independent struggles of the Black masses, and thus the need for Marxist revolutionaries to base their theoretic position on this fact. In the mid-1940s there were a series of resolutions, articles, and debates on these positions within the Workers Party.

Dunayevskaya wrote a number of articles on the Black question. Among them were: "Marxism and the Negro Problem" (June 18, 1944. *RDC* # 259), "Negro Intellectuals in Dilemma—[Gunnar] Myrdal Study of a Crucial Problem" (November, 1944. *RDC* # 271), "Negroes in the Revolution: The Significance of Their Independent Struggles" (May, 1945. *RDC* # 282), and "Industrialization and Urbanization of the Negro" (1946. *RDC* # 311).

Dunayevskaya's studies were rooted: (1) theoretically, primarily in Lenin's writings on the National Question; (2) empirically, in the "economic situation of the Negro problem;" and (3) in "the Negro Movements," independently created. She discussed Lenin's "Thesis on the National and Colonial Question" (1920) and its relation to the Negro Question in America, as well as writings from Trotsky and Marx. She analyzed what she termed the economic remains of slavery found in sharecropping and its "boss and black" relations, industrialization of the Negro North and South, and the mass migrations of Black people north and into southern cities. She hit out against those American Marxists who wished to subsume the mass movements of African-Americans to the class struggle, and thus, did "not understand the significance of the mass struggles of the Negro people" (*RDC* # 285).

The documents of the 1940s were Dunayevskaya's first sustained writings on the Black dimension. She had already been active in the 1920s and 1930s on issues of Black liberation, including working in the office of the *Negro Champion* newspaper of the American Negro Labor Congress in its Chicago years (1925-27). The Black dimension—in America, in the two-way road between Africa and the United States, and in Marx's thought and work—was pivotal to Dunayevskaya's writing and activity throughout her life. The 1940s writings formed an important preparation for her seminal work on the Black struggle, *American Civilization on Trial—The Negro as Touchstone of History*, issued in 1963, on the 100th anniversary of the Emancipation Proclamation.

American Civilization on Trial (*ACOT*) was written under the impact of three kinds of events/experiences: (1) The growing and developing Civil Rights Movement, 1955-1963. From the Montgomery Bus Boycott, the school desegregation struggles, and the lunch counter sit-ins that swept the South in 1960, to the Freedom Rides of 1961 and the emergence of mass freedom struggles in southern city upon city—the Movement, as it became known, transformed America on the Black question in a way not seen since the Civil War.

(2) News and Letters Committees' participation in the Movement. From its founding in 1955, the Committees had actively been involved. Its paper, *News & Letters*, had recorded numerous first hand reports from the civil rights' battlefields. Members were involved in demonstrations, mass marches, picket lines, and other forms of freedom struggles. In 1961 News and Letters members had

been Freedom Riders, and had with others, written the pamphlet *Freedom Riders Speak for Themselves* (*RDC* #3414).

(3) *Marxism and Freedom's* publication in 1958. Structured on the movement from practice to theory, it would provide the theoretical framework for the writing of *American Civilization on Trial*.

This thirty-odd page pamphlet was a concentrated distillation and provocative reading of American history and its Black dimension. In no way can it be summarized. We can only selectively mention a handful of the topics covered.

The Preface written for the second edition issued three months after the first, summed up its thrust: "We . . . have written of past history and of history in the making as one continuous development of the vanguard role of the Negro." Not a party-to-lead but a people, "Black Masses as Vanguard," played a leading role in U.S. history. This formed the basis for the unique Marxist-Humanist conception of vanguard as masses in motion.

In *ACOT's* Introduction the stage was set for presenting that vanguard role historically by noting, that "the self-activity of the Negroes . . . and most of all in the *South*," far more than the established powers in Washington, actively opposed segregation (*ACOT*, 5). The Introduction continued: "So persistent, intense, continuous, and ever-present has been the self-activity of the Negro, before and after the Civil War, before and after World War I, before, during and after World War II, that it has become the gauge by which American Civilization is judged."

ACOT's Part I, "From the First through the Second American Revolution," began "The African, brought here as slave against his will, played a decisive role in the shaping of American Civilization" (8). It then took up slave revolts, "the Ambivalence of the Declaration of Independence," and the fact that with the development of the cotton gin "capitalism was tied to the cotton plantations." Most crucially, in the Introduction and Part I, "Abolitionism: a New Dimension of American Character," was shown as the revolutionary thread that transformed America. The Abolitionists—standing tall "because they stood on the shoulders of the actual mass movement of slaves following the North Star to freedom" (7)—succeeded, with the Black masses, in transforming the Civil War "from a war of mere supremacy of Northern industry over Southern cotton culture to one of emancipation of slaves" (9). David Walker, William Lloyd Garrison, Wendell Phillips, and John Brown were discussed, not as great men, which of course they were, but as inextricably related to the Black masses' striving for emancipation.

Karl Marx's relation to the Abolitionists—"the *spontaneous* affinity of ideas, the *independent* working out of the problems of the age as manifested on one's own country, and the common Humanist goal made inevitable the crossing of the paths of Karl Marx and the Abolitionists" (7)—and his following in detail the progress of the Civil War and the lot of the Blacks, were discussed.

When the Civil War was over, "the four million freedmen remained tied to cotton culture, and therein lies imbedded the roots of the Negro Question" (10). This formed the basis for Part II. "The Still-Unfinished Revolution." Once the Black farmer did not get his 40 acres as Congress failed to pass Thaddeus Stevens' Land Division Act, he had nowhere to go but to the dependent relation of share-cropping: "Cotton remained dominant, semi-feudal relations were inevitable. The division of labor set up by the cotton economy may not be disturbed" (12). *ACOT* described the withdrawal of troops from the South, which allowed a counter-revolution to be solidified. Northern industrialists may have wished to break the monopoly of commercial over industrial capital, but, as *ACOT* demonstrated, they had little interest in shaking up the former slave owners' social-political rule. "Black Codes" were enacted, a cotton economy remained in the hands of plantation owners who had a black labor supply with nowhere else to survive but on those plantations, in what became the "boss and black" relationship.

The several decades post-Civil War were not solely an era of reaction. *ACOT* showed this in discussing Reconstruction, northern labor struggles in railroads and for an eight-hour day, and the emergence in the South and West of the Populist movement that included the National Colored Farmers' Alliance with one and one-quarter million members. *ACOT* quoted the Southern historian C. Vann Woodward: "Never before or since have the two races in the South come so close together as they did during the Populist struggles." Nevertheless, as *ACOT* noted:

> The unity of white and black was soon, in turn, shattered by the combined interests of the Bourbon South with monopoly capital that had won the struggle over labor in the North and spread its tentacles over the Caribbean and the Pacific. Monopoly capital's growth into imperialism puts the last nail in the coffin of Southern democracy and thus not only re-established racism in the South but brings it to the North.

"Imperialism and Racism" formed Part III of *ACOT*. Here the pamphlet examined "'the smell of empire' that combined with the economic remains of slavery to establish racism as a 'permanent' feature of American life" (15). The rise of monopoly capital with the "additive of color" set the ground for America's "Plunge into Imperialism." As *ACOT* summarized the period:

> (1) three full decades of phenomenal industrial expansion followed the end of the Civil War; (2) three full decades of undeclared civil war were waged against labor in the North; and (3) the combined might of Northern capital and the Southern aristocracy was used against the challenge from agriculture—Populism. The removal of the Federal troops was only the first of the steps in this unholy alliance which two decades later jointly ventured into imperialism (16).

ACOT noted that even this period of deep racist reaction—abroad, with white U.S. imperialist intrusion in the Philippines and Cuba, at home, with the horror of Black lynching—did not stop Black intellectuals like W.E.B. DuBois and the Negro press from "actively supporting the recently formed Anti-Imperialist League." The period also gave birth to a new form of radical labor organization, the socialist/syndicalist I.W.W. (Industrial Workers of the World) whose members included tens of thousands of Black workers.

Part IV, "Nationalism and Internationalism" took up the mass migration of African-Americans out of the South during and immediately after World War II, where they were subjected to "the most ill-paid, back-breaking jobs in Chicago stockyards, Pittsburgh steel mills, Detroit auto factories, Philadelphia docks" (19). The racism faced was not alone in industry, but as well in the trade union movement. In fact it was in all aspects of life: "[T]he move from country to city was not really to the big city but to the small, overcrowded ghetto. . . . The social humiliation to which the Negroes were subjected daily, in and out of the factory, in and out of the ghetto, in and out of stores and places of entertainment, was not limited to the Negro migrants" (19).

Confronted with a solid wall of prejudice the Black masses were greatly attracted to the appeal of Garveyism. In a section titled "Garveyism vs. 'Talented Tenth,'" *ACOT* showed how Marcus Garvey's internationalist form of nationalism helped to organize millions of Black people, overwhelmingly proletarian. The movement contrasted sharply with the elitism of DuBois's concept of a "talented tenth," which would supposedly lead African-Americans.

An additional current of thought came to the fore to appeal to the Black movement in this period—Marxism. Drawing upon Dunayevskaya's work from the 1940s, *ACOT* took up Lenin's "Thesis on the National and Colonial Question" that had included "the Negro in America," in contrast to many American socialists and Marxists, who did not recognize an independent Black question. What was particularly illuminating in this section was the citing of the Black poet Claude McKay, who in the early 1920s spoke and wrote of how American Negroes had "found that Karl Marx had been interested in their emancipation, and had fought valiantly for it" (quoted, 21).

In moving to "From the Depression through World War II" (Part V), *ACOT* took up how the CIO changed the industrial face of the nation through industrial unionism, and in the process made "a break in Negro 'nationalism:'" "[W]ithout the Negro, the CIO could not have organized the basic industries where Negro labor was pivotal" (24). Such organizing meant that Black labor moved away from the talented tenth, who were busy claiming that "the best friend" of the Negro was the capitalist, since the "most prejudiced" among the whites was the laborer. The CIO showed the possibility of Black and labor unity.

Part V also discussed the independent Black action of the organizing of a March on Washington protesting continued racism in employment, and then fighting to end Jim Crow in the Army. Particularly revealing was the discussion of the Communists' abandonment of any independent Black movement as soon as the United States entered the war on the side of Russia: "Hitler is the main enemy and the foes of Negro rights in this country should be considered as secondary" was the line of the Communist Party (quoted, 24).

Part VI developed the concept of "the Negro as Touchstone of History:" First at the very birth of the new nation: "Because slavery stained American civilization as it wrenched freedom from Great Britain, the Negro gave the lie to its democracy" (26); then in the post-Civil War period: "The Negro became the touchstone of this class-ridden, color-conscious, defaced civilization which had an ever-expanding frontier but no unifying philosophy" (26).

ACOT summed up the thrust of the argument: "What is pivotal to the study of the role of the Negro in American Civilization is that, at each turning point in history, he anticipates the next stage of development of labor in its relation with capital. Because of his dual oppression, it could not be otherwise" (27).

The role as touchstone was manifest in the "Urbanization of Negroes," which showed that phenomenon was not alone from the South to the North, but by the 1950s and early 60s *within* the South. It was this which helped give rise to the emerging Black struggle in the South—from the Montgomery Bus Boycott (1956) to the deepening of the struggle with the lunch-counter sit-ins (1960) and the Freedom Rides (1961). At the same time came a growing industrialization, now in the South as well. Here too, the African-Americans as touchstone to U.S. history was shown by the racism manifest against being hired, as well as on the job, and in the *permanent* army of unemployed which Black workers were forced to join.

In a section on "The Two-Way Road to African Revolutions," no claim was made for any one-to-one relationship of the movement in America and the African Revolutions. Rather, "the underlying humanism" present signified that:

> [t]he historic greatness of today's development, no matter what the roots are, flowed from the *spontaneity*, the *timing*, the political *maturity* of our *age* and our *world*. It is not just black, or even colored, but white as well. Nor is it directly only against Western imperialism as the East German and Hungarian Revolutions for freedom from Russian totalitarianism showed (28).

American Civilization on Trial ended with Part VII, "Facing the Challenge, 1943-1963." The Part began by calling for no separation between the self-determination of people and ideas. The self-determination manifest in the Civil Rights movement, as in the Hungarian Revolution, had implicit within an underlying philosophy, "a new type of humanism." How to work that out explicitly, in its fullness? "*What is needed is a new Humanism. It is the unifying philosophy of Marxist-Humanism* which, in the years of our existence, has enabled us not only to follow, support and participate in the Negro struggles, but in some ways to anticipate their development" (31).

The final section "What We Stand For—and Who We Are" briefly discussed the development of this human-rooted "philosophy of life" arising from the Marxist and Abolitionist traditions. It quoted from *Marxism and Freedom*: "A new unity of theory and practice can evolve only when the movement from theory to practice meet[s] the movement from practice to theory. . . . The creation of a new society remains *the* human endeavor. The totality of the crisis demands, and will create, a total solution. It can be nothing sort of a New Humanism" (quoted, 33).

What was perhaps as remarkable as the text was the purpose of *American Civilization on Trial*. Far from writing it for an academic journal, or putting it in the form of a textbook for the university, Dunayevskaya and News and Letters Committees sought to have a serious theoretical-historical study of the Black dimension in the United States as a "popular pamphlet" directly within the Freedom Now movement. It was used in many places in the Civil Rights struggle including Freedom Schools in the Mississippi, sold at mass demonstrations and marches, on picket lines, in freedom centers, and at factory gates. So central did Dunayevskaya see *American Civilization on Trial* to Marxist-Humanist thought, that she asked that it be incorporated into the Constitution of News and Letters Committees.

"The Challenge of Mao Tse-tung" Chapter in an Expanded Edition of *Marxism and Freedom*

Three objective-subjective events in relation to China—(1) the emergence of Mao's China as a pole of attraction in the Third World; (2) the growing rift between China and Russia, which posed the possibility of war between these state-capitalist entities claiming to be Marxist; and (3) the presence of Chinese voices from below who dared to speak out on their conditions of life and labor for a few short weeks during the Hundred Flowers period (May to mid-June, 1957)—led Dunayevskaya to write "The Challenge of Mao Tse-tung" Chapter for a second edition of *Marxism and Freedom* (1964).

The immediate political context that began the chapter was the developing Sino-Soviet conflict. Despite the fact that Marxist language framed the battle, Dunayevskaya argued that the rift had little to do with working out an authentic Marxist interpretation of reality:

> [W]e must not let the fact that both contestants call themselves Communist hide their class nature: both are capitalistic to the marrow of their bones. State-capitalism changes the form, not the content, of these totalitarian regimes. . . . Because [they] are involved in a contest for influence over the new African, Asian and Latin-American world, where the Marxian theory of liberation is a

polarizing force for freedom fighters, the battle is fought out in the language of "Marxist-Leninism" (*M&F*, 289).

This ideological battle was taking place after 1956-57 had shown the real battles against state-capitalist regimes calling themselves Communist. The Hungarian Revolution had exposed Russian totalitarianism. The brief opening of the "Hundred Flowers" period ("Let 100 flowers bloom, let 100 schools of thought contend."–Mao) showed the deep opposition within Mao's China. Dunayevskaya presented a number of these "Voices of Revolt" who spoke out during the six short weeks the Hundred Flowers lasted. One voice she quoted, that of Lin His-ling, age 21, called for a "true socialism" which was "highly democratic" and bore little resemblance to China's socialism "sprung from a basis of feudalism." As Dunayevskaya noted, "This opposition was soon ruthlessly crushed" (290).

In this first section of the chapter, "Communist Counter-Revolutions," Dunayevskaya proceeded to take up the disastrous Great Leap Forward that soon followed the Hundred Flowers period. She detailed the mass herding of China's peasantry into "People's Communes" with their oppressive conditions of ten hours labor, two hours ideological study, and lack of privacy and freedom.

Throughout this chapter, Dunayevskaya concentrated on what she termed "The Dialectic of Mao's Thought." She saw Mao's thought as a modern day representation of Hegel's "Spirit in Self-Estrangement:" "the absolute and universal inversion of reality and thought, the entire estrangement, one from the other" (quoted, 291).[3] She concentrated on Mao's "practical" ideological pronouncements not only to characterize Mao philosophically, but because it was Mao's philosophical revision that provided the ideological cover for his unique road to power and "great leaps" in power.

The second section of the chapter traced Mao's thought and action from the defeat of the 1925-27 Revolution to the conquest of power. It began:

> Different conditions produce different modes of thought. The twenty-two year long struggle for power□ from the defeat of the Chinese Revolution of 1925-27 to Mao's assumption of full power in mainland China 1949□ determine the dialectic of "Mao's Thought" as a corollary to Stalin's long series of basic revisions of Marxism which ended in its total transformation into opposite□ the monolithic single party state power of totalitarian Communism. To this, and not to Marxism, Mao made two original contributions: (1) the role of the Army, in and out of state power; and (2) "Thought Reform," that is to say, brainwashing which, as natural adjunct to his "four-class politics," is applied equally to all classes (299).

Here was Mao's original road to power. Dunayevskaya showed that with the defeat of the 1925-27 Revolution, Mao made "guerrilla war, and not peasant revolution . . . into a theory. . . . Military control of an area gave the Party state power over the peasantry" (300). A guerrilla army and Party-controlled peasant soviet characterized this first period of the road to power.

When at the next stage, 1935-45, Japan's occupation meant for Mao a class collaborationist policy with Chiang Kai-shek in a United Front, his "philosophical" justification took the form of two essays, "On Practice" and "On Contradiction." Dunayevskaya analyzed these essays, showing Mao's reduction of theory to mere "practicality," his manipulation of the category of contradiction, thereby denuding the objectivity of development through contradiction in Hegelian-Marxian theory.

In writing about Mao in power, Dunayevskaya argued against any interpretation of Mao's China as a throwback to Oriental Despotism. Rather, she saw Mao's practices in agriculture, in the military and in industry as under the economic compulsion of our present age of state-capitalism.

In turning to the Sino-Soviet dispute, Dunayevskaya analyzed its stages from 1960 through 1963, as they maneuvered and battled for influence over the various Communist powers internationally, and most especially for influence in the Afro-Asian Latin American world. For her, the conflict was another manifestation of "the non-viability of state-capitalism as a 'new' social order . . . proven by the same laws of development as that of private capitalism, that is to say, the compulsion to exploit the masses at home and to carry on wars abroad" (322-23). "The co-existence of oppressor and oppressed is the determining factor . . . in proving the non-viability of Chinese state-capitalism that calls itself Communist" (328).

The final section of the chapter, "In Place of a Conclusion: Two Kinds of Subjectivity," began:

> Two kinds of subjectivity characterize our age of state-capitalism and workers' revolt. One is the subjectivism that we have been considering—Mao's—which has no regard for objective conditions. . . .
> The second type of subjectivity, the one which rests on "the transcendence of the opposition between the Notion and Reality," is the subjectivity which has "absorbed" objectivity, that is to say, through its struggle for freedom it gets to know and cope with the objectively real (326-27).

Dunayevskaya briefly probed these two kinds of subjectivity, which she noted, "is the burden of my new work in progress," (what would become *Philosophy and Revolution*). She saw them in "head-on collision" in the 1956 Hungarian Revolution. As well, she saw them in China, no matter Mao's rhetoric to turn the antagonistic class contradictions into struggles of the "old" and the "new." As against Mao's type of subjectivity, she ended this chapter on the masses' subjectivity:

> The subjectivity of the millions struggling for freedom . . . poses the need for a new relationship between theory and practice. The freedom struggles are not

limited to Hungary or Africa, Russia or China; they include the United States and Western Europe as well. The challenge is for a new unity of Notion and Reality which will release the vast untapped energies of mankind to put an end, once and for all, to what Marx called the *pre*-history of humanity so that its true history can finally unfold (330).

Working out a Marxist-Humanist Concept of Organization at the Time of *Marxism and Freedom*

With the publication of *Marxism and Freedom* (1958), Dunayevskaya strove to build a Marxist-Humanist organization on its theoretical ground.[4] Her concept of a Marxist-Humanist organization was most comprehensively expressed in the presentations she prepared for News and Letters Committee Conventions and Plenums. She sought to work out organizational development in relation to philosophic cognition, to ongoing world events, and to the growing mass movement in civil rights, class struggles on factory floors against automation, as well as forms of organization arising out of the African and East European revolutions. Working to create a philosophic-organizational pole of attraction for the ongoing freedom movements was the task that she undertook.

In 1960 she presented an Organizational Report, "From Organizational Consciousness to Organizational Building" (*RDC* #2767). She argued that a new stage of consciousness for News and Letters Committees had been realized in uniting the spontaneous actions in class struggles with the completion and publication of *Marxism and Freedom*: "The *new* stage of consciousness becomes the foundation for the leap from mere consciousness of organization to the *building* of our organization" (*RDC* #2769).

Dunayevskaya's concept of organization was the polar opposite of any vanguard party-to-lead. The role of a Marxist organization was no substitute for the masses: "*The masses are the makers of history and the only way you can find out whether you can answer history's call—THAT IS TO SAY REPEAT IN YOURSELF THE MIRACLE OF CREATION—is to remove the roadblocks in the way of the masses who are actively reorganizing the world*" (# 2773).

Marxist organization did have a crucial role to play. One of the roadblocks in the way was that the ongoing mass struggle was being "ideologically disarmed" not only by parts of the capitalist class but by so-called vanguard groupings out "to lead," who were "a millstone around the neck of the proletariat." "To remove this roadblock, to have the movement from theory to practice, merge with this movement from practice to theory on the way to the new society, is the *why* of organizational growth and of cadre building" (# 2775).

Her conception of a cadre was not of a specialized group of leaders, but of the whole organization, "not only of leaders, but of ranks." Crucial were the human "limitless possibilities," the "human energy" which, in Marxist-Humanist terms, was not simply activity but "activity within a philosophic-national-international-and-personal context that was comprehensive to all. In a word, human energy is neither just doing and not thinking, nor the reverse. The *relationship* between the two is the decisive factor" (# 2771).

How was this human energy to be released as a Marxist-Humanist?

> Your talents can only be born through organizational growth and organizational growth depends on a cadre and a cadre depends on individuals and individuals depend on the objective situation, which compels the forging of a cadre.
> This is *not* a merry-go-round. All these inter-dependents come from life itself, and life itself includes *both* the struggle for freedom *and* organization building which is to become the struggles' polarizing force (# 2772-73).

This meant releasing one's innate and acquired talents by a *collective* digging, through organization. "The organization, in a word, is a form for the release of the creative energies of the masses as they prepare for this reconstruction of society from the ground up" (# 2777). The creation of such an organization was the historic task that Dunayevskaya saw News and Letters Committees undertaking.

Organization as a form for the creative energies of the masses remained central to Dunayevskaya's writing on organization throughout her life. At the same time she was grappling with how organization could be the form for development of those who considered themselves Marxist-Humanists and who would bring others to that philosophy. It was through organizational growth, becoming "the struggles' polarizing force," that the release of the creative energies of the masses could be fully realized.

In writing about how Marxist-Humanists could build organization and undergo self-development Dunayevskaya put forth a number of themes in the 1960s.

• "The role of Philosophy in Building Organizations"—

> To the Hegelian philosophic heritage of Freedom and Reason, I now wish to add *Organization*.
> Naturally, I don't mean Hegel's opportunism and the organization of the Prussian state to which he capitulated; I am concerned with this dialectical philosophy, and not his personal opportunism. The point is that, though to Hegel the philosopher, organization meant only Organization of Thought, the sense of history is so overpowering, that through the history of thought we get the *actual* development of humanity ("Ideas, Organization and World Development," 1961 News and Letters Perspectives #3178-79).

In this same Perspectives presentation Dunayevskaya briefly looked at the heritage of Marxist organizations, "in order to see what was alike in this inter-relationship of philosophy and politics in all ages—and what each contributed that was *new* in order to see the problems of *today*: the relationship of spontaneity and other organizations to the specifically Marxist-Humanist one" (# 3180). She concluded: "[U]nless there is a underlying philosophy which unites spontaneity and organization in the tradition of Marx, all their shout about 'newness' only brings them to the old whirlpools" (#3183).

• "Africa and 'the Party'"—In 1962 Dunayevskaya had traveled to West Africa. When she returned she noted to two high points from the trip: (1) The Africans saw her as author and as the head of an organization, "philosophy and organization are judged *objectively* rather than on the basis of prestige and number." (2) Their "overwhelming confidence that without an organization nothing can succeed, has shed a new light, where light was badly needed, on the question of the role of a party" (Draft Perspectives, July 1962, #3204).

Dunayevskaya discussed the kind of single party that had arisen out of the historic experience in Africa—the fight against imperialism, and the rise of a nationalist movement—as differentiated from the single party state of Stalinism. In Africa there was also a duality as seen in the rise of Nkrumahism in Ghana and its elite party. At the same time she saw and wrote of the African who spoke "with awe and reverence of the party:"

> He does so not because he is told to do so by his leadership *nor* because of the negative features in the single party state which he does oppose. He does so out of his own volition and because he believes there is absolutely no other way to achieve freedom. *The party, to him, means the organization that has put an end to the fragmentation that imperialism brought.* . . . [The Africans] *have fastened on to the indissoluble link between freedom and organization. It is this which we have to gain for our present development, not as a generalization, but as the concrete growth of our organization*" (# 3212-13).

Flowing out of this discussion Dunayevskaya developed a section of the Perspectives on the "Need for Full-Time Organizers for Marxist-Humanism."

• "The Organization as Molder of History"—*Marxism and Freedom* spoke of Marxism as the unity of theory and practice. Dunayevskaya argued that such a unity "can be neither an abstraction which Hegel called 'a featureless unity' nor merely 'a long-winded weary story of its particular detail. It must have features, that is to say, a human body, *a very specific human body—that of organizers for Marxist-Humanism, full-time and otherwise*" ("Perspectives" 1962, # 3243). She wrote of the actions undertaken by such organizers and by News and Letters Committees as "not some monthly 'action sheet,' which gave people something bite-size to chew on." Rather, it was participation in

> the *actual* live struggles at the point of production and on the civil rights field; with the youth, and against the drive for war, etc., all leading to getting members for the organization, *the only organization that is governed by a total philosophy, the philosophy of Marxist-Humanism, a philosophy that is itself a form of action, as well as the action itself, stemming from many different directions both spontaneously from the workers and consciously from the organization's*

containing a link with history, history of the past in order to mold the history of today, today not tomorrow. . . . Unless we recognize the uniqueness of our contribution of Marxism we will be unable to build an independent organization with its own *reason d'etre*. More precisely put, it is not only a recognition but the action out of OUR ROLE AS MOLDERS OF HISTORY. This, then, is central to the new stage of all of us becoming ORGANIZERS FOR MARXIST-HUMANISM ("The New Stage, or the Organization as Molder of History," from Perspectives Report, 1962, #3246-47).

• "Organizational responsibility for theoretic positions; Individual responsibility for Organization"—

The fact that we are not a party nor lay claim to being one cannot by any stretch of imagination absolve us of responsibility for a body of thought, or, perhaps I should have said a philosophy—a Marxist-Humanist philosophy—that, has a body, a form of *being* as well as a form of expression.

The crux of the dialectic is the dialectical relationship of subject to object in the *process of history*. History is of today's making by live men in their relationships with other men through struggles, class struggles, freedom struggles, struggles of the future inherent in the present *to come to the surface, to become the actual*.

We become molders of history *when* both our mass activity and theoretic activity get spelled out as individual responsibility in a way which erases distinctions between subjective and objective, between mass and organization, between ranks and leaders, between philosophy and revolution ("Theory and Practice as the Turning Point," Perspectives 1964, # 3612-13).

Dunayevskaya here posed a crucial theme that she would return to again and again in the ensuing decades: "Organizational responsibility for the Idea of Marxist-Humanism." For her this meant a two-way road between organization and philosophy, as opposed to organization building without philosophy, or theoretical expression without organizational concretization. She expressed this as "Marxist-Humanist philosophy embodied in an organization."

This necessitated working out the relationship between philosophy, organization, and the mass movement. In this period Dunayevskaya would write: "*Organizational consciousness begins with the realization that none of these analyses, whether in book or pamphlet form, in newspaper or Political Letter form are 'for themselves.' It is conceit to think so. No one can build an organization when they underestimate the reason of the masses to grasp our philosophy organizationally*" ("The Need to Transform Reality," September 1963 Perspectives Report, #3279). This meant building a group where philosophy itself was action. In the 1960s, Dunayevskaya posed how such building needed to be in relation to the Freedom Now movement, to the struggles on the shop floor against speed-up and racism, and to the growing youth movement. These were the forces that could grasp philosophy organizationally.

In turn, just as philosophy gave action its direction, Dunayevskaya saw that theoretical expression itself deepened through organization whose ground was philosophic: "In contrast to the 1902-03 period, where party building meant organizational discipline of intellectuals, *today*, the Marxist-Humanist basis of organization and organizational responsibility for theoretic positions is the way, *the only way, of expanding theory itself*" (1964 Draft Perspectives #3589).

Dunayevskaya argued that, "each generation must restate Marxism for itself *not only theoretically but organizationally*. . . . The real course of the history of Marxism shows that, in *each* historic period, there has been a new relationship between the philosophy of human activity that is Marxism and its organization ("Organization, Philosophy and Reality," Draft Perspectives 1966, #4033).

•

We want to note that Dunayevskaya's projection of organization was unique in that it was rooted historically in philosophic-theoretic work of Marx, and in sharp opposition to the organizational practice of revolutionary organization post-Marx, including some of Lenin's formulations and practice. At the same time, it was concretely determined by the specific needs of the organization she founded, News and Letters Committees.

There was no straight line in this process. News and Letters Committees often experienced tensions in trying to work out its perspectives. In the 1960s, there was an enormous pull toward activism that reflected the reality of the Freedom Movement, where theoretical labors to provide clarity to the movement took a back seat to activity and more activity. Members of News and Letters Committees were not immune from this pull. Dunayevskaya again and again projected that thinking itself, "theoretical preparation for revolution," was the urgent need, not alone for the Freedom Movement as a whole, but for News and Letters Committees in particular. She saw this as organizational responsibility for the Idea, Marxist-Humanism. To theoretically-philosophically arm the organization, and the revolutionary movement as a whole, were seen by her as *the* urgent necessity of our era. Resistance to that task, as well as ongoing objective-subjective events, spurred Dunayevskaya to forge new pathways for its concretization, which could be grasped by News and Letters Committees' members, and hopefully find resonance in the Movement as a whole.

These struggles and tensions were not limited to the 1960s. Dunayevskaya's writings on philosophy's relation to organization was a major theme throughout her life. It came to be a primary focus in her final years as we will see in part V.

•

There was no sharp line between the post *Marxism and Freedom* projections and concretizations, and the origins of Dunayevskaya's second book, *Philosophy and Revolution*. We turn to this work in Part III.

¹ See "1962: Year of the Africa Trip," #3184-3250 and "Africa Trip of 1962," #9573-9677, in the *RDC* for articles, letters and reports.

² Dunayevskaya's own long history of relationship to labor struggles began in the 1930s, and can be seen in activities from the San Francisco General Strike to her support of the Southern Tenant Farmers' Union. Her 1940s analyses of state-capitalism centered on the lot of the laborer in Russia. Dunayevskaya's studies and outlines of Marx's *Capital* formed an important strand for her view of workers as revolutionary subject. As we saw in Chapter 2, it was the Miners' General Strike of 1949-50, which was catalyst for her view of workers as reason, and crucial to her 1953 concept of a movement from practice that was a form of theory. This became explicitly developed in the "Automation and the New Humanism" chapter of *Marxism and Freedom*.

³ For Dunayevskaya's further discussion of Mao and the category of Spirit in Self-Estrangement see her *Philosophy and Revolution*.

⁴ We will discuss only a small segment of Dunayevskaya's writing on organization, drawn from the period 1960-1966. Throughout Dunayevskaya's political-philosophic life she grappled with the form and content of Marxist revolutionary organization, as well as the kinds of organization that emerged from the mass movements. In the last years of her life she was working on a book she had tentatively titled "Dialectics of Organization and Philosophy: 'the party' and forms of organization born out of spontaneity." The book was unfinished at the time of her death. See Volume XIII of the *Supplement to the Raya Dunayevskaya Collection*: "Raya Dunayevskaya's Last Writings, 1986-1987, Toward the Dialectics of Organization and Philosophy." See also Part V of the present work.

Part III

**1960-1976, Philosophy and Revolution:
From Hegel to Sartre and
from Marx to Mao**

Chapter 8

1960-1973: The Process of Writing *Philosophy and Revolution* with Focus on Hegel's Absolutes

Shortly after *Marxism and Freedom* came off the press, Dunayevskaya wrote to Herbert Marcuse that she was thinking of a "supplement," to take up "more rough Ideas" on Hegel's Absolutes, which she had not developed in her first book. Fifteen years later *Philosophy and Revolution* (1973) with its philosophic foundation "Why Hegel? Why Now?" came off the press.

The philosophic focus of Dunayevskaya's work of the 1960s and early 1970s was fourfold: (1) the dialectic of Hegel's Absolutes "in and of themselves;" (2) an exploration of the impact of the Hegelian dialectic on the thought and activity of Marx and Lenin; (3) a critique of recent alternatives in light of Hegelian thought; (4) the positing/concretizing of Hegel's Absolutes within the freedom struggles, and revolutionary problematic of the 1960s and early 1970s.

The decade and a half of exploration and writing yielded a vast tapestry:[1]
• Summary notes on each of Hegel's major philosophic writings;
• Correspondence with philosophers and revolutionaries from the United States, as well as from Africa and East Europe;
• Presentations on dialectics for audiences as varied as Black auto workers in Detroit, anti-war New Left youth in Japan, and women in an emerging Women's Liberation Movement;
• Draft chapters of *Philosophy and Revolution* circulated to and discussed with Marxist-Humanists colleagues;
• The founding of a Marxist-Humanist Archives collection.

This chapter will examine a few strands of the process of writing *Philosophy and Revolution*, with emphasis on her developments of Hegel's Absolutes in relation to ongoing liberation struggles.

1960-61: Letters on Preliminary Notions, Summary Notes Probing Hegel's Philosophic Works

In the early 1960s Dunayevskaya began to work out preliminary conceptions of her new work. "The first broad outline of the new book," she noted in an early commentary, was given in three letters written in October, 1960—one to Herbert Marcuse and the other two to News and Letters colleagues Louis Gogol and Saul Blackman. The letters became the basis for her first philosophic discussion of the new book with the leadership of News and Letters Committees, and are briefly examined:[2]

• "I hope I may intrude upon you with some [thoughts] on the Absolute Idea," Dunayevskaya wrote to Marcuse (October 16, 1960):

> I proceed to work out the philosophic foundations (the Hegelian Absolute Idea and Marx's Humanism) for the present day struggles for freedom in the underdeveloped economies, a sort of counterpart to *Marxism and Freedom* which limited itself to the present-day descent from ontology to technology....
> I would like at once to make clear *what* is the "thesis" I use from Hegel's final chapter. It is found on p. 467 [Johnson and Struthers translation]: "The self-determination therefore in which alone the Idea is, is to hear itself speak." The self-determinations of people are, surely, no less important than the self-determination of the Idea. It is no accident that Nagy, the Petofi intelligentsia, and the Hungarian Workers Councils all fought its ideological battles by unfolding Marxist-Humanism and this same discovery appears in Senegal where Leopold Senghor, for all his apologia for De Gaulle, unfolds the same banner (*PON*, 99).

Dunayevskaya proceeded to "the unfoldment of the Absolute Idea in Hegel's *Logic*, all the way glancing at which point in it, at the various historic stages in the development of the Marxist movement, the Marxists 'got caught.'" Hers was a reading of Absolute Idea in relation to two historic two periods:

(1) The period of Lenin's World War I exploration of *Science of Logic* as he confronted the vulgarized, truncated Marxism of the Second International, as well as the mechanist Marxism of his Bolshevik colleague Nikolai Bukharin.

Quoting from the opening paragraphs of the Absolute Idea chapter, she found that Hegel's discussion of the limitations of inquiring cognition—where "subject, method, and object are not posited as the one identical notion"—spoke to the Second International's neglect and perversion of the dialectic method. Bukharin too, could be fit in here: "Bukharin speaks of 'society' as if indeed it was matter, dead matter" (101).

In contrast, Dunayevskaya posited Lenin's creative, revolutionary reading of Hegel: "[He] saw Hegel laying the premises for historical materialism" (103). She was reading the Absolute Idea chapter, with Lenin's 1914 Notebooks in front of her. At the same time, she pinpointed Lenin's philosophic stopping point in the last paragraph of the *Logic*, and discussed the fact that Lenin did not develop his discovery of the creativity of cognition when he was writing his notes on the Absolute Idea chapter itself. This remaining philosophically on the threshold, spoke to "the dividing point for our epoch" from Lenin's.

(2) Dunayevskaya turned to her own age and the Absolute Idea's dialectic as it illuminated contemporary movements such as the Hungarian Revolution and the African revolutions, and was itself illuminated by these movements. She saw the first paragraph of the Absolute Idea chapter as containing "the stopping point of today's African intelligentsia. If you are versed in their constant reiteration of the 'African personality,' you will recognize them easily enough in Hegel" (100).

Later in the letter, she would "jump to Khrushchev and his state philosophers," who had supposedly "reconstituted the [Hegelian] law of the negation of the negation [earlier thrown out by Stalin who feared its revolutionary meaning against a totalitarian society] . . . . With missile thrust and automated production achieved, they have need of the law *for the natural sciences as they practice them.*"

In relating the *Logic's* Absolute Idea chapter to these two historic periods, Dunayevskaya's conversation with the dialectic spoke to the todayness of Hegel's thought:

> [E]ven if he did reside in ivory towers, there were awfully crowded ones—so much so that today's freedom fighters in Africa find room there too. . . .
> [T]he dividing point for our epoch is precisely on this free, individual, total liberation which shows, both in thought and struggles, what they are aiming [at] and thus compelling me in any case to read and reread that Absolute Knowledge, Absolute Idea, Absolute Mind as each developing struggle on the world scene deepens (102, 103).

She ended by inviting Marcuse to comment on these "thoughts-in-process."

• Dunayevskaya's letter to Louis Gogol (October 12, 1960, *SRDC* #13761) sought his collaboration in working through a number of questions on science, aiding her on a possible chapter for the new book. She began with a critical summary of Gustav Wetter's discussion of modern science in his *Dialectical Materialism*:

(1) She questioned Wetter's leaving out of his presentation on "science," Russia's 1943 revision of the law value and decision to revise the way Marx's *Capital* was to be taught. Dunayevskaya argued that this meant being unaware "of the breaking point in Russian attitudes to the empirical sciences," and demonstrated that "the fragmentation of the worker in our society brings with it the fragmentation of the intellectual."

(2) In accepting the Russian division of Marxian philosophy into two, dialectical materialism and historical materialism, Wetter concerned himself only with the former. Dunayevskaya commented:

The Russians do it for the very same reason that they broke the structure of teaching of Marx's *Capital*—to hide both the inner springs of their society and to transform history itself into an abstraction. That is to say, you consider "societies": slave, feudal, capitalist, "socialist" without seeing the *self developing subject*, the *proletariat*, who alone can bring about "the negation of the negation" and establish a society where the *individual* is the social entity and only proof of its freedom. The Communists as state-capitalists and Wetter as Jesuit want to disregard that "subject." Suppose we let them do it because we "really" want to study science "objectively." The very history of science itself would give the lie to that not only because, taking it from Planck through Einstein, the historic *period* would have a great deal to say on the subject, but because the very *inner* dialectic of science depends on its *continuity and accumulated* knowledge.

(3) In Wetter's dialectic chapter "the 1955 *re-vision* of the negation of the negation [which Dunayevskaya had taken up in *Marxism and Freedom* as "Communism's Perversion of Marx's Economic-Philosophic Manuscripts"] is treated as a *re-establishment* (sic!) of that law." She argued that Wetter had neglected Stalin's omission of negation of the negation, and thereby misrepresented Karpushin's revision of the law.

Despite these critiques, Dunayevskaya felt Wetter could help readers "to see certain of the relations of dialectical laws and natural science." It was this relationship between dialectical laws and natural science that she wished Gogol to take up. She asked him to think about: "(1) To what extent did dialectical materialism, even as perverted as it is by the Russians, help the Russian scientists strike out on their own *in advance* of 'Western Science.'" Here her reference was to the Sputnik. "(2) When they did make their leap, did that, technologically, produce *dis*continuous development so that, far from having 'to catch up' in all spheres, they have sufficient know how in sufficient spheres to become 'superior' in what matters in capitalist society: military, and perhaps even heavy industry[?]" (3) Did "living in the age of 'the unified field theory'" mean that "not only Russia, but even the underdeveloped countries could leap ahead[?]"

• "Philosophic Foundations of Man's Struggles for Freedom in Colonial Countries," was the title Dunayevskaya gave to her preliminary work on her new book in a letter to Saul Blackman (October 1960, *SRDC* # 13768). She wrote of reading heavily on the economics and political movements of Africa, Asia, and Latin America. She asked, "What are the 'colonial countries'?" noting that after Hitler, "colony" could be in Europe as well, and encompassed now those such as Czechoslovakia and Hungary in Russia's domination. "Above all, since I will not divide economic foundation from the struggle for the minds of men, we have, in Marxist Humanism, that which covers America as well as Hungary, Senegal, as well as Cuba."

She saw state capitalism not only in Russia, but what all capitalist countries had in some manner to adopt. In the period 1940-50, with war, state-capitalism led to science wedded to the military, and the splitting of the atom. When wedded to industry, it led to automation, and what she saw as the new of *discontinuous development,* that is, leaps ahead even as other fields lagged behind: "1950-60 then is *all* new. Automation. Outer space. ICBMs. 'Genes'."

Dunayevskaya pointed to agriculture in Russia—Khrushchev's attempt to transform virgin fields in Siberia—as well as to Sputnik, "a world transportation break-through," as possible manifestations of this kind of discontinuous development, which moved "to catch up with capitalism in the *most* advanced country," bringing the colonial world to Russia's shore.

With African countries beginning to achieve independence, Russia suddenly had a new interest in competing with Western imperialism. At the same time, China was following a different path of "communes." One now had "Mao's Thought" vs. "Soviet Marxism." Dunayevskaya formulated these developments in the question she had raised in *Marxism and Freedom*: "'What Happens After?'* There, state capitalism of the era of the scientific break-through has one answer; we and the millions, billions of submerged humanity another."

The letter further discussed the relation of dialectics and nature, and named the Absolute Idea as the self developing proletariat concretely evolving a new society. As with the letters to Herbert Marcuse and Louis Gogol, this letter was part of virgin rock from which Dunayevskaya shaped the ideas for her new work.

These letters and others from the period showed Dunayevskaya "thinking out loud," on philosophy, science, revolutionary subjectivity, and Marxist-Humanist practice, among other themes. Some of the discussion became part of "The Challenge of Mao Tse-tung" chapter of an expanded edition of *Marxism and Freedom*. Other strands were developed within the "Economic Realities and the Dialectics of Liberation" part of *Philosophy and Revolution.*

Notes on *Phenomenology of Mind*

As preparation for writing her new book, Dunayevskaya undertook summary notes on Hegel's major philosophic writings in the 1960s. Her Notes on *Phenomenology of Mind* were written in December 1960; those on *Science of Logic* were composed in January 1961; Notes on the smaller *Logic* from the *Encyclopedia of the Philosophical Sciences* were completed in February 1961 (*PON*, 35-90).

These summaries were not "private notebooks," but shared with her colleagues in News and Letters, and correspondents outside of News and Letters. They were a treatment of the dialectic, a Marxist discussion of Hegel's writing in and of itself, with particular emphasis on sections such as "Spirit in Self-Estrangement" and "Absolute Knowledge" in *Phenomenology* and "The Third Attitude of Thought Toward the Objective World" in the smaller *Logic,* which she felt had particular relevance to the present moment. Her notes on *Science of Logic* took in material from Lenin's 1914 *Abstract*.

We will focus our commentary on her "Notes on Hegel's *Phenomenology*." Dunayevskaya began by dividing *Phenomenology* into two major departments:

> *I. Consciousness, Self-Consciousness and Reason*, being the summation of both the relationship, or rather awareness of a world outside oneself through feudalism to the beginning of capitalism, i.e., commercial capitalism; and *II. Spirit, Religion, and Absolute Knowledge,* which takes us from industrial capitalism and its ideological predecessors covering the field from Christianity through the enlightenment to the Jacobins of the French Revolution, all the way to "the new society" (Absolute Knowledge) with its "predecessor" in Greek Art and the Greek city-state (*PON,* 35).

In *Philosophy and Revolution,* this division into two would be expressed as "What Happens Up to the Day of Revolution?" and "What Happens After the Revolution?" (*Philosophy and Revolution*, 11)

When Dunayevskaya began commentary on the first division she moved from consciousness to the lordship and bondage section of self-consciousness, "a *production* relationship." Her emphasis was on what occurred after the bondman gained "a mind of his own," where "if freedom is not 'a type of freedom which does not get beyond the attitude of bondage,' it must first confront objective reality" (*PON,* 36).

"Various attitudes of mind," in Hegel's *Phenomenology* were what Dunayevskaya traced, often relating them to the contemporary scene. Thus, when she quoted Hegel on unhappy consciousness—a "personality confined within its narrow self and its petty activity, a personality brooding over itself, as unfortunate as it is pitiably destitute"—she referred to her own writing on "the specific personalities of the old radical who cannot find a place for himself in bourgeois society or in the movement as examples of this unhappy consciousness" (36).

When discussing "The Law of the Heart, and the Frenzy of Self-Conceit," she raised the question of,

> the labor bureaucrat and his "earnestness of high purpose, which seeks its pleasure in displaying the excellence of his own true nature, and in bringing about the welfare of mankind." When it meets up against mankind's opposition to this personal interpretation, "the heart-throb for the welfare of mankind passes therefore into the rage of frantic self-conceit, into the fury of consciousness to preserve itself from destruction" (38).

Specific figures—China's Mao, Cuba's Castro, Yugoslavia's Milovan Djilas with his "counter-thesis to the new class"—were critiqued in relation to the section in Hegel called, "Self-Conscious Individuals Associated as a Community of Animals and the Deception Thence Arising: The Real Fact."

While Dunayevskaya discussed moments in the contemporary scene that Hegel's *Phenomenology* illuminated for her, she was not arguing for any one to one relation, or for an exclusivity of interpretation. Rather, as she wrote later in *Philosophy and Revolution*:

> The plenitude (and suffering) of consciousness in self-development that Hegel has gathered together for his "Science of the Experience of Consciousness" allows for a great variety of interpretations (very often by the same discerning reader upon *each* rereading of a passage). But such varied analyses can be made because, and only because, Hegel created his dialectic from a most painstaking and rigorous examination of the movement of no less than 2500 years of history (10).

Dunayevskaya called the second major subdivision, Spirit, "the cornerstone of the entire work." Within this subdivision, the section on spirit in self-estrangement, "which Hegel also defines as 'the discipline of culture," became a major focal point for her commentary:

> [I]t is a critique of everything from the Industrial Revolution to the French Revolution, and including what Marx called the "fetishism of commodities," as well as what Hegel calls a spiritual, but factual, "reign of terror"—the intellectual run amok. Throughout, we will be seeing the contradiction between the individual and society or between what we would call petty bourgeois individualism and the truly social individual (39).

She proceeded both to follow this section in and of itself, and to relate it to historic figures such as Pierre Proudhon, and in her own age to Mao and Trotsky. Her point was not so much to give examples, as it was to speak of the discerning power of the Hegelian dialectic: "[W]hat is so extraordinary about Hegel, that he catches the spirit of an epoch in *crisis*, and, therefore, its ramifications extend into both ages that are marked beyond the one he analyzes, and personality beyond those that he had known in his own period or in history" (40). In her Notes, Dunayevskaya wrote further commentary on Spirit in Self-Estrangement, as well as on other sections of Spirit and on Religion.

Here we turn to her remarks on Absolute Knowledge the final chapter of *Phenomenology,* where she began: "As we reach this apex of Hegelianism—the consummation of experience, of philosophy—we will confront the end of the division between object and subject. This takes the form of making consciousness itself the object" (45). This was not, in Hegel's words, "pure conceptual comprehension of the object; here this knowledge is to be taken only in its development" (quoted, 45).

Dunayevskaya commented: "Development is of the essence. It is the beginning out of which something arises. It is the middle through which something must be passed. It is the end, 'the mediated result,' which is really not an end of anything but a process of development which is the beginning of another process as much as it is the end of a former one" (45). Thus there is movement, action: "This is the movement towards science, that is to say, from individual experience through social experience, to a universal generalization of the experience which goes to make up the action" (46). For Hegel "the actual existence of this Notion, science does not appear in time and in reality till spirit has arrived to this stage of being conscious regarding itself" (quoted, 46).

Dunayevskaya pointed to Hegel's concentration of the philosophical history of that journey in thought in a single page of the Absolute Knowledge chapter, "Hegel sums up the entire development of philosophy and science from Descartes to himself." She summarized the passage to "where Hegel comes in," and then noted: "[t]he last three pages of the *Phenomenology* are an out pouring of 'simple mediating activity in thinking' where the whole process releases itself, History and Science, Nature and Spirit are [quoting Hegel] 'born anew from the womb of knowledge—the new state of existence, a new world and a new embodiment of spirit'" (46-7).

These notes on *Phenomenology* as well as those on the *Science of Logic* and the *Encyclopedia Logic* would undergo far-reaching development over the next decade to take the form of the "Absolute Negativity as New Beginning" chapter of *Philosophy and Revolution*.

A New Philosophic Moment: Absolute Negativity as New Beginning,
I. 1967-1969

In 1987, Dunayevskaya wrote of the new philosophic moment she had created in writing *Philosophy and Revolution*:

> "As new beginning" has no precedent. I don't think I thought of it until after re-reading Absolute Idea in *Science of Logic*, and that was *after* the three final syllogisms in the *Philosophy of Mind*, that I suddenly said to myself: it is not only a new beginning it is *as* new beginning, that Marx clung to Hegel after he discovered his own new continent of thought—*that* was *the* new beginning. Why did no one see it? (What *is* Marxist-Humanism? How to Project it at Momentous Historic Moments?" March 16, 1987 *SRDC* #10875).

"Absolute Negativity as New Beginning" as a new philosophic moment was inseparable from Dunayevskaya's original philosophic exploration of Hegel's Absolutes, her May 12, and May 20, 1953 letters (*PON*, 15-32). She would characterize those letters as finding in Hegel's Absolutes a dual movement, a "movement from practice that is itself a form of theory and a movement from theory that is itself a form of philosophy and revolution" (Letter of January 13, 1987 *RDC* # 10726).

Marxism and Freedom (1958) was her first treatment of Hegel's Absolutes in book form, and had as its emphasis the manifestation of the absolutes in the movement from practice, from French Revolution to the 1950s of East European Revolts, battles against automation, and the Montgomery Bus Boycott.

In the decade following *Marxism and Freedom*'s appearance Dunayevskaya continually returned to her 1953 discussion of Hegel's Absolutes. Three strands were present which led to a deepening of this original philosophic moment of Marxist-Humanism:

(1) Her continual rereading and study of Hegel's thought, particularly his absolutes, in relation of the May 12 and May 20, 1953 letters.

(2) The world objective-subjective situation which on the one hand saw the rise of Third World Revolutions, the intensification of Civil Rights struggles, a growing youth anti-war movement and the beginnings of a new Women's Liberation movement—continual manifestations of the movement from practice. On the other hand, these movements began to face contradictory ideological pulls from without and within (Maoism, Trotskyism, the Sino-Soviet Conflict, bourgeois liberalism and reformism, divisions between leaders and masses) that threatened impasse and retrogression in liberation struggles. Theoretical clarification was the urgent need of the ongoing liberation struggles.

(3) Within News and Letters Committees, Dunayevskaya found that while there was a grappling with the movement from practice and a concretization of it in the pages of the newspaper, there was not a sustained exploration of the movement from theory as related to Hegel's Absolutes. She saw the need for her own colleagues to grapple in a deeper manner with the revolution in philosophy embedded in her 1953 breakthrough on Hegel's Absolutes. *Absolute Negativity as New Beginning* was the philosophic new moment Dunayevskaya worked out in the 1960s.

"Absolute Negativity as New Beginning," was the title of the first draft of what became Chapter One of *Philosophy and Revolutionary*. It was written in January 1967, and was part of a section called "Why Hegel, Why Now?" Soon after completing this draft, Dunayevskaya held a theoretical conference on its contents with the Detroit News and Letters Committee. In a letter sent in preparation for the conference she wrote of the difference between *Marxism and Freedom* and the new book: "[T]he theory [in *Marxism and Freedom*] was so overwhelmingly concerned with workers in production that the so-called strictly philosophic parts in relationship to Hegel were a very small portion of it. This is entirely reversed with the new book, and especially so in the part called 'Why Hegel? Why Now?'" (*SRDC* #13956).

The "Absolute Negativity as New Beginning" chapter would have two additional drafts with considerable expansion of content (second draft, 1968 *RDC* #4190; third draft, 1970 *SRDC* # 13128). Besides the continuous development of the chapter, and the Why Hegel? Why Now? part of *Philosophy and Revolution*, what also became transformed was where this part would be situated in the book. In 1964 Dunayevskaya wrote:

> I wish to continue with some of the philosophic problems of the new book. This time I have an outline of one of the parts [the section on Why Hegel Why Now?] The very fact that I say "one of the" parts rather than the first part shows the problem. If it were for us, it would definitely be part one; for the public, however, I cannot begin straight off with a problem in philosophy; I must show the objective world first so all can see the obvious before I begin saying the not-so-obvious (Letter to Bess and Eugene, Oct 1, 1964 *SRDC* #13890).

By 1968 she had developed a different view:

> The more I work with the thing [the new book], the less I can see starting with the present. It is impossible to reverse history or philosophy, even where looking into the past is only for purposes of illuminating the present. In a word, much as we all groaned under the weight of Hegel, this is precisely where we will have to start. The only way we will be able to make the readers realize the present of Part III, will be by extending the Introduction and that I will do (Dear Friends [of News & Letters] letter of February 20, 1968. *SRDC* #14018).

The factors that led to the forging of the Absolute Negativity as New Beginning chapter—further explorations of Hegel's Absolutes, contradictions in the ongoing freedom movements, the work of News and Letters Committees—were also the factors that impacted Dunayevskaya's decision to begin *Philosophy and Revolution* with the new philosophic moment of Absolute Negativity as New Beginning.

One of Dunayevskaya's fullest discussions of absolute negativity in the period leading up to *Philosophy and Revolution,* was her June 1969 letter to a colleague, Richard Greeman. It was reprinted as "The Newness of Our Philosophic-Historic Contribution" (*RDC* # 4407; major excerpts *PON*, 166). The form of the letter was a response to a presentation Greeman had made on dialectics. Early in the letter Dunayevskaya spoke to what separated *Marxism and Freedom* from her new work:

> What distinguishes *Philosophy and Revolution* from *Marxism and Freedom* is that, instead of dealing, primarily with revolutions, and secondarily, with the underlying philosophies; instead of so bemoaning the intellectual sloth that has accumulated in the revolutionary movement since Lenin's death that one decides *to wait for others* to come with us on that journey of discovery of Hegelian philosophy, we here take the plunge ourselves, deep, deep into "absolute negativity." *No one since Marx, not even Lenin, went that deep.* . . .
> *Philosophy and Revolution* is so new a reinterpretation of Hegelian dialectics, so totally belonging to *our age,* and so linked to the revolutions-to-be, that none but Marxist-Humanists, *specifically us,* could have written it (*PON*, 167-68).

The thrust of her letter centered on what separated her dive into Hegel, particularly on the Absolutes, from other returns to the dialectic, including those of Lenin and Marx. She first took up Lenin:

> [W]hat, *specifically*, philosophically, marks off our age from that of Lenin[?] By the time of the collapse of the Second International, Lenin was sufficiently disgusted with "materialists" to stand in awe of "idealist" dialectics and write: "Cognition not only reflects the world, but creates it." Yet this isn't what he developed. That task is ours. His was, as you well know, transformation into opposite (168).

Dunayevskaya pinpointed the historic moment that signified the new stage in cognition:

> What was new was that the death of Stalin [1953] lifted an incubus from the minds of workers and intellectuals, but first of all and most seriously from workers. And precisely because workers were girding for actual revolutionary struggles, revolutionary intellectuals no longer feared the "ontological Absolute," but began seeing it, instead, as the *concrete universal*. That is to say, the *new* in the Absolute as a unity of theory and practice was that it was being disclosed as a movement *from practice* that was on its way both to theory and a new society....
> This was the *historic* breakthrough to that which separates one era—Lenin's—and another—ours (168-69).

The first concretization of this breakthrough in book form was *Marxism and Freedom*. *Philosophy and Revolution* was a further theoretical preparation for revolution. It focused on "*strictly philosophic* problems in a comprehensiveness never attempted before, and, on the other hand, 'Economic Reality and the Dialectics of Liberation' [as taken up in Part III] appearing in so varied, contradictory forms as to fail to measure up to the challenges of the era."

The "strictly philosophic problems" centered on the Absolutes in Hegel:

> Absolute Knowledge as the unity of history and its comprehension in the *Phenomenology of Mind;* the Absolute Idea as the unity of theory and practice in the *Science of Logic* and Absolute Mind as the unity of the Individual and the Universal in the *Philosophy of Mind*—are approached as new beginnings because our age of absolutes sees something in them that Hegel just guessed at and yet, as genius, caught in the air of the epoch of the French Revolution (170).

This dialectic of the Absolutes came to the fore in the post World War II world with an illumination and a concreteness that was not present in Marx's or Lenin's day. Dunayevskaya noted that Marx hit out sharply against any "Absolute," while at the same time appropriating the Hegelian dialectic. Marx saw Hegel's dialectic "not only as method but as a *critique of reality*," with historical materialism disclosing what was enveloped in "mystical form." Dunayevskaya, writing in the middle of the 20th century found new illuminations in the Absolute:

> What we did that was *new*, and could have only been seen in our era, was to grasp the *division* in the problems dealt with *before and after* the Revolution, in Hegel's case the French Revolution, in our case, the Russian Revolution.
> What we [in 1953] had singled out as new in the Absolute Idea in the *Science of Logic* was the manner in which the *second* negativity becomes "the turning point of the movement of the Notion . . . for the transcendence of the opposition between Notion and Reality, and that unity which is the truth, rest upon this subjectivity alone [*Science of Logic II* p. 477]. With the birth of a new, Third World, the question that had to be solved was: is the new subject of revolution to be found only in the Africa-Asian-Latin American revolutions, or by including in "subjectivity" not only force of revolution, but also *theory in historic continuity,* [do] we retain both the proletariat in technologically advanced lands, as well as the Marxist-Humanism they brought anew onto the historic stage (171).

Dunayevskaya formulated what she saw as the need of the age in relation to the illuminations one obtained from the Hegelian dialectic and from Marx:

> The whole point is that each age has a task, and the drive, the self-movement, *from practice and from theory,* suddenly makes one see points, get illuminations for the tasks that confront the epoch, even from so seemingly closed an "ontological system" as Hegel's. The truth is that it was at the point that Hegel had reached the *unity* of the Individual and the Universal in a way that it seemed no problem at all to depart from Hegel who used the philosopher as yardstick for measuring the development of mankind, where the true Subject is the mass in motion. But without this *internal dialectic* it would have been impossible to work out the *concrete universal.*
> Naturally, this cannot be achieved in thought alone. Naturally, men's actions alone can reconstruct society on new beginnings, can end the prehistory of mankind. Naturally, Marx's concept of *praxis*—the activity of men, mental and manual—and not Hegel's "Absolutes," contains the answer. But everyone from Marxists to anarchists never tires of speaking of *praxis* without ever, at least not since 1917, achieving a social revolution. So a new beginning, a new point of departure, a new unity of philosophy and revolution must be worked out, and it is this we invite all to help us achieve so that freedom finally becomes a reality (172).

II. 1969-1971, The Simultaneity of Writing and Projecting the New Book in the Black Dimension and in Women's Liberation

The writing of *Philosophy and Revolution,* as with *Marxism and Freedom,* was a collaborative project. In addition to carrying on a wide-ranging correspondence, and inviting the direct collaboration of East European thinkers in writing a chapter on the East European revolts, Dunayevskaya held philosophic conferences on the relation of the book to objective-subjective concerns of the time. In 1969 she convened a Black/Red conference in relation to Black revolt in America; in 1971 a News and Letters Women's Liberation conference met.

The Black/Red Conference was held in Detroit, which had experienced a major inner-city rebellion in the summer of 1967. One of the unique dimensions of the Civil Rights Movement in Detroit was the emergence of Black caucuses in the auto plants/auto union. In the late 60s, Black revolt was widespread throughout the United States, and in the fall of 1968 Dunayevskaya issued a Call for a Black/Red Conference—black for the historic, ongoing mass movement in America, red for the coloration of revolution—"in order *to listen* to black thinking, *not* as if were no more than a command to act, but as part of a total *philosophy*, the real pre-requisite to revolution." The participants in the conference were predominantly Black and working class.

Dunayevskaya began her presentation focusing on *man* and *labor*, in contrast to the Nixon Administration's attempt to have everyone focusing on the astronauts who had just visited the moon. "[T]he reason you can go to the moon, but can't solve the housing problem right here in a little slum, is because you have always had, in class society, this division between science and life.... All of the history of mankind can be developed just on the history of labor.... Labor has built everything" (*PON*, 145). The kind of labor she spoke about was not alone manual, but mental:

> [T]his mental activity is not restricted to scientists or to other intellectuals ... What is most important of all is that workers think their own thoughts. And the thoughts that workers think are the thoughts that *move* the world.
> It is all summarized in one word: freedom.... What gets everything changed is thinking how and by what means you can move to freedom, and masses actively moving toward freedom (145-46).

To labor and thought, Dunayevskaya added some colors: "Black and red stand for the actual movement of society." She then began historically with 1831, the year of Nat Turner's Revolt and the year of Hegel's death: "[W]hat Nat Turner did and thought is related to Hegel, though they were of course quite unknown to each other" (146). For Dunayevskaya, the revolt and Turner's Confession—"But cannot you think the same idea which prompted me might prompt others as well as myself to this undertaking [the revolt]?"—were dialectics:

> Here is a supposedly unintelligent man, and he recognizes that as great as is his own struggle for freedom, it is impossible that he, though he heard the voices from heaven, thought of it alone. He is absolutely sure that the Spirit, meaning the objective movement for freedom, and the people fighting for freedom are the same thing.
> How these two movements—objective and subjective, idea of freedom and people fighting for freedom—function together, is what we are going to be learning today. It is called *dialectics* (146).

Dunayevskaya's discussion traced dialectics from Greek times to the French Revolution and Hegel. "[W]hen [Hegel] began to talk about dialectic, it didn't mean only thoughts bumping up against each other, it meant action." She then moved to Marx and the dialectic, particularly his relationship to the Abolitionists in America and the fact that labor could not advance before the Civil War.

Dunayevskaya focused on two moments in 20th century American history which involved the Black question: (1) the Garvey Movement of the 1920s as demonstrating as crucial dimension of Negro nationalism in the U.S.; (2) the formation of the Congress of Industrial Organization, CIO, in 1936, which could not have been built without Black workers.

She then returned to *Philosophy and Revolution* and discussed its Part I, "Why Hegel, Why Now?"

> [Why Hegel, Why Now?] takes up the dialectic as the algebra of revolution, the methodology of what man has done in fighting for freedom. Once you get three things, you have the essence of it: 1) the dialectic—the actual development, through actual class struggle, through actual contradictions; 2) the right Subject—who is resolving these contradictions? Marx said it was the class force, but helped by other forces such as minorities, the Black people, and the youth; 3) how does this movement from below for freedom, from practice, unite with the movement that comes from theory? In other words, the relationship of theory to practice (150).

After continuing discussion on Parts I and II of *Philosophy and Revolution* she took up the part she wished help in writing, "Economic Reality and the Dialectics of Liberation." She conceived it on two levels, the first being the world level discussing the relationship between the advanced countries and the technologically underdeveloped countries. On this level, particularly with the African Revolutions, there was the daring and greatness of those revolutions. But at the same time there was a move back to military regimes and to siding with American imperialism or its Russian counterpart. Dunayevskaya asked whether this was due to African leaders no longer relying on the African masses who had won liberation.

The second level of this dialectics of liberation was being played out in the Black movement in America. Dunayevskaya gave a brief overview of aspects of that movement, including contradictions that had arisen from within. She asked the participants in the conference to discuss the present period in the movement, doing so by becoming theoreticians in response to the newly arising forces.

After Dunayevskaya's presentation, the fifty plus participants engaged in a wide-ranging discussion over several hours.[3] Black caucus in the shops, electoral politics, Black power, the divisions between Black and white workers, the division between youth and adults, the overthrow of the system, were among the topics taken up. One participant asked, "When does theory end and action begin? Capitalism exploits not only black people, but white, and Indian, and Mexican-American. Our problem is how to take over. Power is never given, it always has to be taken. When are we going to start planning to take over and give power back to the people?"

In her summary Dunayevskaya spoke to the role of theory:

> Theory is not just a lot of talking. It is a clearing of your head—it helps you to get the capitalist out of there. That is why it prepares you for your revolution. You will be part of the new book. Even if you don't want theory, theory is going to take you anyhow. . . . It would be fitting to end with one phrase from a white Abolitionist, Wendell Phillips, who said that if you get six people in a room all discussing freedom, you have the first act of revolution. That is what you did today.

•

The Women's Liberation Conference held in Detroit in February 1971, was called to invite the participation of women, members and non-members of News and Letters Committee, in the writing of the final chapter of *Philosophy and Revolution*, "New Passions and New Forces." The first part of Dunayevskaya's presentation (as recorded in a brief summary, *RDC* #4355) focused on the division between "the Idea as such" and "the Idea whose time has come" in relation to women's liberation. For the Idea as such she took up Marx's *Economic and Philosophic Essays* in 1844, and at the time they were translated into English by herself (1958). In the essay on "Private Property and Communism" Marx had written, "the most fundamental relationship of all human relationships is that of man to woman." In 1947, when Dunayevskaya took up this essay, she had stressed Marx's anti-capitalism and anti-vulgar communism, and not man/woman. Dunayevskaya pointed to the transition point between "Idea as such" and "Idea whose time has come" which occurred in the 1950s, "when News & Letters Committees wrote their Constitution and women were singled out as one of the forces of Revolution."

The 1960s signified a totally new stage—Women's Liberation as an Idea whose time had come. Dunayevskaya listed the new aspects to this movement: they were young, out of the Left, the Black dimension was present, and they had no illusion that they represented a majority. However, a disregard for philosophy had brought the women's liberation movement to an impasse. "[*Despite*] *all these things in their favor, the Women's Liberation Movement has found the need for philosophy*." The objectivity of the movement kept it rising up: "The most important point of the whole Movement is that the women are objecting to being *object*, instead of *Subject*, to use the Hegelian term. They are seeking to become *whole human beings*."

Dunayevskaya stressed the need to develop theory for the movement to advance. She discussed two theoretical works on women — Kate Millett's *Sexual Politics*, and Simone de Beauvoir's *The Second Sex* — and then turned to her book-in-progress, ending with the chapter on "New Passions and Forces" on Blacks, youth, and women:

> In the case of the Women, we have not succeeded in hearing quite that many new voices. What we do know is that *self-development means that you will gain a new dimension in yourself, will feel a totality in the new person you are becoming, as you give expression to what you are feeling and thinking.* The proof of Marxist-Humanism will be in your own self-development.

A second section of her presentation took up "the organizational questions flowing from the theoretical groundwork." This involved concrete tasks for News & Letters–Women's Liberation Committee including working with working class women, having voices from below in the pages of *News & Letters*, projecting the philosophy of Marxist-Humanism.

The discussion following Dunayevskaya's presentation took up such questions as the difference between theory and philosophy, whether a definition of class could be broad enough to encompass women, and how to see women's liberation in terms of individuality and universality. A number of the women's liberationists spoke of the status of the women's movement in their various locales.

In her summary, Dunayevskaya spoke of the specificity of News & Letters — Women's Liberation Committee: its concentration on the proletarian and Black dimension within women's liberation; the fact that it had a philosophy which was a total one. And she spoke to its tasks:

> What we have to do is bring out the new dimensions of women as revolutionary force. The greatest strength of the movement is its *spontaneity* — including the need for correspondence with others: to share our ideas, and elicit theirs. . . . You will soon discover why correspondence is the most important activity of all, as you discover that putting down your ideas in black and white, rather than expressing them orally brings out some surprising things. And it *forces* you to clarify your thoughts.

Establishment of the Marxist-Humanist Archives
The Raya Dunayevskaya Collection

In 1969, in the midst of writing the draft chapters for *Philosophy and Revolution,* Dunayevskaya established the Marxist-Humanist Archives. Her concept was one of a fully open and accessible collection, organized by the founder. She arranged for its preservation on microfilm. Two major determinants were present in her establishment of an archives collection: (1) She had experienced and was continuing to experience first hand the lack of availability of Marx's writing more than a three-quarters of a century after his death. It had taken the Russian Revolution to finally make available such crucial writings as the *Economic and Philosophic Manuscripts of 1844,* only to have them pushed aside and reburied with Stalinism. *The Grundrisse,* the original ending of Vol. I of *Capital,* and Marx's *Ethnological Notebooks* were among the works that experienced even longer delays before being made available. The failure to have the whole of Marx's writings was still evident a quarter of a century later, at the time of the centenary of Marx's death—a fact that Dunayevskaya continued to call attention to and fight against.

(2) The crucial necessity of having available not alone the results of a founder's studies, but the *process* of reaching those results. She saw this in relation to Marx and to Lenin. In tracing through Marx's notebooks and correspondence, together with the historic events of his day, the Civil War in the U.S. and the Paris Commune, she was able to discern how he had arrived at *Capital* (1867), and had developed it further in the French edition (1873-75). Dunayevskaya strove to share the process of her work at each stage with her colleagues and wanted to make that process available in documents in the Marxist-Humanist Archives organized by herself. This stood in contrast to what she called Lenin's philosophic ambivalence. He had not shared his Philosophic Notebooks—what Dunayevskaya regarded as Lenin's philosophic preparation for the Russian Revolution—with his Bolshevik co-leaders.

The origin and development of her writings as an archives collection, (*The Raya Dunayevskaya Collection*), were closely tied to specific moments in the development of each of her major writings. Thus, her first "on the record" discussion and organization of her archives, (not at that time for deposit with an institution, but for her colleagues in News and Letters Committees) came in preparation for the first News & Letters Convention after the publication of *Marxism and Freedom* (1958). A letter and a six-page table of contents which described the documents, (gathered by John Dwyer, who was one of Dunayevskaya's Marxist-Humanist colleagues and her husband), was circulated to the committees (*RDC* # 9357-63). The collection spanned 17 years of development, 1941 to 1958.

In her letter, Dunayevskaya wrote of the need to get "acquainted with our own specific heritage . . . the development of the state capitalist theory, the emergence of the philosophic roots so that it first *rounds out* the theory to where it has not only caught the link to history but moves continually forward to the present." She singled out "as study of *method,*" the writings on the book on Marxism *before* the Absolute Idea *and* the miners' strike were absorbed, and *after.*"[4]

The decision to formally organize and deposit the archives, and arrange for their availability on microfilm came as *Philosophy and Revolution* was taking on its final form. The archives, *The Raya Dunayevskaya Collection—Marxist-Humanism: Its Origins and Development in the U.S., 1941 to Today*, were placed at the Wayne State University Archives of Labor and Urban Affairs. In a letter to News and Letters (June 5, 1969, *SRDC* # 14061), Dunayevskaya briefly described the donation and told how material from the 1941-42 analysis of the Russian economy allowed her to speak about the *"whole body of ideas"* as a quarter of a century of *Marxist-Humanism*:

> When I first spoke to the archivists I had thought that 1941-1955 would have to be called "State Capitalist Tendency" and only from the establishment of News & Letters could I call the tendency Marxist-Humanism. The actual compilation came to be a voyage of discovery, for I found that one of the unpublished manuscripts called "Labor and Society," written in 1942 had actually based itself on the Humanist essays [of Marx]. They were then totally unknown in this country. . . . [T]he titling of the volumes of archives, newspapers, pamphlets and the book reflects philosophically and politically a quite consistent, historic as well as American-rooted and black dimension that spans a period impossible of anybody to dispute.

In 1981, as *Rosa Luxemburg, Women's Liberation, and Marx's Philosophy of Revolution* was being readied for publication, Dunayevskaya expanded and reorganized the collection.

In 1986, a new donation was made. One part consisted of documents from 1981 to 1986. The other part created a major "Retrospective and Perspective" section, which reached back to 1924 and added additional documents through each decade to 1986. The collection's subtitled was changed to "Marxist-Humanism: A Half-Century of Its World Development."

After Dunayevskaya's death, additional volumes have been created and deposited as a *Supplement to the Raya Dunayevskaya Collection.*

---

[1] *The Raya Dunayevskaya Collection* and *Supplement* document the array of writings and activities that Dunayevskaya engaged in during this period:
• Three international trips were undertaken. While the one to Europe (1959) was primarily to present the ideas developed in *Marxism and Freedom* to workers, Marxist thinkers and groups, including those with a state-capitalist orientation, the other two trips,

to Africa (1962) and to Japan and Hong Kong (1965-66), were related to her work on what would become *Philosophy and Revolution,* as well as establishing relations between Marxist-Humanist thinkers and organization in the United States with individuals and organizations in Africa, and in the Far East. Dunayevskaya was involved in observing, participating, and dialoguing with the revolutionaries present in the African revolutions of the 1950s and early 1960s. In Japan, she lectured on Marxism, on Hegel's dialectic, and on the movement in the United States, speaking to university students on the New Left, Marxist revolutionaries, and Japanese autoworkers. In Hong Kong she interviewed refugees from Mao's China, developing material which would become part of *Philosophy and Revolution.*

• An important dimension of Dunayevskaya's research can be found in the files she kept for each chapter of *Philosophy and Revolution.* They consist of book notes on her readings, relevant articles, plus a few of her letters and presentations. The material consists of some 1,000 pages.

• Draft chapters of *Philosophy and Revolution* were circulated among her News & Letters colleagues.

• Correspondence, presentations, and notes on the writing of *Philosophy and Revolution* over the span of 15 years.

• Her summaries of Hegel's major writings: on *Phenomenology,* on *Science of Logic,* and on the *Encyclopedia of Philosophical Sciences.*

• Presentations delivered on aspects of *Philosophy and Revolution* in the process of its being written.

• Her Perspectives presentations to News and Letters Committees conventions and plenums in which she discussed her work on *Philosophy and Revolution* in relation to ongoing world objective-subjective events and Marxist-Humanist organizational developments. Among the world events, which she analyzed in this period were the rise of a new generation of revolutionaries as seen in the growing civil rights and then, Black power movements, as well as the anti-Vietnam War movement. She took up the rise of Third World Revolutions, the Cuban missile crisis, the Free Speech Movement, the events of May 1968 in France, as well as Prague Spring and Russia's subsequent invasion, and the Sino-Soviet conflict.

[2] Besides the letters discussed below, see especially her letters to: Charles Denby, March 10, 1960, on Maurice Merleau-Ponty's *Marxism and Philosophy* (*SRDC* # 13734, *Power of Negativity,* 110); Joseph Buttinger, October 20, 1960, on Hegel's *Phenomenology, Science of Logic,* and *Encyclopedia of Philosophical Sciences,* (*SRDC* #13773); Herbert Marcuse, November 22, 1960, on Bukharin's *Historical Materialism* and Hegel's Absolute Idea (*SRDC* #13815), and January 12, l961, on Absolute Idea in Hegel and its ramifications in Marx, in Lenin, and in Dunayevskaya's own work (*SRDC* #13824, *Power of Negativity,* 104); Jonathan Spence, February 27, 1961, on concepts for *Phenomenology* which relate to Mao Tse-tung (*SRDC* #13844), and June 1, 1961, on Absolute Idea (*SRDC #13846, PON,* 112); and Olga Domanski, February 7, 1961, on the Hegelian categories of universal, particular and individual (*SRDC* # 13842). In January 1961 she made a list of "Letters and Summations of Hegelian Philosophy relative to new book," that she had undertaken from October 1960 through January 1961 (*SRDC* #13759). In addition, see her presentation "The Philosophic Foundations for the Struggles of Freedom in the Latin American and Afro-Asian Countries," a transcript of the first talk on the book, November 13, 1960 (*SRDC* # 13782). In February 1961, Dunayevskaya held

a discussion with the Resident Editorial Board of News and Letters on some of the philosophic letters she had written.

[3] For excerpts of the discussion and Dunayevskaya's summary see *RDC* #4338-54.

[4] In 1962, when the Cuba Missile Crisis threatened a world holocaust, Dunayevskaya arranged to send documents of News and Letters to a number of countries for safe keeping.

Chapter 9

Working out the Dialectic of Hegel's Absolutes for Our Age: The Structure and Content of *Philosophy and Revolution*

Where *Marxism and Freedom* was structured on the movements from practice to theory, *Philosophy and Revolution* focused on the theoretic/philosophic framework which illuminated and responded to movements from practice. While the historic period covered—from the French revolution to the latter part of the 20th century—was similar for both works, the approach was quite different. History, particularly the roles of the masses in transforming society and impacting theoretic expression, was central to *Marxism and Freedom*. In *Philosophy and Revolution*, the historic moments of mass praxis were more implicit, while the philosophic exposition was explicit, particularly in the first two parts.

Put differently, the meaning of historic moments were seen in relation to the clash of ideas. Part I, "Why Hegel? Why Now?" presented the philosophic moment of our age grounded in the thought of Hegel, Marx and Lenin. Part II, "Alternatives," probed the thought of Mao, Trotsky and Sartre, which Dunayevskaya viewed as Alternatives that had not established continuity with the dialectic as presented in Part I. Part III, "Economic Reality and the Dialectics of Liberation," in a sense returned to viewing the movement from practice as it examined the 1960s and early 70s in Africa, East Europe and the United States. However, this was done within the philosophic structure established in Part I. Two questions came to the fore: (1) How could the revolutionary dialectic be re-created to meet the new movements from practice that emerged in the post-World War II World? (2) How could the movements from below unite with a philosophic expression of liberation as they faced the stark social and economic realities present?

Part I: Why Hegel? Why Now?

In exploring the questions "Why Hegel? Why Now?" Dunayevskaya took a journey through Hegel's major philosophic writings, Marx's plunge into the Hegelian dialectic in founding historical materialism, and Lenin's study of the *Science of Logic* in the aftermath of the outbreak of the First World War and the collapse of established Marxism.

Far from being merely a question of "correcting" idealism's abstractions, Dunayevskaya's journey demonstrated that "the pull of objective history grounded Hegelian philosophy in the principle of freedom" (*Philosophy and Revolution*, 4). At the same time, she would show that Marx's and Lenin's philosophic labors cast illumination on and helped give rebirth to the dialectic at historic moments in the 19th and 20th centuries.

"Encounter[ing] Hegel on his own ground—the Absolute Method" characterized Dunayevskaya's journey. It began in the opening chapter of *Philosophy and Revolution*, "Absolute Negativity as New Beginning—The Ceaseless Movement of Ideas and History." The Absolute Method, she argued, "is the dialectic of the Subject, the continuous process of becoming, the self-movement, self-active, self-transcending method of 'absolute negativity'" (7). In exploring Hegel's major philosophic works Dunayevskaya took up a number of critical overlapping themes, including: (1) the relationship between reality and the Idea, (2) seeing a new beginning as opposed to a closed ontological system within each of Hegel's works, and (3) a concentration on the Absolutes at the end of each work as philosophic moments that spoke powerfully to the world of the latter half of the twentieth century.

•

In her commentary on the *Phenomenology*, she wrote: "It becomes impossible to separate reality and spirit, not because Hegel had imposed spirit upon reality, but because spirit is immanent in reality" (8). This was not simply because each phenomenological development could be linked with a corresponding historic stage, "but also that thought molds its experience in such a manner that it will never again be possible to keep these two opposites in separate realms. The method of uniting the two dialectically is irresistible because it comes from within (9)." Thus, far from being merely an idealistic abstract system, history was within Hegel's philosophic categories: "In a word, Marxist and non–Marxists alike have grasped . . . the deeply rooted historical content of Hegelian philosophy" (10).

Dunayevskaya summed up this movement of ideas and reality that was captured in the Hegelian dialectic:

> The constant reappearance of one and the same movement—the dialectic as a continuous process of self-development, a process of development through contradiction, through alienation, through double negation—begins with sense-certainty and never stops its ceaseless motion, not even at the apex, Absolute

Knowledge. It is the development of mankind's history from bondage to freedom. It is the development of thought from the French Revolution to German Idealist philosophy. It is Hegel transforming the dialectics of the French Revolution into "Absolute Method" (10).

When Dunayevskaya turned to the *Science of Logic* with its abstract philosophic categories, she called attention to the fact that those categories do not "depart from the principle of freedom in which his entire philosophic system is grounded"(19). Furthermore, "a unique single dialectic process contains Thought and Actuality" (19). The *Science of Logic*, Dunayevskaya noted, had as well a polemical movement. This often came in the form of "Observations." These "Observations" were a battle of ideas with other philosophers—Hegel's engagement with the world in his philosophic system.

Dunayevskaya discussed Hegel's critique of Jacobi and Kant. She pointed out that what was first an observation on Jacobi in the Doctrine of Being in the *Science of Logic* (1812), developed into an entire "Third Attitude to Objectivity" when Hegel took up Jacobi in the 1827 edition of the smaller *Logic*. Her expanded commentary on the Third Attitude was due to her view that Jacobi's intuitionalism was not only an important attitude present in Hegel's day, but intutitionalism impacted the reality of the post-World War II world. For Hegel, intuitionalism, "has no other basis than subjective knowledge, and the assertion that we discover a certain fact in our consciousness, what we discover in our own consciousness is thus exaggerated into a fact of consciousness of all and even passed off for the very nature of the mind."

Dunayevskaya discussed Hegel's critiques of Kant, where Kant recognized the "relation of thought to sensuous existence," but "'stopped dead' by putting an impenetrable 'thing-in-itself' between thought and experience" (27). In contrast to Jacobi and Kant, Dunayevskaya argued that Hegel's dialectical attitude united thought and reality.

She continued exploring the interpenetration of the Idea and reality in her commentary on Hegel's *Philosophy of Mind*, quoting from the opening section, Mind Subjective—Free Mind: "When individuals and nations have once got in their heads the concept of full-blown liberty, there is nothing like it in its uncontrollable strength, just because it is the very essence of mind, and that as its very actuality." Dunayevskaya argued against those who claimed that Hegel's concept of freedom was only conceptual.

•

In showing that the dialectic was a self-movement, a dialectic of self-development through double negation, Dunayevskaya not only hit out against the static triadic form of thesis-antithesis-synthesis that some interpreters have sought to impose upon Hegel's dialectic, but posed the dialectical positive contained in the negation as "the path to a *new beginning*. . . . It is ceaseless movement, a veritable continuous revolution. . . . It is the nature of development. It is a fact of life" (13).

She saw within each of Hegel's major works new beginnings. From *Phenomenology*: "The 'ultimate' turns out to be *not the Absolute, which has just suffered its Golgotha, but a new beginning, a new point of departure*" (18). From the *Science of Logic,* quoting Hegel on the movement of the Notion as "the universal and absolute activity, the self-determining and self-realizing movement," she wrote, "once again there is a need for *new beginnings.*" From *Philosophy of Mind* Dunayevskaya commented on the three final syllogisms, showing that Hegel did not end with his system, the Logic, as the final mediating agent. Rather "Logic is altogether replaced by the self-thinking Idea." She read this to be the entrance to the new society, *the* new human beginning.

The dialectic method was a method of absolute negativity, not a nullity, but a continual process of becoming, a new beginning as its being, essence, and notion. Because Hegel's dialectic of negativity was the permanent path of new beginnings, Dunayevskaya saw Hegel's Absolutes *as new beginning—Absolute Negativity as New Beginning.*

•

Dunayevskaya's reading of Hegel, was a reading through the Absolutes. It was a reading of Absolute Knowledge to the Golgatha of Absolute Spirit, which she saw as a new beginning; a reading of the Absolute Idea in the *Science of Logic* to "absolute liberation," in contrast to Lenin's commentary which halted before this free release of the Idea; a reading of the Absolute Mind section of the *Philosophy of Mind,* upon which Marx did not comment, as the entrance to the new society. The Absolutes in each work were not seen by Dunayevskaya as separate from the whole of Hegel's philosophic body of thought. Rather, because the Absolutes were at one and the same time a recollection or retrospective, and a perspective, indicating a new sphere to enter, the Absolutes contained the whole—summation as new beginning.

• Dunayevskaya's point of concentration in the *Phenomenology* turned to its final chapter Absolute Knowledge. Here, where many interpretations have argued that Hegel's Absolute absorbed all traces of the actual, and some Hegel scholars argued for "a speculative theocracy," she contended: "The truth is that nowhere is the historic character of Hegel's philosophic categories more evident than in Absolute Knowledge" (11).

In Absolute Knowledge, Dunayevskaya noted, Hegel drew out what was quintessential for not only *Phenomenology,* but for his as yet unwritten *Logic*: "The object as a whole is the mediated result (the syllogism) or the passing of universality into individuality through specification, also the reverse process from the individual, to universal through cancelled individuality or specific determination."

It was this self-movement, this ceaseless movement through double negation, which characterized all of *Phenomenology* not excluding Absolute Knowledge. As opposed to what Hegel called "the arbitrary caprice of prophetic utterance," the movement through the Hegelian categories—"the transforming of that inherent nature into explicitness, of Substance into Subject"—was history. Dunayevskaya quoted Hegel: "The process of carrying forward this form of knowledge of itself is the task which spirit accomplishes as actual History."

So pervasive and all encompassing was this movement, that Absolute Spirit itself was transformed. Quoting the last paragraph of the chapter, Dunayevskaya called this to our attention: "In truth, as we see, we have reached not heaven, but the Golgotha of Absolute Spirit! . . . Absolute Knowledge was not after all, the end. . . . The 'ultimate' turns out to be *not the Absolute, which has just suffered its Golgotha, but a new beginning, a new point of departure"* (17-18).

• In *Science of Logic*, Dunayevskaya called attention to the fact that arriving at Absolute Idea did not mean that the movement had reached its ultimate and simply ceased: "Hegel unequivocally states that 'the Absolute Idea contains the highest opposition within itself'" (27). Rather, it was in the Absolute Idea chapter that Hegel would write: "The self-determination, therefore, in which alone the Idea is, is to hear itself speak." The movement through this internal "highest opposition" is the Idea's self-determination. It is the method of that self-determination that is the unity of Absolute Idea and Absolute Method.

Dunayevskaya followed Hegel's consideration of "the universal element of its form—*the method.*" "The development of what the dialectic method is," she argued, "is as far removed from the mechanical triplicities of thesis, antithesis, synthesis (which never were Hegel's formulations) as earth is from heaven" (28). Instead she pointed to "the earthly character of liberation" which made up Hegel's universals, and "give us insight into the movement of history itself." Hegel's own Absolutes were subjected to this dialectic of development, so that they arrived at "the universal and absolute activity, the self-determining and self-realizing movement." Dunayevskaya noted: "The concrete Universal manifests itself as absolute activity, activity without restriction, either external or internal; for the method is the form of the Absolute Idea, self-movement as method" (29).

What was immanent in the entire objective movement that Hegel unfolded for us—from the Doctrine of Being, through the Doctrine of Essence, to the Doctrine of Notion—turned out to be "its own Other," or what Dunayevskaya termed, "[f]ree creative power [which] is the unifying force of this final chapter on the Absolute Idea, the unity of the theoretical and practical idea, to that form of life which is the activity of the Notion" (32).

• In examining *Philosophy of Mind,* Dunayevskaya concentrated on the final three syllogisms of the "Absolute Mind" chapter (paragraphs 575, 576, 577), where, "Hegel has us face the self-thinking Idea." In probing each of these final paragraphs in their syllogistic form, Dunayevskaya discerned "ceaseless absolute negativity." Thus, where the three books of the *Encyclopaedia*, Logic-Nature-Mind, are depicted in the first syllogism, what becomes crucial is the movement: "The logical principle turns to Nature and Nature to Mind." Nature as middle turn is the mediating, the sundering agent. As she noted, Nature became "negation." In the second syllogism the form is Nature-Mind-Logic. Here Dunayevskaya turned to one Hegel scholar's interpretation which expressed this syllogism as a manifestation of *Phenomenology*: "a systematic philosophy of history . . . therefore a system of (evolving) subjectivity" (301, footnote 98).

In the final syllogism (paragraph 577), Dunayevskaya pointed out that the sequence was interrupted. It was not Mind-Logic-Nature. Instead Logic was replaced by *the self-thinking Idea.*

In her May 20, 1953 letter on *Philosophy of Mind* she took this movement through the final three syllogisms to mean: "We have entered the new society." In *Philosophy and Revolution* she wrote: "It was on the eve of the East Germany uprising in June, 1953 that I commented on Hegel's final three syllogisms. I considered Hegel's formulation, "the logical principle turns to Nature and Nature to Mind," as the movement not only from theory to practice, but also from practice to theory as well as the new society" (300, footnote 91).

Dunayevskaya's travels through Hegel's Absolutes led her, in the concluding paragraphs of "Absolute Negativity as New Beginning," to pose the question "Why Hegel? Why Now?" in a different, and most provocative manner: "Is it possible for another age to make a new beginning upon Hegel's Absolutes, especially absolute negativity, without breaking totally with Hegel?" (45). Her journey through *Philosophy and Revolution* via the dialectic of Marx and of Lenin, and then to the "new passions and new forces" of our day, presented her response.

•

In the second chapter "A New Continent of Thought—Marx's Historical Materialism and Its Inseparability from the Hegelian Dialectic," Dunayevskaya took up three moments of Marx's work—the *1844 Manuscripts*, with emphasis on "Critique of the Hegelian Dialectic;" the 1857-58 *Grundrisse,* with discussion of the "Pre-Capitalist Economic Formations" and "Machinery" sections; and *Capital*, 1867 to 1872-73, with focus on the development of the "Fetishism of Commodities" section of Chapter One:

> We propose . . . to trace the development from the birth of Historical Materialism and of proletarian revolution, 1844-48, through the 1850s when the *Grundrisse* will reveal Marx not merely as 'scientific economist' but as dialectical analysis of liberation from the pre-capitalist Orient through the industrial workers' battles with the machine, to authorship of *Capital*, Marx's greatest theoretical, dialectical, historical, philosophical as well as economic work (*P&R*, 50).

Dunayevskaya's immersion into Marx was no abstract academic discourse. It was a deep probing, and at the same time a battle of ideas with others, particular state-capitalist vulgarizers of Marx's thought. The polemic movement occurred in the context of the ongoing reality of Third World Revolutions, the

Sino-Soviet conflict, and automation. The Hegel-Marx relation was examined not alone as indebtedness and critique, but as transcendence and re-creation.

In the 1840s, Dunayevskaya saw Marx undergoing "a triple break—from classical political economy, from Hegelianism, and from the 'old' materialism" (53). In their place, Marx forged a new Humanism: "We see here how thoroughgoing Naturalism or Humanism distinguishes itself both from Idealism and Materialism, and is, at the same time, the truth uniting both" (quoted, 53).

As opposed to those who wished to make a sharp break between the "young" Marx of 1844 and "mature" Marx of *Capital*, Dunayevskaya argued for a continuity of his philosophy of liberation:

> [T]he proof that Marx never jettisoned his Humanist vision when he allegedly became, "instead,"—a "scientific economist," is in the very process of becoming, of originating *Historical* Materialism in the 1844 Manuscripts and not merely in philosophic categories, not even when they are as basic as Alienation and Reification. There is no philosophic category in Marx that is not at the same time an economic one. And there is no economic category that is not at the same time a philosophic one (56).

Dunayevskaya concentrated on Marx's "Critique of the Hegelian Dialectic," showing "how 'economic' this 'strictly' philosophic essay is" (56). She singled out Marx's movement beyond a Feuerbachian critique of Hegel. Where Feuerbach dismissed "negation of the negation" as mystification, Dunayevskaya quoted Marx: "[I]nasmuch as Hegel comprehends the negation of the negation in accordance with a positive relation, which is immanent in it . . . to that extent he has discovered though only as an *abstract, logical and speculative* expression, the movement of history" (56). This movement of absolute negativity became an expression of the unity of economics and philosophy as Dunayevskaya took up Marx's expression: "communism is humanism mediated by the transcendence of private property. Only by the transcendence of this mediation, which is nevertheless a necessary presupposition, does there arise *positive* Humanism, beginning from itself" (quoted, 54). Marx had already hit out against a vulgar communism's reduction of liberation to a change in property forms. Here he stated the need to go beyond communism to Humanism.

This emphasis on "positive Humanism" was the dividing line as Marx separated himself from other tendencies and gave birth to his world historic vision. To Dunayevskaya it served as ground for the ideological battles of the post-World War II world. She referred to the Russian Communists' attempts "to separate 'the young Marx' tainted by 'Hegelianism' from the 'mature economist,'" (55), as East European revolts burst forth, and, as well, to Mao's attempt to appropriate the concept of "contradiction" for his own purposes, even as the objectivity of this Hegelian-Marxian category challenged his rule.

The richness of her dialogue with Marx illuminated the birth of historical materialism in the 1840s. Against the attempts to separate the young Marx from the mature Marx, the philosophic Marx from the scientific Marx, the Hegelian Marx from the economic Marx, Dunayevskaya strove to present the multi-linear strands of Marx's development in the 1840s: (1) his discovery of a new Subject, the proletariat, who neither Hegel, nor the Hegelians of Marx's day, or the classical political economists, recognized as Subject; (2) his separation both from a materialism which failed to recognize absolute negativity as "the moving and creating principle" in the dialectic, and from a vulgar communism which negated the individual in society; (3) all this became concretized in Marx's profound relation to the Hegelian dialectic: his critique of Hegel's dehumanization of philosophy, his break with Hegel's philosophic abstractions went hand in hand with a transcendence and re-creation of the dialectic as a new Humanism. At the same time that Dunayevskaya cast illumination on the creation of historical materialism, she appropriated Marx's new Humanism as ground to do battle with a wide range of tendencies, including state-capitalism using Marxist language.

•

The frontispiece of *Philosophy and Revolution* quoted from Marx's *Grundrisse*, his Notebooks of 1857-58:

> When the narrow bourgeois form has been peeled away, what is wealth, if not the universality of needs, capacities, enjoyments, productive powers, etc., of individuals, produced in universal exchange? What, if not the full development of human control for the forces of nature—those of his own nature as well as those of so-called "nature"? What, if not the absolute elaboration of his creative dispositions, without any preconditions other than antecedent historical evolution which makes the totality of this evolution—i.e. the evolution of all human powers as such, unmeasured by any *previously established yardstick*—an end in itself? What is this, if not a situation where man does not reproduce himself in any determined form, but produces his totality? Where he does not seek to remain something formed by the past, but is in the absolute movement of becoming?

The grandeur of Marx's vision was what Dunayevskaya strove to give flesh and blood to in this chapter, which swept from Marx's 1840s to the 1870s. For her, the late 1850s of the *Grundrisse* held a pivotal, revealing, place in that landscape.

(1) "This rough draft is, in many respects, more total a conception than the logical, precise *Capital*" (65). An outline within, and Marx's correspondence, showed that he wished to cover the ground for six books: Capital, Landed Property, Wage Labor, the State, Foreign Trade, the World Market. (Marx did not live to work out all of what he had projected in these notebooks.) Dunayevskaya continued:

> [The *Grundrisse*] manifests a tremendous world-historic view, not only an analysis of the existing society, but a conception of a new society

based on expanding human forces, during a century in which the whole cultivated world thought of expanding material forces as the condition, activity, and purpose of all liberation (65).

(2) The manner of presentation in the *Grundrisse,* and in the subsequent *Critique of Political Economy,* left Marx dissatisfied, and he began anew the process of working out *Capital*. Dunayevskaya traced this process with respect to Marx's discussion of Machinery. In so doing she examined the relation of dialectics to an emerging Subject: "[U]nless the Subject himself (the proletariat) recreates or rather creates anew the dialectic as it emerges *from practice,* there is no forward movement. Nowhere is this seen more clearly than in the section on Machinery [in the *Grundrisse*]" (69).

The 1850s were a relatively quiescent period, without the strikes and uprisings of the first Working Man's International, the Civil War in the U.S., and the Paris Commune that characterized the mid 1860s and early 1870s. This reality influenced the form of Marx's presentation: "What was at issue was the appearance of the totally contradictory phenomenon of the insufficiency and, at the same time, the indispensability of the Hegelian dialectic" (65).

To "recast" the *Grundrisse* as *Capital,* Marx had to break with the concept of theory as a debate among theoreticians. In *Marxism and Freedom,* Dunayevskaya had shown that Marx's focus on the working class struggles of the 1860s meant a new concept of theory—the interchange between a revolutionary theoretician and the mass struggles from below. Now she showed the specificity of this for Marx's writing on machinery:

> [T]he last word on the subject of Machinery is not in *Grundrisse,* but in *Capital.* Not that there is anything "wrong" with what Marx analyzed in the *Grundrisse.* It simply is not *concrete* enough. Not only is the truth always concrete, but the specificity of the dialectic, of Subject (the proletariat), is irreducible. The simple, the profound truth is that the actual class struggles naturally were at their most intense in the turbulent 1860s. . . . [A]s against *Capital's* graphic description of the workers' resistance to the discipline of capital in the process of production itself, the *Grundrisse* still stresses the *material* condition for the solution of conflict and contradictions" (69-70).

Dunayevskaya traced Marx's work on the chapter on Machinery in the 1860s—from rereading his notebooks on technology, to attending a practical course for workers, to asking Engels questions about work in his factories. His emphasis now was on the conflict of technology with the worker rather than on technology's continual development. This could be seen most clearly in the growing class struggle. Dunayevskaya quoted Marx from *Capital*: "It would be possible to write quite a history of the inventions made since 1830 for the sole purpose of supplying capital with weapons against the revolts of the working class" (72). She commented:

Marx followed hawklike every strike of workers. Concrete, concrete, concrete—this sums up the scrupulousness with which Marx followed the strife of the worker, making it inseparable from its opposite: the concentration and centralization of capital as well as from the machine's development....
We are in a very different world from the one where machines were described in the *Grundrisse*. The *Grundrisse* is proof of the limitation but also the indispensability of the dialectic. The limitation is not caused by deficiencies in the dialectic "as method".... Rather, the limitation resides in the fact that the dialectic is not an "applied" science. It has to be recreated as it spontaneously emerges from the developing Subject (72, 73).

(3) At the same time Dunayevskaya was elucidating the dialectical structure and vision of Marx's work of the 1850s and 60s, she carried on a polemic against interpreters who misread or misused Marx's works. Thus, in relation to another section of the *Grundrisse* she regarded as pivotal, "Pre-Capitalist Economic Formations," she hit out against Karl Wittfogel's theory of Oriental Despotism. She questioned Eric Hobsbawn's view that Marx's historical development in *Pre-Capitalist Economic Formations* was not history "in the strict sense."

Perhaps most crucially, she felt the *Grundrisse* argued decisively against Marx interpreters who divided a young "Hegelian" Marx from a mature "scientific" Marx:

[The *Grundrisse* showed] it simply was not true that the Hegelian dialectic had been dropped by Marx when he became 'economist' and theorist as well as participant in proletariat revolution....
The *Grundrisse* has made clear beyond any doubt a great deal more than the simple truth that the mature Marx, like the young Marx, considered the Hegelian dialectic the source of all dialectic, his own included (62, 75).

(4) Finally, Dunayevskaya returned again and again to Marx's vision and the manner whereby he concretized it:

The reconstructed science [Marx's journey from the *Grundrisse* to *Capital*] meant not only that his original discoveries made all the difference, but also that these original economic categories were so philosophically rooted that a new unity was created out of economics, philosophy, revolution. The historic rationality Marx discovered as immanent in the hope of people meant, in turn, that it is living people who work out the meaning of philosophy by making the theory of liberation and the struggle to be free a unity. So much is *free* man the true subject of history that Marx called the period in which he lived, and the one in which we still live, the *pre*history of mankind. Man's true history does not begin until he is free, can develop all his innate talents, which class society, especially value-producing capitalism, throttles (74).

•

"The Adventures of the Commodity as Fetish" was the final part of the Marx chapter. In meticulous detail Dunayevskaya traced the origins and working out of the Fetishism of Commodities section of Chapter one of *Capital*, arrived at in its final form only after the Paris Commune in the French edition of *Capital* (1872-75). We will not here try to summarize the comprehensive treatment Dunayevskaya gave to Marx's extraordinary unmasking of capitalist's real spirit (see *P&R*, 76-94). We limit ourselves to two points.

(1) In following Marx's work on fetishism of commodities, Dunayevskaya had in mind the state-capitalist regimes calling themselves Communist. She called attention to Stalin's sudden decision to break with *Capital's* dialectical structure in its "teaching," by skipping the first chapter on commodities. The Stalinist theoreticians concluded "that just as 'commodities' existed before capitalism, so will they after, *and* they also exist under 'socialism'" (78). Dunayevskaya hit back as this perversion:

> By denuding the commodity-form of a product of labor of its specifically capitalistic class character, the Russian revisionists paved the path for the startling reversal in the Marxian analysis of the law of value as the mainspring of capitalist production. Where heretofore, to Marxist and non-Marxist alike, that law was inoperative under socialism, the Stalinist theoreticians now admitted that the law of value did indeed operate in Russia and that it was at the same time "a socialist land" (78).

(2) Dunayevskaya drew the strands of "Why Hegel? Why Now?" together for Marx's day, in showing the necessity for the Hegelian dialectic in Marx's thought as well as the necessity for Marx's revolutionary break from Hegel, and the points of Marx's return to Hegel.

> [T]here is a great deal more to Marxian dialectics than the "application" of Hegelian dialectics to economic data. To whatever extent the Hegelian dialectic enabled Marx "free movement in matter," Marx could not have disclosed the fetishism of commodities except by *transcending* not only Hegelian idealism but also "abstract materialism" and the historian-compilers of collections of lifeless facts (90).
>
> Marx noted, directly in *Capital* itself (not only his greatest but most original work, that in content was as far removed from Hegel's works as earth is from heaven), that Hegelian dialectics was the source of *all* dialectics (obviously his own included). It was written when Marx was wholly in his new continent of thought, not merely at first discovery, but fully developed at *his* most creative moment, when Marx was individual genius and proletarian revolutionary as well as historical "recorder" of the masses in action at *their* greatest point of creativity—the Paris Commune. Even at this apex Marx found the Hegelian *notional*, dialectic self-development through absolute negativity (91).
>
> It is true, of course, that Marx had to break with Hegel's Absolutes before he could discover the materialist concept of history. But this hardly explains Marx's return to Hegel; and no simplistic reduction, that it was only for pur-

poses of "standing Hegel right side up," can possible eradicate the deep organic, persistent relationship. . . .

[I]n the same manner that Marx's development of the form of the commodity was related to Hegel's syllogistic Universal, Particular, Individual, or the Doctrine of Notion in general, so "the absolute general law of capitalist accumulation" is Hegel's Absolute Idea *made concrete for one very concrete, very specific, very transitory historic social order* (93, 94).

•

"The Shock of Recognition and the Philosophic Ambivalence of Lenin" formed the final chapter of Part I "Why Hegel? Why Now?" Two major moments were treated: (1) commentary on Lenin's *Abstract on Hegel's Science of Logic*, 1914-15; (2) examination of Lenin's 1915-1923 writings and activities post his direct study of Hegel. Dunayevskaya was a crucial interpreter of Lenin as revolutionary theoretician in this last decade of his life. She was the original translator of Lenin's Philosophic Notebooks on Hegel into English, probing their meaning for more than three decades. Because of Lenin's philosophic ambivalence—"Lenin had not prepared his *Philosophic Notebooks* for publication, and in this resided his philosophic ambivalence (106)"—the relationship between those studies and Lenin's subsequent writings on imperialism and on self-determination of nations, as well as his practice in revolution 1917-1923, were not explicitly tied together prior to her studies. Dunayevskaya discerned the strands leading from Lenin's *Philosophic Notebooks* to his revolutionary praxis post-1914.

In *Marxism and Freedom*, Dunayevskaya had taken up the objective-subjective circumstances that led to Lenin's return to the Hegelian dialectic—the collapse of established Marxism with the outbreak of the First World War that led to socialists taking sides in a capitalist war. Lenin felt the compulsion to find the philosophic roots of Marxism that could illuminate the betrayal. *Philosophy and Revolution* probed Lenin's new philosophic vantage point in Hegel: "[W]hat was put into question was the old materialism, lacking the principle of the 'transformation into its opposite,' 'the dialectic proper. This was what Lenin was to emphasize in the Hegelian dialectic" (96-97).

Dunayevskaya took up Lenin's commentaries on each of *Science of Logic's* three major divisions, the Doctrines of Being, Essence and Notion. She showed Lenin's catching of movement and self-movement as the core of Hegelianism; of Lenin's singling out "The idea of the transformation of the ideal into the real is *profound*. Very important for history." She commented: "It was this discovery of the relationship between the idea and the material in Hegel which led Lenin to see that the revolutionary spirit in the dialectic was not superimposed upon Hegel by Marx, but was in Hegel" (98). This was the most profound aspect of the shock of recognition—Lenin's experience in finding the revolutionary dialectic in Hegel.

Dunayevskaya summed up that experience—

Lenin's *Abstract of Hegel's Science of Logic* reveals a mind in action, arguing with itself as well as with Hegel, advising him "to return to" Hegel, "to work out" ideas, history, science, Marx's *Capital*, current theories, and leaping into the Notion which he translated as "NB. Freedom = subjectivity ('or') goal, consciousness, striving N.B" (100).

—as she posed the "Why Now?" of "Why Hegel?" with regard to Lenin: "So strong is the illumination cast on the relationship of philosophy to revolution in Lenin's day that the challenges of our day also become translucent, exposing the ossification of philosophy, the stifling of the dialectics of liberation" (100).

At the same time, Dunayevskaya was in a battle with the Russian state-capitalist theoreticians, who for their own political purposes sought to pervert the meaning of Lenin's *Philosophic Notebooks*. She attacked them: (1) for their attempt to ahistorically combine Lenin's 1908 vulgarly materialistic *Materialism and Empirio-Criticism* with his 1914-15 *Abstract of Hegel's Science of Logic*, thus trying to render meaningless Lenin's *philosophic* great divide in Marxism; and (2) for their vulgar reductionism of Lenin's magnificent "Alias: Man's cognition not only reflects the objective world, but creates it," to what Dunayevskaya termed "philistine talk of semantics."

When Dunayevskaya took up Lenin's notes on the Doctrine of Notion, she singled out "his comments on the close relationship between Marx's *Capital* and Hegel's *Logic*":

> If Marx did not leave a Logic (with a capital letter), he left the *logic* of *Capital*, and this should be especially utilized on the given question. In *Capital*, the logic, dialectic and theory of knowledge of materialism (3 words are not necessary: they are one and the same) are applied to one science, taking all that is valuable in Hegel and moving it forward (quoted, 102).
>
> It is impossible fully to grasp Marx's *Capital*, and especially its first chapter, if you have not studied through and understood the *whole* of Hegel's *Logic*. Consequently, none of the Marxists for the past half century have understood Marx!! (quoted, 103).

Dunayevskaya summed up the meaning of Lenin's philosophic breakthrough, his "philosophic preparation for revolution:" "Lenin had gained from Hegel a totally new understanding of the *unity* of materialism and idealism. *It was this new understanding that subsequently permeated Lenin's post-1915 writings in philosophy, politics, economics, and organization*" (103).

When Dunayevskaya turned to Lenin's post-1914 period, her emphasis was not on his fight against the betrayers, but against the revolutionaries who did not betray but remained in the old materialism, the old categories. The nature of imperialism, and the infusion of the self-determination of nations with new content were two crucial areas of Lenin's activities that Dunayevskaya examined.

Bukharin was one of Lenin's Bolshevik co-leaders with whom Lenin disputed. Dunayevskaya contrasted Lenin's and Bukharin's works on imperialism:

> [A]s opposed to Bukharin's concept of capitalist growth in a straight line, or via a quantitative ratio, Lenin's own work holds on tightly to the dialectical principle, "transformation into opposite." The key point in tracing the *subject's* self-development instead of an "objective" mathematical growth is that you thus see the simultaneity of the transformation into opposite, of competitive capitalism into monopoly, *and* part of labor into an "aristocracy of labor." Above all, you become conscious that this is but the "first negative." The development through *this* contradiction compels finding the "second negative," or as Marx expressed it, going "lower and deeper" into the masses to find the *new* revolutionary strata (108).

For Lenin this meant discerning new national revolutionary forces as "bacilli" for proletarian revolution: "Where Lenin saw in the stage of imperialism a new urgency for the slogan of national self-determination, Bukharin vehemently opposed the slogan as both 'impossible of achievement' and 'reactionary'. . . . This plunge to abstract revolutionism . . . Lenin called nothing short of 'imperialist economism'" (108-09).

Dunayevskaya contended that the debates were not solely limited to political differences on the nature of imperialism and the role of self-determination of nations. Lenin's political position, she argued, flowed from his immersion in "the dialectic proper." The transformation of capitalism from competition to monopoly and its extension into imperialism could be seen by Lenin from the vantage point of the Hegelian transformation into opposite. The need to go lower and deeper within the working class, to find newly emerging Subjects of revolution in the age of imperialism, found philosophic ground within the concept of second negativity. Lenin had found the revolutionary dialectic in Hegel: "Lenin's rediscovery of dialectics, of self-activity, of Subject verses Substance at the very moment of the collapse of the Second International, simultaneously disclosed the appearance of counter-revolution from *within* the Marxist movements and the new forces of revolution in the national movements" (110).

The debates over national self-determination did not end after the 1917 Russian Revolution. Dunayevskaya followed the dispute over self-determination within the Russian state: "This time Bukharin contended that it was no longer possible to admit the right of self-determination since Russia was now a workers' state, whereas nationalism mean bourgeois and proletarian together, and 'therefore' a step backward" (111). She quoted Lenin's response: "We cannot deny it [the right of self-determination] to a single one of the peoples living within the boundaries of the former Russian Empire." Dunayevskaya's point of concentration was a refusal to separate the political from the philosophic:

> Lenin . . . refused to depart in his debates with Bukharin from that single word, dialectic, as the relationship of subject to object, dialectics as the movement

from abstract to concrete. In place of the mechanistic bifurcation of subject and object, Lenin joined the two in a new concrete universal—TO A MAN (112).

Dunayevskaya returned to probing Lenin's *Philosophic Notebooks* to draw tighter the distinction between these two Bolshevik co-leaders, a distinction that led Lenin to write in his "Will" (1923) that Bukharin had never understood the dialectic. At the same time she returned to ramifications of Lenin's philosophic ambivalence: "Though the theoretical preparation for revolution seemed clear from the *political* works that followed his unpublished *Philosophic Notebooks*, the disputes among Bolsheviks revealed that, in truth, none of the underlying philosophy was understood" (114). Dunayevskaya's conclusion was stark and sobering: "The duality in Lenin's philosophic heritage is unmistakable" (117). To her this meant the imperative necessity of recovering the heritage of those *Philosophic Notebooks* for the revolutionary movement in the post-World War II period. But first one had to face the theoretic void that Lenin's death meant, "which Leaders stood ready to fill with Alternatives."

II. Alternatives

"Alternatives" referred to theoretic currents—Trotskyism, Maoism, and Sartrean Existentialism—that emerged out of the objective situation of the mid 20th century as alternatives to the dialectics of liberation of Hegel, Marx and Lenin that were forged in the 19th and early part of the 20th centuries. Dunayevskaya described the period in a short Introduction, "On the Eve of World War II: Depression in the Economy and in Thought." Three chapters followed: "Leon Trotsky as Theoretician," "The Thought of Mao Tse-tung," and "Jean-Paul Sartre—Outsider Looking In."

•

The chapter on Trotsky as theoretician opened with a quote from Hegel: "In every dualistic system . . . the fundamental defect makes itself visible in the inconsistency of unifying at one moment, what a moment before had been explained incapable of unification." Dunayevskaya argued that Trotsky's theoretic positions—beginning from his Theory of Permanent Revolution, extending to his view of the nature of the Russian economy under Stalin, and to the relationship of leadership, i.e. the revolutionary Party and masses—were plagued with such dualism.

She began with the Theory of Permanent Revolution, quoting excerpts from its main thesis to the effect that a revolution could occur in a country economically more backward, allowing for the working class to take power sooner than in a country more capitalistically advanced; that such a revolution in Russia would need the state support of a European working class to remain in power and become socialist; and that such a first revolution in Russia could act as a force of revolutionary idealism for the proletariat in Western countries.

At the same time, it was Trotsky's view that the rural population "will be drawn into the revolution and for the first time obtain political organization only after the proletariat has taken the helm of government" (quoted, 131). To Dunayevskaya this meant that methodologically, Trotsky "had developed the theory of permanent revolution without a self-developing Subject" (129), without the peasantry as central, and hence, the dualism. In her view: "Theoretically, [Trotsky's] whole life can be said to be a series of postscripts to these 1904-06 theses" (131).

To create a theory of revolution in relation to underdeveloped lands without a self-developing Subject ended up in "abstract revolutionism." In place of the peasantry came, not so much the vanguard role of the proletariat, but the Marxist organization having "influence over the proletariat." Dunayevskaya contrasted Trotsky's positions to that of Lenin's striving to create "new points of departure for theory, should the continuation of October on a world scale emerge 'via Peking rather than via Berlin'" (132).

After Lenin's death, China became an important testing ground for Trotsky's theory—in the 1927 Revolution and in the 1930s. Despite the fact that the Chinese peasantry played a central role in the developing revolutionary ferment in China, Dunayevskaya showed that Trotsky's unchanging position was of a peasantry that could not gain even a national consciousness, much less a socialist consciousness.

With regard to "The Nature of the Russian Economy," Dunayevskaya followed Trotsky's refusal to recognize the reality of Russia's transformation from a worker's state to a state-capitalist one: "Trotsky continued making an abstraction of the Russian state, even after Stalinism had transformed it into its opposite, a state-capitalist society. . . . Like all fetishisms, the fetishism of state property hid from Trotsky the course of the counter-revolution in the relations of production" (142). Dunayevskaya searched out the philosophic error that had Trotsky as theoretician trapped in the abstraction that nationalized property equals socialism:

> To a revolutionary theoretician, what is important is that the new stage of economic development, no matter what it is called, is always considered *in strict relationship* to the subjective development, the new form of workers' revolt, i.e., the new strata in the population that continue to oppose that stage of capitalist development. And flowing from this relationship comes the working out of a new relationship between theory and practice in a way that the philosophy of revolution and its forces and passions do not get separated (143).

Instead of such concrete revolutionary methodology, Trotsky's methodology took the particular of nationalized property and transformed it into a universal of socialism, what Dunayevskaya termed, "Making a Fixed Particular into a

New Universal." For Trotsky, it meant a continuation of his dualism, this time "between [his] *theory* of world revolution and the *practice* of defending 'socialism in one country,' as if indeed it were a socialist land" (145).

In the chapter's final section, "Leadership, Leadership," Dunayevskaya brought together the dualisms at the center of Trotsky as a theoretician:

> The duality between the concept of world revolution and that of defense of Stalinist Russia; between socialism as a classless society that can only realize itself as a world society, and socialism = nationalized property isolated from the world economy; between workers as the vanguard and workers who need to submit to "the militarization of labor" (!); between Party as leader of the proletarian revolution and Party as ruling over workers' own instincts and demands—all these dualities, as we have seen, were compounded by the contradiction between the dialectics of the revolution and the specific Subject who constituted the majority of "the masses," when they happened to be peasant rather than proletarian (148).

•

Philosophically, Dunayevskaya regarded the thought of Mao Tse-tung as a form of retrogressionism. Two quotes from Hegel—one from the Spirit of Self-Estrangement section of *Phenomenology*, the other on intuitionist philosophy from "Third Attitude to Objectivity" of the smaller *Logic*—opened the chapter. She commented: "[T]he modern version of the intuitionist and voluntarist alternative to dialectics has indeed led down a retrogressionist path of primitive accumulation of capital" (162).

Dunayevskaya reached this conclusion by tracing Mao's actions and thought at various moments before and after obtaining power, primarily in the first two sections of the chapter, "Discontinuities and Continuities," and "From Contradiction to Contradiction to Contradiction." On one level the discontinuities included a break from the Marxian concept that the overthrow of the old class-based society would mean the entrance to a new human one. Dunayevskaya quoted Mao's view: "the complete victory of socialism cannot be brought about in one or two generations; to resolve this question thoroughly requires five or ten generations or even longer." Even "several centuries" might be needed for full Communism (quoted, 153, 154).

The discontinuity continued with Mao's manipulation of a crucial strand of objectivity in the Hegelian-Marxian dialectic—the category of contradiction. Dunayevskaya discussed the Maoist version of the theory of contradiction—"The Principal Contradiction" and "The Principal Aspect of Contradiction"—how primary can become subordinate, and secondary primary. By the time Mao was finished with his "complexity" and "unevenness," as well as "special" parts, Dunayevskaya wrote: "[N]ot only has he [Mao] 'outflanked' the objectivity of the Hegelian theory of contradiction; *he has totally denuded the Marxian theory of its class nature and its historicity*" (163).

These discontinuities on the vision of a new society, and on the concept of contradiction, were not abstraction questions. Dunayevskaya argued that for Mao "the *practicality* of theory" was of the essence, governing his willingness to break with the past:

> Whether we talk of him as practitioner or theoretician the crucial point is the *break* with the past, not the points of similarity. That is what is decisive in "The Thought of Mao Tse-tung" as it is decisive in objective development. It is crucial, not because the break is "irrational," but because it will reveal the objective *class* compulsion tugging at Mao's Thought, and disclose the gulf between the Chinese reality—its technological backwardness in production despite the advance in H-bombs—and the reality of the advanced industrial nations in automated production (153).

Thus on a second level, the chapter followed Mao's discontinuities with his own past:

- The period of the "100 Flowers Campaign," followed by the forced mass labor of "the Great Leap Forward," as Mao's response to what he saw not as flowers but as 1,000 weeds;
- The Sino-Soviet Conflict, as Mao issued a challenge for leadership of the Third World;
- Launching "The Great Proletarian Cultural Revolution" from above against his own leadership;
- Mao's attempt to forge "a new world axis—Peking-Djakarta—to break up the bipolar world."

These discontinuities were a manifestation of Mao's actual continuity: his reduction of theory to its "practicality," and thus his constant break with the past when he deemed it expedient.

Dunayevskaya returned again and again to what she saw as the retrogressionism of Mao's thought, his "uninterrupted revolution," which:

> has nothing to do with spontaneous proletarian revolutions which lead to classless societies. Quite the opposite . . . When he calls for "revolution," he is calling for more and more production. This is what Marx called primitive accumulation of capital. . . . No, the qualitatively new phenomenon in the "Thought of Mao Tse-tung" protrudes from the proclamation that "for a very long historic period after the proletariat takes power the class struggle continues as an objective law independent of man's will;" "for decades or even longer after socialist industrialization and agricultural collectivization" *both* "the class struggle" and the "ideological struggles" go on (154, 155).

In contrast to Mao's retrogressionism, particularly his view of the Chinese masses as "poor and blank," Dunayevskaya, in a final section, "Alienation and Revolution," presented a view of the revolutionary opposition within China. This took two forms. First, she presented excerpts of an interview with a Chinese refugee in Hong Kong who had returned to China after the revolution to participate in building a new society. Although she had begun with great enthusiasm, her experiences—in following the Hundred Flowers debates, participating in the mass labor of building a dam, watching as Russia went from the greatest friend to "revisionist"—left her with a view that things were reeling backward: "The trouble was, the more I read, the more I began to doubt some of Mao's statements, because my own experience, which kept intruding into my study, didn't jibe either with his practice or theory. But I didn't dare to say so out loud, not even to myself" (quoted, 173).

Sheng Wu-lien was the other opposition inside China that Dunayevskaya called attention to: "In Hunan, Mao's 'own' district, immediately after his visit there in the autumn of 1967, twenty organizations arose, calling themselves the Hunan Provincial Proletarian Revolutionary Great Alliance Committee" [abbreviated as Sheng Wu-lien] (176). She quoted a number of paragraphs from their document "Whither China?" which critiqued the emerging "Red capitalist class," and called their opposition "the Challenge from the Left."

Sheng Wu-lien wrote:

> To really over throw the rule of the new aristocracy and thoroughly smash the old State machinery, it will be necessary to go into the question of assessment of the past seventeen years [since the 1949 Revolution] . . . the real revolution, the revolution to negate the past seventeen years has basically not yet begun. . . Where China goes also determines where the world goes. China will inevitably go toward the new society of the People's Communes of China! (quoted, 178).

•

In taking up Jean-Paul Sartre, characterized as an "Outsider Looking In," Dunayevskaya focused on Sartre's 1950s effort, in Simone de Beauvoir's words, "to reconcile [Marxism] with his basic Existentialism" as seen in his *Question de méthode*, Sartre's introduction to *Critique de la raison dialectique*:

> [T]o comprehend fully the new Sartre as he weighs the attraction and repulsion between Existentialism and Marxism, we must understand his preoccupation with methodology as it concerns "the unique character" of what he calls "The Progressive-Regressive Method." It is this which, in Sartre's eyes, justifies his retention of the autonomy of Existentialism until the time when it will be "integrated" into Marxism (191-192).

Despite Sartre's wish to reconcile existentialism and Marxism—indeed his view of existentialism reduced to the role of a "parasite" on Marxism—Dunayevskaya argued that Sartre's "Progressive-Regressive Method" with its category of the "practico-inert," had greater kinship to Sartre's categories in his existential work *Being and Nothingness* than to the Marxism of Marx:

> Just as Sartre's disregard of History in *Being and Nothingness*, far from allowing him to embrace the human condition in its totality, closes all exits to reso-

lution of contradictions, so his "embrace" of History *sans* the masses as Subject in the *Critique* makes it impossible to open any doors to revolution (194-95).

Just as in *Being and Nothingness*, despite the language of opposition, there is no higher ground emerging from the contradiction in the Hegelian sense of Idea, so in the *Critique* there is none in the Marxian sense of spontaneous revolts and actual class struggles. Where in *Bring and Nothingness* the process of collapse is everything, in *Critique* the terror of the "collectivity" becomes everything. Out of neither does there emerge a method, a direction, a development (195).

Sartre *may* have destroyed as many dogmatisms as he claims. But one unstated yet all-pervading dogmatism continues to be the underlying motif of all Sartre thinks, writes, does. It is the dogmatism of the backwardness of the masses now called "practico-inert" and including the individual as well as the masses (200).

Just as in *Being and Nothingness* the Being-in-itself and Being-for-itself remain as apart at the end as at the start, so in *Critique* there is no self-development though the individual is now social man, and the past is not rejected but recognized as History and with a capital H (201).

Dunayevskaya critiqued *Question de méthode*, taking up Sartre's discussion of contemporary events—particularly the Hungarian Revolution of 1956—and his discussion of Marx. While Sartre opposed the bloody suppression of the Hungarian Revolution, he did not make a category of its workers councils: "[T]he Insurrection was much too brief and too troubled for us to be able to speak of an organized democracy" (quoted, 198). In contrast to Marx's methodology, Dunayevskaya characterized Sartre's "empty abstraction which has helped cover up soured revolutions and failed to disclose new roads to revolution in theory, not to mention in fact. . . . The philosophy of existence . . . remained Subjectivity without a Subject" (209-210).

Sartre's failure to posit historical revolutionary human subjectivity within existentialism, combined with his failure to grasp Marx's philosophy of revolution as rooted in concrete human forces, left him with no viable pathway in his struggle to unite existentialism with Marxism.

III. Economic Reality and the Dialectics of Liberation

In the 1940s Dunayevskaya had studied the economic reality of the first three 5-year State Plans of Stalin's Russia, coming to the conclusion that the so-called Soviet Union was a state-capitalist society. In doing so she had followed the lot of the Russian workers, including resistance to their conditions of life and labor. Economic reality and worker resistance were held as one. In Part III of *Philosophy and Revolution,* the view of the material world and the forces of resistance were extended and deepened geographically, with regard to human subjectivity, and in philosophic expression. Geographically, Africa, Eastern Europe, and the West, were taken up. Subjects of revolution encompassed not only the proletariat, but the activity of African masses in the countryside and city, the Black revolt in the U.S., as well as the anti-Vietnam War youth, and an emerging Women's Liberation movement. Philosophically, the self-determination of peoples and the self-determination of the Idea, were seen as a single dialectic—a dialectics of liberation. The interrelationship between economic reality and the dialectics of liberation was the theme probed.

The three chapters of this final part—"The African Revolutions and the World Economy," "State Capitalism and the East European Revolts," and "New Passions and New Forces: The Black Dimension, the Anti-Vietnam War Youth, Rank-and-File Labor, Women's Liberation"—on one level returned to the structure established in *Marxism and Freedom*: a probing of the movement from practice. At the same time, this return to the movement from practice to theory, extended to the 1960s and early 1970s, was explored from the vantage point of the dialectic in Hegel, Marx, and Lenin—the Absolute Method—and from the vantage point of Marxist-Humanism's philosophic contribution—Absolute Negativity as New Beginning.

This was evident from the opening sentence of the Africa chapter: "The African revolutions opened a new page in the dialectic of thought as well as in world history" (213). Dunayevskaya argued that whether one looked at revolutions in Africa or in East Europe, "in the decade which ended the 1950s and began the 1960s, the struggles for freedom were clearly also searches for a total philosophy, a new humanism, and a new world" (215).

For Africa, the economic reality was stark. Dunayevskaya showed that neo-colonialism was not an illusion but "a fact of existing world capitalism" (222). The technologically advanced world not only had a basic productive wealth far greater than the underdeveloped world, but its rate of growth in the 1950s and 60s outdistanced the Third World. It was the developed world, not the underdeveloped world that attracted the bulk of capital investment. Furthermore, Dunayevskaya argued that "*so long as the motive force of production continues to be the accumulation of surplus value (or unpaid hours of labor)*" there was insufficient capital "to industrialize the 'backward' lands" (227).

At the same time, the tragedy of the African revolutions was not alone the capitalist economic reality: "The tragedy of the African revolutions began so soon after revolution had succeeded because leaders were so weighed down with consciousness of technological backwardness that they turned to one of the two poles of world capital. The isolation from the masses deepened so that the new rulers began to look at them as mere labor power" (218).

Dunayevskaya argued that it was the power of a dialectics of liberation—the upsurge of the African revolutions—which enabled the African states to break free of the direct domination of imperialism. At the same time, it was the failure to deepen this dialectics of liberation *after* revolution that allowed neocolonialism to so quickly take hold in Africa. Historical developments and the ongoing objective/subjective reality in Nigeria, Ghana, and Senegal were discussed, as Dunayevskaya developed her ideas on the power of a dialectics of liberation and the grave contradictions that threatened to hinder its deepening on the African continent.

•

In "State Capitalism and the East European Revolts" the focal point for economic reality and the dialectics of liberation became "the East." Dunayevskaya began by tracing the dialectic of the Polish revolt to 1970-71, protests involving Gdansk shipyard workers and originally sparked by a rise in food prices. To Dunayevskaya, Poland 1970 was part of a continuity of revolt in East Europe, "the very nearly ceaseless struggles over two decades."

She termed this movement—including East Germany 1953, Hungary 1956, Czechoslovakia 1968, and Poland 1970—"The Movement from Practice that Is Itself a Form of Theory." The kinds of struggles engaged in, the organizational forms that arose, the questions asked and demands posed—all pointed to the maturity of the practice that in fact became an actual form of theory. There was the continuous nature of East European revolt and Dunayevskaya's creation of a philosophic category that spoke to the meaning of the revolutionary events. She saw this as the recreation of the dialectic for the post-World War II world, a striving for the unity of mass revolt and dialectical philosophy.

Dunayevskaya discussed a number of the revolts: the decentralized from of workers' councils that sprang up in Hungary, the kinds of discussions which took place in Yugoslavia prior to the student-sparked rebellion of 1968. She contrasted the revolts and emergence of a new stage of cognition to the official Communist theoreticians, whose theoretical utterances only served as ideological rationalizations for the Communist regimes' exploitative practices.

Dunayevskaya pointed to a different form of theoretical discussion that arose among East European thinkers—among them Karl Kosik and Milan Prucha of Czechoslovakia, and Bronislaw Baczko of Poland—who raised dimensions of humanism, and who considered themselves Marxist or Socialist Humanists. She quoted from their discussions probing the meaning of current East European events in relation to the humanism of Marx.

At the same time, Dunayevskaya warned against "some of those who hail new forms of revolt still do not see the masses as Reason. Instead, they interpret these upsurges as if *praxis* mean the *workers practicing what the theoreticians hand down*" (265). She saw the new stage of cognition which had been born out of mass worker *praxis*, as not alone a challenge to the ruling powers, but to revolutionary theoreticians who saw themselves aligned with the masses: "[I]t is high time for a new relationship of theory to practice to be worked out with due intellectual humility. . . . Is it not time for intellectuals to begin, with where the workers are and what they think, to fill the theoretic void in the Marxist movement?" (266).

•

In *Philosophy and Revolution's* final chapter, "New Passions and New Forces," Dunayevskaya's concentration was on the Black Dimension as seen in "the African Revolutions and the Black Revolution in America," on anti-Vietnam war youth, on the women's liberation movement, and on rank-and-file labor—as each emerged and developed in the 1960s and early 1970s. "We do have what no other age has had in such depth—the movement from *praxis* whose quest for universality does not stop with practice but hungers for a uniting of theory to practice" (285).

Dunayevskaya took up the movement from *praxis* beginning with the Black movement of the 1960s, including the slogan of "Black Power," and the rebellions in the cities. She commented on and critiqued the rebellion in France, May 1968, and on the new moment represented by the Cuban revolution. In writing of women's liberation she noted: "The uniqueness of today's Women's Liberation movement is that it dares to challenge what is, including the male chauvinism not only under capitalism but within the revolutionary movement itself" (280). Drawing the various strands of the movement from practice together, she wrote:

> What the movement from practice has revealed over these two decades of revolt and striving to establish new societies . . . was that the masses wish not only to overthrow exploitative societies, but they will no longer accept cultural substitutes for uprooting the old *and* new managers over their conditions of labor *and* life. Anything short of a *total* reorganization of life, totally new human relations was now retrogressionist. . . . The new frontiers opened with the end of illusions, with the start of revolutions *within* the successful revolutions, with the permanence of self-development so that there should end, once and for all, the difference between the Individual and the Universal. Philosophic-political maturity marks the uniqueness of our age. The need for "second negativity," that is, a second revolution, has become *concrete* (285-86).

•

In the final pages of *Philosophy and Revolution*, Dunayevskaya summed up its journey:

> What we have shown throughout is this: There is a dialectic of thought from consciousness through culture to philosophy. There is a dialectic of history from slavery through serfdom to free wage labor. There is a dialectic of the class struggle in general and under capitalism in particular—and as it develops through certain specific stages from competition through monopoly to state, in each case it calls forth new forms of revolt *and* new aspects of the philosophy of revolution. . . .
> It is true, of course—and indeed there would be something fundamentally amiss if it were otherwise—that Marx and Lenin solved the problems of their age, not ours. But powerful foundations have been laid for this age which we would disregard at our peril. . . .

The *new* that characterizes our era, the "energizing principle" that has determined the direction of the two decades of the movement *from practice* simultaneously rejects *false* consciousness and aborted revolution.

The reality is stifling. The transformation of reality has a dialectic all its own. It demands a unity of the struggles for freedom with a philosophy of liberation. Only then does the elemental revolt release new sensibilities, new passions, and new forces—a whole new human dimension.

Ours is the age that can meet the challenge of the times when we work out so new a relationship of theory to practice that the proof of the unity is in the Subject's own self-development. Philosophy and revolution will first then liberate the innate talents of men and women who will become whole. Whether or not we recognize that this is the task history has "assigned," to our epoch, it is a task that remains to be done (287, 290, 291-92).

Chapter 10

Philosophic Concretization and Projection: Organizational Ramifications and Contradictions

> *"Philosophic analysis . . . is itself a form of activity even as the movement from practice is itself a form of theory."*

Philosophy and Revolution's publication released new forms of activity in News and Letters Committees:

 • Political-Philosophic Letters on current events written by Dunayevskaya were issued beginning in 1976.

 • A series of six lectures on "Women as Thinkers and as Revolutionaries," was presented by her in 1975 (*RDC* #5363), while *Working Women for Freedom*, a Women's Liberation—News and Letters Committees pamphlet was issued in 1976 (*RDC* #5370).

 • New expressions of the Black Dimension included *Indignant Heart: A Black Worker's Journal* (1978), a greatly expanded version of Charles Denby's 1952 autobiography incorporating his more than two decades as editor of *News & Letters*, as well as the pamphlet *Frantz Fanon, Soweto, and American Black Thought* (1977, *RDC* #5305).

 • Revolutionary forces in American history were examined in pamphlets on the American Revolution (*America's First Unfinished Revolution*, 1976, *RDC* #5527), and on the St. Louis General Strike of 1877 (*Then and Now: On the 100th Anniversary of the First General Strike in the U.S.* 1977, *RDC* # 5577).

 • The newspaper, *News & Letters*, was expanded to include several 12-page issues each year, while the Draft Perspectives for News and Letters national meetings were published as a public document within the pages of the paper beginning in 1977.

- An important philosophic presentation by Dunayevskaya in this period was her address to the Hegel Society of America, "Dialectics of Liberation in Thought and in Activity: Absolute Negativity as New Beginning," a paragraph-by-paragraph interpretation of the final chapter on Absolute Idea in Hegel's *Science of Logic* (1974 RDC #5631).

At the same time as these concretizations/projections of *Philosophy and Revolution*, there emerged a gap between the philosophic leap the book embodied and the organizational expression of this new stage. The needed organizational development of News and Letters Committees flowing from *Philosophy and Revolution*'s publication became a focal point of Dunayevskaya's discussions. She spoke of being "the *organizational* author" of *Philosophy and Revolution* (RDC #5622), and saw philosophy's concretization in ongoing objective-subjective events as a crucial force of revolutionary change. How philosophy became concretized—its politicalization as it became foundation for building a Marxist-Humanist organization—was an explicit point of concentration in the mid-1970s. One way Dunayevskaya formulated the task was in the 1976-77 Draft Perspectives Thesis:

> The concretization of philosophy gives an altogether new meaning to politicalization. That is to say, whether it's an activity in the class struggle, or Women's Liberation or racial equality, or international solidarity, philosophic analysis is not something "appended" to a "main thesis," *but is itself a form of activity even as the movement from practice is itself a form of theory* (RDC # 5689).

The labor to concretize philosophy and thus develop its organizational expression, became manifest in a number of spheres in this period: (1) projection within the women's liberation movement, including the publication of a pamphlet, *Working Women for Freedom*; (2) issuing of Political-Philosophic letters which analyzed ongoing world events; and (3) transformation of News and Letters Committees into a *philosophic nucleus* through a focus on Marxist-Humanism's original contribution to the dialectic: Absolute Idea as New Beginning, and projecting it through politicalization. In each sphere, Dunayevskaya found the organizational response and development contradictory.

Projection in the Women's Liberation Movement

In the fall of 1975 Dunayevskaya gave a series of six lectures on "Women as Thinkers and Revolutionaries." These formed an important strand in the development of Dunayevskaya's third book, *Rosa Luxemburg, Women's Liberation, and Marx's Philosophy of Revolution* and will be discussed in Chapter 11. Excerpts from one of the lectures formed part of an appendix to the pamphlet *Working Women for Freedom* (1976, RDC #5370).

Working Women for Freedom, was a collectively written pamphlet issued by Women's Liberation—News and Letters Committees. It was a history pamphlet and at the same time captured a wide range of the voices of women in the 1970s. It told stories of working women from factories, farm fields, hospitals, and offices, including working and organizing in a shirt factory and an electrical plant, a social agency office, and an auto plant. The pamphlet presented working women speaking for themselves on their conditions of labor, how they had to often fight not only the boss but the union bureaucracy, and at times male workers' sexism. It gave voice to Black, Latina, and Native American women telling of their specific oppression and of their thoughts for a different future. Its international dimension touched on Portugal and Italy, as well as China and Nigeria. Reports of women's liberation demonstrations and meetings were presented.

Among the crucial themes taken up was how deeply entwined were the Black movement and women's liberation. Black women activists from the 1950s, and '60s—Rosa Parks and Fannie Lou Hamer among them—were shown as initiators and leaders. The same was true historically in the activity and thought of a Sojourner Truth, who did not hesitate to speak out not only against slavery, but for Black women's rights and not alone Black men's rights.

Another theme was that of women being hidden from history. Several pages of women's history were brought to the fore, including garment worker struggles of the early 20th century and women active in the birth of the Congress of Industrial Organization (CIO) in the 1930s.

The theme of women hidden from history was deepened to their being hidden from philosophy with the inclusion of an essay by Dunayevskaya, "Women as Thinkers and as Revolutionaries," as an appendix. She began with Part I on Mass Creativity and the Black Dimension, telling the story of the Women's War in East Nigeria in 1929. The market women, facing a new tax by the occupying British Empire, organized resistance, which developed into a revolt across tribal divisions. The British restored "order" by firing into a demonstration killing 40 women. Dunayevskaya called attention to "the self-organization of the women," which was so often underestimated, not only in this historic incident but in many other revolutionary activities and thinking of women.

In Part II of her essay, Dunayevskaya took up Russia, February 1917, where the Petrograd women textile workers who took to the streets in celebration of International Women's Day became the spark that brought forth the overthrow of the Tsar. She asked, "What can we learn from women *as masses in motion,* initiating nothing short of the overthrow of that reactionary Russian colossus, Tsarism?" After a brief description of the events in Russia, she wrote:

> What had happened in action, what had happened in thought, what had happened in consciousness of the mass participants—all this is ground on which we build today. Or should be. But even if some still insist on playing down women *both* as masses in motion and as leadership, let them consider the Ger-

man Revolution, January 1919, led by Rosa Luxemburg. None questioned that she was the leader (*Working Women for Freedom*, 52).

Dunayevskaya described Luxemburg as revolutionary and as theoretician from the end of the 19th century to her murder in 1919. She then challenged the Women's Liberation Movement to learn from Luxemburg: "[S]hould not the corpus of her works become the real test of woman as revolutionary and as thinker and as someone who has a great deal to tell us as women's liberationists of today?" (54)

In the final part, Dunayevskaya took up "An Ongoing Revolution and Today's Women Theorists." The ongoing revolution was the Portuguese of the mid-1970s, where the struggles of women had played an important role for some two decades, and one of the leaders of a revolutionary political organization was a woman.

Dunayevskaya noted that while women theorists had done considerable work in exposing male chauvinism, "the weak point was that none of them were in any serious way related to working class women, their activities, their thoughts, their aspirations." The one exception was Sheila Rowbothan's *Women, Resistance and Revolution*. But even there, philosophic roots of the movement were not taken up, and Luxemburg was unmentioned. The challenge of working out a relation of women's creativity to a philosophy of liberation remained: "What we do need is a *unity* of philosophy and revolution. Without it, we will not be able to get out from under the whip of the counter-revolution" (56).

As *Working Women for Freedom* (*WWFF*) was being projected to an outside audience, Dunayevskaya spoke to her News and Letters colleagues on the nature of that projection:

> [W]e cannot, say, separate *WWFF* from [its] "Appendix" merely by the "declaration" that there is no such division. No, we either understand that *WWFF as mediation* meant both the elicitation from below AND News & Letters' contribution, not as something "at the end" but something that created the very ground for elicitation. The unnamed authors have themselves to *recognize* that *they* have gained a new dimension because of our "mediation," or we succeed neither in bring the outside inside, nor the inside outside (Excerpts for Executive Session of N&L Convention, Sept. 5, 1976, "Dialectics of Leadership as the Creation of a Philosophic Nucleus in History's Mirror, and Today's Objective World *or* Self-Thinking Idea as the Self-Bringing Forth of Liberty," *SRDC* #15019).

The Meaning of Political-Philosophic Letters

Political-Philosophic Letters were begun in 1976 as a supplement to the monthly *News & Letters*. In the first year the Letters covered a wide range of topics. Among them, the Portuguese revolution, the UN Resolution on Zionism, Post-

Mao China, Kissinger's African Safari, and on "Today's Global Crisis, Marx's *Capital*, and the Marxist Epigones Who Try to Truncate It and the Understanding of Today's Crisis" (*RDC* #5181-5299).

In taking up world events, the Letters' focus was to manifest politicalization as a concretization of philosophy and thus, to help develop "a nucleus of philosophic leadership" in News and Letters Committees. "The whole new series of political-philosophic letters was started as one of the ways to get to the philosophic nucleus that is so very badly needed" (*RDC* #5622).

By 1977 Dunayevskaya expressed a critique of the Committee's practice of politicalization:

> Needed Politicalization. It's time we got down to the concrete weaknesses that I see as the main weakness in the leadership. Think of it. We have produced the Philosophic Political Letters which were supposed to be the transition point from *Philosophy and Revolution* to challenging other analyses on the world scene. We sold some and we certainly had local discussions on each and we no doubt know "exactly" what each says. And yet I insist we do not know them at all, because what we know are the results of, *not* a process, *not* the methodology, not a projection especially as a battle of ideas (Resident Editorial Minutes, June 15, 1977, *RDC* #15062).

In those same minutes she also noted, "[I]t is a fact that the mediation between philosophy and organization is that needed politicalization, i.e. not just expressing *Philosophy and Revolution* 'in general,' but specifically the analysis of current events and battling with other tendencies."

Dunayevskaya's critique of the work with the Political-Philosophic letters was related to what she felt was the central problem—the failure of the Committees to grasp the original philosophic contribution of Marxist-Humanism, the dialectic of Absolute Negativity as New Beginning.

Organizational Critique and New Beginning

In 1976 Dunayevskaya gave a presentation titled "Our *Original* Contribution to the Dialectic of the Absolute Idea as New Beginning: In Theory, and Leadership and Practice." Delivered to the East Coast National Editorial Board of News and Letters (April 10, 1976 *RDC* #5622), it was one of Dunayevskaya's most comprehensive summations in the post *Philosophy and Revolution* period of her philosophic contribution in relation to those of Marx and Lenin. In preliminary form, it was what she wished to present to the executive session of the 1976 News and Letters Convention on the relation of Chapter One of *Philosophy and Revolution*, "Absolute Negativity as New Beginning" to the development of a nucleus of philosophic leadership in News & Letters.

In the introduction to the East Coast NEB presentation she wrote: "[W]e have not grasped Chapter 1 of *Philosophy and Revolution* at its origin and root, much less thought of working out its ramification. Because the originality of our philosophic contribution is not fully grasped. . . . *we have yet to develop what I call a nucleus of philosophic leadership" (#5622).*

The full presentation had three parts:

> I. The new in our contribution, first as it relates to Marx and Lenin; secondly, as it relates to Chapter 1 of *Philosophy and Revolution.*
> II. The needed philosophic nucleus which will be leadership, proletarianization, politicalization.
> III. The problems at the Convention, which in one respect simply repeat politicalization, proletarianization, and Chapter 1, but in another respect, spell out the question of what is meant by totality as a new beginning.

Because of the uniqueness of Part One's philosophic projection it is printed as appendix to this chapter. Part One asked "*What* is this original contribution?" Parts Two and Three asked "*How* does it relate to a philosophic nucleus; *Why* is politicalization one of these ways of getting to a philosophic nucleus?" (#5622) To probe those questions Dunayevskaya distinguished her view of politicalization of philosophy from other Left tendencies' wish to "popularize" philosophy. The challenge was to "present the totality of our philosophy in our politicalization" (#5627).

Several months later, at the Convention's executive session she expressed the difficulty within the Committees, and the challenge faced in the period after *Philosophy and Revolution's* publication:

> Because the originality and profundity of our *historic* contribution to Marxism have not, I believe, been creatively grasped by our leadership we were risking a veritable philosophic stalemate in the very year of our best organizational growth. Which is why we didn't act as challengers, not alone in the movement from practice—there we were most active—but in relationship to all other Tendencies in the movement, though they had not even attempted, much less actually filled, the void since Lenin's death, whereas we produced both *M&F* [*Marxism and Freedom*] and *P&R* [Philosophy and Revolution], especially *P&R*.
> It is for this reason that the Political-Philosophic Letters were started—to fill the need for politicalization and the imperative nature of the creation of a philosophic nucleus (*SRDC* #15019).

•

The task of working out the gulf between the Marxist-Humanist vision of *Philosophy and Revolution* and its organizational concretization/projection and political expression in News and Letters Committees continued throughout the 1970s and into the 1980s. Dunayevskaya recognized the task not alone as the specificity of News and Letters Committees, but historically as an objective-subjective challenge for the Marxist movement—the needed fusion of the organization of philosophic thought with an organization of living revolutionaries. Her full labors over the last decade of her life, first on *Rosa Luxemburg, Women's Liberation, and Marx's Philosophy of Revolution*, and then on the uncompleted "Dialectics of Organization and Philosophy," were brought to bear on this task. We turn to these labors in Parts IV and V.

Appendix

Part I, "The new in our contribution, first as it relates to Marx and Lenin; secondly, as it relates to chapter 1 of **Philosophy and Revolution**,*" excerpted from "Our Original Contribution to the Dialectic of the Absolute Idea as New Beginning: In Theory, And Leadership, and Practice," April 10, 1976 (RDC #5622).*

•

We have to begin with what is new in our contribution, because we have been so anxious to stress we are a *continuity* from Marx and Lenin (and we certainly are), and we've been so anxious to stress that we couldn't possibly have been without Marx and Lenin (which again, we couldn't have been), that we have underplayed what is absolutely new, not just in relationship to a lot of nobodies who call themselves Marxists, but in relationship to our founders themselves. And because we have overemphasized their contribution, without which we couldn't possibly have been, it is necessary to then think backwards right now.

No one was greater than Marx. No one needs to be convinced of that fact. However, when it comes to the Absolute Idea, it isn't only that the young Marx got so thoroughly disgusted with Absolutes by the time he discovered his new continent of thought, that he said that's the end of that, I'll return to it some other time. It is that when he did return—and in his greatest work he did—it was already as practice, and not as something that would help us grasp it by having a foundation.

For example, at the height of *Capital*, we see him breaking up the Absolute Idea by speaking about the general absolute law of capitalist accumulation. But its opposite was always taken to be only the unemployed army—and not the absolutely, totally opposite which we take it to be now. Marx only mentioned it as "the new passions and new forces for the reconstruction of society." The negation of the negation at that point certainly wasn't spelled out.

Lenin certainly paid a lot more attention to Absolute Idea. We have that chapter commented on more than any other chapter in *Science of Logic*. But he, too, had to concentrate, as all of us have to concentrate, on what is concrete for our age. What was concrete for his age was, as we know, the transformation into opposite. But he threw out the last half of the last paragraph of Absolute Idea and said, that doesn't make any difference. It *did* make a difference, and my Letters on the Absolute Idea of 1953 spend something like 12 pages arguing against him for leaving out that last half a paragraph.

Even more important, Chapter 1 of *Capital* was always in Lenin's mind as he was reading. We have stressed that Lenin says Universal, Particular, Individual was exactly what Marx had in mind when he wrote *Capital*. But Lenin never says anything about *fetishism*. When he was referring to Universal, Particular and Individual, he was referring to the section just before the fetishism of commodities, when Marx explains how we came to sales to money to capital.

In other words, the fetishism of commodities, as the dead labor sucking the living labor, and as the fact that you not only were exploited, but you actually had become an appendage to a machine—that was not concrete for Lenin. In fact, at one point—even though it wasn't at the stage where he was working with the Absolute Idea—he was "taken in," so to speak, by the Taylor system. He wondered whether that was just capitalistic or whether it could be used if you had soviets and you saw that it wasn't exploitative, and so forth.

So that whether we take our very founders, Marx and Lenin, or any of the Hegelian Marxists: Lukács when he was at his best, Marcuse when he was at his best, Adorno when he was at his best, the East Europeans when they were at their best—in an actual revolution—no one, *no one,* had formulated or even given us any indication that if you are going to break your head over Absolute Idea, *it would be as a new beginning. That's our original contribution.*

It isn't only that we did this great thing by saying Absolute isn't absolute in the ordinary sense of the word—it's the unity of theory and practice; Absolute isn't absolute in the bourgeois sense of the word—it's the question of the unity of the material and the idea. But who ever said Absolute was a new beginning? None but us. And if we don't understand that original contribution—*that we have to begin with the totality*—then we won't know what a new beginning is. A new beginning could just be that we discovered the four forces of revolution. We're certainly very proud of that—but that isn't all we're saying.

In fact, I would say that if there's anything we *do* understand, it's the movement from practice. We certainly have that imbedded in our being. We do understand that part of the absolute. We do not understand the other part, Absolute Idea as second negativity. And until we do understand it, we will not be able to project. Therefore we must return to Chapter 1 of *Philosophy and Revolution*, and read it with altogether new eyes. It is not just that we're challenging, or threatening, or saying something that sounds great and philosophic, but all the ramifications of that.

Hegel died in 1831. He was the greatest philosopher that ever lived. It is now 1976, and it was 1953 when I broke through on the three last syllogisms in the *Philosophy of Mind*. I never bothered to look up the philosophic scholars. I was sure they had dealt with it in their bourgeois way. I found out that nobody in the world had done it. It was then I found out that Hegel himself hadn't put them in until 1830, the year before he died. He had left it at Paragraph #574 in 1817. I think the first time I saw anything written about it was in the 1960s and that was a whole decade after I developed it.

Paragraph #575 says "this is a summation of what I did, and what I did explains my conclusions, Absolute Idea." So why did he suddenly decide to add three paragraphs? To say "a summation" evidently didn't satisfy him the year before he died. In the first of the three, Paragraph #575, Logic, Nature, Mind (the three volumes of the *Encyclopaedia of the Philosophical Sciences*) are not simply the names of what Hegel wrote. Nature, the center part, is not just the second book. The center part, the middle, contains the whole; it looks both forward and backward, and therefore, that is really the key point.

Marx said that any proletarian could have told Hegel that he should have begun with material things first. Everyone says it's a good thing Lenin didn't know that's what Marx said, because he wouldn't have dared say, "isn't that great that Hegel goes from Logic to Nature—he's extending a hand to historical materialism. Therefore, that chapter is the most central. The most ideal is really the most practical—terrific and magnificent!"

I came to this part and said, if it turns both backward and forward, it isn't just the remembrance of things past, but he's also seeing the future imbedded in there. That means there must be a movement from practice to theory that's itself a form of theory. This was on May 12, 1953.[1] There hadn't yet been the June 17th revolt. Everybody thought I was crazy—all this worry about what Stalin's death meant and that it wasn't going to stand still. It is the period from March to June when Stalin died and when the East German revolt broke out that we're concerned with—those few months. When I broke through on the Absolute Idea, May 12 and 20, it was in anticipation of what was actually occurring.

In the next paragraph, #576, Nature becomes first, Mind becomes second, and Logic is the end. So now Mind is the middle, the mediation, the center, the greatness from which the whole flows. What did that mean to us in the JFT? [Johnson-Forest Tendency] I said it meant we had to dig deeper into philosophy; we couldn't stop with state-capitalism. We must see that this was *new*—this movement *from practice* and this movement *from theory* are a unity.

Paragraph #577 is even crazier than #575 and #576 were. Hegel has lived all his life on Logic, but when he comes to #577, instead of turning it to let Logic now become the center, Hegel just throws it out altogether. He says what we're dealing with is Self-Thinking Idea. In the whole thing, he has one single tiny sentence on eternity *after* the Self-Thinking Idea, which has thrown out, replaced, Logic.

Now if that's what it means—and Hegel throws out his Logic—what could be greater? He says the Self-Thinking Idea is the self-bringing forth of liberty. That's when we already have it, the revolution is here, and everything is ready for not putting things off for the day after. It's right here and you better go do it and think it and everybody be part of the dialectic.

*   *   *

What do we mean by the cogency of dialectics of negativity for the period of our period of mass revolutions? What do we mean by Absolute Idea as new beginning? When we keep stressing, correctly, that it's a unity of theory and practice, we do not know the double negation as being within us. . . . I have stated many, many times that second negativity is not just when you come to the Absolute Idea, but that you experience second negativity at every single stage—and since everybody's always saying, "don't give your first reaction, wait for second negativity," you would think we certainly understand second negativity. But until it becomes concrete, we don't.

There is one thing I want to include here, in relationship to Sartre and Fanon on the question of Particular. We've always talked against the fixed Particular, nationalized property=socialism. But Universal, Particular and Individual are the three main categories of the Doctrine of the Notion. Particular is your first negation of the Universal when it's abstract, and Individual is the total concretization when it's Individualism which let's nothing interfere with it's Universalism, that is, Freedom.

The idea is that when it's *not* fixed, Particular is the way to get to the second negativity; there is no other way to get to it. And what Fanon expressed so passionately was that he did not mean that Negroes are not a Particular. He meant that Negritude is the Particular which *is* Universal. That is what he meant by "national consciousness that is not nationalism but is a form of internationalism." He certainly did some very beautiful things of the difference between national consciousness that makes you proud of your heritage or makes you realize that this is a contribution, and nationalism which he absolutely rejected because he was a total internationalist and revolutionary.

I think that part of the politicalization will also be on that. The fixed Particular is absolutely wrong and will kill you. But when it's not fixed, when it's a stage in the development of the concretization, that is the only way to get to second negativity.

What I'm trying to stress here now are certain stages in Chapter 1 [of *Philosophy and Revolution*], which must be grasped as concrete. You have to say to yourself if Absolute Idea means new beginnings, it means that in talking to such and such a person, I have to present the whole of philosophy and Marxist-Humanism. It is not enough to say, "we agree with you on the question of welfare or whatever." The question of welfare or whatever becomes a way not only of you learning something from them, but of them having an awful lot to learn from you, because they get an entirely new interpretation of the problem that had been bothering them.

---

[1] Dunayevskaya discussed Hegel's final three syllogisms from *Philosophy of Mind* in her May 20th, not May 12th, letter.

Part IV

1975-1982, Rosa Luxemburg, Women's Liberation, and Marx's Philosophy of Revolution

Chapter 11

Development of Luxemburg Book, 1975-1982: Strands from Women's Liberation, Luxemburg, and Marx; Relation to Iran's Revolution/Counter-Revolution, and to *News & Letters* as Theory/Practice

One starting point for the development of the third major work, *Rosa Luxemburg, Women's Liberation, and Marx's Philosophy of Revolution*, was a series of six lectures on "Women as Thinkers and as Revolutionaries" Dunayevskaya delivered in the fall of 1975 [1]

The concept of the work deepened in the latter half of the 1970s through a series of explorations of Rosa Luxemburg as theoretician, revolutionary and feminist. By May 1976, her studies yielded a new title for her projected book. No longer "Women as Reason and Force," or "Women as Thinkers and Revolutionaries," but "Rosa Luxemburg, Today's Women Theorists, and the Women's Liberation Movement," became the working title. In May 1977 she made a "Rough Outline of RL Book" (*SRDC* #14795). The five pages of notes were devoted to a discussion of Luxemburg. At the same time, the last paragraph of the outline spoke of reconnecting with Marx, his philosophy of revolution, as well as ending with today's women's liberation movement.

As the study evolved, the strands of Luxemburg and of women's liberation became intertwined with and measured against Marx's philosophy of revolution. The title of the book in progress underwent half a dozen changes between 1975 and 1979. By 1978, the title encompassed Luxemburg, Women's Liberation and Marx. Dunayevskaya articulated the relationship in a report she made to the Resident Editorial Board of *News & Letters* in June 1978:

> [T]he work on Rosa Luxemburg, which is by no means only Rosa Luxemburg, great and important as she is in her own right, nor is it only Rosa Luxemburg in relationship to the Women's Liberation movement of today, crucial as it is to see where we are going. No, what the times, objective and subjective, demand is the relationship of both these subjects to Marx's theory of revolution (*SRDC* #15087).

The full emergence of the three strands—Rosa Luxemburg, women's liberation, and Marx—as separate parts in the book would not be fully realized until 1981.[2]

This eight-year development of the book took place in the context of Dunayevskaya's analysis of ongoing world events, particularly Iran's revolution and counter-revolution, and her organizational activities as National Chairwoman of News and Letters Committees, including the deepening of *News & Letters* as a theoretical as well as practical voice for human liberation.[3]

A Re-examination of the Relationship of Marx and Engels

As part of the work, Dunayevskaya began to examine anew the totality of Marx's thought, particularly in relation to post-Marx Marxists beginning with Engels. In 1978 she wrote a letter to the Scottish Marxist-Humanist Harry McShane discussing the relation of Marx and Engels:

> I would like to have a little theoretical discussion with you on the difference between theory and philosophy, and on the difference between a "leader" and a *founder*.... I wish to go as far back as THE founder of all of us, ENGELS and Lenin included. Note, I include Engels of Marx's own time and place him alongside Lenin or anyone post-Marx, because it is most decisive to realize MARXISM IS MARX'S CONTINENT OF THOUGHT AND ONLY OF MARX, AND NOT OF MARX AND ENGELS (June 30, 1978, *RDC* #6432).

Dunayevskaya here prefigured the formulation "Post-Marx Marxists as a Pejorative, Beginning with Engels," which became central to the new book and to her projection of Marxist-Humanism in the 1980s. In the letter she critiqued those intellectuals who write "nonsense" on Engels "betraying" Marx, and, "the opposite side of the same coin," those who hyphenate Marx-Engels as if it were the same.

She pointed to how at the point of origin—the 1844 *Economic-Philosophic Essays*—"it was Marx alone, and not Marx and Engels, who is responsible for the new continent of thought Marx first called 'a new Humanism.'" The methodology of a Marx was not found in an Engels, not only at the origin of their relationship, "but both in maturation and at the very climactic point of writing after Marx's death, and the very book socialist feminists surely have accepted as the best of all for that era: *Origin of the Family, Private Property, and the State*." She raised a point that would become central to her work on the book: Marx's writings on pre- and non-capitalist societies, which she was in the midst of studying, were far different than what Engels later constructed in *Origin of the Family*.

By late fall 1978, Dunayevskaya developed her view of the relationship of Marx and Engels into the first draft chapter of the new book: "Relationship of Philosophy and Revolution to Women's Liberation: Marx's and Engels' Studies Contrasted" (*RDC* #6467). She critiqued the attempt of the Marxist writer Hal Draper to make an amalgam of Marx's and Engels' positions on women through her examination of Marx's *Ethnological Notebooks* in relation to Engels' writings on women. The draft chapter was published in *News & Letters*, January-February 1980.

This marked new ground in the development of Marxist-Humanism journalism, moving to turn *News & Letters* more fully into a theoretical as well as activist newspaper. It was also a deepening of Dunayevskaya's method of writing as a collectivity. Meetings were held in News and Letters Committees on the chapter with commentary going to her.

The publication of the chapter in *News & Letters* and the subsequent meetings, return us to Dunayevskaya as *organizational* author. Her specific methodology of writing, from the time of *Marxism and Freedom* to *Philosophy and Revolution*, and now to the new book, was one involving a collectivity of her colleagues in News and Letters Committees. This could be seen as well in a Dear Sisters Letter to Women's Liberation-News & Letters (October 15, 1978, *RDC* #6434), written as she was drafting this first chapter. After pointing to the fact that Engels quoted only a few paragraphs of Marx's Abstract of Morgan's *Ancient Society* in his *Origin of the Family*, whereas Marx's Notebooks on Morgan and other ethnologists, written in the last years of his life, numbered some 254 pages, she ended the letter: "I thought you might want to be with me in the process of working out the new book rather than be confronted with its worked-out views, even if as presently expressed they are not all too clear." Later she created a section in the Archives, "Letters from Dunayevskaya on process of writing *Rosa Luxemburg, Women's Liberation and Marx's Philosophy of Revolution*, 1978-81" (*RDC* #6432).

The original draft chapter on Marx and Engels was the starting point for what became a full part, "Karl Marx—From Critic of Hegel to Author of Capital and Theorist of 'Revolution in Permanence.'" The catalyst for this transformation was the category of post-Marx Marxists, which encompassed not alone Engels, but Lenin, Luxemburg, Trotsky, and Ryazanov, and indeed all post-Marx Marxism in relation to Marx's archives.

In a Dear Colleagues letter (November 3, 1980) Dunayevskaya wrote:

> The so-called last chapter, the one on Karl Marx's philosophy of revolution, just wouldn't get written. It refused to be confined into a single chapter. The

subject demanded more, and not alone because it has always been central to everything we do, but because specifically in relation to Rosa Luxemburg, precisely because she was such a great revolutionary, the lacuna of philosophy in her concepts came to a very sharp near-breaking point on the question of the 1917 Russian Revolution and 1919 German Revolution (*RDC* # 6461).

The letter went on to give an outline of the three chapters she was proposing for the Marx part. The part subsequently became four chapters.

An Evolving View of Rosa Luxemburg

After writing the draft chapter on Marx's and Engels' studies contrasted, Dunayevskaya concentrated on Luxemburg. Two draft chapters on Luxemburg appeared in *News & Letters* in 1980: "Before and After the 1905 Revolution" (*News & Letters*, Jan.-Feb. 1980, *RDC* #6420), and "The Break with Kautsky, 1910-11" (*News & Letters*, April 1980, *RDC* #6426).

These chapters were part of an evolving view of Luxemburg. Dunayevskaya had written on her as a revolutionary theoretician in the 1940s.[4] She again had taken up Luxemburg's theory of accumulation in *Marxism and Freedom* (1957). By the mid-1970s in the context of a growing women's liberation movement, Dunayevskaya returned to a study of Luxemburg. In part she wished to challenge the women's movement to explore the thought and activity of this great early 20th century revolutionary. In the process of her research, Dunayevskaya uncovered an ignored and forgotten feminist dimension of Luxemburg's political activities, and in her personal life. Luxemburg as theoretician, as revolutionary activist, and as feminist, became multiple points of departure for Dunayevskaya's study.

The emphasis was now not alone on her 1913 theory of accumulation, but on seeing her as revolutionary activist as well as a theoretician. Dunayevskaya began to explore the many dimensions of Luxemburg: fighting reformism within the Marxist movement, participating in and writing on the 1905 Revolution, critiquing the leader of the German Social Democracy, Karl Kausky, as early as 1910, as well as anti-war activist jailed in the midst of World War I, and as leader and martyr of the 1919 German Revolution.

In the late 1970s Dunayevskaya's study of Luxemburg continued to be a major focal point. What emerged was a multi-dimensional Luxemburg as revolutionary personality, "an original character," as serious Marxist theoretician, as passionate human being living life to its fullest under extreme circumstances. Not the least of the dimensions discussed was Luxemburg as a feminist. Dunayevskaya saw her as connecting in a challenging manner to the growing modern women's liberation movement.

The Objectivity of and Challenge to the Women's Liberation Movement

In response to the Women's Liberation Movement that emerged in the 1960s, arising in part as a critique of male chauvinism in the Left, News and Letters Committees and Dunayevskaya were active in the movement, forming a Women's Liberation—News & Letters Committee, creating a regular women's liberation page in *News & Letters*, participating in debates and conferences, and issuing several pamphlets: *Working Women for Freedom* (1976), *Sexism, Politics and Revolution in Mao's China* by Dunayevskaya (1977), and *Revolutionary Feminism—Women as Reason* (1978).

Inherent within the origins of the new book being Dunayevskaya's lecture series "Women as Thinkers and as Revolutionaries" was her recognition of the revolutionary subjectivity of women as an idea whose time had come. This meant a challenge for the women's liberation movement: how to express Women as Reason in the fullness of a social uprooting; how women as revolutionaries meant as activists *and* as theoreticians. To help meet that challenge, Dunayevskaya asked the women's liberation movement to grapple with three tasks, three ways of seeing:

(1) The need to dive into the fullness of Luxemburg, particularly to recognize her greatness as refusing to be "pigeon-holed" into only the "women's question" by the male theoreticians of the Second International, while at the same time recognizing Luxemburg as a feminist in taking up women's issues as inseparable from the fullness of revolution, and in her independent relationship with her comrade and lover Leo Jogiches. Dunayevskaya created a specific chapter on Luxemburg as Feminist.

(2) The need to dig into Marx's views on women as not only different from Engels, but rich with revolutionary possibilities. Whether it was Marx's view of man/woman relations as seen in his 1844 *Economic-Philosophic Manuscripts* revealing the exploitative relations of human beings to human beings in class society, or his critique of the early family as carrying the seeds of slavery and feudalism, or Marx's commentary on the greater equality Iroquois women had in Native American Society in his 1880s *Ethnological Notebooks*—all, argued Dunayevskaya, provided revolutionary points of departure for the modern women's liberation movement.

(3) The need to trace the movement of women's liberation as past, present, and future, with emphasis on the dimensions of color, class, revolution, and theory. In a Dear Colleagues letter Dunayevskaya wrote to the leadership of News and Letters, with a copy to the Women's Liberation Committee:

> One more new moment has arisen in relationship to the "RL [Rosa Luxemburg] book." Where, previously, I had insisted that WL was not a separate part, but only a chapter (and I did so in order to stress that the book is a *totality*, rather

than three different parts), I have now decided that the totality is best seen when there is a separate part. Here is what I mean: What was chapter 6, "Women's Liberation, Then and Now," is not only a matter of "Then and Now" i.e. different historic periods but also and above all, so totally different a concept that it transforms the whole question of "timing." Naturally, the different historic periods are important. . . . But we cannot limit the concept of Women's Liberation to a contrast of different historic periods, important as that subject is. Rather, Marx's concept of the Man/Woman relationship, which we quote so often, instead of being "taken for granted" must first be worked out for all periods.

We must roll the historic clock back, not just to questions of the women's movement, but back to the post-Marx Marxists, beginning with Engels himself. I now see that *Engels'* "philosophy," when it comes to Women's liberation, is only a form of *"biologism."* . . . Clearly, the new Part II that I am proposing will not be just a critique of modern women's liberationist theoreticians but a critique of all post-Marx Marxists, beginning with Engels' *Origin of the Family.* . . .

The new Part II I'm proposing will probably be entitled: The Women's Liberation Movement as Revolutionary Force and Reason . . . [It] will affect also the section I called "Luxemburg's Activity in the Women's Movement" (Letter of January 30, 1981, *RDC* #6465-66).

A chapter, "Luxemburg as Feminist, Break with Jogiches," was written for the section on Women's Liberation. Throughout the development of the book, Dunayevskaya continually wrote letters, made presentations to, and sought commentary from the Women's Liberation Committee of News and Letters. She saw the working out of the book and its projection closely related to the development of women's liberation within News and Letters, and towards having an impact upon the ongoing women's liberation movement.

In one Dear Sisters Letter to Women's Liberation–News & Letters (Nov. 24, 1978, *RDC* #6439), she discussed entering into debate with theorists such as Eleanor Leacock and Evelyn Reed on the basis of the draft chapter on Marx and Engels. Another letter (*RDC* # 6420) sharply critiqued Mary-Alice Walters' introduction to *Rosa Luxemburg Speaks* for failing to take up either the 1919 German Revolution (Spartakus uprising) or Luxemburg on the woman question. Dunayevskaya urged the Marxist-Humanist women to engage in a battle of ideas. One manifestation of this was seen with the translation of a number of Dunayevskaya's writings on women into Farsi in the midst of the Iranian revolution (*Women as Reason and as Force of Revolution*, issued for International Women's Day, March 8, 1980. *RDC* # 6092).

The Unfolding Revolution and Counter-Revolution in Iran as well as the Transformation of *News & Letters* to a 12-Page Paper—Both in Relation to Work on the New Book

In 1979-80, as the Iranian masses overthrew the Shah and almost simultaneously had the revolution usurped by Islamic fundamentalism, Dunayevskaya wrote a series of Political-Philosophic Letters on the events of revolution, counter-revolution and imperialist intrusion (*RDC* #5998- 6036). Far from being in a separate realm from her work on the book, she saw a relationship between the two:

> [When you see Luxemburg's] hatred of imperialism, of great feeling for all the peoples of all the world whom capitalism was oppressing, of the truly human warmth for the cries of the Hottentot women and children that she kept hearing from the Kalahari Desert as if they were they were just around the corner from her home, then you wish to lash out against the so-called 'New Left' which seems to feel nothing but its own narrow sloganeering, and its all-too-willing tailendism of state powers. It is for this reason that I felt it necessary to take a day off and talk to you about Iran (Dear Colleagues Letter, November 26, 1979, *RDC* #6444-45).

The Political-Philosophic Letter written the next day was titled "Grave Contradictions in the Iranian Revolution" (*RDC* #6013). A second letter (Dear Colleagues letter, December 2, 1979, *RDC* # 6446), related work on the book to the ongoing events in Iran: "In jumping the gun on myself by disclosing to you a very difficult philosophic problem that I, myself, have not yet worked out . . . I do so only because the concreteness of the political crisis and *counter*-revolutionary move with theocratic constitution that the Iranian masses will now be pushed to adopt, makes philosophy more *practically* urgent than any 'political line.'"

The letter discussed the fact that all the revolutionaries after the 1905-07 Revolutions failed to relate themselves to Marx's concept of "revolution in permanence." This in turn was taken up in the context of the need for those in News and Letters Committees to relate to Marx's philosophy of revolution "as manifestation of a *New Continent of Thought*." Dunayevskaya argued that the urgency of the moment in Iran was not solved by getting the latest in-person reports of Khomeini's rise in counter-revolution, but *"instead in having, in the very organism of himself/herself, the knowledge that the immediate is first understood because you are grounded in Marx's philosophy of revolution as spelled out for us in Marxist-Humanist Political-Philosophic Letters for today."*

Dunayevskaya was not arguing any one-to-one relationship between work on the new book and the events in Iran. Rather, what gave life to the relationship was how Marxist-Humanism dug into historic-philosophic moments from

Marx's and Luxemburg's day and placed them in the context of the present moment.

•

The concept and practice of Political-Philosophic Letters helped to create the ground for the 1980 expansion of *News & Letters* into a 12-page "theory/practice" journal as Dunayevskaya was working on the new book. At the same time, her "rediscovery" of Marx's *Wage Labor and Capital,* as having its first appearance as a series of articles in the daily *Neue Rheinische Zeitung,* the "Organ of Democracy" that Marx was editor of in the midst of revolutions/counter-revolutions of 1848-49, was seen as speaking to the tasks of News and Letters Committees in 1980:

> Now, please tell me, where, no matter how had I looked at today, could I have found so relevant to the convention's projection of a *new N&L [News & Letters]* combining theory and practice as the publication of *Wage Labor and Capital* in the popular daily, *Neue Rheinische Zeitung* on April 4, 1849. There is hardly a day that the work on the RL [Rosa Luxemburg] book doesn't throw some new illumination on the problematic of our day, be it on Iran or WL, be it on Theory/Practice or Youth, be it on Black dimension or *N&L* projection of a 12-pager. Naturally, this doesn't mean that the subjects, topics of the book, *as such* "call forth" such a relationship. Rather it is the way Marxist-Humanism recreates it. But, since truth is concrete, it is no accident whatever that it is these subjects and that historic period and this stage of our organization's growth and the way we prepare for the convention and the new tasks it will set that coalesced (Dear Friends Letter, March 5, 1980, *RDC* #6450-51).

A month later, in an extensive letter written in preparation for giving a lecture on 40 years of Marx's creativity, Dunayevskaya wrote of "scheduling, at one and the same time, a new book *and* projecting the transformation on *News & Letters* into a theoretical as well as an activist organ" (Dear Friends letter, April 8, 1980, *RDC* # 6454).

As will be seen, Dunayevskaya's labor to transform *News & Letters* and the Committees would intensify with the publication of *Rosa Luxemburg, Women's Liberation, and Marx's Philosophy of Revolution.*

---

[1] The titles of the six talks were: (1) Russia 1917; Germany 1919; Portugal 1975 (2) Working Women in America—from Abolitionism to the Women's Liberation Movement Today (3) Today's Women Theorists: Simone De Beauvoir, Kate Millett. Shiela Rowbothan, Juliet Mitchell, Maria Borreno (4) The Black Dimension: In Africa and in America (5) Literature and Revolution (6) Philosophy and Revolution: Women as Reason and Force.

For a summary of the lectures see Dear Friends Letter by Olga Domanski, November 6, 1975, *RDC* #5363. For audio tapes of lectures see The Raya Dunayevskaya Audio-Visual Tape Collection, Wayne State University Archives of Labor and Urban Affairs.

[2] For a listing of the development of various titles, parts and table of contents see *SRDC* # 14192-14202.

[3] The Archives of *The Raya Dunayevskaya Collection* contain well over 1,000 pages of documents in relation to the book. (*RDC*, Volume X; *SRDC* #14191-15377) Draft chapters, chapter research files, expanding table of contents pages, scores of letters discussing various chapters as they were being written, new discoveries such as materials from the 1907 Russian Social Democratic Labor Conference (the first after the 1905 Russian Revolution), a previously unavailable English translation of a Luxemburg writing ("Theory and Practice"), Dunayevskaya's commentary on the newly transcribed *Ethnological Notebooks of Marx*, as well as presentations to News and Letters Committees on the book as it evolved are among the materials in the Archives.

[4] See especially her "Luxemburg's Theory of Accumulation, How It Differed with Marx and Lenin" *RDC* #436-447.

Chapter 12

The Categories Post-Marx Marxism and Revolution-in-Permanence in Relation to the Structure and Content of the Luxemburg Book

Post-Marx Marxism

The category of post-Marx Marxism was a central theme of *Rosa Luxemburg, Women's Liberation, and Marx's Philosophy of Revolution* (*RLWLKM*). Within the book's index, Engels, Lenin, Luxemburg, Ryazanov, and Trotsky, were listed under post-Marx Marxists. For Dunayevskaya, the category meant critically examining the relation of Marx's thought to Marxists post-Marx. She saw revolutionaries at each historic moment post-Marx needing to recreate his dialectic, comprehending the totality of Marx's Marxism, his philosophy of revolution, as point of departure. In her view, post-Marx Marxism had fragmented Marx's thought, leading to an application or popularization of it, rather than a re-creation. The results were truncated, and at times vulgarized, conceptions of Marxism. Decades of debris had been heaped upon Marx's thought, and needed to be cleared away.

To present Marx's Marxism was not simply an accumulation of facts, but a comprehension of his methodology. It meant working out anew his philosophy of revolution at subsequent historic moments. This was the historic challenge for the greatest Marxist revolutionaries, let alone the Marxist epigones.

The concept of post-Marx Marxism encompassed a view of Engels, Marx's closest collaborator and loyal follower who prepared Volumes II and III of *Capital* after Marx's death, as not having projected the fullness of Marx's "new continent of thought," in such works as *Origin of the Family*. It meant a deep appreciation of Luxemburg as always a revolutionary, while at the same time manifesting a critique of her "tone-deafness" on philosophy. The category post-Marx Marxism included singling out Lenin's philosophic reorganization of his own concept of Marxism post-1914, while pointing to his philosophic ambivalence in not sharing his philosophic breakthrough with his fellow revolutionaries, or extending it to the question of organization. With regard to Trotsky, Dunayevskaya recognized his historic role in the revolutions of 1905 and 1917, and at the same time critiqued the lack of a self-developing Subject in his theory of permanent revolution, and his conciliationism on matters of revolutionary theory.

She saw revolutionaries in our age as being the first to have almost the totality of Marx's works before them, and thus able to become rooted in his philosophy of revolution rather than be bound to post-Marx Marxism's truncated conceptions. This was not a question of erudition or setting the record straight on Marx. Rather, it was a way of reaching for the future. Revolutionary thinkers and activists, and movements such as women's liberation, could reach for that new, *human* future with Marx's assistance. "Without his philosophy of revolution, neither Women's Liberationists nor the whole of humanity will have discovered the ground that will assure the success of the revolution" (109). Each of the three parts of *Rosa Luxemburg, Women's Liberation, and Marx's Philosophy of Revolution* would counter-pose Marx's revolution-in-permanence to post-Marx Marxism.

Part I: Rosa Luxemburg as Theoretician, as Activist, as Internationalist

What emerged from Part I, "Rosa Luxemburg as Theoretician, as Activist, as Internationalist," was a portrait of Luxemburg's passionate, multi-dimensional life of revolutionary thought and activity. Dunayevskaya began her critical analysis with Luxemburg's entrance on the German scene at the turn of the 20th century and continued until her murder in the midst of the 1919-20 German Revolution. The range of moments taken up—before and after the 1905 Revolution, the 1910-11 break with Kautsky, Marx's and Luxemburg's theories of accumulation of capital, debates on the National Question and her prescience on imperialism, disputes with Lenin on organization in relation to spontaneity and consciousness, the period of war, prison and revolution, discussion of Luxemburg as feminist—all enable us to see the creativity and profundity, as well as the contradictions, of this "original character," Rosa Luxemburg. At the same time, this human, intellectual biography of Luxemburg became a *biography of the idea of revolutionary Marxism* in Luxemburg as well as in Lenin through three early 20th century revolutions—the 1905 and 1917 Russian Revolutions, and the 1919-20 Germany Revolution.

Luxemburg's contributions to world Marxist thought commenced with her entrance into the world of the German Social Democracy at the end of the 19th century. Her 1898 *Reform or Revolution*, written when she was 27, "became the classic answer to Revisionism" (*RLWLKM*, 1). At the same time came her prescient "flash of genius on imperialism as *the* global shift in politics" (4). Dunayevskaya quoted from an 1899 Luxemburg letter: "The conquest and partition of all Asia became the goal which European politics pursued. . . . It's clear that the dismemberment of Asia and Africa is the final limit beyond which European politics no longer has room to unfold" (5). Dunayevskaya called this period of critical writing and insight a turning point in Luxemburg's life prior to the 1905 Russian Revolution, her development as a theoretician-activist on the international scene.

The year 1905 revealed Luxemburg's multi-dimensional talents as a writer-revolutionary in the midst of a mass social upheaval. Dunayevskaya wrote of her plunge "into a whirlwind of activities" in revolutionary Poland in 1905-06, where she now "began to 'speak Russian'—Russian and Polish—rather than German." The general political strikes of masses of Russian and Polish workers turning everything upside down, had a profound impact:

> No wonder that the whole concept of "backward" and "advanced" underwent a total transformation in the ongoing revolution. Luxemburg now saw the so-called "backward" Russian working class as the vanguard—not only of their own revolution, but of the world working-class movement . . . . the actual events that gave rise to the so-called theory of spontaneity were happening before her very eyes (6).

Luxemburg's *The Mass Strike, the Party and the Trade Unions*, emerged from that period. Not only was the mass strike a worker-form of political struggle that could "speak German," but "far from the pamphlet's being restricted to the topics in the title, Luxemburg was, in fact, beginning to question not just the conservative trade union leadership, but the relation of Marxist leadership to spontaneity. . . . [S]pontaniety was a driving force, not only of revolution but of the vanguard leadership, keeping it left" (17). Her attempt to take the lessons from Russia to the German scene was met with a cold reception by the German Social Democracy. It would prefigure her disputes and break with Karl Kautsky in 1910-11. But first Dunayevskaya took up Luxemburg's participation in the 1907 Russian Social-Democratic Labor Party Congress, the first after the 1905 Revolution.

Referring to "the Pivotal Year 1907," Dunayevskaya argued that this ignored Congress, (when compared to all the attention and commentary on the 1903 Congress with its walkouts and splits), was crucial to study precisely because it revealed attitudes to revolution on the part of the important revolutionaries of the period. She quoted discussions and speeches from a number of the participants, publishing one of Luxemburg's speeches as appendix to her book. In her talk, Luxemburg analyzed the revolutionary activity of Marx in the 1848 revolutions in relation to 1905: "Yes, Marx supported the bourgeoisie in the struggle against absolutism, but he supported it with whips and kicks." For Luxemburg, the Russian proletariat of a half-century later launched a "revolution [that] is not just the last act of a series of bourgeois revolutions of the nineteenth century, but rather the forerunner of a new series of future proletarian revolutions" (quoted on 9).

Dunayevskaya's Luxemburg emerged as activist and as thinker, as internationalist revolutionary in debate and discussion with revolutionaries from Russia, Germany, and Poland, as pamphleteer and polemicist. This became further concretized in Dunayevskaya's description of Luxemburg's return to the German scene in disputes with Kautsky in 1910-11 on the nature of revolutionary transformation in Germany, and on German Social Democratic silence (cowardice?) in face of Germany's growing imperialist reach.

•

Dunayevskaya excerpted and summarized the extensive polemic between Kautsky and Luxemburg as part of Chapter 2, "The Break with Kautsky, 1910-11: From Mass Strike Theory to Crisis over Morocco—and Hushed-Up 'Woman Question.'" The central theme of the dispute was over the applicability of the political mass strike in Germany. Luxemburg saw a huge gap between the theoretical pronouncements of the German Social Democratic leadership and the paucity of their practical work and vision. Opportunism was present not only among trade union leaders and reformists, but in the leadership of the established Marxist organization. Dunayevskaya showed how Kautsky used his leadership position to try and censor Luxemburg as he launched polemics against her. She pointed to Luxemburg's refusal to be intimidated, quoting her trenchant responses. Far from being a personal dispute, the exchanges anticipated Social Democracy's outright betrayal four years later at the outbreak of the First World War.

The German Social Democracy's opportunism could be further seen as the dispute shifted from the domestic scene to the international one. Dunayevskaya pinpointed the 1911 "Morocco Incident," when a German gunboat sailed to Morocco. The established socialist leadership played down the militaristic incident, keeping comments "private." Luxemburg refused to go along, publishing the leadership's "private" letter. Dunayevskaya showed that though the leadership tried to divert the issue to Luxemburg's "breach of discipline," Luxemburg continued to focus on the Morocco incident's relationship to the *"internal* development of German militarism . . . and German's urge for world power." As Dunayevskaya noted, "[I]nstead of a serious Marxist analysis of a burning issue, [Luxemburg] said, they were getting 'Socialist-Democratic political twaddle'" (25).

Not only were sharp diversionary polemics issued as the Social-Democracy sought to hide its opportunism, but male chauvinism became a partner in the disputes. Dunayevskaya quoted from the exchanges of letters of the Social Democratic leadership during this period, which referred to Luxemburg as "the poisonous bitch," "the wretched female's squirts of poison," and that Luxemburg and Clara Zetkin, "the two females and their followers are planning an attack on all central positions." These comments came from, among others, Kautsky, and August Bebel, author of *Women and Socialism* (!). At the same time Dunayevskaya wrote of Luxemburg's "tone deafness to male chauvinism," refusing to take up the question in relation to herself. Despite Luxemburg's break with Kautsky and with Bebel, there was no break with the party.

"[Luxemburg] decided that the new crisis caused by the phenomenon of imperialism had to be probed further, much further" (28). Dunayevskaya turned to Luxemburg's great theoretical work, *Accumulation of Capital* (1913), in Chapter 3, "Marx's and Luxemburg's Theories of Accumulation of Capital, its Crises and its Inevitable Downfall."

•

Dunayevskaya's writing here rested between two vantage points: (1) a recognition of, and deep appreciation for, Luxemburg as a serious Marxist theoretician, determined to extend Marx's theory to the new phenomenon of imperialism:

> The long road Luxemburg traveled to develop from mere agitation to serious theory is important to note. To begin with, she had been pivotal in both of the great debates which determined the direction of Marxism: the first against the first appearance of reformism, and the second against the acknowledged leading orthodox Marxist, Karl Kautsky. . . . Whether one thinks her theory right or wrong, it is utterly fantastic to act as if it can be dismissed as a mere *tour de force* and not a serious theory—that is to say, brilliant but not profound (32).

(2) A sharp, detailed, critique of Luxemburg being so overwhelmed by the *phenomenon* of imperialism, as to leave behind and lose sight of Marx's painstaking theoretical study of the laws of capital accumulation. She thus ended up without Marx's grounding to help discern the direction of capital accumulation in the age of imperialism.

There simply is no way to summarize Dunayevskaya's illuminating commentary on Luxemburg's and Marx's theories of capital accumulation found in the sections "Encounter with Marx's Theory of Expanded Reproduction" and "Luxemburg's Critique: Reality Vs Theory; Phenomenology Vs Philosophy." The reader is urged to journey through these pages (33-42). In commentary after completing *RLWLKM*, Dunayevskaya wrote:

> Chapter III of Part One jams up the different views of Luxemburg and Marx on "Accumulation of Capital" in order to show that the new events which Luxemburg called "reality," which she contrasted to Marx's "theory," could have been so contrasted because she failed to fully work out dialectic methodology—which would have revealed a single dialectic in both objective and subjective worlds ("New Thoughts on *Rosa Luxemburg, Women's Liberation and Marx's Philosophy of Revolution*," August and September 1983, included as prefatory material to the 1991, second edition of *RLWLKM*).

In the same presentation, Dunayevskaya developed the question of dialectic methodology further by writing two new paragraphs to be added to this section of *RLWLKM* on the "dialectic of movement both in [Hegel's] *Phenomenology of Mind* and in the *Philosophy of Mind*." The chapter ended with "Crises and the Breakdown of Capitalism," Dunayevskaya's discussion of Marx's "general contradiction of capitalism" in contrast to Luxemburg's view.

What emerged from these first three chapters was that "dialectics of revolution" in relation to Marx's Marxism became the manner to view and measure Luxemburg's profound multidimensionality. Dunayevskaya concretized this further in the two chapters that ended Part One: Chapter 4, "From the 'National Question' and Imperialism to the Dialectics of Revolution; the Relation of Spontaneity and Consciousness to Organization in the Disputes with Lenin, 1904, 1917;" and Chapter 5, "War, Prison, and Revolution, 1914-19."

•

Luxemburg's internationalism was, of course, one of her foremost revolutionary attributes. The rise of imperialism made this particularly concrete for Luxemburg as she continually exposed and fought capitalism's imperialist extension to Africa and Asia. Dunayevskaya called attention to her solidarity against colonialism's murderous subjection of various peoples. Yet what was called into question was not Luxemburg's internationalism, but her failure to rethink what that meant in terms of her position on the national question. In Dunayevskaya's view, what was at stake was dialectics of liberation. If imperialism was super-exploiting colonial peoples, then a Marxist revolutionary's vision needed to encompass colonial peoples as more than a suffering mass. All senses needed to be attuned to the possibility of colonial peoples as a new revolutionary force emerging alongside the proletariat of advanced lands. Rather than the national question being seen as a reactionary a la Luxemburg, its possibility as a pathway to internationalism needed to be grasped—a concrete working out of dialectics of revolution.

However, for Luxemburg, such a pathway never opened. Dunayevskaya discussed Luxemburg's continuing opposition to nationalism as expressed in her Junius writing in the midst of the First World War. She quoted Lenin's critique of certain formulations of the writing, characterizing them as a "half-way dialectic," and as "imperialist economism." Dunayevskaya also brought to bear the later developments of the Third World theorist Franz Fanon, who, rather than counter-posing internationalism and nationalism, wrote, "national consciousness which is not nationalism is the only thing that will give us an international dimension."

Dunayevskaya argued that the duality of Luxemburg on nationalism and internationalism was found in another manner in "the ambivalence of her position of spontaneity and organization." On the one hand, in her 1904 critique of Lenin, she held up high spontaneity and consciousness of the masses, extolling their ability to learn from their mistakes and learn the historical dialectic themselves, as opposed to her characterization of the "infallibility" of any "central committee." But on the other hand was the fact that "Luxemburg herself very nearly made a fetish out of the principle of a unified party" (60). She quoted Luxemburg's 1908 statement that "the worst working-class party is better than none," and added, "clearly, there was too much organizational Lasalleanism in Luxemburg as there was in Lenin" (61).

Dunayevskaya called attention to that fact that even Luxemburg's 1910-11 break with Kautsky and Bebel on the general strike and on imperialism, did not mean her leaving the party. She did not forge a break of the Spartakus, a fully organized tendency, until the actual outbreak of the German Revolution. Rather, Luxemburg continued with a concept of a unified party, a unified International, even in face of the betrayal of the Second International.

Dunayevskaya took the question back to dialectics of revolution: "What were the dialectics of revolution? Was spontaneity/consciousness the equivalent of philosophy and revolution in the full Marxian sense, or did it stop at a Lassallean sense of spontaneity/organization?" (62)

This did not negate Dunayevskaya's view of Luxemburg as revolutionary raising critical questions. After the Russian Revolution broke out Luxemburg began drafting a pamphlet, *The Russian Revolution*. She did not shirk from warning: "Freedom only for the supporters of the government, only for the members of one party—however numerous they may be—is no freedom at all. Freedom is always and exclusively freedom for the one who thinks differently." At the same time, "Lenin and Trotsky with their friends were the *first* to set the example before the world proletariat. . . . In Russia the problem could only be posed. It could not be solved in Russia, it can only be solved internationally. And *in this sense*, the future everywhere belongs to 'Bolshevism'" (quoted, 64).

•

Luxemburg as indomitable revolutionary was what flowed out of Dunayevskaya's final chapter of Part One, "War, Prison, and Revolution, 1914-19." Here we see first Luxemburg's revolutionary anti-war stance. When almost the whole leadership of the German Social Democracy capitulated to war, Luxemburg, with her colleagues Clara Zetkin, Karl Liebknecht, and Franz Mehring, issued a public statement of opposition. When imprisoned in February 1915, her anti-war writing and agitation only became more intense. The Junius pamphlet,

> this first great antiwar pamphlet—which was, at one and the same time, propagandistic in the bravest sense, seriously theoretical, and straight out of Germany itself—was more than just a breath of fresh air for isolated antiwar Marxists the world over. It was the genuine opening of a new epoch, of a new path to revolution. Lenin was among those heaping praise upon the pamphlet for its courage; but he felt strongly that it was worked out in isolation (69).

In prison Luxemburg continued her theoretical work on accumulation of capital, writing her *AntiCritique*. When finally the German Revolution erupted November 1918, Luxemburg was freed. Dunayevskaya recorded "Luxemburg's inexhaustible energy" in the two and a half months before she was murdered: "The red thread that runs through it all is, of course, the abolition of capitalism and the creation of socialism. There was no middle road. It was either barbarism or socialism." A Communist Party of Germany was founded. Even as "Spartakus Week" faced counter-revolutionary armed might she spoke of "the future victory [that] will blossom from out of this 'defeat'" (73-75).

Dunayevskaya's portrait of Luxemburg continued in "Luxemburg as Feminist," in Part II, "Women Liberation Movement as Revolutionary Force and Reason," and in Dunayevskaya's measuring of all post-Marx Marxists, including Luxemburg, against Part III, "Karl Marx—From Critic of Hegel to Author of Capital and Theorist of 'Revolution in Permanence.'"

Part II: The Women's Liberation Movement as Revolutionary Force and Reason

Dunayevskaya's chapters in this part encompassed: (1) a spirited journey through selected moments of the women's movement in the 19th and 20th century with emphasis on the dimension of Black women and on creativity of masses in motion; (2) an examination of the unexplored and unappreciated feminist dimension of Luxemburg; and (3) a challenge to the present women's liberation movement as to how to continue and deepen its contributions to revolutionary social transformation, beginning with a plunge into Marx's philosophy of revolution.

In "An Overview by Way of Introduction; the Black Dimension," Dunayevskaya asked the women's liberation movement to grapple with a number of concepts. First was one of "perceiv[ing] the Black dimension as Reason in our age" (81). She quoted Marie Steward, "the first America-born woman, white or Black, to speak publicly" (1831), addressing "Ye daughters of Africa" to awake and use "their minds and talents" and not allow "a mean set of men flatter us." Dunayevskaya turned to the thought of a Sojourner Truth, the "generalship" of a Harriet Tubman before and during the Civil War, both of whom were willing to challenge a Frederick Douglass when suffrage came only to Black men and not to women. She wrote of the "Women's War," tens of thousands of Ibo market women in southeastern Nigeria challenging British imperialism, as well as their own African chiefs in 1929. All were manifestations of the revolutionary dimension of Black women.

The concept of the Black Dimension was interwoven with a second theme, the relation of individualism and masses in motion. The "Women's War" was "the collective action of Ibo women" (84). It was not that there was not individual grass-roots leadership among the Ibo women, or that a Rosa Luxemburg was not, in Dunayevskaya's view, "an original character." Rather, she posed the relationship between the individual and masses in motion: "What illuminates the contributions both of an original character and of the masses in motion is the way those masses in motion uproot the old and create the new" (84). This was what released or made possible original characters who, as Luxemburg, felt the compulsion "to throw one's whole life on the scales of destiny" (83). For Dunayevskaya, the challenge was to put together two seemingly opposite facts: "the individuality of each woman liberationist is a microcosm of the whole, and yet that the movement is not a sum of so many individuals but *masses in motion*" (83).

A third concept Dunayevskaya put forth was that of "world-historic moment." How it released and revealed so much in terms of individual creativity and passion, masses in motion, and the creation of philosophic moments of freedom. The case in point was the 1840s. She described how, out of the 1840s came a Margaret Fuller moving beyond Transcendentalism, participating in the 1848 Italian Revolution and becoming "an enthusiastic Socialist." She pointed to the Seneca Falls 1848 Woman's Right Convention at the time of the European Revolutions of 1848, and to a Flora Tristan calling in 1843 for a Workers' International of men and women. Dunayevskaya related these world historic moments of the 1840s to Marx's 1844 articulation of the relation of man to woman as expressing to what degree our "species has become human—part of his revolutionary world view, 'a throughgoing Naturalism or Humanism.'"

What she asked was, "what is the root of theory, its true beginning?" (82), and recognized its origins within "masses in motion," as revolutionary individuals such as Luxemburg, and as a revolutionary philosopher, Marx, sought to give word to it.

•

In exploring "Luxemburg as Feminist; Break with Jogiches," Dunayevskaya argued that *the* determinate for Luxemburg was revolution: "although she might sometimes appear as a reluctant feminist, she is always revolutionary" (85). While refusing "to be pigeonholed by the German Social-Democracy into the so-called Woman Question" (89), Dunayevskaya noted and cited her writing and activity on this theme both before and after the 1905 Revolution. Of particular importance was Luxemburg's relationship with Clara Zetkin, "who is recognized by all as the founder of women's liberation as a *working class, mass movement*, as well as theoretician and editor of the greatest mass circulation women's newspaper [*Gleichheit (Equality)*] to this day" (89).

Dunayevskaya argued that the 1905 Revolution was determinate in Luxemburg's relation with her comrade and lover Jogiches. They separated as lovers, though never as political comrades, shortly after 1905. The impact of the Revolution on Luxemburg was immense: a deepening of her view of the creativity of the spontaneous action of the masses, and a new interest in the question of organization when it meant mass organization, something she had previously left in the hands of Jogiches. Equally, the Revolution impacted the man/woman relation in her relationship to Jogiches. Dunayevskaya noted:

A birthtime of history manifests itself not only in great social changes but in original characters, and Luxemburg was an original. Her further self-development was reaching new heights without leaning on Jogiches for either theory or organization. A new historic period had been reached—and differences in the attitude to revolution appeared, not because one wished to play a different "role" than the other, but because the revolution is an overwhelming force that brooks no "interference" from anyone. Luxemburg needed to be free, to be independent, to be whole (92).

Dunayevskaya took issue with biographers of Luxemburg who felt the break up with Jogiches defined her life: "Her greatest intellectual accomplishments occurred after the break. To say that her whole life was changed because of the breakup is a typical male attitude, i.e., thinking that a woman's life stops when the break in a love relationship occurs" (93-94).

•

The final chapter of this part was titled "The Task That Remains To Be Done: The Unique and Unfinished Contribution of Today's Women's Liberation Movement." Dunayevskaya began by singling out its unique appearance in the 1960s: "Not only did it come out of the left but it was *directed against it*, and not from the right, but *from within the left itself*" (99). She surveyed its presence in the U.S. in the 1960s and 70s, emerging from the Civil Rights Movement and the leftist Students for a Democratic Society, and involving Black, Chicana, American Indian, Puerto Rican as well as white women. She singled out its global dimension, whether in Portugal and Iran in the midst of revolutions, or the writings of women from the Middle East, the Congo, and East Timor.

Because of its uniqueness in challenging the male Left, Dunayevskaya in turn challenged the movement to grapple with seeing the fullness of Marx as a revolutionary who had a concept of man/woman. To do this meant separating one's views from the modern myth of certain writers that Marx and Engels were "one," particularly when it came to the woman question. To Dunayevskaya, Engels' *The Origin of the Family* was far away from the spirit of Marx's writings on man/woman whether as seen in his 1844 *Economic-Philosophic Manuscripts* or his *Ethnological Notebooks* of the 1880s. She cited two "Engelsianisms" that were no concepts of Marx: (1) "'The world historic defeat of the female sex,' which Engels grounds in a transition from matriarch (or at least matrilineal descent) to patriarchy, *is no expression of Marx's*" (105). (2) This was related to the so-called "primordial division of labor between the sexes," which puts off women's freedom to the far distant future, and "is *not* Marx's concept."

In contrast, Dunayevskaya argued that "new revolutionary paths to liberation, could be found in seeing Marx's "philosophy as action:" "[W]e must turn to Marx—the whole of Marx. Without his philosophy of revolution, neither Women's Liberation nor the whole of humanity will have discovered the ground that will assure the success of the revolution" (109).

Part III: Karl Marx—From Critic of Hegel to Author of *Capital* and Theorist of "Revolution in Permanence"

Each of Dunayevskaya's three books—*Marxism and Freedom, Philosophy and Revolution* and *RLWLKM*—had major treatments of Marx. What distinguished her discussion in *RLWLKM* was two-fold: (1) the presentation on Marx came within the context of "Post-Marx Marxism as a Pejorative," the category she developed in the process of writing the book. It became the lens for viewing, not betrayers, but revolutionaries beginning with Engels; (2) the range of her Marx presentation now encompassed the "whole" of Marx, from his 1841 doctoral dissertation to the previously unknown *Ethnological Notebooks* of the 1880s. In her view of Marx, Dunayevskaya refused to fragment Marx's economics, philosophy, organizational work, revolutionary journalism, political and historical analysis, one from another. All were seen as an integrated whole, fused by Marx into a philosophy of revolution.

In "Marx Discovers a New Continent of Thought and Revolution," the first chapter of Part III, Dunayevskaya viewed Marx's first decade of revolutionary thought and activity. "Prometheus Bound, 1841-43" focused on Marx's doctoral thesis, "The Difference between the Democritean and Epicurean Philosophy of Nature." She saw this work as expressing "the originality and radical departure of thought Marx was making for his own period . . . —the desire to illuminate the contemporary post-Hegelian period by examining a parallel age in the history of Greek philosophy, the post-Aristotelian period" (122).

Marx was on his way to a new beginning and was challenging Hegel's accommodation to the reality of the German state. Dunayevskaya noted: "One must analyze the accommodation not merely to expose it, but in order thereby to discover the inadequacy of the principle which *compelled* the accommodation. Only in that way could the critique produce an advance in knowledge which would create the possibility of a new beginning" (122). Marx was seeking new ground: "Marx himself had not yet discovered 'another element,' a new beginning, a Subject; but that is what he was searching for—and Freedom was the ground" (123). "Freedom is so much the essence of man that even its opponents realize it," wrote Marx in his early revolutionary journalism. "No man fights freedom; he fights at most the freedom of others. Every kind of freedom has therefore always existed, only at one time as a special privilege, at another time as a universal right" (quoted, 124).

In "Prometheus Unbound, 1844-1848," Dunayevskaya dove into Marx's new beginning. Her concentration was on the year 1844, in the months *before* his lifelong collaboration with Engels began: "The year was the most eventful not because of objective developments, but because of the type of subjective self-development that initiated a genuine birth-time of history and thought that Marx called a new Humanism and that was later to be called Marxism" (125). It was the year Marx moved to Paris and began to immerse himself in the new subject, the working class. "You have to have participated in one meeting of the French workers to be able to believe the virgin freshness and nobility among these workworn men" (quoted, 125). Dunayevskaya wrote: "That Subject—labor—became the turning point for the rest of Marx's life. It emerged as, at one and the same time, he studied the *enragés* in the French Revolution (he was planning to write a study of the Convention), and met the workers of the period" (125). She continued:

> His break with bourgeois society had not stopped either with the break with religion or the break with Hegel's Philosophy of the State and Law and bureaucracy. It was Marx's concept of Alienated Labor which broke through all criticism. *That* discovery changed all else. *That* "self-clarification," stretching from April to August, disclosed the inner connection between philosophy and economics, philosophy and politics, subjective and objective; it created a new beginning, a new totality of theory and practice (125).

Moving between each of Marx's major topics from the *1844 Manuscripts*—"Alienated Labor," "Private Property and Communism," "Critique of Hegel's Dialectic and Philosophy as a Whole"—Dunayevskaya showed the development of Historical Materialism, a "self-determination of the Idea" into a philosophy of revolution: (1) She took up Marx's critique of political economy showing how it skewed those who attributed all to property relations and ignored the human condition in the production process. (2) For her, Marx's analysis of labor spoke to the vulgar communism of his day, and the Socialists and Communists of our day, who, "speak of labor as an abstraction instead of seeing that labor under capitalism 'materializes itself in an inhuman way' (Marx)" (126). (3) She pointed to Marx's critique of Hegel, "Marx argued that Hegel had thrown a mystical veil over the actual movement of history, turning man into a form of consciousness," while at the same time emphasizing Marx's view that, "the greatness of the Hegel's *Phenomenology* . . . is the dialectic of negativity as the moving and creative principle" (127).

For Dunayevskaya, Marx's break point from the old became key: "What sets off one age from another—the birthtime of history or the birthtime of a total philosophy—cannot be grasped by singling out 'influences' but by seeing that the breaking point, the point of departure from the old, becomes the translucent direction forward" (128).

That break point came as Marx found a new Subject in "actual corporeal Man." Only then "will we actually get the deep internal dialectic and first be able to transcend, *historically* transcend, the Hegelian dialectic (which nevertheless remains the source of all dialectic), *and* classical political economy, *and* vulgar communism" (127).

It is not possible to do justice here to the thought-dive into the early Marx that Dunayevskaya achieved in this chapter. Hers is a synthesis of his early work, often related to the problematic of Luxemburg's and Lenin's age as well as her own.

Dunayevskaya took up Marx's major writings of the 1850s and 1860s in "A Decade of Historic Transformation: From the *Grundrisse* to *Capital*." In this chapter the profound transformation of Marx's "economics," as seen in the *Grundrisse* and then in *Critique of Political Economy*, to what became the manuscript of *Capital*, was examined in relation to methodology. (See as well Dunayevskaya's discussion on *Capital* in *Marxism and Freedom*, and her discussion of both the *Grundrisse* and *Capital* in *Philosophy and Revolution*.) Her discussion of the *Grundrisse* emphasized the section on "Pre-Capitalist Economic Formations" as having great relevance in the latter part of the 20th century. Here we will focus on her discussion of *Capital*.

The opening paragraph of "*Capital*: Significance of the 1875 French Edition of Volume 1," distilled Dunayevskaya's view of *Capital*:

> *Capital*, not the *Grundrisse*, is the *differentia specifica* of Marx's Marxism, its apex. Marx's greatest theoretical work, in fusing economics, history, dialectics, discloses ever new aspects of each along with new-won forces of revolt. Thus, history is not so much a history of theories as of class struggles, civil wars, and battles at the point of production. Economics is a matter not only of the economic laws of the breakdown of capitalism, but of the strife between the worker and the machine against dead labor's domination over living labor, beginning with *hearing* the worker's voice, which had been stifled "in the storm and stress of the process of production." This voice will never be still. In the last part of the work, "Accumulation of Capital" as we approach the most "economist" and "scientific" development—"the organic composition of capital"—Marx reminds us all over again that this organic composition cannot be considered outside of its effects "on the lot of the laboring class." Dialectics, of course, is the method of development of each and of all, objective and subjective, whether that new-won force came out of the actual struggle for the shortening of the working day, or in discerning the law of motion of capitalism, with both a look back to precapitalist formations—from the communal form through slavery and feudalism—and a look forward at what will follow capitalism: "freely associated labor" taking destiny into its own hands (140).

Dunayevskaya proceeded to focus on Chapter One, "Commodities." She viewed this as, "the Great Divide between the Marxian and the Hegelian dialectic" (142), even as one could trace the central categories of Hegel's *Logic* within its pages. Dunayevskaya was working out Marx's break with and indebtedness to Hegel at a most profound level—within *Capital* itself. *Capital* was a great divide from Hegel because the Subject was the living laborer: "It is that Great Divide because, *just because*, that Subject—not subject matter, but Subject—was neither economics nor philosophy but the human being, the masses" (143).

Capital was where Marx most definitively overthrew Hegel's dehumanization of the Idea. And yet at the same time, for Dunayevskaya, a discussion of Chapter One was best framed through the Hegel's categories of Being, Essence, and Notion. Marx's infusing of these categories with the human subject was the most profound, revolutionary reorganization of the dialectic. "*This* dialectic is therefore totally new, totally internal, deeper than ever was the Hegelian dialectic which had *de*humanized the self-development of humanity in the dialectic of Consciousness, Self-Consciousness, and Reason" (143).

Although Chapter One on commodities, "meant we were in the phenomenal sphere only, in the market, in exchange," Dunayevskaya stressed the uniqueness of the dialectic in Marx's hands:

> [S]o distinctive is the Marxian dialectic from the Hegelian that, even when we have not yet reached the Subject, the labor*er*—directly after being told that the commodity is the unity of capitalist wealth that is characterized by two factors—use-value and exchange-value—we are informed that this is only appearance, that in fact this is a manifestation of the dual character of labor itself, and that this is so crucial that though we will not meet labor until we get to the process of production, we must know about it before. In a word, we have now moved from Appearance to Essence (143).

Dunayevskaya proceeded to discuss Marx's development of the fetishism of commodities, wherein "material relations between persons and social relations between things" had become the actual relations in capitalist society. Marx argued that only "freely associated" producers could release humanity from fetishistic commodity production, and establish a society of new human relations. Dunayevskaya wrote: "*[W]hat Marx confronts us with in the very first chapter is not only Appearance and Essence but Notion*" (144).

What we come face to face with is that Marx was at his most dialectical in *Capital* when he was breaking with Hegel's dehumanization of philosophy, the non-dialectical element in Hegel: "That path to freedom both separates the Marxian dialectic from the Hegelian and transforms Hegel's revolution *in philosophy* into a philosophy *of revolution*, so that even in economics, i.e., in the production sphere, with Marx's guidance we follow the actual form of the proletarian revolt" (145).

The second major focus of Dunayevskaya's discussion of *Capital* was the section on Accumulation of Capital. This section too, underwent substantial revision in the French edition edited by Marx. Dunayevskaya demonstrated that within Accumulation of Capital, particularly when one is cognizant of the additions to the French edition that were left out of the subsequent English edition, were many of the questions taken up in Volume 2 of *Capital*. Luxemburg and other theoreticians of the Second International failed to dig deeply into Marx's changes in the French edition, which could have provided a crucial perspective for an analysis of imperialism and the emergence of new revolutionary subjectivity in the colonial lands.

For Dunayevskaya, the question was not this or that individual paragraph, or the presence or absence Hegelian "language." Rather, it was to see the whole of *Capital* as simultaneously economics and philosophy, history and dialectics, because it was forged under the impact of humanity's struggle for freedom, objectively and subjectively, a "negation of the negation" that was at one and the same time, the logic of capitalism's development *and* its downfall through the intervention of masses in motion.

•

In the chapter, "The Philosopher of Permanent Revolution Creates New Ground for Organization," Dunayevskaya first examined Marx's *Critique of the Gotha Program*. This 1875 critique of a so-called socialist unity program between followers of Marx and those of Lassalle, was in fact based on Lassallean doctrines. Marx felt compelled to disassociate himself from these doctrines and did so by comprehensively critiquing them. Dunayevskaya's reading of Marx's *Critique* saw it as by no means limited to the critique of a particular tendency. Rather, it raised the relationship between one's principles and revolutionary organization. As such, it transcended its particular historic moment. Indeed, Dunayevskaya pointed to Lenin's transforming Marx's *Critique* as well as *The Civil War in France* into his own *State and Revolution* in the midst of the Russian Revolution. For Lenin, the lessons he drew revolved around the need to smash the bourgeois state, and to form "the revolutionary dictatorship of the proletariat." However, he did not read *Critique* as new philosophic ground for organization.

Lassalle's organizational practice had a strong pull on Luxemburg and other revolutionaries. Dunayevskaya commented on an article, "Lassalle and the Revolution," which Luxemburg had written in 1904. Luxemburg wrote that Lassalle entered history for organizing the workers into "an independent class party." Dunayevskaya asked why Luxemburg, who was such a firm internationalist, would seemingly put Lassalle's national party on a higher level than Marx's First International:

> [W]hy was it that Lassalle, who founded the General Association of German Workers in the early 1860s as the first independent mass political organization, should still tower above Marx after he founded the International Working Men's Association? Was there a national strain from the start? How could Rosa Luxemburg, who was the greatest internationalist, not have seen any of this? It could not have been *national* vs. *international*. It could have only been *activism* vs. *philosophy* (157).

Dunayevskaya then added: "[N]o revolutionary took it [*Critique of the Gotha Program*] as a point of departure for working out a theory of organization."

Even Lenin did not grapple with "the inseparable relationship of philosophy to organization itself. That means that Lenin's philosophic reorganization remained in a separate compartment from the concept of the party and the practice of vanguardism" (157).

Dunayevskaya now turned to "Marx's Theory of Permanent Revolution, 1843-1883." She traced Marx's use of the expression from his 1843 essay on the Jewish question, where its context was the need to move beyond bourgeois rights to the fullness of new human relations, to his 1850 Address to the Communist League, where, after the defeat of the 1848-49 Revolutions, he proclaimed: "Their battle cry must be: The Revolution in Permanence."

For Dunayevskaya, far from the key being merely the words "permanent revolution," reducing it to an agitational slogan, what was at stake was the fact that in Marx's "constant search for revolutionary allies the vision of the revolutions to come was in no way changed"(161) at each historic moment. Whether it was Marx's concluding that to support the proletarian revolution in Germany there needed to be "a sort of second edition of the peasant war," or whether, as Dunayevskaya noted, with the 1882 Preface to the Russian edition of the *Communist Manifesto,* "the concept was worked out anew as the relationship between advanced and underdeveloped countries" (162), *permanent revolution* was the warp and woof of Marx's body of thought and activity.

In a chapter afterword, "Trotsky's Theory of Permanent Revolution," Dunayevskaya traced his writings on the theory in the period after the 1905 Revolution and the 1917 Revolution, critiquing Trotsky's writing of that history, and pointing to the grave contradictions within the theory, which was on the one hand a brilliant prognostication of revolutions in underdeveloped lands, but on the other utterly dismissed any independent revolutionary role for the peasantry.

•

The final chapter of the book, "The Last Writings of Marx Point a Trail to the 1980s," gave Dunayevskaya's reading of Marx's last decade. Unlike some commentators who characterized the last period on Marx's life as "a slow death," Dunayevskaya saw it as containing "new moments" ranging from his *Ethnological Notebooks,* to his writings on the Russian peasant commune and the relation of revolution in technologically developed and underdeveloped countries.

Dunayevskaya's opening section was a discussion of post-Marx Marxists and what they did with the unpublished archives of Marx. This included Engels, who did prepare Volumes 2 and 3 of *Capital,* but also buried Marx's last writings on pre-capitalist societies as a few paragraphs in his own *Origin of the Family,* and David Ryazanov, who did bring out the early writings of Marx, but when it came of Marx's last decade, characterized his systematic note taking and commentary as "inexcusable pedantry."

Dunayevskaya turned to present her own survey of some of these last writings, beginning with Marx's *Ethnological Notebooks*—his notes and commentary on a number of ethnographers, including Lewis Henry Morgan. In viewing

Engels' uncritical, enthusiastic response to Morgan verses Marx's more measured, critical appreciation, she contrasted Marx's and Engels' view of social transitions:

> Nothing less than the vital question of transitions is at stake in the difference between Marx's and Engels' views. Marx was showing that it is *during* the transition period that you see the duality emerging to reveal the beginnings of antagonisms, whereas Engels always seems to have antagonisms only at the end, as if class society came in very nearly full blown *after* the communal form was destroyed and private property was established. *Moreover, for Marx the dialectical development from one stage to another is related to new revolutionary upsurges, whereas Engels sees it as a unilaterial progression* (180).

In taking up a number of Marx's specific commentaries in the *Ethnological Notebooks,* Dunayevskaya not only contrasted Marx and Engels, but showed the liberties taken by the 1941 Russian translation of Marx's text on Morgan, which translated "the career of property" as "private property," and inserted "hallowed path of private property," both serving to narrow capitalist accumulation of wealth to collective vs. private property. Her critique was not alone of statist-Communism, but post-Marx Marxists who accepted the Communists' narrow definition of socialism.

Two of Marx's writings on Russia from the 1880s occupied Dunayevskaya's attention: (1) the drafts and letter to Vera Zasulich in response to a question of the future of the Russian Commune as a possible path to communism without going through capitalism; (2) the 1882 Preface to the Russian edition of the *Communist Manifesto.* Both writings, in Dunayevskaya's view, showed Marx's concern with the "needed Russian Revolution."

In probing these writings, Dunayevskaya saw Marx as searching out paths to social revolution. In his investigation of the Russian peasant commune's specific forms he was asking whether the commune could serve as a basis for a socialist reorganization of society without going through all the vicissitudes of capitalist development. Marx concluded that this was possible but involved not alone preservation of the commune form but a "needed Russian Revolution." The focus on revolution was as well present in Marx's and Engels' Introduction to the Russian edition of the *Communist Manifesto* where they projected that Russia could have a proletarian revolution ahead of the West.

Dunayevskaya argued that the last decade of Marx's life yielded "the type of profound writings that, at one and the same time, summed up his life's work and created new openings" (188). She returned briefly to three "new moments of the revolutionary philosophic-historic concepts by Marx in the last decade of his life"—additions to the French edition of *Capital*, the *Critique of the Gotha Program*, and his *Ethnological Notebooks*—to show Marx's summations that created new openings.

Finally, in "A 1980s View," she argued that a 1980s rediscovery of the totality of Marx's thought, whose "decisive determinant . . . was 'revolution in permanence,'" could cast new light on today's revolutionary problematic in so many areas: from revolts in state-capitalist tyrannies to revolutions in colonial lands to the man/woman relationship. Dunayevskaya ended *RLWLKM* as follows: "What is needed is a new unifying principle, on Marx's ground of humanism, that truly alters both human thought and human experience. . . . Every moment of Marx's development, as well as the totality of his works, spells out the need for 'revolution in permanence.' This is the absolute challenge to our age" (195).

Part V

1980-87, Reaching for the Future: Dunayevskaya's Re-examination of a Half-Century of Marxist-Humanism, and the Projection of a New Work on Dialectics of Organization and Philosophy

Part V

1980-87, Reaching for the Future: Dunayevskaya's Re-examination of a Half-Century of Marxist-Humanism, and the Projection of a New Work on Dialectics of Organization and Philosophy

Dunayevskaya's 1980s Vantage Point of Marxist-Humanism's Multi-lineal Origins and Pathways of Development

During the 1980s Dunayevskaya turned to examine the whole body of Marxist-Humanist thought, developed over the course of more than four and a half decades, "Marxist-Humanism emerging out of Marxist-Humanism." She viewed such retrospectives as the needed vantage point for forging perspectives in the 1980s:

• Her retrospectives-perspectives began with the pamphlet *25 Years of Marxist-Humanism in the U.S.* (1980), penned as she was in the midst of writing the chapters of *Rosa Luxemburg, Women's Liberation, and Marx's Philosophy of Revolution* (1982).

• They continued with new Introductions for 1980s editions of several works on the Black Dimension: *American Civilization on Trial—Black Masses as Vanguard* (1983); *Nationalism, Communism, Marxist-Humanism and the Afro-Asian Revolutions* (1984); and *Frantz Fanon, Soweto and American Black Thought* (1986).

• Dunayevskaya created a collection of her writings on women over a 35-year period, *Women's Liberation and the Dialectics of Revolution* (1985), and wrote an Introduction/Overview.

- The pamphlet *The Coal Miners' General Strike of 1949-50 and the Birth of Marxist-Humanism in the U.S.* (1984) included her essay "The Emergence of a New Movement from Practice that is Itself a Form of Theory."
- She wrote a retrospective on thirty years of *News & Letters*, first printed in the paper, and then published in the pamphlet *The Myriad Global Crises of the 1980s and the Nuclear World Since World War* II (1986).
- New Introductions were written for the 1982 editions of *Marxism and Freedom* and *Philosophy and Revolution*.
- In 1986 she added a volume to the Marxist-Humanist Archives titled, "Retrospective and Perspective—The Raya Dunayevskaya Collection, 1924-1986."
- These labors formed important pathways to her intensive 1986-87 studies for a work tentatively titled, "Dialectics of Organization and Philosophy: the 'Party' and forms of organization born of spontaneity." The book remained unfinished at the time of her death.

It was her efforts to bring seemingly disparate moments—of Marxist-Humanist philosophy and organizational practice, of the contradictory origins and development of her body of thought as a discontinuity with "orthodox" Marxism that established a continuity with Marx's thought, of new organizational beginnings emerging from Hegel's Absolutes, of post-Marx Marxism as a pejorative vs. Marx's Marxism—into a whole that characterized Dunayevskaya's 1980s.

In a presentation to the Resident Editorial Board (December 1, 1986) she wrote, "The point is that all the strands from the paper to the Archives to the objective situation [are] integral to the book-to-be" (*SRDC* #10680). She titled one of her "Talking To Myself" writings, "The Organization, the Paper, the Book—All Equal Philosophy of Marxist-Humanism—All were grounded in May 1953" (May 11, 1987, *SRDC* #10917). The breakthrough she *experienced* in 1953 with her Letters on Hegel's Absolutes, became the *concept* that determined her development through more than three decades. In the 1980s, this 1953 "Philosophic Moment of Marxist-Humanism" fused with the category of post-Marx-Marxism as pejorative, to become the determinate of the last-half decade of her work. This unity of the first and the last, as it impacted Dunayevskaya's new beginnings in the 1980s, is what we are exploring in this final part.

Among the crucial strands of her work in the 1980s:

- She reexamined Marx's new moments, particularly from his last decade, and saw them as speaking to the 1980s, releasing further development of her critique of post-Marx Marxism.
- She probed once again Lenin's 1914 encounter with *Science of Logic*, and came to a new view of his philosophic ambivalence with regard to Hegel's Absolutes.
- She compiled a collection of her writings on women over 35 years, *Women's Liberation and the Dialectics of Liberation: Reaching for the Future*, with a special Introduction/Overview.

This singling out of a particular subject of revolution in relation to the whole body of Marxist-Humanist thought was found as well in the challenges Dunayevskaya issued to youth, and to the Black dimension in the 1980s, and with regard to labor in *The Coal Miners' General Strike of 1949-50 and the Birth of Marxist-Humanism in the U.S.*

• She returned to the origins of Marxist-Humanism through a reexamination of the philosophic developments and contradictions in the Johnson-Forest Tendency, 1949-53, and 1953-55, which became full-fledged differences and a break with C.L.R. James.

• She made numerous returns to her 1953 Letters on Hegel's Absolutes, re-examining each of her "trilogy of revolution"—*Marxism and Freedom, Philosophy and Revolution,* and *Rosa Luxemburg, Women's Liberation, and Marx's Philosophy of Revolution*—in light of these Letters.

In 1986-87, these returns, together with the development of the category of post-Marx Marxism as a pejorative, led to a deeper probing of the philosophic dimension of organization within the 1953 Letters, resulting in her work on "Dialectics of Organization and Philosophy."

• What characterized this period as well, was Dunayevskaya's probing of the tensions that arose between her working out of the body of ideas in the 1980s as New Beginnings, and the way her News and Letters colleagues, at times, compartmentalized and fragmented, rather than projected the fullness of Marxist-Humanism's movement of becoming. She discerned a gap between her development of Marxist-Humanism and its organizational projection.

Though we are singling out particular strands of her 1980s Retrospective/Perspectives, we need to be aware of their interconnectedness. These themes were often taken up simultaneously in the documents of the period. Subjecting objective reality, as well as Marxist thought and practice outside and inside Marxist-Humanism, to the category of post-Marx Marxism as a pejorative in fusion with the Philosophic Moment of Marxist-Humanism, characterized the methodological foundation of her work in the 1980s. These labors were the new moments of Dunayevskaya's Marxist-Humanism.

In 1986 Dunayevskaya wrote of "the inter-connections at our birth" focusing on the multiple stands of her work:

> Take a few of the inter-connections at our birth and you will see that even when you list a single point of departure, it turns out to be a multiple point. Thus, 1950, is most often given by us because it is the Miners' General Strike. But actually not only was it activity, articles, new human relations which become integral to *Marxism and Freedom*, 1957, but you really have to return back a full decade to 1947. In taking 1947 to '49 as the point of departure you see that a trip to France [by Dunayevskaya] to present the state-capitalist position meant meeting that magnificent Camerounian, and learning about the spontaneous outpouring of Yaounde. And at the same time we learn of the great contradictions in Palestine about to become Israel. And at the same time I am digging

into methodology both in Marx's *Capital* and that in our age of state-capitalism. And again at the same time, I am wrestling with the categories of Hegel's *Science of Logic*, which all ended in a series of Absolutes. To see in the Absolute, not a system, *not* a hierarchy, but new beginnings, *new beginnings of such phenomenal importance as to become the determinant of the end*—an end that will only come to the future, when masses-in-motion become Reason.—No need to belabor the point that this is very far from anything "accidental." It signals a new historic epoch, a new relationship of capital to labor, race to class, man to women, youth both in action and as the future in the present.

To Marxist-Humanism it poses the task of developing what this sudden outpouring meant (Letter to G. and J. Sept. 21, 1986, *SRDC* #11572).

To emphasize this integrality of Dunayevskaya's work in the 1980s, we have chosen in our treatment not to divide this final part into chapters. Rather we have created three sections: I. Projecting and Extending *Rosa Luxemburg, Women's Liberation, and Marx's Philosophy of Revolution*. II Retrospective of Marxist-Humanism—Its Origins and Development. III. Towards Dialectics of Organization and Philosophy.

I. Projecting and Extending *Rosa Luxemburg, Women's Liberation, and Marx's Philosophy of Revolution*

The publication of *Rosa Luxemburg, Women's Liberation, and Marx's Philosophy of Revolution*, led to two kinds of projections/extensions: (1) An extensive tour during the 1983 centenary of Marx's death was taken with *Rosa Luxemburg, Women's Liberation, and Marx's Philosophy of Revolution* in hand. The tour allowed Dunayevskaya to interact with thousands of listeners, contrasting Marx's new moments to post-Marx Marxism. Out of that interaction and her own rethinking of her work, she wrote a number of paragraphs to be added to specific sections in the book. In a subsequent edition of the Luxemburg book, these paragraphs have been added to the text. She sought to practice what she had articulated as the title for the book's final chapter, "The Last Writings of Marx Point a Trail to the 1980s." (2) A new book on women's liberation, *Women's Liberation and the Dialectics of Revolution: Reaching for the Future*, a collection of essays written by Dunayevskaya over a 35 year period, was published.

Projecting Marx's New Moments in Relation to Post-Marx Marxism

"[I]n challenging post-Marx Marxists, we are articulating Marx's Marxism for our age" ("Not By Practice Alone: The Movement From Theory" 1984, *PON*, 283). In many of her presentations of the 1980s, Dunayevskaya focused on new moments of Marx's last decade as a trail to our age. In her 1982 "Battle of Ideas" Political-Philosophic Letter, she singled out Marx's reading and commenting on Morgan's *Ancient Society*, his visiting of Algiers and awareness of what we now call the Third World, and his refusal to make the "Historical Tendency of Capital Accumulation" into a universal, citing Russia as having the possibility of a different pathway. She wrote of how in *Rosa Luxemburg, Women's Liberation and Marx's Philosophy of Revolution*, "I trace a trail to the 1980s from the 1880s and focus on Marx's 'translation' of absolute negativity as the revolution in permanence, calling that the absolute challenge to our age" (*PON*, 246).

In her presentation "Marxist-Humanism: The Summation That Is A New Beginning, Subjectively and Objectively," 1983, she spoke of "four new moments in Marx that are the 1980s trail":

(1) A paragraph from the Marx-edited French edition of *Capital*, which showed that even the predominance of foreign over internal trade including annexing "vast lands in the New World, in Asia, in Australia," wouldn't abate the general crisis of capital, only intensify it. In the same period, Marx wrote of how revolution could occur in the less developed "East" ahead of the "West."

(2) Marx's 1850 call for "revolution in permanence" needed to be related "to Marx's continuing concretization of the dialectic of negativity, as the dialectic of revolution." This was manifest in the *Grundrisse*:

> It is no accident that it was there where Marx stopped speaking of only three universal forms of human development—slave, feudal, and capitalist—and included a fourth universal form: the "Asiatic mode of production." That post-Marx Marxists failed to have that ground for working our the reality of their age, and thus anticipate what we now call a whole new Third World, is exactly what this age is still suffering from (*PON*, 260).

(3) Marx's new moment on

> organization—was not only not grasped but actually *rejected*. Post-Marx Marxists were always "proving" that, because Marx had not worked out a "theory" or organization, while Lassalle knew how to build a mass party, he left them no model to practice. . . . The whole truth is—and that is first and foremost—Marx never separated organization forms from his total philosophy of revolution (261).

(4) The man/woman relation seen in Marx's *Ethnological Notebooks*, which can then return one with new eyes to Marx's 1844 concept of man/woman as well as Marx's relation to the dimension of women in the Paris Commune, followed by his proposal for autonomous women's sections in the First International.

Arguing that grasping Marx's creation of new moments was key for comprehending the whole, Dunayevskaya showed Marx's totality as a new beginning:

> The crucial truth is that the question: How to begin anew? informed the whole of Marx's dialectic methodology—even *after* his discovery of a whole new continent of thought, even *after* the publication of the first edition of *Capital* as well as the 1875 edition, *after* the Paris Commune, *when* he took issue with Mikhailovsky who had written what turned out to be what all *post*-Marx Marxists likewise accepted as the climax of the work, that is the "Historical Tendency of Capitalist Accumulation" as a universal. Marx, on the other hand, held that the summation of Western capitalist development was just that—the particular development of capitalism—which need not be the universal path of human development. Here we have the unique way Marx practiced summation as a new beginning (257-58).

The methodology Dunayevskaya discerned in Marx's practice—the uniqueness of his summation as new beginning—was the methodology she strove to practice as Marxist-Humanism in the 1980s. "How to begin anew?" commenced with probing of the whole of Marx. What was at stake was "Marx's world Promethean vision," which the post-Marx Marxists proved incapable of following out.

Even someone as crucial to Marx as Engels had not fully grasped this "unchained dialectic." In Dunayevskaya's 1980s view, Engels's narrow unilinearism verses Marx's multilinearism was present in their differing discussions of the man/woman relationship, as well as in how each approached the transition from primitive communism to class society. Marx, she argued, saw the dualities inherent within primitive communism, in its dissolution and transition to the next stage, not merely after the fact. Marx's was a re-creation of the dialectic open to newly arising self-active human subjectivity. In contrast, Engels's tended more toward an application as in his *Dialectics of Nature*. When he did discuss the man/woman relation, Engels's conclusion on the movement out of primitive communism was "the world historic defeat of the female sex," which Dunayevskaya argued, was no expression of Marx's.

The critique extended from Engels to all post Marxists, Lenin and Luxemburg included. Her point of departure was the manner wherein these revolutionaries seized upon or failed to catch Marx's new moments, including Marx's prescience on capitalism's relations with non-capitalist lands, and in not seeing the relation of philosophy and revolutionary organization that Marx was hewing out in *Critique of the Gotha Program*.

Dunayevskaya's polemic reached to Marxist epigones of her own day as well as non-Marxists. The historic and contemporary category of "post-Marx Marxism" was projected by her during an extensive speaking tour she took on the occasion of the centenary of Marx's death, 1983, giving more than 40 lectures, primarily on university campuses. The audience ranged from students, to Black intellectuals and activists, to women's liberationists, including a Third World women's conference, to activists who had participated in the 1949-50 Miners' General Strike. The topics encompassed "Marx and the Liberation of Women," "Rosa Luxemburg as Theoretician, as Activist, as Internationalist," "On the Marx Centenary: Facing the Challenge to all Post-Marx Marxists," and on "Marx and the Black World." In critiquing post-Marx Marxists and non-Marxists, Dunayevskaya was challenging the 1980s generation of revolutionary thinker/activists to forge a new beginning.

New Paragraphs Added to *Rosa Luxemburg, Women's Liberation, and Marx's Philosophy of Revolution*

For Dunayevskaya each of her books was a living document, subject to rethinking and development, and to which she returned again and again in her public talks, in dialogue with her Marxist-Humanist colleagues, and in her own study. The result was a continual expansion and self-critique written onto various pages and chapters of each work. A number of her personal copies with marginalia are on deposit as part of the *Supplement of the Raya Dunayevskaya Collection*.

With *Rosa Luxemburg, Women's Liberation, and Marx's Philosophy of Revolution*, this process took on a special form. Shortly after its publication, Dunayevskaya undertook her Marx Centenary tour with the work in hand. She began to formulate new paragraphs that came from questions posed as well as her own speaking preparations. After the tour she addressed a letter to her colleagues (August 1983, *SRDC* #15370) listing and discussing the new passages, including the specific pages where she wished to place them. The 1991 edition of her book excerpted this letter and the passages.[1] The passages were summations or expansions of key categories Dunayevskaya had developed in the book. They included:

(1) *Post-Marx Marxism:* Noting that she did not want readers of wait until the last chapter to discuss this central category of the book—post-Marx Marxism as a pejorative, beginning with Engels—she added two paragraphs to the Introduction discussing the fact that Engels, and later the Marx archivist, Ryazanov, had rushed to their own interpretation of Marx's *Ethnological Notebooks* without truly knowing all of what Marx had left unfinished. To her this was

characteristic of post-Marx Marxism: "Isn't it time to challenge all of the post-Marx Marxists, when even those who have achieved great revolutions (and none was greater than the 1917 Russian Revolution) did not, in thought, measure up to Marx? Isn't it time to dig into what Marx . . . had to say himself?" (*RLWLKM,* xxiv).

(2) *The Philosophic Dimension of Luxemburg's Economic Error:* Dunayevskaya had devoted a chapter to discussing the differences between Luxemburg's and Marx's theories of the accumulation of capital. In the added paragraphs she wished to summarize the philosophic root of Luxemburg's error in being blinded by the appearance of imperialism and in not being attuned to revolutionary subjectivity in colonial countries. For Dunayevskaya, it resided in the difference between the movement of the dialectic in *Phenomenology of Mind* vs. its movement in *Philosophy of Mind*:

> [A]s against the phenomenology of imperialism being merely a reflection of new surfacings of oppression, new appearances surface as so profound a philosophy of revolution as to disclose that what inheres in it is a living Subject that will resolve the great contradiction of its absolute opposites, imperialism and national oppression. It is this, which Marxist-Humanists call the new revolutionary forces as Reason. Therein is the nub of the Great Divide between *Phenomenology* and *Philosophy*—and because it is no abstraction, but a live Subject, *it unites rather than divides theory and reality* (xxxiv-v).

(3) *Marx's Multilinearism vs. Engels' Unilinearism:* In further developing the contrast between Marx and Engels, Dunayevskaya discussed the question of the transition between one historic stage and another, in which "Marx always related it to new revolutionary upsurges," and saw "a multilinear view of human development as well as *dialectical duality within each* formation."

> As against Marx's multilinear view, which kept Marx from attempting any blueprint for future generations, Engels's unilinear view led him to mechanical positivism. By no accident whatever, such one-dimensionality kept him from seeing either the communal form under "Oriental despotism" or the duality in "primitive communism" in Morgan's *Ancient Society*. No wonder, although Engels had accepted Marx's view of the Asiatic mode of production as fundamental enough to constitute a fourth form of human development, he had left it out altogether from *his* analysis of primitive communism in the first book he wrote as a "bequest" of Marx—*Origin of the Family*. By then Engels had confined Marx's revolutionary dialectics and historical materialism to hardly more than Morgan's "materialism" (xxvi).

(4) *Marx and the Black World:* Dunayevskaya wanted the reader to consider Marx's many references to the Black dimension as a totality and thus developed the following additional paragraph:

> With this dialectical circle of circles, Marx's reference in the *Ethnological Notebooks* to the Australian aborigine as "the intelligent black," brought to a

conclusion the dialectic he had unchained when he first broke from bourgeois society in the 1840s and objected to the use of the word, "Negro," as if it were synonymous with the word, "slave." By the 1850s, in the *Grundrisse*, he extended that sensitivity to the whole pre-capitalist world. By the 1860s, the Black dimension became, at one and the same time, not only pivotal to the abolition of slavery and victory of the North in the Civil War, but also to the restructuring of *Capital* itself. In a word, the often-quoted sentence: "Labor cannot emancipate itself in the white skin where in the black skin it is branded," far from being rhetoric, was the actual reality *and* the perspective for overcoming that reality. Marx reached, at every historic turning point, for a concluding point, *not* as an end but as a new jumping off point, a new beginning, a new vision" (xxxvii).

(5) *The Organizational Question and Marx's "Revolution-in-Permanence:* The original ending of the book called for a new unifying principle based on Marx's humanism and his spelling that out as "revolution in permanence." In an additional paragraph Dunayevskaya wished to unite the question of organization with the concept of "revolution in permanence." While form of organization was important, particularly working out a non-elitist committee-form as opposed to the "party-to-lead," they were "not absolute opposites." Revolutionary philosophy needed to be a determinant: "[T]he challenge demands that we synthesize not only the new relations of theory to practice, and all the forces of revolution, but philosophy's 'suffering, patience and labor of the negative,' i.e., experiencing absolute negativity." Only then could one approach the new society: "That which Hegel judged to be the synthesis of the 'Self-Thinking Idea' and the 'Self-Bringing-Forth of Liberty,' Marxist-Humanism holds, is what Marx had called the new society. The many paths to get there are not easy to work out" (xxxvii-viii).

The paragraph anticipated the labor Dunayevskaya would undertake in 1986-87 on "Dialectics of Organization and Philosophy." At the same time it singled out Marxist-Humanism's labor to establish a continuity with Marx's humanism in his re-creation of Hegel's dialectic.

Women's Liberation and the Dialectics of Revolution

Several months after the Marx Centenary Tour, Dunayevskaya gathered together a collection of her writings on Women's Liberation from 35 years. For this new book, *Women's Liberation and the Dialectics of Revolution—Reaching for the Future* (1985) she wrote an "Introduction and Overview."

Dunayevskaya began her introductory essay by situating women's liberation in the post-World War II age: "What distinguishes the newness and uniqueness of Women's Liberation in our age is the very nature of our epoch, which signified, at one and the same time, a new stage of production—Automation—*and* a new stage of cognition. The fact that the movement from practice was itself a form of theory was manifested in the Miners' General Strike of 1949-50" (*Women's Liberation and the Dialectics of Revolution*, 1). Even before women's liberation became a movement, she had written on the dimension of women in this miners' general strike, and in Left political organizations in the post-World War II world.

As women's liberation became a movement in the late 1960s, Dunayevskaya called for its recognition as reason as well as force. The breadth of this collection, historically and globally, demonstrated the objective significance of woman as revolutionary subject. She challenged the women's liberation movement to undertake the needed theoretical/practical labor, including probing Hegel and Marx, for unchaining the present moment in reaching for the future. The full significance of women's liberation encompassed a relationship to emancipatory philosophy. Only thereby would it reach towards a dialectics of revolution.

Her early women's liberation writings mentioned above were in Part I, "Women's Labor and the Black Dimension." The collection, however, was not arranged chronologically. Rather, each part consisted of writings from the different decades. Dunayevskaya wished to stress totality and new beginning. In a presentation which included commentary on her Introduction and Overview, she developed this: "Clearly, I wanted each part to be a totality, but even that is not the answer, because we can get there only when totality is a new beginning, and that new beginning is in philosophy" ("Responsibility for Marxist-Humanism in the Historic Mirror: A Revolutionary Critical Look," December 30, 1984, *RDC* #8335-8347).

In this presentation she gave a "reading" of the Introduction and Overview before it was printed in book form, singling out six "dialectics of revolution." Women's Liberation was the first dialectic of revolution presented, "*when* it is relation—when it comes out of—the new epoch itself, which we declared philosophically to be a movement from practice that is itself a form of theory, and absolutely inseparable from revolution" (#8343). Other forces of revolution, the Black dimension as a determination of the dialectic, and youth, were brought forth. In each case, new revolutionary forces were presented in unity with reason. "How absolutely necessary it is to uproot all the old so that Reason as the new consciousness and the revolutionary force as the new consciousness comprise the second dialectic of revolution" (#8344-45). "Yet," she warned, "even that, even naming more than one force of revolution, and even not following the chronological order does not really cover reason and revolution, the very heart of the Marxian dialectic" (#8345).

In discussing Part II of the collection, "Revolutionaries All," Dunayevskaya brought forth what she termed the third dialectic present in the Introduction and Overview: "masses in motion" as expressed in the 20th century revolutions begun in the 1905 Russian Revolution, extending East to Persia, and at the same time carrying over to our own day as summarized in her *Philosophy and Revolution*.

The fact that in the Introduction and Overview Dunayevskaya linked the excerpts on New Passions and New Forces from the final chapter of *Philosophy and Revolution*, to her discussion of Hegel's Absolutes in Chapter One, was the basis of "the fourth dialectic . . . the return to Hegel." This became expressed by quoting Gramsci on "the philosophy of praxis is consciousness full of contradiction in which the philosopher . . . posits himself as an element of the contradiction" so that dialectics is "knowledge and therefore action."

The Introduction now discussed Part III, "Sexism, Politics and Revolution—Japan, Portugal, Poland, China, Latin America, the U.S.—Is There an Organizational Answer?" Here Dunayevskaya noted "[T]he whole question of organization as non-elitist and demanding the practice of new relations between men and women were not connected by the Women's Liberationists to Marx's philosophy of 'revolution in permanence' as ground for organization." At the same time she defended their demands for new organizational relations as against the male chauvinism inherent in the Left. The importance of organization was its link to a concept of revolution-in-permanence: "The fifth dialectic . . . is that without revolution-in-permanence as ground for organization, it doesn't make any difference. Whether you have an organization or not, you will fail" ("Responsibility for Marxist-Humanism..." *RDC* #8345).

Dunayevskaya identified the sixth dialectic in Part IV, "The Trail to the 1980s." This final dialectic is "the need for a total uprooting, including that of the family." Here her discussion of Marx ranged from his critique of the bourgeois family, to the multi-linear pathways of human development he wrote of in the *Grundrisse*, including the expression "the absolute movement of becoming,' to his *Ethnological Notebooks*. In contrast, were the views of Engels in *Origin of the Family, Private Property and the State*, as well as other post-Marx Marxists. Dunayevskaya was concerned with the process of arriving at how deep and total the uprooting had to be. For her it meant thought-dives into Marx and re-creating the Hegelian dialectic of Absolutes as New Beginning, and a separation from post-Marx Marxism even as one grasped crucial moments within, as in Lenin's 1914 return to Hegel. The uprooting required presence within the new emerging moments: Promethean vision and reaching for the future fused with listening to new voices from below.

The six "dialectics of revolution" Dunayevskaya discerned in her Introduction and Overview to *Women's Liberation and the Dialectics of Revolution*, were not posed by her as any "answer." It was part of a continuing dialogue she felt the necessity of having with Marxist-Humanist colleagues in the 1980s. She was asking them to grapple with Absolute Method, whether in reading a collection of her essays on women, in projecting *News & Letters* newspaper, or in participating in various freedom movements. In the final paragraph of this presentation, "Responsibility for Marxist-Humanism in the Historic Mirror," she spelled it out anew:

Today I declare that Absolute Method, though it is the goal from which no private enclaves can escape, is still only "the road to" the Absolute Idea or Mind. That is still *the* only answer which transcends method—or expresses it, if you wish. And that needs concretization. That concretization is the name of the Absolute Idea for our age: Marxist-Humanism, further pinpointed as News and Letters Committees in the U.S., but by no means limited to the U.S. It is a world concept, a world concretization. And it is that historical look at it, and the looking at ourselves, that will assure revolution-in-permanence to be (#8347).

II. Retrospective of Marxist-Humanism— Its Origins and Development

Dunayevskaya's 1980s View of the Johnson-Forest Tendency

Dunayevskaya returned again and again to examine the origins of Marxist-Humanism within the State-Capitalist (Johnson-Forest) Tendency. She explored how state-capitalist theory in the 1940s was a needed point of departure for the Tendency to begin its exploration of the Hegelian dialectic and the early Marx, but by 1953 proved to be insufficient without a comprehensive dive into Hegel's Absolutes. Initially the leaders of the Tendency had seemed to be on the same wave length. In the early 1940s Dunayevskaya had made sight translations from "Lenin's Abstract on Hegel's *Science of Logic*." She had found and read Russian translations of the 1844 Marx. By 1947 Grace Lee had made rough translations of essays from Marx's *Economic-Philosophic Manuscripts* of 1844. In 1948 James wrote his *Notes on the Dialectic*.

In a series of retrospectives from the 1980s—the Prologue to *25 Years of Marxist-Humanism in the U.S.* (1980), the Postscript to the "Battle of Ideas" Political-Philosophic Letter (1982), "Marxist-Humanism: The Summation That Is a New Beginning, Subjectively and Objectively" (1983), "The Emergence of a New Movement from Practice that Is Itself a Form of Theory" in *The Coal Miners General Strike of 1949-50 and the Birth of Marxist-Humanism in the U.S.* (1984), and "Not by Practice Alone: The Movement from Theory" (1984)—Dunayevskaya reexamined the period 1948-1954.

She explored the tensions within the Johnson-Forest Tendency that had arisen from 1949 to the split of 1955. She took up differing attitudes to Lenin's *Philosophic Notebooks*, to the mass movement from below as signified by the 1949-50 Miners' General Strike, to the concept of Marx's Humanism, to the role of a workers' newspaper and revolutionary Marxist organization in the political events of the time, and to the meaning of Hegel's Absolutes for the revolutionary movement.

Differing Readings of Lenin's Philosophic Notebooks

C.L.R. James' *Notes on Dialectics* inspired me to translate Lenin's *Abstract of Hegel's Science of Logic* . . . Although I was unaware that my brief comments [to James] in submitting the translation of Lenin's *Philosophic Notebooks* signaled a difference in an interpretation of the historic and philosophic significance of those Notebooks, the truth is that that *is* the beginning of philosophic differences *within* the Johnson-Forest Tendency ("Battle of Ideas" 1982, *PON*, 247).

In 1980 she recalled:

> On Feb. 18, 1949 I sent the translation of Lenin's notes on the Doctrine of Being. The covering note refers to the "Notes on the Dialectic" Johnson had written in 1948, which had then impressed me very much, but which in 1949 made me call attention to the fact that Johnson "practically skipped over the first book." The same note focused on Lenin's new appreciation of the "self-development of the concept," no matter how "idealistic" that sounds . . . It is with this new appreciation I felt for Lenin's *Philosophic Notebooks* that a philosophic division started to emerge between the two founders of the State-Capitalist Tendency—Johnson and Forest (*25 Years of Marxist-Humanism in the U.S.*, 1, 2).

On March 12, 1949 she concluded the translation of Lenin and sent it to Johnson along with another note:

> My covering note for it no doubt shocked him: "Let me say at the start that although you have entered into this 'conspiracy' with Lenin, the outstanding difference between the two 'versions' (of the Dialectic) is striking. You will note that Lenin's notes on the Notion are as lengthy as those on the Introduction, and Doctrines of Being and Essence combined . . . although you spent that much time on Notion, and included its practice, the thing you chose most to stop at and say: *hic Rodus, hic salta* to was the Law of Contradiction in Essence . . . (but Lenin) chooses to single out the section on the Idea" (*25 Years of Marxist-Humanism*, 2).

When Dunayevskaya looked back at the correspondence from James and Lee that followed her translation of Lenin, she found that whereas she had concluded that "Lenin no longer 'feared' the Absolute [in the Doctrine of Notion], seeing it both as unity of theoretical and practical idea, as the *method* of absolute cognition, and as criticism of all Marxists, including himself," they had concluded, "the key of Lenin's notes on *Logic* is this relation to Essence" (*25 Years of Marxist-Humanism*, 2). She continued:

> It is very nearly beyond comprehension to find how they could make such a claim in the face of the fact that Lenin's commentary on the Doctrine of Notion

was more comprehensive than what Lenin had written on all the rest of the *Logic* combined. . . .

Perhaps we can understand part of the reason why when we read the letter in which Johnson finally (on June 10, 1949) first acknowledged the translation of Lenin's *Philosophic Notebooks* and my commentaries. He wrote: "You are covering a lot of ground and it is pretty good. But after conversations with [Grace] & reading (carefully, this time) your correspondence, I feel that we are still off *the* point . . ." Clearly, it is not I with whom they disagreed as hotly as they did with Lenin (*25 Years of Marxist-Humanism*, 2).

Differing Attitudes to the Miners' General Strike

At the same time that Dunayevskaya was translating Lenin, there were stirrings in the coal fields, where the Johnson-Forest Tendency, then in the Socialist Workers Party, was active. These erupted several months later into a general strike in the region (discussed in Chapter 2). In the 1980s, Dunayevskaya reexamined this period in several writings including *The Coal Miners' General Strike of 1949-50 and the Birth of Marxist-Humanism in the U.S.* which she co-authored with Andy Phillips, who had been a miner and Tendency member in that period. Her contribution was titled "The Emergence of a New Movement from Practice that Is Itself a Form of Theory."

Dunayevskaya wrote: "The dialectic of the 1949-50 Miners' General Strike, as it was transformed from a Lewis-authorized strike that already had lasted some six months into a challenge to John L. Lewis himself, laid the ground for new ways of thinking" (*Coal Miners General Strike*, 33). The new ways of thinking for Dunayevskaya meant vantage points for the book on "Marxism and State-Capitalism" she was working on. One of those vantage points was to have a worker be part of the discussions of the draft of the book with the co-leaders of the Johnson-Forest Tendency. As we saw in Chapter Two, Dunayevskaya's theoretical work was related to strike activities, including discussions with the miners on Marx's description of alienated labor, and helping to set up a miners' relief committee to establish relations between the striking miners and rank-and-file production workers in other industries. In 1984 she wrote: "With our new pamphlet on the 1949-50 miners' general strike, we can see *as a unity* the spontaneous activity and what philosophic problems were being worked out simultaneously" ("Not by Practice Alone," *PON*, 284).

In the same document she discussed another mass self-activity of the period, the Bolivian Revolution of 1952. Its uniqueness lay in its being the first post-war national revolution in Latin America with a peasant dimension, and particularly in the fact that,

> miners on strike and peasants in revolt—*jointly* challenging the big imperialist behemoth of U.S. imperialism as well as its own rulers—made the revolution of such new *world* importance that, along with all the new passions and forces in 1950 and the final break [of the Johnson-Forest Tendency] with Trotskyism in

1951, the Latin American dimension nudged us to that new second great divide in post-Marx Marxism—Marxist-Humanism (*PON*, 275).

In contrast to Dunayevskaya's attitude toward the movement from below was James' attitude. When the Tendency left the SWP in 1951 to begin a new organization and newspaper, tensions immediately surfaced:

> The shock was that it was also the beginning of the end of a united Johnson-Forest Tendency. Where I proposed that the first issue of the new paper we planned to issue should be devoted to the new miners' seniority strike, Johnson (James) opposed. He insisted that "our membership and their friends are the only audience I have in mind for the paper . . . If a mighty bubble broke out, 500,000 miners vs. John L. Lewis, and shook the minefields, I would not budge from our program." We then went "underground," publishing only a mimeographed paper until 1953 (*Miners General Strike*, 38).

As Dunayevskaya noted, "it is there, *precisely there*, where those two 'subjectivities'—Johnson and Forest—in their attitude to the *masses in motion*, acted totally differently" ("Not By Practice Alone: The Movement From Theory" 1984, *PON*, 275).

"Deep depoliticalization" was occurring within the Tendency, not only in the face of new movements from below, but with an ongoing Korean War and McCarthyism raging. Dunayevskaya summed up the contradictions in the Tendency in face of new movements from below:

> [H]ow different were the views of C.L.R. James and Raya Dunayevskaya toward these movements from below when we were on the threshold of breaking through to the Absolute Idea which had led us to Marxist-Humanism. . . .
> A new sense of objectivity cried out to be released, but none were there to embrace it as two kinds of subjectivity engaged in *internal* tensions, inevitable but nevertheless diversionary from the objectively developing new situation. We were nearing the eve of 1953, that is to say, the philosophic breakthrough in the Absolute Idea ("Not by Practice Alone," *PON*, 274, 275).

Philosophic Differences on Humanism

In the late 1940s the Tendency was grappling with philosophic questions. Grace Lee made rough translations of the early Marx, James wrote his *Notes on Dialectics*, Dunayevskaya translated Lenin's *Philosophic Notebooks*. All three had begun digging into Hegel. A three-way philosophic correspondence took place in 1949-51. And yet, philosophic differences were emerging. *State-Capitalism and World Revolution* (1950), their summing up of their experience in Trotskyism, did not limit itself to political conclusions, but had a section on the philosophy of state-capitalism, written by Lee. However, it centered on Contradiction, rather than on the Absolute Idea they had been reaching for in their philosophic correspondence. In "Not by Practice Alone: The Movement From Theory,"(1984) Dunayevskaya wrote:

> *State-Capitalism and World Revolution*, in its section on philosophy, focused on Contradiction rather than second negativity and Absolute Idea, which would have brought us to Marx's Humanism. Grace [Lee], who is the author of that philosophic section, considered Humanism merely as either Christian or Existentialist Humanism, naturally rejecting both. In so doing the Tendency went no further than analyzing "The Philosophy of State-Capitalism." Indeed, that is what it openly called that section. In a word, it went no further philosophically than we had already worked out in economic and political terms for the decade of 1941-50.
>
> There was a possibility of another direction: the ongoing miners' strike and our listening to the voices from below, as we worked out philosophically the meaning of that strike. Instead, we "stopped dead," to use Hegel's phrase against Kant, who was on the threshold of the dialectic, being the first to reintroduce it into modern philosophy, but had not worked the dialectic out fully, i.e., concretely at the same time. In a political way, that is what was happening to the Johnson-Forest Tendency as differences began to surface between Johnson and Forest (*PON*, 281).

What Kind of Newspaper? What Kind of Politics?

As noted above, when Dunayevskaya proposed that the first issue of the paper the Tendency would issue be devoted to a new miners' seniority strike in 1951, James proclaimed that was not the kind of paper he had in mind. In the 1980s, Dunayevskaya called this kind of underground existence "deep depoliticalization." It would presage the conflicts of the Tendency:

> 1953 saw, at one and the same time, the emergence, *in* the Johnson-Forest Tendency, of open divergences toward objective events (be it Stalin's death, the East German revolt, the Beria purge, *or* McCarthyism), as well as towards the subjective idea of what type of paper *Correspondence* was to be and what was its relationship to Marxism. . . . *Everything changed with the death of Stalin on March 5, when suddenly, it wasn't only the objective situation that had so radically changed, but divergences appeared between Lee and me within the Tendency* (25 Years of Marxist-Humanism, 1, 3).

Dunayevskaya went on to describe how she wrote an analysis of Stalin's death and, after discussions with Charles Denby on the workers' reactions in the factory, wrote a second article putting the 1920-21 Trade Union debate between Lenin and Trotsky in the context of both Russia and the U.S, 1953. Lee, who was editor of *Correspondence* for that issue, and had a very different view of what kind of analysis of Stalin's death was needed, "so 'editorialized' my analysis and so passionately stressed the alleged indifference of the American proletariat to that event, that the article became unrecognizable" (3).

In "Not By Practice Alone: The Movement From Theory"(1984), she wrote of the political crisis within the Johnson-Forest Tendency following Stalin's death:

> Suddenly what was disclosed as the apoliticalization which deepened when, after our final break with Trotskyism in 1951, we failed to face the public either with our theory of state-capitalism, or the magnificent experience in the Miners' General Strike followed by the seniority strike in 1951. As against Johnson's co-leader, Grace, who wished to continue with the so-called "underground" apolitical existence, Charles Denby saw so great an affinity of the America workers' daily battles against the labor bureaucracy that he asked me to reproduce my analysis of the 1921 Trade Union Debate between Lenin and Trotsky, in the context of the ramifications of the 1953 death of Stalin and the workers' revolts that were sure to follow (*PON*, 285).

It was in the month following this controversy that Dunayevskaya wrote her two Letters on Hegel's Absolutes. Six weeks later, the June 17th East Germany Revolt occurred. That momentous world-shaking event shook up the post-Stalin Russian leaders, who proceeded to execute "Beria, the head of the Secret Service and the most hated man of the totalitarian bureaucracy; and institute some mild reforms." It led to further tensions within the Johnson-Forest Tendency as Dunayevskaya's analysis of the Beria purge, the lead of the first issue of a printed *Correspondence*, was critiqued for several issues by the followers of Johnson and Lee:

> The analysis of both Stalin and Beria were written while McCarthyism was raging in the country. All three events brought about a sharp conflict between Johnson and Lee on the one side, and me on the other. It was clear that in the two years between leaving the [Socialist Workers Party] and the appearance of *Correspondence* there had developed in the followers of Johnson a great diversion from Marxism as well as from the American revolution (*25 Years of Marxist-Humanism*, 4).

•

The philosophic culmination of the 1949-53 period within the Johnson-Forest Tendency was Dunayevskaya's May 12 and 20, 1953 Letters on Hegel's Absolutes. Her philosophic breakthrough revealed differing attitudes to Hegel's Absolutes on the part of Johnson and Forest. By 1955 the Johnson-Forest Tendency split apart. To explore this we turn to Dunayevskaya's reexamination of her 1953 Letters on Hegel's Absolutes

Creating the Category "Philosophic-Moment of Marxist-Humanism" for the 1953 Letters on Hegel's Absolutes

The Philosophic Separation from James

In the 1980s, Dunayevskaya returned with a new intensity to her 1953 letters. This brought forth a deeper comprehension of her philosophic differences with James. From her 1949 translation of Lenin's *Abstract on Hegel's Science of Logic* forward, Dunayevskaya was determined to journey into Hegel's Absolutes as containing the philosophic new beginning for the post World War II world. Where James and Lee focused on finding "dialectic of the party" within Hegel's Absolutes, Dunayevskaya allowed dialectics' absolute negativity to determine her philosophic labors. Here was how she articulated that difference in her 1982 "Battle of Ideas" writing:

> [H]ard as I tried to continue in the context that preoccupied James and Grace—the "dialectics of the party"—I was bound in a very different direction once I concentrated on Hegel's "dialectic *mediation*" rather than any sort of "media*tor*," whether the Party or otherwise (*PON*, 248).

Even when in the beginning of her May 12 letter, she tried to stay within the confines of "the Party," the dialectic was taking her to a far different concept of organization than where James had been heading: "I am not touching upon the mass party; the workers will do what they will do and until they do we can have only the faintest intimation of the great leap . . . I am not concerned with spontaneity verses organization . . . I am concerned only with the dialectic of the vanguard party [or] of the *type* of grouping like ours, be it large or small, and *its* relationship to the mass."

In her 1987 "Presentation on the Dialectics of Organization and Philosophy," she commented on this section of her May 12 letter:

> [W]hat happens to a small group "like us" who know that nothing can be done without the masses, and are with them, but [such small groups of] theoreticians always seem to be around too. So, what is the *objectivity* which explains their presence, as the objectivity explains the spontaneous outburst of the masses? In a word, I was looking for the objectivity of subjectivity (*PON*, 7).

In this same 1987 presentation, Dunayevskaya contrasted James' attitude to Hegel's *Philosophy of Mind* to her own. She referred to the fact that James "said that he looked into *Philosophy of Mind*, he concluded that he found nothing there 'for us'" She then added, "I must have felt dissatisfied, since that is where I went" (*PON*, 7).

In Dunayevskaya's May 12, 1953 letter, she asked Grace Lee to get her a copy of *Philosophy of Mind*, adding, "[N]ow that I believe the dialectic of the Absolute Idea is the dialectic of the party, I feel that Mind is the new society gestating in the old, and I feel sure we could get a lot of very valuable dialectical developments there" (*PON*, 24).

In her May 20 letter on *Philosophy of Mind*, she began with an outline of the development of the vanguard party and its relationship to the mass movements. But by the time she reached Absolute Mind and its concluding four paragraphs, 574-577, she had left dialectic of the party behind. She was within Hegel's final syllogisms, where Mind becomes "the mediating agent in the process." The references to the Paris Commune and Soviets were not about organizational form, but a movement from practice that she saw as a form of theory. Commenting in her 1982 "On the Battle of Ideas" essay she wrote, "It becomes necessary to stress here, over and over again, that I had not a single word to say about the Party or the Soviets or any form of organization. On the contrary. Here is what I then concluded [in the May 20, 1953 Letter]: "We have entered the new society" (*PON*, 240).

In a 1987 Talking to Myself document, after once again reviewing and quoting from the May 12 and 20, 1953 letters she wrote: "So it is *Philosophy of Mind* i.e., the May 20 rather than the May 12 Letter, that completely frees me from CLR [James] *and* from concern with party, as with the final three paragraphs of *Mind*, I end not with the form of organization, but instead say, 'we have entered the new society'" (*SRDC* # 10923).

The Philosophic Moment as Determinant for Three Decades of Marxist-Humanism

> *In Hegelian dialectics, the philosophic moment is a determinant; even if the person who was driven to articulate the Idea of that "moment" was very nearly unconscious as to its depth and its ramifications, it remained the element that governed the concretization that follows the laborious birth that poured forth in a torrent nevertheless.*
> Specifically and concretely, in our case the moment I'm referring to is May 12 and 20, 1953. The Idea is in demystifying the Absolute as either God or the closed ontology, as the unity I singled out, a dual movement, from theory to practice, from practice as well as from theory ("Presentation on the Dialectics of Organization and Philosophy," June 1987 PON, 5).

In 1987, Dunayevskaya's reexaminations of her 1953 Letters on Hegel's Absolutes led to the category "The Philosophic Moment of Marxist-Humanism" to express the meaning of that breakthrough. This category was the culmination of her many returns to the 1953 Letters in the 1980s that sought to explore the impact of 1953 on the entire body of Marxist-Humanist thought.

In particular, the dual movement from practice and from theory that she had discerned in Hegel's Absolutes was examined in the 1980s in relation to the writing of her trilogy of revolution.

With regard to *Marxism and Freedom*, she commented:

Once I saw that movement from practice as a philosophic category, which was not alone for our age but for Marx's as well, I could structure the whole of *Marxism and Freedom* in the context of the movement from practice, beginning with the age of revolutions—industrial, political, philosophic—and subtitling the whole work: "From 1776 until Today." ("On the Battle of Ideas," 1982, *PON*, 244).

In relation to *Philosophy and Revolution*:

With *Philosophy and Revolution*, we had a new situation. It is not alone all the new passions and forces of the 1960s with which the book ends, but the fact that the philosophic predominates over the historic, the theory over the practice; indeed, the very fact that the structure is the exact opposite of what *Marxism and Freedom* was—that is, not the movement from practice, but the movement from theory—gave the whole question of Hegelian dialectics "in and for itself" a totally new meaning, in the sense that it demanded detailing not only the movement from practice but that from theory. That movement from theory becomes the uniqueness of Marxist-Humanist philosophy and our original contribution to *Marx's* Marxism ("Not By Practice Alone: The Movement From Theory" 1984, *PON* 282).

For the Rosa Luxemburg book:

With the availability of Marx's *Ethnological Notebooks* and, in general, "new moments" Marx discovered in his last decade making it possible finally to view Marx's Marxism *as a totality*, it is clear also that our own contributions to *Marx's* Marxism helped articulate Marxism for our age. . . . This is what makes it imperative that, to work out the new relationship of practice to theory, and theory to practice, we do not stop with Hegel's Absolutes—Knowledge, Idea, Mind—but recreate, as Marx did, Absolute Method—the unchained dialectic. In challenging post-Marx Marxists, we are articulating Marx's Marxism for our age ("Not By Practice Alone: The Movement From Theory" 1984, *PON*, 282, 283).

In working out the meaning of the philosophic moment as a determinate of what followed, "the ground and roof," Dunayevskaya wrote:

Everyone has heard so much about 1953 as the stage of breakthrough on the Absolute Idea that you may think: what else is there to be said? The whole point, however, about the philosophic point that became a philosophic determinant—and not just the ground of [it], but became so startlingly new and clear with Marx—[is] that looking at it for this age, specifically [in relation to] ourselves, it began to appear in an altogether new way. Here is what I mean.
Heretofore what we stressed when we pointed to 1953 as source was the important point of 1955, when there was an actually organizational break-up [of Correspondence Committees and founding of News and Letters Committees]. Then what became clearer was that actually, insofar as the words "Marxist-Humanism" are concerned, we couldn't say 1955, but as it was expressed in

written form in *Marxism and Freedom* in 1957. Now what is clear is not that any of the other dates are wrong, but that each time it is a specific period that makes one realize that actually what wasn't clear was what was in *the* philosophic moment, and *only when* the objective and subjective merge is it "proven." Oh, the source, the ground, really also had a roof. But the context in between, the structure, couldn't be controlled without the objective situation. But that, on the other hand, made it very clear that we are back to focusing on the philosophic moment (Presentation on the Dialectics of Organization and Philosophy," *PON*, 6).

The 1953 Letters on Hegel's Absolutes formed a crucial dimension of Dunayevskaya's work on Dialectics of Organization and Revolution. This will be taken up shortly here in the final section of Part V.

Critiquing the Gap Between Philosophic Expression and Organizational Practice of Marxist-Humanism in the 1980s: I. 1983-85

A concept of critique and self-critique was central to Dunayevskaya at each stage of the development of Marxist-Humanism. She saw Marxist-Humanism emerging out of Marxist-Humanism as the point of departure for revolutionary new beginnings in the 1980s. However, this was not a given. Marxist-Humanism itself had to be tested by its own category of Absolute Negativity as New Beginning. Submitting Marxist-Humanism to absolute negativity was a determinate for her philosophic-organizational labors of the 1980s as she dug deeply and critically, into its origins and development.

In the 1980s, Dunayevskaya: (1) reexamined the origins of Marxist-Humanism in the Johnson-Forest Tendency; (2) singled out the category "philosophic moment" for Marx of 1844, and for Marxist-Humanism in the 1953 Letters on Hegel's Absolutes; and (3) projected her trilogy of revolution as a living body of ideas via new concretizations of its categories, including material added to the text after publication. Here we want to examine how Dunayevskaya subjected Marxist-Humanist organization to critical retrospective that helped to forge new revolutionary perspectives, including work on Dialectics of Organization and Philosophy.

After each of Dunayevskaya's major works a gap seemed to emerge between the philosophic stage reached and its organizational projection. With her third work, *Rosa Luxemburg, Women's Liberation, and Marx's Philosophy of Revolution*, her critique of post-Marx Marxism, became, as well, a self-examination of Marxist-Humanism. Dunayevskaya concluded that this crucial category was not being creatively projected by her News and Letters colleagues, and that there was danger of a gap developing between the philosophical expression and the organizational practice of Marxist-Humanism.

One period that manifested this difficulty was 1983-85, as *Rosa Luxemburg, Women's Liberation, and Marx's Philosophy of Revolution* came off the press and was being projected. She found that her colleagues were not following the same manner of projection that she undertook in the Marx Centenary tour:
* In 1983, she wrote a letter to the youth of News and Letters Committees "On the Needed Total Uprooting of the Old and the Creation of New Human Relations," August 13, 1983, appealing to them to become "thought-divers":

> [T]o engage in this battle of ideas ... it is not only the post-Marx Marxists we challenge but *all* alternatives to *Marx's* Marxism.... What has made this appeal to the youth appear so urgent to me is that, at one and the same time, we not only confront the objective situation of a nuclear world filled with economic recession and political retrogression as well as altogether too many aborted, unfinished revolutions turned into their very opposite, but also the fact that Marx's all encompassing revolution in permanence, which desires to becomes ground also of organization, has, until *RLWLKM* been left at the implicit stage (*PON*, 288).

The following year she wrote another letter to the youth comrades, "On Listening to Marx Think as Challengers to All Post-Marx Marxists" (June 5, 1984 *RDC* #8185). She began this letter expressing why Marxist-Humanism had singled out youth as a revolutionary force and recalled early work of projection after *Marxism and Freedom* was published. In turning to the 1980s she quoted from the 1982 Perspectives: "philosophy itself does not reach its full articulation until it has discovered the right organizational form." Then she spoke to the difficulties the youth and all the committees were having in projecting Marxist-Humanism organizationally:

> It is that organizational form, News and Letters Committees, which is the test of whether you fully understand *what* the "body of ideas" called Marxist-Humanism *is*. To discuss this year's expression of it is surely not an administrative matter (for example, who will do the column?) Rather, it is a question of: What ideas, what challenges are to be projected in the column. . . . How will our work in Latin American support committees or the anti-nuclear movement be expressed differently from other years when the uniqueness of Marxist-Humanism got subordinated to activity *sans* philosophy? . . . And, above all, how could *self*-development become so separated from the Universal, or what is even worse, made the equivalent of the Universal? Isn't it because the *organizational* form of Marxist-Humanism, of philosophy of revolution in permanence, isn't made primary in our own minds? . . .
>
> Since you didn't seem to be overly pre-occupied with such tasks last year, permit me to quote the final paragraph of my letter of Aug. 13, 1983: "When we talk about 'thought-divers' we can see that Marx was the greatest of all. That's what I'm really appealing to the youth to do. Becoming a thought diver and an activist in this period demands nothing short of *practicing* the challenge to all post-Marx Marxists, and thereby creating such new ground for organization,

such concretization of Marx's revolution in permanence, as to find a new way to let the actual revolution *be*."

- In a letter to Women's Liberation–News & Letters Committee in 1982 after *Rosa Luxemburg, Women's Liberation, and Marx's Philosophy of Revolution* has gone to press she proposed a new paragraph for the text on women's liberationists as both "revolutionary force *and* Reason." She then continued:

> My point in making these two suggestions for additions is that this sort of thing must be in each one's mind very nearly every time they speak on the new book. Each one must not only concretize the book further, day in and day out, for it's only in that way that the projection of *Rosa Luxemburg, Women's Liberation and Marx's Philosophy of Revolution* will result not only in organizational growth, but, indeed, in helping to lay the ground for the American Revolution (August 20, 1982, *SRDC* #15320).

In 1984, after the Luxemburg book had been out more than a year, Dunayevskaya sent out a Dear Revolutionary Sisters letter, which announced that a collection of her work on Women's Liberation would be published. She then added:

> Despite my vehement opposition to the Kantian category, "ought," I'm forced to use it because there is no other way to express the need I feel for us to confront the reality that during the whole period since the publication of *Rosa Luxemburg, Women's Liberation and Marx's Philosophy of Revolution*, there has not been a single breakthrough review in the so-called feminist press. To me, that signifies that a more *philosophic* breakthrough on Women's Liberation must somehow be worked out, without waiting for the publication of this new collection of old writings with a new introductory summation. I would like to propose that you take advantage of the pre-convention period to write out a short of balance sheet from which a new concretization—I mean new projection—of Marxist-Humanism for the WLM can flow....
> Let's see what comes "out of" individual self-criticism (*RDC* #8183).

- The most comprehensive critique Dunayevskaya made for News and Letter Committees in this period was within the 1984-85 Perspectives, "The Movements from Theory as Well as from Practice vs. the Great Artificer, Ronald Reagan, for whom the Whole World is a Stage." After delivering the talk (July 7, 1984), Dunayevskaya felt compelled to rewrite the entire third section, "Not By Practice Alone: The Movement From Theory" (*PON*, 273). No summary or synthesis of this document could do justice to its comprehensiveness. Its thrust was to trace the movement from theory, which was present in each of Dunayevskaya major writings: "That movement from theory becomes the uniqueness of Marxist-Humanist philosophy and our original contribution of *Marx's* Marxism."

The practice of News and Letters Committees in the 1980s was not projecting the uniqueness of Marxist-Humanist philosophy at a time when *Rosa Luxemburg, Women's Liberation and Marx's Philosophy of Revolution* had been published, creating a "trilogy of revolution," with *Marxism and Freedom* and *Philosophy and Revolution*. Dunayevskaya's dissatisfaction gave birth to the "Not By Practice Alone the Movement from Theory" rewritten section of the Perspectives to provide a pathway for her colleagues to reorganize.

In one of her Talking to Myself documents from 1987, "What *Is* Marxist-Humanism? How to Project It At Momentous Historic Moments?," she wrote of the period when the Luxemburg book came out, and what she found lacking among her colleagues was her type of Marxist-Humanist projection that led to her rewriting of the "Not By Practice Alone" section of the 1984-85 Perspectives:

> *What was missing in 1983 was not just the single element but the totally new category—Post-Marx Marxism.* I began suddenly feeling that there couldn't have been this big division between what I was saying and what our comrades were hearing *if* from the Center as well as at the Locals, there was a profound comprehension of that little phrase, Post-Marx Marxism. Shadowing somewhere in the background seemed to be emerging a difference, not just between Marxist-Humanists and non-Marxist-Humanists, but *within* Marxist-Humanism. Indeed, it held over until the Convention, which is why I felt so utterly mad and insisted on re-writing the final section, "Not by Practice Alone."
>
> Marxist-Humanism was hungering for some [Marxist-Humanists] to experience a shock of recognition of its Uniqueness, Universality, rather than particular and smartness, for the moment when the Self-Determination of the Idea and the Self-Bringing Forth of Liberty finally become one.
>
> I also felt that each one of us took a single element in *RLWLKM*—a single element only—like the Women, [Women's Liberation], or making [Rosa Luxemburg] the heroine, or the Black Dimension, or Organization—rather than the book as a totality, and that totality as a new beginning for all to work out, seeing that it is rooted in '57-'59 as the founder of [Marxist-Humanism] projected it (*SRDC* #10869, 10873, 10874).

III. Towards Dialectics of Organization and Philosophy

"I'm not ready to give any definitive answer on the philosophic-historic question on organization—I'm already thinking a whole new book is necessary for that before we would concretize organizational responsibility for the philosophy we have founded. Let's all start thinking seriously of what exactly is involved in accepting organizational responsibility for the philosophy of Marxist-Humanism"—Resident Editorial Board Minutes, October 22, 1984.

"Philosophy itself does not reach its full articulation until it has discovered the right organizational form"—Marxist-Humanist Perspectives, 1982-83.

In the mid-1980s, Dunayevskaya began research on a new work on organization. Her entire revolutionary life had been lived within Marxist organization. From Communist youth organizations in the 1920s, to Trotskyist organizations in the 1930s and 1940s. The State-Capitalist Tendency which she co-founded, while remaining in the Trotskyist movement in the 1940s, came to reject the vanguard party form of organization. Upon leaving Trotskyism (1951), the Tendency formed Correspondence Committees as a de-centralized form of organization. In the late 1940s, the three co-leaders of the Tendency, under the prodding of James, began to seek out "dialectic of the party" within Hegel's writings. As we have seen, Dunayevskaya in her 1953 Letters, began with the Tendency's search for dialectic of the party. However, in reaching the three final paragraphs of *Philosophy of Mind*, she had moved beyond the party: " We have entered the new society." After the split between Dunayevskaya and James, she and her colleagues formed News and Letters Committees.

The Committees began *News & Letters* newspaper and assigned Dunayevskaya the task of restating the philosophy of Marxism anew in book form. *Marxism and Freedom* (1957) discussed revolutionary organization in a number of different ways. Of particular importance were the various forms of self-organization of masses from the early worker organizing of the 1840s to the 1848 Revolutions of spontaneous worker organization as well as the Communist League. Later forms were seen in the Paris Commune, the Russian Soviets, the East Europe Revolts and Revolutions, as well as the self-organization involved in the 1955-56 Montgomery Bus Boycott. The book explored radical political organizations of the 19th century, such as the Communist League, the First Working Men's International, and Lassalle's General German Worker's Association. A special category was made of the Second International by Dunayevskaya, which she called Organizational Interlude. For the 20th century, one chapter on Russia was titled "Forms of Organization: The Relationship of the Spontaneous Self-Organization of the Proletariat to the Vanguard Party."

Philosophy and Revolution (1973) continued discussion of spontaneous forms as well as the vanguard party. In addition, the question of organization and its relation to Marxist-Humanist philosophy was taken up in many different ways in the Perspective Theses and Organizational Reports for News and Letters national gatherings of the period, as well as in discussions in the Resident Editorial Board of News and Letters Committees.

A new stage was reached with Dunayevskaya's writing of *Rosa Luxemburg, Women's Liberation, and Marx's Philosophy of Revolution*. In forging the category post-Marx Marxism as pejorative, Dunayevskaya had worked out a chapter titled "The Philosopher of Permanent Revolution Creates New Ground for Organization." This chapter was an important point of departure in Dunayevskaya's decision to probe the question of organization anew.

In the 1981 Perspectives to News and Letters Committees, delivered as the manuscript for *Rosa Luxemburg, Women's Liberation and Marx's Philosophy of Revolution* was being readied for publication, she wrote:

> The philosophic concept of leadership becomes correctly, with us, the projection of Marx's Humanism. That is to say, philosophy of revolution rather than the vanguardist party. It becomes all the more imperative that we project all the new moments in Marx that we did discover. And that is not limited to the new in organizational form—committee-form against the "party-to-lead"—*that didn't separate theory from practice.*
> We have all too often stopped at the committee-form of organization rather than the inseparability of that from philosophy. And it is the philosophy that is new, unique, our special historic contribution that enabled us to find historic continuity, the link to Marx's Humanism. It is this which is totally new, *not* the committee-form of organization, as crucial as that is (reproduced in 1991 edition of *Rosa Luxemburg, Women's Liberation and Marx's Philosophy of Revolution*, xxxi).

In 1983, after publication, Dunayevskaya added a paragraph just before the final paragraph for the entire text. It read:

> This is the further challenge to the form of organization which we have worked out as the committee-form rather than the "party-to-lead." But, though committee-form and "party-to-lead" are opposites, they are not absolute opposites. At the point when the theoretic-form reaches philosophy, the challenge demands that we synthesize not only the new relations of theory to practice, and all the forces of revolution, but philosophy's "suffering, patience and labor of the negative," i.e., experiencing absolute negativity. *Then and only then* will we succeed in a revolution that will achieve a class-less, non-racist, non-sexist, truly human, truly new society. That which Hegel judged to be the synthesis of the "Self-Thinking Idea" and the "Self-Bringing Forth of Liberty," Marxist-Humanism holds, is what Marx had called the new society. The many paths to get there are not easy to work out (reproduced in 1991 edition of *Rosa Luxemburg, Women's Liberation and Marx's Philosophy of Revolution*, xxxviii).

Dunayevskaya ended her August 26, 1983 letter accompanying this paragraph as follows: "With this final addition we have come to the question of Organization as likewise inseparable from the concept of 'revolution in permanence.'"

The door was opened for her labors on her new work on organization. In 1986-87 multiple strands were created by Dunayevskaya's new studies:

(1) She again examined her May 12 and 20, 1953 Letters on Hegel's Absolutes to trace out "the many universals inherent in it." One dimension that came forth was a changed view of Lenin's philosophic ambivalence. A second dimension was working out more precisely her separation from C.L.R. James on the dialectic. Thus the difference between his "dialectic of the party," and her 1986-

87 working out "dialectics of organization and philosophy" could be seen as originating in her Letters on Hegel's Absolutes.

(2) She returned to Hegel's writings, particularly his *Phenomenology of Mind*. Within the final paragraph of its ultimate chapter, Absolute Knowledge, she found a discussion of organization that spoke to the problematic of Dialectics of Organization and Philosophy. She also returned to the Third Attitude to Objectivity in the smaller *Logic*, finding new insights on organization.

(3) Marx's concept of organization, particularly his work in the First International and on the Paris Commune was probed.

(4) She researched post-Marx concepts of organization, and she asked a number of her colleagues to assist on research in areas from the First International, to Council Communism, to forms of organization arising from the Spanish Civil War and other mass movements.

(5) She continued a critical examination of the philosophical-organizational practice of News and Letters Committees.

Her extensive work of 1986-87, which remained unfinished at the time of her death, has been preserved as Vol. XII, *Supplement to the Raya Dunayevskaya Collection*, and totals close to 1,000 pages of letters, presentations to her News and Letters colleagues, and journalism. Of particular importance were Talking To Myself documents, which consisted of notes, drafts of works, various critiques. These were often dictated to one of her secretaries. A few were written out by her. It is from this body of material that strands of her unfinished work are discussed here. This discussion is a limited one, presented to give an indication of the direction of Dunayevskaya's work on Dialectics of Organization and Philosophy. There is no substitute for one's own probing Volume XII of the *Raya Dunayevskaya Collection*.

New Perspectives on Lenin's Philosophic Ambivalence

In 1985 Dunayevskaya expressed one of the strands that would be important in her new work on organization.

> [I]n 1973 *Philosophy and Revolution* was mild on Lenin's ambivalence . . . [I]n embryo, I began arguing with Lenin in 1953, criticizing him for leaving out the final paragraph of AI [Absolute Idea], but even in '83 in *Rosa Luxemburg, Women's Liberation, and Marx's Philosophy of Revolution* when we had made clear through the years that we had separated ourselves from Lenin's vanguard party, I didn't tighten Lenin's failure philosophically to deal with the Party. And that is why the fifth book is more necessary than ever (Resident Editorial Board Minutes, June 17, 1985 *SRDC* #16652).

By 1986 Dunayevskaya began to work out the philosophic source of Lenin's failure to reorganize his organizational conceptions. It was no longer sufficient to work out the political reasons for his organizational attitude. Her studies on Lenin's philosophic ambivalence gained a new perspective. The center of her sharper critique was not on Lenin's failure philosophically to deal with the Party, but on the fact that in his 1914-15 Notebooks on Hegel's *Science of Logic* Lenin remained *philosophically* on the threshold of the Absolute Idea, in the chapter on the Idea of Cognition. Lenin's ambivalence was rooted in the incompleteness of his journey into the final Absolute Idea chapter of the *Logic*.

In her May 12, 1953 Letter on the Absolute Idea chapter of *Science of Logic* she had called attention to Lenin's stopping:

> I am shaking all over for we have come to where we part from Lenin. I mentioned before that, although in the *approach* to the Absolute Idea Lenin had mentioned that man's cognition not only reflects the objective world but creates it but *within the chapter* he never developed it. Objective world connections, materialism, dialectical materialism it is true, but not the object and subject as one fully developed—that's what he saw. Then he reaches the last paragraph [of the *Science of Logic*]: "For the Idea posits itself as the absolute unity of the pure Notion and its Reality, and thus gathers itself into the immediacy of Being; and in doing so, as totality in this form, it is Nature."
>
> There Lenin stops—it is the *beginning* of the last paragraph—and he says: "This phrase on the *last* page of the Logic is exceedingly remarkable. The transition of the logical idea to *Nature*. Stretching a hand to materialism. This is not the last phrase of the *Logic*, but further till the end of the page is unimportant."
>
> But, my dear Vladimir Ilyitch, it is not true; the end of that page *is* important; we of 1953, we who have lived three decades after you and tried to absorb all you have left us, we can tell you that (*PON*, 22).

Dunayevskaya proceeded to quote from the final paragraph after Lenin stopped, including "the Notion . . . arises to perfect its self-liberation in the Philosophy of Spirit, and to discover the highest Notion of itself in that logical science of the pure Notion which forms a Notion of itself." It is to *Philosophy of Spirit (Mind)*, especially its final three paragraphs, that Dunayevskaya proceeds to in her May 20 Letter.

In the years after 1953 Dunayevskaya did not publicly pursue Lenin's shortening of his journey into *Science of Logic*. In *Marxism and Freedom* (1958) her "Lenin and the Dialectic: A Mind in Action" presented Lenin's encounter with Hegel's dialectic as the ground for what she termed the Great Divide in Marxism. In *Philosophy and Revolution* (1973), her chapter on Lenin, "The Shock of Recognition and the Philosophic Ambivalence of Lenin," the discussion of ambivalence was not about Lenin's commentary in his *Notebooks* but about his failure to publish them and discuss them publicly, his ambivalence toward his own work. However, in the mid-1980s Dunayevskaya began a further study. In 1985 she called her 1973 *Philosophy and Revolution* "mild on Lenin's ambivalence."

In a 1986 letter to a non-Marxist Hegel scholar she developed her new perception of Lenin's philosophic ambivalence by following in detail his *Notebooks* as he approached the end of the *Logic*, and instead of continuing there, switched to the briefer, less developed smaller *Logic*, preferring its end in paragraph 244 to that of the *Science of Logic*:

> The truth is that Lenin had begun seriously to consult the smaller *Logic* at the section on the Idea, which begins in the smaller *Logic* with paragraph 213. When Lenin completed Chapter 2, "The Idea of Cognition," he didn't really go to Chapter 3, "The Absolute Idea," but first proceeded for seven pages with his own "translation" (interpretation). This is on pp. 212-19 of Vol. 38 of his *Collected Works* (Excerpts from the letter were reproduced as part of "New Thoughts on Dialectics of Organization and Philosophy," *Philosophy and Revolution* 1989, 2003 editions).

Dunayevskaya briefly commented on Lenin's interpretation and then noted: "But I consider that he is still only on the *threshold* of the Absolute Idea. Indeed, all that follows p. 219 in his Notes shows that to be true, and explains why Lenin proceeded on his own after the end of his Notes on the Absolute Idea, and returned to the smaller *Logic*" (*P&R* xxxviii).

1980s Views of Hegel's *Phenomenology* and Smaller *Logic* with Regard to Organization

• A return to Hegel, particularly his *Phenomenology of Spirit*, became an important focal point of Dunayevskaya's studies of 1986-87. In a Talking to Myself document of June 1986, she wrote:

> [W]e haven't understood that *Phenomenology of Mind* (1807, not 1830) projected *ground* for the Absolutes, and they haven't understood that *ground* because it was the French Revolution. And Hegel was saying very passionately: "look at what happened in France, and we haven't even developed a single dialectical category, and we are talking philosophy time and time again." The whole philosophy of 2,500 years has to find a new language, and here it is. Academics had no vision then and they have no vision now. The whole truth is that between 1807 and 1831 (death) it was a matter of developing that movement, *historic* movement, and that vision Marx alone saw. And he saw it because he was in a new age and needed a new language to express the forces and the Reason of Revolution both *con*tinuity and *dis*continuity of the dialectic and of the new European Revolutions (1840s) (*SRDC* #10769).

In September 1986, in a "Random Thoughts While Working on *Dialectics of Organization*" she wrote:

> The one thing that is new and surprised me for being new this first week of working on the book is that somehow the difference is *not* on the difference between Party and forms of organization born out of spontaneity, *both* of which

are organization. Rather, it is the dialectics of philosophy and dialectics of organization.

It is this that makes me think that I have too long neglected *Phenomenology*; that it is not only out of "defense" of Hegel that Marx considered that as the greatest work and the most creative of Hegel. Rather, it was because dialectics as methodology and not merely as instrument or tool was actually more creatively developed there then when it was detailed as categories and ended in Absolutes (*SRDC* #10770).

She then made notes on Gustav Emil Mueller's commentary on *Phenomenology* from Walter Steinkraus' *New Studies in Hegel's Philosophy*. The following day she made notes on her 1960 study of Hegel's *Phenomenology*. She commented on her own way of dividing *Phenomenology:*

> The whole idea of the present is the Dialectic of Philosophy itself, and how no matter how "great" we were—and it took plenty of chutzpuh to have divided the whole of the *Phenomenology* into just two parts: I. Comprising Consciousness, Self-Consciousness and Reason; and II. Comprising Spirit, Religion, and Absolute Knowledge.
> The point was, that, politically, what was preoccupying us was the before and after of a revolution that goes so perversely in such opposite directions as did the Russian. It has "cleansing" in the sense that it removes all rubbish the erudition thrown ones way—quantity of facts *ad nauseum*, and leaves out turning points that historic [history] directs.
> On the other hand, or at the same time, the "cleansing" unfortunately turns you away from philosophy *as philosophy*, in this case dialectics proper, METHODOLOGY (*SRDC* #10772).

Dunayevskaya continued to discuss her notes, and then turned to a 1982 academic discussion on the meaning of Absolute Spirit by Louis Dupré, H.S. Harris and Quentin Lauer. Excerpting and commenting on their discussion, she wrote:

> The whole point *is the timeliness* of this discussion is not that it is a commemoration of 150 years. Quite the contrary. It is precisely because, rather than a commemoration, it actually answers today's problems and in doing so actually elicits *organizational* questions that you wouldn't think is anywhere near the interest of Hegel either in his time or in ours, is what makes it so contemporary (#10777).

In November 1986, Dunayevskaya decided to reproduce her 1960 summary of *Phenomenology* with a new introduction. "In a fundamental sense, an Introduction is also an Overview, though that overview be not the overview of the specific subject reprinted, but what others especially when that other is a Karl Marx, have said on the subject" (#10822). The 1960 summary notes were published in a special issue of *News & Letters,* May 8, 1987, with a new introduction. Dunayevskaya considered this to only be Part I of the introduction she intended to write. Notes for a projected Part II of "Why Hegel's *Phenomenology*? Why Now?" are found in *SRDC* #10883.

At a Resident Editorial Board Meeting of March 23, 1987 (*SRDC* #10727) Dunayevskaya spoke of a new reading she had been working out on Hegel's use of the word organization twice on the final page of *Phenomenology*:

> I turned back to Hegel's *Phenomenology* focusing fully on the last page with its very difficult, abstract climax that leads, at one and the same time, to the Absolute and its Golgotha.
> For the first time, I abbreviated that whole page (p. 808 in Baillie's translation, p. 492-93 in Miller's) into two sentences and suddenly saw that in Hegel's use of the word Organization, twice in the same paragraph, something that could be considered the actual ground for our concept of the relationship both of spontaneity and the party *and* its inseparability from organization of thought. Read it for yourself and see what you can work out, but here is what I saw, precisely because I'm working on a book on Dialectics of Organization and Philosophy: The two types of organization Hegel has in mind are, first "as free existence" in its varying "historic form," what we would call the movement from practice at historic turning points. Secondly, Hegel is defining "intellectually comprehended" organization and concludes, "the two together, or History intellectually comprehended form as once recollection and the Golgotha of Absolute Spirit." My point is that it was no accident that Marx judged the *Phenomenology of Mind* as the most creative act of all of Hegel's works, and where he began not just a critique of the Hegelian Dialectic, but the finding of a new continent of thought and revolution; both indeed had become the ground for what we are working out on the Dialectic of Organization and Philosophy.

While Dunayevskaya considered the way Hegel introduced Organization twice in the last paragraph of *Phenomenology* as "central to me now" (April 3, 1987 *SRDC* #10880), she did not develop this further before her death.

• A second return to Hegel in this period with regard to organization was to a new reading of the Third Attitude to Objectivity found in the smaller *Logic*. This attitude, which contained Hegel's critique of intuitionism had, as we noted earlier, been an important dimension of Dunayevskaya's work on Hegel as far back as her 1961 summary notes on the smaller *Logic* (*PON*, 82) as well as a significant discussion in her *Philosophy and Revolution*. In those readings she had pointed to Hegel's view of intuitionism as a step backward to the separateness of thought and being. She noted Hegel calling such intuitionism in the hands of the philosopher Jacobi "reactionary."

In her new return to the Third Attitude in November and December 1986, she saw how the dimension of organization, in this case the church, entered into Hegel's critique.

> What excited me most about this attitude to objectivity is the manner in which Hegel brings in Organization. As early as paragraph 63 Hegel had lashed out against Jacobi's faith, in contrast to Faith: "The two things are radically dis-

tinct. Firstly, the Christian faith comprises in it an authority of the Church; but the faith of Jacobi's philosophy has no other authority than that of personal revelation." As we see, Hegel now has suddenly equated Organization to Principle, Doctrine: "And secondly, the Christian faith is a copious body of objective truth, a system of knowledge and doctrine; while the scope of the philosophic faith [intuitionism] is so utterly indefinite, that, while it has room for faith of the Christian, it equally admits belief in the divinity of the Dalai Lama, the ox, or the monkey" (reproduced in "New Thoughts on Dialectics of Organization and Philosophy," Introduction to Third Edition of *Philosophy and Revolution*, xxxvi-xliv).

For Dunayevskaya it was not the specificity of religious doctrine and the church that was her focal point, but the relationship of a body of ideas and its organizational expression: "[As to] my latest self-critique on Organization . . . on that question I also see Hegel in a new way. That is to say, the dialectical relationship of principles (in this case the Christian doctrine) and the organization (the Church) are analyzed as if they were inseparables" (*P&R*, xliii).

Critiquing the Gap Between Philosophic Expression and Organizational Practice of Marxist-Humanism in the 1980s: II. 1986-87

As Dunayevskaya reached toward a summation of the Marxist-Humanist Idea as a new beginning, she saw a gap between what she was projecting and the practice of News and Letters Committees. Earlier we presented manifestations of the gap as Dunayevskaya articulated it in the mid 1980s. Here we want to examine the gap as it was manifested in 1986-87, a time when the twin perspectives of the organization were preparing for and issuing a bi-weekly *News & Letters*, and "how the organization as a whole is part of the collectivity of working out The Dialectics of Organization and Philosophy" (SRDC #10677).

• In the Spring of 1986, as the News and Letters Committees were preparing to transform *News & Letters* to a bi-weekly, Ronald Reagan launched a missile attack against Libya. Though the April *News & Letters* was almost ready to be printed, Dunayevskaya immediately responded, asking for changes to be introduced into the lead article and the editorial. She then turned to write a *"Special, Special, Special,* Preliminary Marxist-Humanist Statement on the Last 48 Hours," sharing with her colleagues the response and presenting its context and meaning. "[The changes were made] *as if [News & Letters] were a daily paper.* Such challenges are the proof that philosophy is action and action is Marxist-Humanist organization as it responds to the objective situation as well as the immediate subjective re-organization needed" (March 27, 1986 SRDC #11003). The question was not of an isolated imperialist action of the Reagan administration, but could it be as well preparation for full-scale war?

On a much larger historic scale, Dunayevskaya recalled the period of the Spanish Civil War, when some dissident Trotskyists were asking whether "the actions of the Stalinists were not only those of murderous bureaucrats 'factionally' getting rid of the Trotskyists in Spain. . . . couldn't . . . involve more than just Spanish fascism? Couldn't both Stalin's Russia and Hitler's Germany be testing their weapons for World War?" Dialectical method revealed the need to pose this broader context. It was this type of context that Dunayevskaya asked her colleagues to consider: "What it involves is the whole concept of Archives. It is that which demonstrates our historic right to exist. It is not just a question of being an independent Marxist-tendency. Marxist-Humanism is epochal in that it sums up the three decades of a movement from practice to theory which is itself a form of theory, and is inseparable from the full-blown philosophy of revolution."

Two weeks later Dunayevskaya addressed a Dear Colleagues letter to the leadership of News and Letters Committees: "I would like to discuss with you . . . what has been disturbing me ever since it appeared to me that the uniqueness of the Marxist-Humanist analysis in my 'Special, Special, Special' seemed to have escaped some of us." She reviewed and expanded upon her "Special" letter, noting that "though I did not separate that sudden objective new event from Marxist-Humanism's tasks as revolutionary socialists on the road to this bi-weekly . . . it became separated in the discussion" subsequently carried on by her colleagues. Her focus was on *"organizational responsibility for Marxist-Humanism."* Rooting herself in the context of Hegel's "attitudes to objectivity" she noted:

> The attitudes involved in discussions on the "Special," by not making inseparable the events and our concrete tasks—from distributions of the April *N&L*, through finances for the bi-weekly, to practicing organizational responsibility for Marxist-Humanism, for *N&L*, as if it were part on one's *daily* life—simply don't measure up to the uniqueness of Marxist-Humanism, which considers the Universal and concrete as one" (April 10, 1986 *SRDC* #11005).

In a second Dear Colleagues letter (April 28, 1986 *SRDC* #11009), she again posed the gap between the philosophy of Marxist-Humanism and organizational practice:

> No member would deny organizational responsibility for the philosophy of Marxist-Humanism; indeed, the leadership may feel deeply insulted to have ABC's cited. Yet isn't it as much ABC to practice self-critique concretely as objective crises arise and demand that they be related to such "internal" questions as preparing for a bi-weekly?
> Was that really everyone's preoccupation at the time Ronald Reagan assaulted Libya from the Gulf of Sidra? It is true that everyone at once acted against Reagan. But was there a simultaneous projection of the uniqueness of the Marxist-Humanist analysis at the mass demonstrations? Was there a total grasp

of the "Special-Special-Special," which had been written within 48 hours, as well as of the changes in the Lead and Editorial of the April *N&L* as it was on the presses?

• Another manifestation of Dunayevskaya's perception of the gap in News and Letters Committees can be seen in her discussion of the relation of preparation for the bi-weekly and organization growth of the Committees:

> In thinking about what part of *Dialectics of Organization and Philosophy*, I will be able to give a whiff of to the REB when I return Dec. 1, and at the end of the year in the sum-up, I became more and more conscious of the very near-disappearance from our vocabulary of the phrase "organizational growth." The fact that we totally opposed the old radicals' "recruitment mentality" should not (I repeat should *not*) exclude organization growth for Marxist-Humanists. The very opposite is the case. The deeper we delve into philosophy the more urgent as well as inseparable does organizational growth become. Indeed, the Dialectic of philosophy—and I have been doing a lot of deep diving into it—has opened an altogether new vista to organizational growth (Dear Colleagues letter, Nov. 3, 1986 *SRDC* #11574).

She saw the need for her colleagues to recognize the difference between those who identify with one or another aspect of News and Letters writings and yet not to the *idea* of Marxist-Humanism. Individual "self-development" was not a substitute for the kind of development that would occur by joining revolutionary organization "as part of the creation of a totally new human being, of a new society." "Organizational growth" could not be allowed to disappear as a goal.

In another letter, Dunayevskaya solicited the views of two of her colleagues,

> on those inseparables that seem to be hard to see as inseparables—organizational growth and the bi-weekly to which it is integral. The integrality of organizational growth with the bi-weekly, as the integrality of the Archives with philosophy of Marxist-Humanism is "taken for granted" in the belief that since we are all Marxist-Humanists, no concretization is need for either the Archives or the Dialectic. . . . It came as a shock to me to suddenly realize, as I was working of the Dialectic of Philosophy on the same level as the Dialectic of Organization (the book-to-be), that the phase, "organizational growth," had very nearly disappeared from our vocabulary. And yet, that is *precisely* why I was so anxious in proposing the transformation of *N&L* into a bi-weekly (Letter to I. and G. November 30, 1986 *SRDC* #11580).

She continued discussion of contradictions in the projection of Marxist-Humanism in the Resident Editorial Board meeting of March 23, 1987 with a report titled "What Has Happened to our Projection of Marxist-Humanism—that a difference seems to have emerged in two aspects of the dialectics of organization between: 1) the concept, and 2) organizational growth as a 'practical question'? We have to see that this doesn't develop, because nothing short of the task of projecting [Marxist-Humanism] is the issue" (*SRDC* #10727).

It was in this meeting that she presented her new reading of the final paragraph of Absolute Knowledge in *Phenomenology* as speaking to the question of organization. This was not accidental. Dunayevskaya's concept of critique when it was a self-critique of Marxist-Humanism was rooted in dialectics as negation of the negation. The first negation or critique of what is, was inseparable from a second negation, a posing of a pathway forward. This was not a psychological question of finding something to "feel good about." Rather it was at the heart of dialectical thinking.

She articulated a concept of organizational responsibility in relation to philosophic responsibility:

> What I'm trying to say is when there is a group, whether it is two or 20 that feels so strongly about the present and the future, there you have an organization that feels responsible for that body of ideas, in this case, the post-WW II world. [Added in handwriting:] Not just organizationally but philosophically responsible to History as to Today as well as to future. (#10728).

Finally, in the presentation prepared on Dialectics of Organization and Philosophy (June 1, 1987 *The Philosophic Moment of Marxist-Humanism*),[2] Dunayevskaya asked the organization to consider changing the form of *News & Letters* to a 12-page monthly form rather than a 8-page bi-weekly as what the organization needed at that present moment. Aspects of this presentation will be taken up in the following section.

"One Possible Outline for Dialectics of Organization and Philosophy"

It was no accident that Dunayevskaya's 1953 Letters on Hegel's Absolutes, thirty-four years after they were written, were, at one and the same time, designated by her as the Philosophic Moment of Marxist-Humanism, and seen as integral to the process of working on Dialectics of Organization and Philosophy. Marxist-Humanism was the name Dunayevskaya gave to the philosophic re-creation of Marx's Marxism in the post-World War II world as her first book, *Marxism and Freedom*, was finished. But the designation of the Letters on Hegel's Absolutes as Philosophic Moment only came as part of her 1986-87 work on organization, as she returned once again to 1953 to probe was she called the many universals inherent.

In returning to the 1953 period, Dunayevskaya examined what separated her from C.L.R. James. By 1950 both James and Dunayevskaya had turned away from the elitist vanguard party to lead as the form for revolutionary organization. What was it to be replaced with? James felt they needed to search out dialectic of the party in Hegel's Absolutes. His colleagues, Lee and Dunayevskaya, followed his lead. In the process Dunayevskaya came to a far richer reading of Hegel's Absolutes. In 1953 she articulated this as a movement from practice to theory as well as from theory to practice. In 1973 she deepened this development, articulating it as Absolute Negativity as New Beginning.

By 1986-87 Dunayevskaya, rooted in 1953's philosophic moment, sought to work out the dialectics of organization after more than three decades of philosophic and practical labor.

She found inherent in her 1953 Letters a view of organization that was poles apart from James's "dialectic of the party." She returned to James's *Notes on Dialectics*, where he had sought to relate spontaneity and organization as opposites as follows: "Now, however, we shall, to conclude Essence, take a term that is on all lips: Lenin's concept of organization. Organization. *You know nothing about organization unless at every step you relate it to its opposite, spontaneity* . . . That is something *new*. Merely to *say* that" (quoted in "Key to CLR's Notes on the Dialectic." *SRDC* #10825).

To James, the spontaneous mass struggles were the opposite of the vanguard party to lead. They alone created a different organizational form and therefore solved "dialectic of the party." Indeed, though in his 1948 *Notes on Dialectics* he had probed Absolute Idea, when he turned to Hegel's *Philosophy of Mind* he felt there was nothing there "for us." The philosophic probing stopped. The right organizational form was seen by James as the answer to "dialectic of the party."

In contrast, Dunayevskaya not only embraced the spontaneous mass struggles historically, as her writings on the Black struggles and miners' struggles during World War II show, but concretely practiced that conception in her relation to the Miners' General Strike of 1949-50. She had theoretically structured all her books, beginning with *Marxism and Freedom* to embrace the movements from practice and their mass organizational form, which she saw as a form of theory. However, at the same time she did not shift all responsibility for theory or organization onto the shoulders of the masses. The mass struggles from below became catalyst for her continued philosophic digging. In her May 12, 1953 letter she stated "I am concerned only with the dialectic . . . of that *type* of grouping like ours, be it large or small, and *its* relationship to the mass" (*PON*, 16). In her May 20, 1953 letter she saw Absolute Mind as "We have entered the new society."

Within Dunayevskaya's 1953 letters there was a dialectics of organization that held as one spontaneous forms from below and the dialectic "of that *type* of grouping like ours." They both strove toward a new society: the masses implicitly in their practice; the revolutionary grouping through its philosophic-organizational labor to project revolution in permanence. With her 1986-87 work on Dialectics of Organization and Philosophy, Dunayevskaya was seeking to bring to full flowering what had been implicit on organization in the 1953 letters.

Here are several articulations of Dunayevskaya's evolving view of the problematic of dialectics of organization and philosophy as she saw it in 1986-87:

* The one thing that is new and surprised me for being new this first week of working on the book is that somehow the difference is *not* on the difference between Party and forms of organization born out of spontaneity, *both* of which are organization. Rather, it is the dialectics of philosophy and dialectics of organization (Sept. 24, 1986 *SRDC* #10770).
* What I'm driving at, is that unless we work out the dialectic in philosophy itself, the dialectic of organization, whether it be from the vanguard party or that born from spontaneity, would be just different forms of organization, instead of an organization that is so inseparable from its philosophic ground that form and content are one (Oct. 6, 1986 *SRDC* #10789).
* The most difficult of all tasks that confronts us, indeed, that has confronted all post-Marx Marxists who have tried to get out from under some form of statification—and none more so than those like us who have been hewing a road back to Marx's Marxism—is to project that it is not the Party or the leader or leadership, but *philosophy*, the body of ideas, the dialectic of ideas and organization, as against the party as well as distinct from forms of organization born out of spontaneity. While these, of course, are correct, as against the elitism and ossification of the Party, the truth is that these forms also search for an organization different from their own in the sense that they want to be sure that there is a totality of theory and practice against the establishment of a power that has stopped dead with its conquest of state power—in short, altogether new beginnings ("The Year of Only 8 Months" January, 1987 *SRDC* # 10699-700).

In a Talking to Myself Document of Nov. 15, 1986 (*SRDC* #10815), Dunayevskaya wrote "Now then, the book to be, in the tentative sense in which I am willing to whisper about it now, is likewise finally developing the Dialectic *IN* philosophy, which makes us grasp that it is not that Party and form of spontaneity, though opposites, are absolute opposites[,] but that the absolute opposites that must be transcended but transcended in unity are organization and philosophy."

Doesn't this argue that dialectics of organization and dialectics of philosophy are not "stages," in which one is transcending first one and then the other? To separate philosophy and organization is to put a barrier in place of transcending. Philosophically, one gets thrown back to the threshold of the Absolutes, to the Idea of Cognition, caught in the practical idea, a "solving" of the organizational question. You cannot think about solving the dialectics of organization as a dialectics of the party, and only then move to a dialectics of philosophy. The two—organization and philosophy—need to be transcended together. Otherwise, you cannot philosophically move through Absolute Idea to Absolute Mind, and enter the new society as the actuality of a self-liberation.

In May 1987, Dunayevskaya had dictated "One possible outline for *Dialectics of Organization and Philosophy*." It is reproduced as deposited in the *Supplement to the Raya Dunayevskaya Collection* (#10922):

5/11/87

(Keep for pre-Plenum)

One possible outline for **Dialectics of Organization and Philosophy**

Parts

I **On Spontaneous forms of Organization vs. Vanguard Parties**

*Begin with our age

problem from Marx's day to ours.

Here include:

whole ? of PMM on org.
- Mx on organization, esp. IWA and relation to **Paris Commune**
- Engels and 2nd International→Erfurt
- Lenin on **What is to be Done?** → **State and Revolution** → last years, especially Trade Union debate
- Soviets as spontaneous forms of organization (Kronstadt?) NO? [& Rosa Luxemburg]
- Council Communism-- Pannekoek
- Spanish Revolution and Hungarian Revolution this NB

(?? Again, brings us to our age but can't solve here)

II **Hegel and Marx** -- on dialectics of philosphy and organization

- Hegel's **Phenomenology**, esp. Absolute Knowledge, esp. last paragraph on ? of Organization and Erinnerung
- Marx's "Critique of the Hegelian Dialectic" & vs. Lukacs' Young Hegel on end of **Phenomenology**
- Relation of Hegel/Marx-- **Critique of the Gotha Program** as ground but not sufficient itself.

III **Hegel and Lenin**

- ? of **forms** of organization is not answer
  --**What is to be Done?**/ **State and Revolution**'
- Lenin's **Philosophic Notebooks**-- not as in 1953 **or** 1973, but 1987.
- ? of "**Idea of Cognition**" and "**Absolute Idea**" in Lenin's **Philosophic Notebooks** --(as in letters)
- Hegel's own difference (**Science of Logic**/ Smaller **Logic**)
- (On Attitudes to Objectivity) in Hegel, in Lenin, in our age

IV **Dialectics of Organization and Philosophy in Post-World War II World**

- Miners' general strike/Cameroonian-- Third World revolutions (vs. CLR James)

(? ground & roof?) -- 1953 letters on Absolute Idea -- concentration on organization **and** on 3 final syllogisms

Dual movement is not alone, but Self-Thinking Idea= MHism

- MHism's **concept** of organization (Constitution)
- Introduction/Overview (of trilogy of revolution??)

This is on **ourselves**...

The outline was not a definitive form for Dunayevskaya's work. We cannot know the full direction and development that her work would have taken. Dunayevskaya did not see her book providing "the answer" to the question of organization: "[T]he book will not contain the answer, i.e., any kind of blueprint or any kind of finality of what type of organization is needed. That cannot possibly be known until it appears" (Talking to Myself Notes March 30, 1987 *SRDC* #10877). Indeed, after she had written what became Chapter 11 of *Rosa Luxemburg, Women's Liberation, and Marx's Philosophy of Revolution* "The Philosopher of Permanent Revolution Creates New Ground for Organization," she decided not to end with this chapter but to add a Chapter 12, "The Last Writings of Marx Point a Trail to the 1980s." In part this was because she did not wish the chapter on organization to be the final chapter and thus considered "the answer."

In the "In Lieu of Minutes of [Resident Editorial Board Meeting] of August 5, 1986 on Executive Session" she wrote,

> Or take the one reference . . . I listed as the Dialectic of the Party. For heaven sakes, what [a] way of hiding the really new and making it appear as if it is the 1987 answer to 1902-03. Believe me, I am not writing a new *What Is To Be Done* and taking that ground to answer the 'opposite' of the elitist party. . . . This is what we have rejected and this concept of the elitist party will be totally uprooted in the new book on the Dialectic of Organization (*SRDC* #10668).

What we do have on dialectics of organization and philosophy is the vast amount of material she had been working on prior to writing any draft chapters. The many strands of that work are present to study. They, together with the entire body of work of Raya Dunayevskaya, philosopher of Marxist-Humanism, form a rich tapestry for future labors. What she brought us toward was not an organizational answer, but the task of entering the new society:

> The negation of the negation will not be a generality, not even the generality of a new society for the old, but the specific of *self*-liberation, which is the humanism of the human *being*, as well as his philosophy (final sentence of "Rough Notes of Hegel's *Science of Logic*," *PON*, 73).
> The burning question of the day remains: What happens the day after [the revolution]? How can we continue Marx's unchaining of the Dialectic organizationally, with the principle he outlined in his *Critique of the Gotha Program?*
> The question of "What happens after?" gains crucial importance because of what it signals in self-development and self-flowering—"revolution in permanence." No one knows what it is, or can touch it, or decide upon it before it appears. It is not the task that can be fulfilled in just one generation. That is why it remains so elusive, and why the abolition of the division between mental and manual labor sound utopian. It has the future written all over it ("The Year of Only 8 Months," *SRDC* #10700).

¹ The paragraphs were published with further modifications by Dunayevskaya as the final chapter of her *Women's Liberation and the Dialectics of Revolution—Reaching for the Future* (1985).

² I am referring to the presentation as printed in *The Philosophic Moment of Marxist-Humanism* because it is presented in a more complete form than as excerpted in *Power of Negativity*.

Selected Bibliography

Works by Raya Dunayevskaya discussed

Archives
The Raya Dunayevskaya Collection and Supplement to the Raya Dunayevskaya Collection.
Wayne State University Archives of Labor and Urban Affairs, 5401 Cass Ave. Detroit, MI 48202.

Guides to the Collection and Supplement to the Collection, available from The Raya Dunayevskaya Memorial Fund, nandl@igc.apc.org

This collection is the definitive depository of the vast majority of Dunayevskaya's writings. It is divided into two parts: The *Raya Dunayevskaya Collection* was organized directly under Dunayevskaya's supervision in the 1970s and 1980s. The *Supplement* to the collection was organized after her death through the Raya Dunayevskaya Memorial Fund. The collection as a whole currently contains seventeen thousand pages and is available on microfilm.

Books

Marxism and Freedom, from 1776 until Today
original edition (New York: Bookman, 1958)
most recent edition (Amherst, New York: Humanity Books, 2000)

The Marxist-Humanist Theory of State Capitalism
(Chicago, News & Letters, 1992)

Philosophy and Revolution, from Hegel to Sartre and from Marx to Mao
original edition (New York: Delacorte, 1973)
most recent edition (Lanham, Maryland: Lexington, 2004)

Power of Negativity, Selected Writings on the Dialectic in Hegel and Marx
Edited by Peter Hudis and Kevin Anderson
(Lanham, Maryland: Lexington, 2002)

Rosa Luxemburg, Women's Liberation, and Marx's Philosophy of Revolution
original edition (New York: Humanities Press, 1982)
most recent edition (Champaign-Urbana: University of Illinois Press, 1991)

Women's Liberation and the Dialectics of Revolution
original edition (New Jersey: Humanities Press, 1985)
most recent edition (Detroit: Wayne State University Press, 1996)

Newspapers

Early newspaper writings
Many articles appeared in Trotskyist journals in the 1930, 40s and 50s. Some are available in the *Raya Dunayevskaya Collection*.

Correspondence, 1953-1954
Dunayevskaya wrote articles for a mimeographed and then printed *Correspondence* before *News & Letters* was founded. Selected articled available in the *Raya Dunayevskaya Collection*.

News & Letters, 1955-1987
Newspaper founded by Raya Dunayevskaya and her colleagues in 1955. Dunayevskaya wrote a column in each issue, originally titled Two Worlds; later called Theory/Practice. In addition, she wrote various lead articles and editorials. From 1975 onward, the Draft Perspectives for News and Letters Committees, authored by Dunayevskaya for the Resident Editorial Board of *News & Letters,* was published in the paper. Her writings from the paper are available in the *Raya Dunayevskaya Collection*. After Dunayevskaya's death, *News & Letters* has continued to publish many of her writings under the title "From the Marxist-Humanist Archives."

Selected Pamphlets

Many of Dunayevskaya writings were published as separate pamphlets issued by News and Letters Committees. Presently, some are available only in *The Raya Dunayevskaya Collection*.

American Civilization on Trial, 1963 (first edition), News & Letters.
Miners' General Strike of 1949-50 and the Birth of Marxist-Humanism, *(with Andy Philips),* News & Letters, 1984.

The Myriad Global Crises of the 1980s and the Nuclear World since World War II. News and Letters, 1986

Nationalism, Communism, Marxist-Humanism and the Afro-Asian Revolutions, News and Letters, 1959, expanded edition 1961.

Outline of Marx's Capital, Volume One. RDC # 324, mid 1940s.

Outline of Marx's Capital, Volume Two. RDC # 385, 1945.

The Philosophic-Moment of Marxist-Humanism, News and Letters, 1987.

Russia as a State-Capitalist Society, 1973, RDC #4760.

Working, Women for Freedom, includes essay, "Women as Thinkers and as Revolutionaries," by Dunayevskaya.

25 Years of Marxist-Humanism in the U.S.—A history of worldwide revolutionary developments, News and Letters, 1980.

Selected Articles, Presentations, Translations
(arranged by date.)

"The Union of Soviet Socialist Republics is a Capitalist Society," Workers Party Internal Discussion Bulletin. February, 1941. Reprinted by News and Letters, October, 1992.

"An Analysis of the Russian Economy," part of "The Nature of the Russian Economy," November, 1942. *RDC* #69. Reprinted in *The Marxist-Humanist Theory of State Capitalism*. News & Letters.

"Politics and Economics," November 1942 *RDC* #102.

"Labor and Society," 1942? *RDC* #87. Reprinted in *Marxist-Humanist Theory of State-Capitalism*.

"The Law of Value and Capitalist Society," August 1943, *RDC* #8895.

"A New Revision of Marxian Economics," *American Economic Review*, September 1944, *RDC* #209.

Correspondence with C.L.R. James and Grace Lee (Boggs), 1948-52.

RDC #1595-1744, #9209-9327.

Translation of Lenin's Abstract on Hegel's *Science of Logic*, 1949, *RDC* #1492. Appendix to *Marxism and Freedom* (1958 edition).

"Discussion led by Raya Dunayevskaya on the new form of book-in-the-making from two vantage points: American proletariat and Lenin's Philosophic Notebooks." Feb. 15, 1950, *RDC* # 1585.

"Stalin: Why He Behaved as He Did," in mimeographed *Correspondence* 1953, *RDC* #2194.

"Then and Now, 1920 and 1953," in mimeographed *Correspondence.* April 16, 1953, *RDC* #2184.

Letters on the Absolute Idea, May 12 and 20, 1953, *RDC* # 1797. Reprinted in *Power of Negativity.*

"Our Organization," July 1953, *RDC* #2042.

News & Letters, Vol. 1 No. 1 June 17, 1955. Dunayevskaya, chairperson National Editorial Board

"Letter Writing and New Passions," first Dunayevskaya column in *News & Letters,* June 24, 1955.

"Introductions" to *Philosophic Notes* pamphlet, November, 1955, *RDC* #2433-4, *SRDC* #12061-62.

"Theoretical and Practical Perspectives: Where to Begin," Perspectives Report to first News and Letters Convention, July 1956, *RDC* #2566,

"Constitution," News and Letters Committees, July 8, 1956 *RDC* # 2587.

"The American Roots of Marxism in the World Today and Our Development," Plenum report to News and Letters Committees, Labor Day weekend, 1957, *RDC* #2597.

"From Organizational Consciousness to Organizational Building," 1960, *RDC* #2767.

"Summary Notes on *Phenomenology of Mind,*" January 1961, *RDC* #2806. Reprinted in *Power of Negativity.*

"Ideals, Organization and World Development," 1961 News and Letters Perspectives, *RDC* #3178.

"Draft Perspectives," 1962, *RDC* #3204.

"The Time Is Now," Perspectives Report, 1962, *RDC* #3243.

"The Need to Transform Reality," Perspectives Report, September 1963, *RDC* # 3279.

"The Challenge of Mao Tse-tung," chapter added to *Marxism and Freedom,* 2nd edition, 1964.

"The Turning Point," Draft Perspectives, July, 1964, *RDC* #3577.

"Theory and Practice at the Turning Point," Perspective Report, 1964, *RDC* #3591.

"Organization, Philosophy and Reality," Draft Perspectives, 1966, *RDC* #4033.

"The Black/Red Conference Presentation," Jan. 12,1969, *RDC* #4338. Reprinted in *Power of Negativity.*

"The Newness of Our Philosophic-Historic Contribution," June 1969, *RDC* #4407. Major excerpts reprinted in *Power of Negativity.*

"The Women's Liberation Conference, summary of presentation," February 1971, *RDC* #4355.

"Political-Philosophic Letters, begun in 1976, *RDC* #5181-5299.

"Our *Original* Contribution to the Dialectic of the Absolute Idea as New Beginning: In Theory, and Leadership and Practice," presentation to East Coast National Editorial Board of News and Letters, April 10, 1976, *RDC* #5622.

"National, International, Objective-Subjective Crises Are Testing Revolutionaries," Draft Perspectives, July 1976, *RDC* # 5689.

"Relationship of Philosophy and Revolution to Women's Liberation: Marx's and Engels' Studies Contrast," draft chapter for *RLWLKM*, 1978, *RDC* #6467.

"The Dialectic of Today's Crises and Today's Revolts," Perspective Report to News and Letters Committees Convention, Sept. 2, 1978, *RDC* #5791.

"On the Battle of Ideas: Philosophic-Theoretic Points of Departure as Political Tendencies Respond to the Objective Situation," Political-Philosophic Letter, October 1982 *RDC* #7489. Reprinted in *Power of Negativity*.

"Marxist-Humanism: The Summation That Is A New Beginning, Subjectively and Objectivity," January 1, 1983, *RDC* #7639. Excerpts reprinted in *Power of Negativity*.

"In Memoriam, Charles Denby," 1983. Reprinted 1989 edition of *Indignant Heart: A Black Worker's Journal*.

"Not by Practice Alone: The Movement from Theory," section of "The Movements from Theory as Well as from Practice vs. the Great Artificer, Ronald Reagan, for whom the Whole World is a Stage," Perspectives Report, July 7, 1984. *RDC* #8193. Reprinted in *Power of Negativity*.

"The Emergence of a New Movement from Practice that Is Itself a Form of Theory" in *The Coal Miners' General Strike of 1949-50 and the Birth of Marxist-Humanism,* News & Letters, 1984.

"Responsibility for Marxist-Humanism in the Historic Mirror: A Revolutionary Critical Look," December 30, 1984, *RDC* # 8335.

"Dialectics of Revolution: American Roots and Marx's World Humanist Concept," March 21, 1985. *RDC* #10219.

"Introduction/Overview to Volume XII of *RDC*, February 28, 1986. *Guide to Raya Dunayevskaya Collection*, p. 57.

"Retrospective/Perspective: Thirty Years of News & Letters," News & Letters 1986. Reprinted in The Myriad Global Crisis of the 1980s and the Nuclear World since World War II. News & Letters, 1986

"The Year of Only 8 Months," Presentation to expanded Resident Editorial Board Meeting, January 1987, *SRDC* #10690.

"Presentation on the Dialectics of Organization and Philosophy," June 1987, *SRDC* #10737. Reprinted in *The Philosophic Moment of Marxist-Humanism*, News & Letters, 1987. Major excerpts reprinted in *Power of Negativity*.

Other Works discussed

Anderson, Kevin
Lenin, Hegel, and Western Marxist: A Critical Study (Urbana: University of Illinois Press, 1995).

Denby, Charles.
Indignant Heart, 1952.
Indignant Heart: A Black Worker's Journal, 1978.
Workers Battle Automation, News & Letters, 1960.

Engels, Frederick
The Origin of the Family, Private Property and the State (New York: International Publishers, 1942)

Hegel, G.W.F.
History of Philosophy, (New York: The Humanities Press, 1974).
Phenomenology of Mind, trans. by J.B. Baillie (London: Allen & Unwin, 1931).
Philosophy of Mind, trans. by William Wallace (Oxford: Clarendon Press, 1971).
Science of Logic, trans. by Johnson and Struthers (New York: MacMillan, 1929).

James, C.L.R.
Notes on Dialectics, Hegel, Marx, Lenin (Westport, Connecticut: Lawrence Hill & Co., 1980; original typescript, 1948.

Johnson-Forest Tendency
State-Capitalism and World Revolution (1950). August 1950, *RDC* #1333.

Lenin, V.I.
"Abstract on Hegel's *Science of Logic*," in *Marxism and Freedom*, appendix to first (1958) edition. Also in *Collected Works,* Vol. 38 (London: Lawrence & Wishard).

Luxemburg, Rosa
Accumulation of Capitalism (London: Oxford University Press, 1951).

Marcuse, Herbert
Reason and Revolution, (New York: Oxford, 1941)

Marx, Karl
Capital, Vol. I, Moore-Aveling trans. (Chicago: Charles H. Kerr, 1909).
A Contribution to the Critique of Political Economy, trans. By N.I. Stone (Chicago: Charles H. Kerr, 1904).
Critique of the Gotha Program, (London: Lawrence and Wishard, n.d.).
Economic-Philosophic Manuscripts, 1844, appendix to *Marxism and Freedom,* first (1958) edition. Also, *Marx-Engels Collected Works,* Vol. 3 (New York: International Publisher, 1975).
Grundrisse trans. Martin Nicolaus (London: Penguin Books, 1973).

Sartre, Jean-Paul
Search for a Method, trans. By Hazel E. Barnes (New York: Alfred A. Knopf, 1965).
Being and Nothingness, trans. By Hazel E. Barnes (New York: Philosophic Library, 1956).

Women's Liberation—News and Letters Committees
Working Women for Freedom, News & Letters, 1976, *RDC* #5370.

Acknowledgements

Wayne State University Archives of Labor and Urban Affairs prepared and made available microfilm of *The Raya Dunayevskaya Collection* and the *Supplement* to the collection. The Raya Dunayevskaya Memorial Fund and News and Letters prepared Guides for the collection.

I thank Roger Hollander for his meticulous proofreading and editorial suggestions.

Expanded Table of Contents and Index

Introduction -- Hegel, Marx, Lenin, Luxemburg, and Revolution in the Thought and Passion of Raya Dunayevskaya
* *Facing the Present Moment*
* *A Biographical Note, 1910 to 1941*
* *Facing the Crisis in Marxism as Capitalism Took New Form and Revolution Became Transformed into Opposite*
* *The Concept of Critique: Battle of Ideas and the Development of Marxist-Humanism*
* *Dunayevskaya's 1980s Philosophic Labors as Our Vantage Point*

Part I: *1941-1956, From the Origins of State Capitalist Theory to Letters on Hegel's Absolutes to the Founding of News and Letters Committee*

Chapter 1 -- The Hitler-Stalin Pact, the Outbreak of the Second World War, and the Theory of State Capitalism: Manuscripts from Its Initial Projection, 1941-43
* *Prologue: The 1930s—The Spanish Civil War and Dunayevskaya as Secretary to Leon Trotsky*
* *Early Writings on State-Capitalism in Relation to Marx's Writings*
  "The Union of Soviet Socialist Republics is a Capitalist Society"
  "An Analysis of the Russian Economy"
  "Politics and Economics"
  Marx's early writings in relation to "Labor and Society"
  Writings on Marx's Economics, Particularly the Law of Value
  "A New Revision of Marxian Economics"
* *Drawing Together Strands from the Theory of State-Capitalism Documents of the 1940s*

Chapter 2 -- Translation and Initial Probing of Lenin's Notebooks on Hegel's *Science of Logic*: Theoretical Ramifications, 1949-51; Relation to the 1949-50 Miners' General Strike

• *From State-Capitalist Theory to Philosophic Correspondence Via Lenin's Hegel Notebooks*
    Letters Accompanying the Lenin Translations
    Exploring Lenin's Breakthrough
    "The dialectic of Marx's plan for *Capital*."
• *The Coal Miners' General Strike and the New Form of the Book-To-Be*

Chapter 3 -- Dunayevskaya's 1953 Breakthrough on Hegel's Absolutes in Relation Momentous World Events: the Death of Stalin and the June 17, 1953 East German Revolt

• *The Letters on Hegel's Absolutes*
    May 12, 1953—From the Dialectic of the Party to the Threshold of the New Society
    May 20, 1953 "We have entered the new society."
• *The Letters on Hegel's Absolutes and the Break-Up of the State-Capitalist Tendency, 1953-54*

Chapter 4 -- Founding of News and Letters Committees, 1955-1957, in the Context of East European Revolts, Workers' Struggles Against Automation, and the Montgomery Bus Boycott

• *Where to Begin? Theoretical and Practical Perspectives*
• *News and Letters Committees: Its Constitution and Organizational Form*
• *News & Letters, a Marxist-Humanist Newspaper*
    The Revolutionary Journalism of Raya Dunayevskaya
• *Charles Denby: Autoworker, Editor of News & Letters, "Worker's Journal" Columnist, Author of Indignant Heart: A Black Worker's Journal, Colleague of Raya Dunayevskaya*
• *The Organization of Thought, Which Determines Organizational Life: News and Letters Perspectives as Marxism and Freedom Is Completed*
• *Viewing News and Letters, 1955-57, Under the Shadow of the Johnson-Forest Tendency*

Part II: 1955-1964, Marxism and Freedom . . . from 1776 until today

Chapter 5 -- Origins of *Marxism and Freedom* as World Events Unfold: Montgomery, Alabama 1955-56, Hungary 1956, Mao's China, 1957

- *A Collective Effort in the Writing of <u>Marxism and Freedom</u>: News and Letters Colleagues and Committees; Working People as Co-Authors*
- *Dialogue with Herbert Marcuse*
- *Appendix: A 1957 Dunayevskaya Commentary on <u>Marxism and Freedom</u>*

Chapter 6 -- Elucidating the Philosophical Foundations of Marxism: The Structure and Content of *Marxism and Freedom*

- *Part I, From Practice to Theory: 1776 to 1848*
- *Part II, Worker and Intellectual at a Turning Point in History: 1848 to 1861*
- *Part III, Marxism: The Unity of Theory and Practice*
- *Organizational Interlude*
- *Part IV, World War I and the Great Divide in Marxism*
- *Part V, The Problem of our Age: State Capitalism vs. Freedom*

Chapter 7 -- Projection and Concretization of *Marxism and Freedom* as Objective-Subjective Turning Points Develop: the African Revolutions, Automation Battles, and the Civil Rights Movement

- *Ideological-Philosophic Pulls as Africa Transformed Itself: <u>Nationalism, Communism, Marxist-Humanism and the Afro-Asian Revolutions</u>*
- *The American Proletariat Speaking for Itself: <u>Workers Battle Automation</u>*
- *<u>American Civilization on Trial</u>: Dunayevskaya and the Black Freedom Movement*
- *"The Challenge of Mao Tse-tung" Chapter in an Expanded Edition of <u>Marxism and Freedom</u>*
- *Working out a Marxist-Humanist Concept of Organization at the Time of <u>Marxism and Freedom</u>*

Part III: *1960-1976, Philosophy and Revolution: From Hegel to Sartre and from Marx to Mao*

Chapter 8-- 1960-1973: The Process of Writing *Philosophy and Revolution* with Focus on Hegel's Absolutes

- *1960-61: Letters on Preliminary Notions; Summary Notes Probing of Hegel's Philosophic Works*
    Notes on <u>Phenomenology of Mind</u>
- *A New Philosophic Moment: Absolute Negativity as New Beginning,*
    I. 1967-1969
        II. 1969-1971, The Simultaneity of Writing and Projecting the New Book in the Black Dimension and in Women's Liberation

- *Establishment of the Marxist-Humanist Archives—<u>The Raya Dunayevskaya Collection</u>*

Chapter 9-- Working out the Dialectic of Hegel's Absolutes for Our Age: The Structure and Content of *Philosophy and Revolution*
- *Part I: Why Hegel? Why Now?*
- *Part II. Alternatives*
- *Part III. Economic Reality and the Dialectics of Liberation*

Chapter 10 -- Philosophic Concretization and Projection: Organizational Ramifications and Contradictions
- *Projection in the Women's Liberation Movement*
- *The Meaning of Political-Philosophic Letters*
- *Organizational Critique and New Beginning*
- *Appendix*

Part IV: 1975-1982, Rosa Luxemburg, Women's Liberation, and Marx's Philosophy of Revolution

Chapter 11 -- Development of the Luxemburg Book, 1975-1982: Strands from Women's Liberation, Luxemburg, and Marx; Relation to Iran's Revolution/Counter-Revolution, and to *News & Letters* as Theory/Practice
- *A Re-examination of the Relationship of Marx and Engels*
- *An Evolving View of Rosa Luxemburg*
- *The Objectivity of and Challenge to the Women's Liberation Movement*
- *The Unfolding Revolution and Counter-Revolution in Iran as well as the Transformation of <u>News & Letters</u> to a 12-Page Paper—Both in Relation to Work on the New Book*

Chapter 12 -- The Categories of Post-Marx Marxism and Revolution-in-Permanence in Relation to the Structure and Content of the Luxemburg Book
- *Post-Marx Marxism*
- *Part I: Rosa Luxemburg as Theoretician, as Activist, as Internationalist*
- *Part II: The Women's Liberation Movement as Revolutionary Force and Reason*

- *Part III: Karl Marx—From Critic of Hegel to Author of <u>Capital</u> and Theorist of "Revolution in Permanence"*

Part V: 1980-87, Reaching for the Future: Dunayevskaya's Re-examination of a Half-Century of Marxist-Humanism, And the Projection of a New Work on Dialectics of Organization and Philosophy

Dunayevskaya's 1980s Vantage Point of Marxist-Humanism's Multi-lineal Origins and Pathways of Development

    I. Projecting and Extending *Rosa Luxemburg, Women' Liberation, and Marx's Philosophy of Revolution*

- *Projecting Marx's New Moments in Relation to Post-Marx Marxism*
- *New Paragraphs Added to <u>Rosa Luxemburg, Women's Liberation and Marx's Philosophy of Revolution</u>*
- <u>*Women's Liberation and the Dialectics of Revolution*</u>

    II. Retrospective of Marxist-Humanism—Its Origins and Development

- *Dunayevskaya's 1980s View of the Johnson-Forest Tendency*
- *Creating the Category "Philosophic Moment of Marxist-Humanism" for the 1953 Letters on Hegel's Absolutes*
- *Critiquing the Gap Between Philosophic Expression and Organizational Practice of Marxist-Humanism in the 1980s:I. 1983-85*

    III. Towards Dialectics of Organization and Philosophy

- *New Perspectives on Lenin's Philosophic Ambivalence*
- *1980s Views of Hegel's <u>Phenomenology</u> and Smaller <u>Logic</u> with Regard to Organization*
- *Critiquing the Gap Between Philosophic Expression and Organizational Practice of Marxist-Humanism in the 1980s: II. 1986-87*
- *"One Possible Outline for Dialectics of Organization and Philosophy"*

A

Abolitionists see Black Dimension
Absolute(s) (see also Dialectic; Dunayevskaya; Hegel; Marx), 115-117, 126, 279, 306
Anderson, Kevin, 64n2, 121
Archives see Dunayevskaya (works)
Raya Dunayevskaya Collection
Automation (see also Denby (works) 88, 89, 111-113, 156, 164-165

B

Black Dimension, 96-99, 161-171, 195-197, 229
   abolitionists, 103, 157
   American history, in, 167-171
   Marx and, 276-277
   Montgomery Bus Boycott, 88,109-110, 154
Bureaucratic Collectivism, 25
Burharin, Nikolai, 154, 184, 215-217

C

Capitalism (see also Marx, State-Capitalism), 1-3
China (see also Mao Tse-tung; Sino-Soviet Conflict), 110, 114-115, 171-174. 219-221
Civil Rights Movement see Black Dimension
Classical Political Economy, 127-128
Coal Miners' General Strike (1949-50) (See also Philips, Andy), 57-63
Correspondence Committees see Organization

D

Denby, Charles, 65-66, 96-99,164-164, 284-285

Denby Charles (works)
Indignant Heart: A Black Worker's Journal, 96-99
Workers Battle Automation, 97, 164-165
Dialectics (see also Dunayevskaya; Hegel; Lenin; Marx; Organization), 1, 3-4
"Dialectics of Organization and Philosophy" see Dunayevskaya
Dialectic of Party see Organization
Domanski, Olga, 111-114
Dunayevskaya, Raya,
   "absolute negativity as new beginning," 14, 190-198, 204-208, 233-236
   absolutes, on, 12, 14, 78-81, 279
   Africa, on , 8, 223-224
   biographical note, 6-9
   black dimension, and, 6, 7, 8, 23, 103, 165-171, 176, 195-197, 229
   concept of critique, 5-6, 11-14, 15
   "dialectics of organization and philosophy," 15-16, 81, 174-178, 274, 292-308
   Engels, critique of, 241-242, 258
   Fanon, relation to, 236
   Hegelian dialectic, relation to, 12-13, 50, 54-55, 184-184, 187-190, 204-208, 234-236, 297-300
   internationalist, as, 11,159, 200n1
   Lenin, relation to, 13-14, 33-34, 45-53, 161-163,184-184, 233-234,295-296
   "Letters on Hegel's Absolutes," 68-78, 208, 286-289, 296-297
   Luxemburg, relation to, critique of, 240, 242,245, 250-256, 275-276
   organizational person, as, 90, 174-179
   Mao Tse-tung, critique of, 13, 219-221
   Marcuse, dialogue with, 12-13, 115-123

Marx, relation to, 23, 35-36, 37-39, 53-57, 73, 120-121,129-131, 132-133, 134-146, 208-214, 233-234, 258-259, 259-266
Marx-Engels relation, on, 240-241, 274, 276,
post-Marx Marxism, critique of, 14-15, 249-250, 259, 285-287
revolutionary journalism of, 93-96
revolutionary subjectivity, and, 10-11, 23, 173-174, 194, 222-226, 277-279
Sartre, critique of, 221-222
state-capitalist theory, and, see State-Capitalist Theory
Trotsky, critique of, 154-155, 217-219, 250, 264
Trotsky, secretary to, 7-9
Spanish Civil War, and, 22
women's liberation, and, 197-198, 228-230, 239, 240-242, 243-244, 246n1, 256-259, 290-291
workers, and, 7-8,57-63,65-66,77-78, 85,, 95-96, 96-99, 100-102, 109, 111-113, 121-122, 141-142, 179n2, 282-283
youth, and, 290
Dunayevskaya, Raya (works)
American Civilization on Trial, 165-171
"The American Roots of Marxism in the World Today and Our Development," 99-105
"An Analysis of the Russian Economy," 26-32
"The Challenge of Mao Tse-tung," 171-174
"The Emergence of a New Movement from Practice that Is Itself a Form of Theory," 60-61
"Labor and Society," 35-36
"The Law of Value and Capitalist Society," 37-39
"The Lenin Book," 68
"Letter Writings and the New Passions," 95-96
Marxism and Freedom, 45-46, 90, 109-123, 125-157,159-179

"A 1957 Commentary on *Marxism and Freedom*," 119-122
"Our Original Contribution to the Dialectic of the Absolute Idea as New Beginning ," 233-236
Nationalism, Communism, Marxist-Humanism and the Afro-Asian Revolutions, 160-163
"A New Revision of Marxian Economics," 39-41
"Notes on *Phenomenology of Mind*," 187-190
Philosophy and Revolution, 183-202, 203-226, 227-236
Political and Political-Philosophic Letters, 160, 230-231, 245
"Politics and Economics," 32-34
The Raya Dunayevskaya Collection, 16, 21-22, 199-200, 200-201n.1, 247n3
Rosa Luxemburg, Women's Liberation, and Marx's Philosophy of Revolution, 239-247, 249-266, 272-279, 289-292
"State-Capitalism and Marxism," 41
"Theoretical and Practical Perspectives," 84-89
"The Union of Soviet Socialist Republics is a Capitalist Society," 24-25
Women's Liberation and the Dialectics of Revolution, 277-279
Dwyer, John, 199

E

East German Revolt (June 17, l953), 77-79
Engels, Friedrich, 240-242, 258
Engels, Fredrich (works)
Origin of the Family, Private Property and the State, 241, 258

F

Fanon, Franz, 236
Forest, Freddie see Dunayevskaya

G

German Social Democracy see
    Organization
Gogol, Bess, 114
Gogol, Louis, 93, 185-186
Gramsci, Antonio, 5
Greeman, Richard, 192

H

Hegel, G.W.F., 13-14, 126-127
    Absolutes, 12-13, 14, 69-74,
        183,189-190, 204-208
    Spirit in Self Estrangement, 172
    Third Attitude to Objectivity, 205
        299-300
Hegel, G.W.F. (works)
    Phenomenology of Spirit (Mind), 3,
        70, 187-190, 206-207, 297-299
    Philosophy of Spirit (Mind) 73-74,
        74-88, 205,207-209
    Science of Logic, 47-49, 69-74, 126,
        194, 205, 207, 280-281
Hitler-Stalin Pact, 8, 9, 22-23

J

James, C.L.R., 9, 42n3, 63, 64n7, 68,
    73, 78, 286-287, 303-304
James, C.L.R. (works)
    "Notes on Dialectics," 47, 49-50, 68-
        69, 280, 394
James, Freddie see Dunayevskaya
Johnson, J.R. see James, C.L.R.
Johnson-Forest Tendency, 9, 12, 46-53,
    59, 67-69,, 68-69,78-80, 86, 105-
    106, 280-285, 285-287

L

Labor see Workers
Lassalle, Ferdinand, 133-134, 263
Lee, Grace, 9, 53, 55, 62, 67, 68, 78,
    280, 283-84
Lenin, V. I., 161-163, 214-217
    Burharin, critique of, 154, 215-217

    Hegelian dialectic, relation to, 47-
        53,184-185, 215
    Marx, relation to, 50, 52, 73,
    Russian Revolution, and, 149-150
    trade union debate, and, 32-34
Lenin, V.I. (works)
    Imperialism, 48, 150
    "Notes on Hegel's *History of*
        Philosophy, 47
    Philosophic Notebooks (Abstract on
        Hegel's *Science of Logic*), 13-14,
        45-53, 60-61, 64n1, 71-73, 149-
        150, 280-281, 295-297
Luxemburg, Rosa, 5, 240, 242, 243-
    244, 245, 250-256, 257-258, 275-276
Luxemburg, Rosa (works)
    Accumulation of Capital, 48, 253-254
    The Mass Strike, the Party and the
        Trade Union, 251
    Reform or Revolution, 250-251

M

Mao Tse-tung (Mao Zedong), 13, 110,
    114-115, 172, 219-221
Marcuse, Herbert, 12-13, 115-123, 184-
    185
Marcuse, Herbert (works)
    Eros and Civilization, 117
    "Preface to *Marxism and Freedom*,"
        118-119
    Reason and Revolution, 115, 122
Martin, Felix, 98
Marx, Karl, 208-214, 240-242, 259-
    266, 272-275
    black dimension, and, 167, 276-277
    civil war (U.S.), and, 134-135
    Engels, and, 14-15, 274, 276
    fetishism of commodities, and, 138-
        139
    Hegelian dialectic, and, 54-56, 73,
        209-210, 213-214, 262
    humanism, and 23-24, 35-36, 62,
        129-131, 139, 209-210
    last decade of, 264-266
    permanent revolution, theory of, 264,
        277
    revolutionary subjectivity, and, 4,
    workers, relation to, 212

Marx, Karl (works)
  Capital, 24, 37-38, 40, 41, 53-57, 63, 73, 87, 134-146, 210-214, 261-263, 273-274
  Communist Manifesto, 132
  Critique of the Gotha Program, 39-40
  Critique of Political Economy, 56-57, 134
  Economic and Philosophic Manuscripts of 1844, 35-36,62, 120, 129-131,197, 209-210, 260
  Ethnological Notebooks, 241, 258, 273
  Grundrisse, 210-212, 273
  Wage Labor and Capital, 246
Marxism see Marx; Marxist-Humanism; post-Marx Marxism
Marxist-Humanism, 4, 10, 11-14,, 15-16, 17, 21, 41-42, 79, 84, 162-163, 300-303
McShane, Harry, 240
Miners, see Workers

N

News and Letters Committees (see also Organization), 9, 15, 79-80, 81n2, 86-106, 109, 110-114,, 166-67, 174-178, 191, 199-200, 271-272, 288-289, 289-292
News & Letters newspaper, 83, 92-97, 106, 241, 300-302

O

Organization
  Correspondence Committees, 46, 78-79, 90
  Communist League, 132
  dialectic of the party, 68-69, 74, 80
  "dialectics of organization and philosophy," 15-16, 69, 73-74, 81, 174-178, 274, 292-308
  First International (International Workingmen's Association), 263

form of, 4, 148-149, 151-153, 174-178, 293-294
General Association of German Workers, 263
German Social Democracy (betrayal of), 45-46, 148, 252-253
Johnson-Forest Tendency, 9, 12, 67-68, 78-80 ,86, 280-287
News and Letters Committees, 9, 15, 79-80, 81n2, 109, 113, 174-178, 199-200, 231-233, 289-292, 300-302
Paris Commune, 136-139
Second International (betrayal of), 45-46, 121, 147-148
Socialist Workers Party, 9, 46. 60, 64n9, 81n4
soviets, 148-149, 152
Trotskyism, 25
vanguard party, 71, 74, 89, 90, 121, 151-153
Workers Party, 9, 25, 26, 42n2, 42n4, 43n5, 46, 64n9

P

Paris Commune see Organization; Revolutions
Philips, Andy, 57-60, 112
Post-Marx Marxism, 240-242, 249-250, 259, 273, 292
Proudhon, Pierre, 128-129

R

Raya Dunayevskaya Collection see Dunayevskaya (works)
Revolutions
  African, 160-163, 176, 223-224
  Chinese (1925-27), 172
  Chinese (1949), 172
  Cuban (1959), 160
  East European, 224
  East German Revolt (June 17, 1953) 77-78
  French (1789-93), 126
  French (1848), 131-133
  Hungarian (1956), 110, 156

Iranian (1979), 244, 245
  Paris Commune (1871), 136-139
  Russian (1905), 148-149, 251
  Russian (1917), 24
  Spanish (Civil War, 1937-38), 22, 300-301
  underdeveloped lands, in, 160-163
Ricardo, David see Classical Political Economy
Russia (See also Lenin; Stalin; Stalinism; State-Capitalism), 8-9, 65-67, 77-78,, 185, 251-252
  agriculture, 29-30
  Five-Year plans, 26-43
  Hegel, attack on, 127
  Marx, perversion of, 130-131
  peasants, 30
  science in, 1895-187
  Stakhanovism, 31-32
  state-capitalist theory, and, 22-43, 162, 213, 215
  trade union debate in, 33-34, 66-67
  turnover tax in, 28-29
  workers in, 27-29, 30-32, 156
Ryazanov, David, 35

S

Sartre, Jean-Paul, 221-222
Second International see Organization
Shachtman, Max, (see also Organization, Workers Party), 25
Shlyapnikov, Aleksandr, 34
Sino-Soviet Conflict, 171-173
Smith, Adam, see Classical Political Economy
Socialist Workers Party see Organization
Soviet Union see Russia
Spanish Civil War see Revolutions
Stakhanovism, 31-32
Stalin, Joseph, 8, 9, 31, 65-68, 155
Stalinism, 22-43, 72
State-Capitalist Tendency see Johnson-Forest Tendency

State-capitalism, theory of, 3, 9-10, 22-43, 164-156
  world phenomenon, as, 23, 34-35, 41
  Marxist-Humanism, and, 42
Stone, Ria see Lee, Grace

T

Terrano, Angela, 88, 92
Trotsky, Leon, 7-9, 154-155, 162, 217-219, 250, 264
  defense of Soviet Union, and, 8-10, 22-23, 26
  Spanish Civil War, and, 22
  trade union debate, and, 32-3
Trotskyism (see also Organization; Shachtman), 7, 22-23

U

United States, 224-225
  Civil War, in, 62, 134-135
  hegemony of, 1-3
  workers, 57-63, 95-96

W

Wetter, Gustav, 185-186
Wetter, Gustav, (works)
  Dialectical Materialism, 185-186
Women's Liberation, 197-198, 228-230,239,, 243-244, 256-259, 277-279
Workers
  American ,57-63, 66-67, 85, 95-96, 96-99, 134-137, 164-165, 195-197, 282-283, 284-285,
  East German, 78-79
  Russian, 148-149, 153-154
Workers Party see Organization
World War I, 45-46
World War II, 9, 22-23

About The Author

Eugene Gogol served as a secretary to Raya Dunayevskaya in the 1980s, as well as managing editor of the Marxist-Humanist newspaper *News & Letters*. His political activity began in the 1950s as a youth member of News and Letters Committees and within the Civil Rights Movement.

In the 1960s he worked with the Congress of Racial Equality (CORE) in Los Angeles, and participated in the Mississippi Summer Project in 1964, teaching Black history in Jackson, Mississippi. He co-authored *The Free Speech Movement and the Negro Revolution* (1965) with Raya Dunayevskaya and Mario Savio. In the mid-1960s he edited *The Marxist-Humanist* on the UCLA campus. He was a participant-observer in the events in Paris in May-June 1968, and authored the pamphlet, *France, Spring 1968: Masses in Motion, Ideas in Free Flow*. In addition to working in News and Letters Committees in the '60s, he was a member of Students for a Democratic Society (SDS), which he left when it degenerated into Maoism.

Gogol participated in the Anti-Vietnam War Movement and in the 1970s, returned to school in the area of Latin American Studies, and later completed a study on the ideas of José Carlos Mariátegui in relation to Karl Marx, which was published by the Universidad Nacional Autónoma de México as *Mariátegui y Marx: La transformación social en los países en vías de desarrollo*.

Gogol's travels in Latin America include visits to Chiapas Mexico several times since the Zapatista rebellion of 1994. He has written a major study on Latin America, *The Concept of Other in Latin American Liberation: Fusing Emancipatory Philosophic Thought and Social Revolt* (Lexington, 2002).

The author welcomes dialogue and debate on the ideas presented in this study. He can be contacted at egogol@hotmail.com.

www.ingramcontent.com/pod-product-compliance
Lightning Source LLC
Chambersburg PA
CBHW071229230426
43668CB00011B/1365